Lifting the Veil:
The True Faces of Muhammad and Islam

Volume I: Chapters 1 to 100

I.Q. Al Rassooli

authorHOUSE®

AuthorHouse™
1663 Liberty Drive, Suite 200
Bloomington, IN 47403
www.authorhouse.com
Phone: 1-800-839-8640

©*2008 I.Q. Al Rassooli. All rights reserved.*

No part of this book may be reproduced, stored in a retrieval system, or transmitted by any means without the written permission of the author.

First published by AuthorHouse 12/9/2008

ISBN: 978-1-4343-9202-2 (sc)

Printed in the United States of America
Bloomington, Indiana

This book is printed on acid-free paper.

Based upon the series: Idiots' Guide to Islam
www.youtube.com/ahmadsquran3
Our Blog: www.the-koran.blogspot.com
Our Website: www.inthenameofallah.org

This book is DEDICATED to ENLIGHTEN HUMANITY .

Contents

Intoduction 1
We Accuse 3
Does Islam mean Peace 6
Who is a Muslim 8
Who is Allah 10
Women in Islam 14
Meccan Period 20
Madina Period 23
Jihad in Islam 26
Islamophobia 30
Was M a Prophet 33
Challenge 36
The Black Stone 40
What is the Ka'ba? 45
Hijab 50
Quran Against Christians 54
Night Journey or Laylat al Isra 59
Quran Against Jews 67
Predestination in the Quran 72
Abrogating & Abrogated Verses in the Quran 76
Quran Against Unbelievers 80
Islam & African Slavery 84
Myth of Islamic Civilization 89
Quran Against Arabs 93
Quran vs Bible Contradictions 97
Satanic Quran 102
Suicide in Islam 107
The Charter of Umar 110
Foreign Words in Quran 114
Was Muhammad the Last Prophet? 120
The Satanic Verses 124
The 72 Virgins 129
Taqiya/ Islamic Subterfuge 134
And Then it was Revealed 139
Muhammad's Compassion & Mercy 145
Khadijah & Muhammadan Islam 150
Fifty Prayers a Day 156
Compilation of the Quran 161
Biblical Corruption Allegations 168

Muhammad & Knowledge	173
Arab & Islamic Imperialism	178
Allah's 10% Share of Muhammad's Plunder	183
Muhammad the Sinful	187
Mein Kampf & Quran	192
Muhammad the Forgetful	198
Was Muhammad Illiterate?	201
Jews of Arabia	205
Jews of Arabia	211
Altered Revelations	215
Ancestry of the Arabs	218
Male Muhammadan Characteristics	221
Isaac OR Ishmael	227
Battle of Yamama	232
Biblical Names in the Quran	236
The Christians of Arabia	239
Allah & his Aposle Know Best	244
Seven Versions of the Quran	247
Muhammad & Arabia's News Media	251
Made to Order Revelations	256
Jizya or Poll Tax	260
A Quran Unravelled	266
B.Quran Unravelled	271
Muhammad the Coward	275
Anything New in the Quran? Anything?	281
Fight/Kill/Slay in the Quran	285
Allah's Chosen People	288
No Compulsion in Religion	294
Is Islam a Cult or a Religion?	298
Ka'ba or Solomon's Temple?	302
Gabriel or Jibril	307
Dilemma of Muhammadan Muslims	311
Hagar & Ishmael	315
Ilm OR Knowledge	320
Read OR Recite	324
Good & Bad Muslims ?	330
Promised Land in the Quran	334
Apostasy or Ridda Wars	338
Muhammad's Psychological Profile	343
Plagues OR Commandments?	349
Debating Muhammadans	355

Miriam OR Mary ?	360
Missing Verses in Quran	365
Fall of Adam	370
Muhammad's Sunna	375
Poitier: Saviour Battle	380
Was Muhammad Predicted?	385
Messengers & Prophets	389
Islam Before Muhammad	395
Muhammad's Surgeries	399
Mu'allaqat/ Pre Islamic Poetry	403
Jesus in the Quran	409
Days of Creation in the Quran	413
Muhammad & Astronomy	417
Errors in the Quran	422
Slew the Whole World	427
Slew the Whole World	427
Suckling a Grown Man/Rath'at al Kabir	431
Muhammad the Pagan	436
Rajam/ Stoning Verse	442
Muhammad & Deception	447
Let There be Light	453
Muhammad & Gabriel	458
Paradise is Under the Shades of Swords	464
Safa & Marwa: 'Islam' & Paganism	467
Muhammad's Megalomania	473
References	479
Links	483

#1. INTRODUCTION

The purpose of this series of talks is to inform, explain and enlighten people all over the world about the origins of the **Quran and Muhammadan Islam.** We want to challenge the knowledge of the listeners to such a degree that they will try to find fault, lies, misinformation or disinformation in the contents.

It is our desire for you the listeners to independently investigate the sources mentioned here as well as other sources. To compare, contrast and reflect upon the most **astounding, outrageous, revolutionary, unconventional and controvertial** statements and conclusions arrived at in this series, that have ever been expouded anywhere in academia.

The audience should be reminded of a very obvious fact:

No human being is born **evil.**

Every human being, past, present and in the future, is the product of **indoctrination;** a process that starts with the parents, then by the relatives, the siblings, friends, school and the state.

We are all **end products,** and not a single one of us has ever had a choice to whom and where we are borne. Not a single one of us has ever had the freedom to choose our religion, our beliefs, our thoughts, our colour or our race.

Even when we are grown up and have the ability to investigate, to read, to compare and contrast other beliefs, other philosophies, other ideas and opinions, the programming that has been instilled in our brain from birth to maturity has been so intense, that most probably we would still ignore reality and facts.

This series is in the format of **Questions & Answers** and the person being interviewed grew up in an Arab country, his mother tongue is Arabic and has for the last **23 years** been studying and researching the subjects of the Quran, Hadiths, the New Testament, the Hebrew Bible, Arab & Islamic histories.

I.Q. Al Rassooli

We shall explore almost every aspect of Muhammadan Islam from its very beginnings till modern times, relying almost **entirely** upon the Arabic and Islamic sources themselves to prove the statements and conclusions here in declared.

We shall endeavour to do our best to comprehensively explain, investigate and discuss the meaning of words, terms and expressions used in the Quran and by the followers of Muhammad.

#1a. The Accusations

You our listeners must remember that **belief,** any **belief** is **not** a negotiable item. That belief is not subject to analysis, facts, reality or nit picking. It is not **rational.** It is **all** or **nothing.** None the less, what distinguishes humanity from all of the others in the Animal Kingdom, is our ability to think and rationalize for ourselves and all we request is that the listeners **question** matters, study and investigate them themselves and hence arrive at their own **unimposed** conclusions.

This series will be in the format of **Questions** and **Answers** putting **Muhammad** and his **Quran** on **trial** and under intense scrutiny and analysis.

We shall prove our assertions beyond any reasonable doubt and based **entirely** upon all the relevant Arabic and other sources, documentation and information that is available to all.

<u>The accusations against Muhammad and his Quran are:</u>

1. Islam was not Muhammad's creation because the concept **preceded** Muhammad by at least 25 centuries.

2. Allah is **not God** and most certainly is not the God of Israel and Jesus

3. Allah was only the **name** of the supreme rock god of the **Ka'ba** personified by the **Black Stone**

4. Allah was **only** a **stone** and hence could not possibly have revealed anything to Muhammad or to anyone else for that matter.

5. In fact, the Quran is Muhammad's own Alter Ego cleverly projected into the **unsuspecting** mouth of Allah, the **Black Stone,** to make it **sound divine.**

6. Gabriel never passed any messages to Muhammad since Allah was actually **only** the **name** of a rock god.

7   Muhammad deliberately, maliciously and with forethought, continuously and relentlessly, deceived his unsuspecting, gullible and superstitious followers into believing that he was the messenger of Allah.

8   Muhammad was not even a **prophet** since he did not predict any future event that turned out to be true.

9   Muhammad showed utter contempt and an incredible degree of **depraved indidifference** for the lives of his followers by knowingly sending many of them to certain death to do his bidding in what he termed as *" Jihad fi sabil^Allah"* that is *"Struggle in the cause of Allah"*

10 Because no god ever 'revealed' the Quran to Muhammad, it took him 23 years to put it together, especially since there were so called 'revelations' for as long as he was alive and able to invent and concoct them with his usual Abrogating and Abrogated verses whenever he changed his mind about any subject.

11 Almost All the worthy **Concepts, Precepts, Thoughts** and **Ideas** in the Quran were **Plagiarised, Pirated, Plundered** and or **Perverted** by Muhammad from the Scriptures, Traditions and Fetishes of the Jews, Christians, Zoroasterians and the Pagan Arabians.

We furthermore accuse Muhammad and his Quran of:

12 Warmongering since they **unilaterally** declared **total** and **relentless** against all of **humanity** because they do not share their beliefs.

13 Hatemongering

14 Assassination

15 Treachery & Treason

16 Deception

17 Betrayal of Trust

Lifting the Veil

18 Aggression

19 Mass Murder

20 Slavery

21 Discrimination

22 Plagiarism on a massive scale

#2. Does Islam mean Peace

Q: We are repeatedly told that Islam means peace. Is this true?

A: We have to explore this mantra on three levels: Linguistic, Historical & Actual

Linguistically: Islam does not mean peace and never meant peace; this disingenuous explanation is spread by people who are either utterly ignorant of the Arabic language or to purposefully deceive the unwary listener or reader.

In Arabic, **Islam** has its root in the verb **Aslama** which actually means only one thing: **Submission,** that is, *submission to the will of one god,* as the Quran as well as the Muhamnmadan exegetes assert this.

Historically: according to the Quran, Ahadith, Arab & Islamic records, the spread of Muhammadan Islam in the Jazeera al Arabia – the Arabian Peninsula – was achieved by the shedding of a **sea** of Arabian blood to start with, followed later on with the Arabian conquests through the shedding of an **ocean** of blood of the conquered and subjugated peoples.

Actually: as we see, listen to and read in all the world's media, almost **95% of all acts of terror and war** around the world from the Philippines and Indonesia to India, Pakistan, Afghanistan, and Iraq to name just a few in Asia, then to Africa, Europe and the Americas, are all committed by Muhammadan Muslims.

These acts of wanton and indiscriminate terror target not only Jews, but also Christians, Buddhists, Hindus, Animists and fellow Muhammadan Muslims **who are of a different sect.**

In fact more Muslims are killed by other Muslims than by any outsiders to the faith of Muhammadan Islam.

Muhammadan Muslim Males exhibit almost identical characteristics irrespective of race, culture, or sect and these are as follows:

An Obscene degree of **Hypocrisy, Racism and Mendacity** compounded with a **Pathological Depraved Indifference** to **Facts, Reality, Logic, Veracity, Loyalty, Morality, History, Mercy, Friendship, Compassion, Justice** and to **Language**

The greatest tragedy in modern times is their **culture of denial;** the **denial** of **Facts** and the **denial of Reality** in spite of the horrendous pictures that we see almost daily on TV and read about in the newspapers.

This state of mental **denial,** is similar to one who had suffered a traumatic experience that would be too horrible to rethink.

In the case of **Muhammadan Islam,** the solution to this particular problem requires a world wide concerted effort with the use of **draconian** and extreme legal, educational, theological and physical measures.

#3. Who is a Muslim?

Q: Who according to the Quran is a Muslim?

A: For the last 1450 years, Muhammad and his followers have arrogantly but falsely appropriated the term **'Muslim'** only to themselves thus excluding several other groups who were - by the definition of the word **Islam** – themselves Muslims centuries **before** Muhammad, his Quran and his version of Islam.

Let us explore the Arabic and 'Islamic' chronicles themselves to prove the above statement.

Before Muhammad was born, there were people in Arabia, both men and women, who believed in the **God of Abraham only** without being of the faith of the Jews or of the Christians. They are called **Hanifs** in Arabic.

The most illustrious Hanif was actually **Khadijah,** the first wife of Muhammad. She was a **Hanifiya,** that is one who believed only in the God of Abraham although I must add, that her uncle, Waraqa bin Nawfal, was a Christian.

Now, as we ascertained earlier that Islam means **submission** to the will of **One God,** then as a corollary, any **creature** from anywhere in the Universe who declares that 'it' believes in **One God Only,** is **automatically** a **Muslim.**

Let us now look at the Quranic verses themselves:

In Surat al Baqara/ Chapter 2, of the Cow or Heifer, verses 126 to 137 say, in the Arabic of the Quran that Abraham was a **Muslim,** Ishmael was a **Muslim** Issac was a **Muslim** Jacob was a **Muslim al asbat/ the tribes** of Israel were **Muslimoon.**

Other verses of the Quran assert that Jesus was a **Muslim** Miriam/ Mary, the mother of Jesus was a **Muslima,** and the disciples of Jesus were also **Muslimoon.**

Further Quranic verses also assert that Moses, Aaharon, Adam, Job, King Solomon, King David, Yahya/ John the Baptist, etc, etc, were all **Muslims.**

One does not need a **Phd degree** to conclude that, since all the **Biblical** characters mentioned above existed on the world scene between 2500 to 640 years **before** Muhammad's alleged revelations in his Quran, then it means that they were all believers in the **One and Only God,** which of course they all were.

Hence **contrary** to the **indoctrination** of the world by the followers of Muhammad and other **ignorant** academicians, **Islam** did not, does not and must never be the domain of the followers of Muhammad only.

In fact in a nutshell, all the **Israelites** and **Jews** that have ever lived, all the **Jews** of the present time and all the **Jews** in the future, were, are and forever will be **Muslims, that is believers in the One and Only God of Israel.**

#4. Who is Allah?

Q: We are told repeatedly that Allah is God. Is Allah, God?

A: This is another **deliberate** misrepresentation of both language and facts to confuse and deceive people who are ignorant of the language and history of the Arabs.

In Arabic **al Ilah or Ilah** means **GOD. Allah** on the other hand is just the **name** of a god, just like Jupiter was the king among the gods of the Romans or Zeus among the Greek gods.

Aphrodite, Venus, Hercules, Odin etc etc are **names** of pagan deities. Similarly, the name of the Supreme rock god of the Ka'ba among the tribe of Muhammad, the Quraysh in Mecca, was called **Allah** . They are all **not God** but the names of pagan gods.

Muhammad's father, for example, who was a pagan, that is before Islam, was called **Abd Allah** meaning the **Slave of Allah.**

Hence the name Allah was not Muhammad's invention or inspiration because it was already in existence centuries before Muhammad and his Quran.

To further prove my point, take the **Shahada** of the Muhammadan Muslim, that is his declaration in his belief which says:

*" There is no **God but Allah** and Muhammad is the messenger of **Allah**"*

In Arabic it goes like this *" **La ILAH illa Allah** wa Muhammad Rassool **Allah**"*

Which literally means that Allah is the **name** of **God/ Ilah** and that Muhammad is the **name** of the **messenger** of Allah.

If on the one hand Allah is God then it should have said:

*" There is no **Allah but Allah** and Muhammad is the messenger of **Allah**"*

Lifting the Veil

Or on the other hand

*"There is no **God but God** and Muhammad is the messenger of God"*

But the Shahada does not say that, because in reality Allah is only the **name** of a god.

In his Quran, Muhammad actually **Metamorphosed** the supreme rock god of Arabia, **Allah,** into the **God of Israel** and the **God** of **Jesus.**

Q: You keep mentioning the expression " The supreme rock god of the Ka'ba", what do you mean by that?

A: When Muhammad finally subjugated the Quraysh tribe and ordered the destruction of about **360** rock gods and goddesses, in the year 632AD, he left only **ONE stone** unmolested in the **Ka'ba.**

Most **Muhammadan Muslims** have **never** been told or are ignorant of the following fact as recorded in the tradition of the Arabs themselves:

That the holiest **Rock god of the Ka'ba** has always been and still is, what they call the **Black Stone,** a meteorite that was venerated by the **Pagan Arabs** centuries before **Muhammad Islamized** it by wrapping it up with a new and totally concocted historical and theological background that he plagiarised, plundered, pirated and or perverted from the **Bible.**

It would have been **inconceivable** and utterly **illogical** for the **Pagan Arabs NOT** to have a representation of their supreme rock god. It was because the **Black Stone** represented the spiritual home of the Supreme rock god of the pagan Arabs that Muhammad – who according to the Ahadith actually **venerated** it - had no choice but to keep it; the **Black Stone.**

Q: Will you please tell me why you use the expressions 'Muhammad's Quran' instead of just 'the Quran' and Muhammadan Muslims?

I.Q. Al Rassooli

A: What has eluded the understanding of most of humanity is that there is not a single letter, let alone a word, a verse/aya, a paragraph or a chapter/sura in the whole of the Quran that could have been 'revealed' by any **Omniscient, Merciful or Compassionate** divinity. The Quran contains no Mercy or Compassion towards any human being not even if they are followers of Muhammad.

It is very important that the listeners should know that the greatest enemy, threat and scourge of **Muhammadan Islam** is **Knowledge;** that the best friend, aid, supporter and saviour of **Muhammadan Islam** are **Ignorance** and **Stupidity.**

Hence, based **entirely** upon the Muhammadan Islamic sources themselves, in the Quran, in the Ahadith and in the literature of the Muhammadan exegetes, I can assert that without a shadow of a doubt and in reality, every letter, every word, every aya/ verse, paragraph and surah/ chapter in the Quran are actually the product of Muhammad's fervent imagination reflecting his personal thoughts, his fears, his hatreds, his lust, his anger, his jealousy, his needs and his ideas.

The Quran in short is Muhammad's own **ALTER EGO** projected into the unsuspecting mouth of Allah, the supreme rock god of the Quraysh embedded in the corner wall of the Ka'ba called the **Black Stone.**

As far as I know, rocks, whether black, meteorites or gems do not and cannot inspire human beings with revelations.

That is why I repeatedly mention **Muhammad's Quran** since he was its author and in fact **Muhammad, Gabriel, Satan and Allah** are actually one and the same because Muhammad used Gabriel and Allah as tools and red herrings to give his words divine sanction.

I also mention **Muhammadan Muslims** because they follow the **Cult of Muhammad.**

Muhammadan Islam is not a **Religion** but only a **Cult.**

In the oxford dictionary, **Religion** is the belief in the **Divine.**

A **Cult** is the belief in and emulation of, **a human being.**

Both the Quran and the Ahadith assert and instruct, especially the **males** of Muhammadan Islam to **slavishly** emulate the deeds, thoughts, manners and ideas of Muhammad since he allegedly represented the **perfect** male **Human Being**. This by and of itself represents **cultism.**

Most important of all, there is not a single **new Practical** and **Spiritual Precept, Concept, Thought** or **Idea** in the whole of the Quran that had not been **Plagiarised, Pirated, Plundered** and or **Perverted** from the **Scriptures** of the **Jews, the Christians,** the **Zoroasterians,** the **Pagan Arabians,** their **Traditions** and their **Fetishes.**

The only new items in it are the enormous number of **Hatemongering, Warmongering, Racist, Torture** and **Hellish** verses that permeate most of its pages.

#5. Women in Islam

Q: We are told by Muhammadan Muslims – mostly male – that women are treated extremely well in Islam. We also see interviews with some Muhammadan women, who are almost completely covered except for their face and sometimes with only their eyes showing, confessing that they are 'liberated' by their faith. Is this the reality ?

A: Muhammad had a very conflicted attitude towards women; although several verses in the **Quran** display some compassion towards them, none the less, other verses - **which abrogate/ over rule the earlier ones** - show a distinctly low esteem for them in general.

They are looked upon primarily as an **object** for **sexual gratification** and **procreation.** This is reflected in many verses of the Quran and many more - even more derogatory - in the Ahadith.

*Al Baqara 2: 223 Your wives are as a **tilth** unto you; so approach your tilth **when or how ye will***

*** Muhammadan Islam relegates womanhood to the level of a field suitable for ploughing and sowing seed, and the man as the tiller.

The Muslim wife is only a sex object for the Muslim husband's pleasure and desires, when, where and how it suits him. What are mandated under **Shari'a law** are immoral, unjust and unacceptable instructions such as:

That women can be sexually **'violated'** in any manner, time or place that the **'Muslim' man** deems fit.

That a husband may beat his wife with or without a reason, at will.

That a woman cannot sue for divorce on any grounds, etc., etc.

Women are invariably considered as objects for the Muhammadan man's pleasure and gratification; his plaything ***

Al Nisa 4:3 "If you fear that you shall not be able to deal justly with orphans, marry women of your choice who seem good to you, **two or three or four...**"

11 "Allah directs you in regard of your Children's (inheritance): to the male, a portion equal to that of *two* females..."

34 Men are the **protectors and maintainers** of women .. the righteous women are devout .... As to those women on whose part ye fear disloyalty and ill-conduct admonish them, refuse to share their beds, **beat them**

43 "Believers, ..If you are ill, or on a journey, or come from answering the call of nature, or you have **touched a woman,** and you find no water, then take for yourselves clean dirt, and rub your faces and hands

***The Quran claims that **women** are so unclean and polluted that they **are worse than dirt** ***

Al Ahzab 33:59 "Prophet! Tell your wives and daughters and all believing women that they should **cast their outer garments** over their persons

*** As usual in the translation and interpretation of the Quranic verses, the Muhammadan scholars, all male, created rules and regulations to humiliate and make women subject to the dictates of the Muhammadan male chauvinists under all circumstances.

These were and are nefarious, oppressive and inhumane acts of **control** and **subjugation.**

I have absolutely no doubt that the listeners would be utterly shocked to know that nowhere in the whole of the Quran is there any mention whatsoever of the **veil (hijab)** as a covering of women.

The idea, that only a woman's eyes should be exposed out of her whole body, is not only morally bereft of justice and equality, but **is utterly obscene and totally ungodly.**

God did not create women so that only men should be allowed to strut on the face of the earth not fully covered as the women.

Another remarkable story is buried in the Tradition that Aisha, the wife of Muhammad, related that he did not force his wives to wear the hijab as in-

Sahih Al-Bukhari Hadith 8.257 Narrated by Aisha

'Umar bin Al-Khattab used to say to Allah's Apostle

"Let your wives be veiled." **But he did not do so.**

Sahih Al-Bukhari Hadith 1.301 Narrated by Abu Said Al Khudri

Once Allah's Apostle went out to the **Musalla** (to offer the prayer) on 'Id-al-Adha or Al-Fitr prayer. Then he passed by the women and said**, "O women! Give alms, as I have seen that the majority of the dwellers of Hell-fire were you (women)."**

They asked, "Why is it so, O Allah's Apostle?" He replied,

"You curse frequently and are ungrateful to your husbands. I have not seen anyone **more deficient in intelligence and religion than you.** A cautious sensible man could be led astray by some of you."

Sahih Al-Bukhari Hadith1.493 Narrated by Aisha

The prophet said: The things which annul prayer were mentioned before me (and those were):

a dog, a donkey and a woman. I said, "You have compared us (women) to **donkeys and dogs.**

Sahih Al-Bukhari Hadith 7.33 Narrated by Usama bin Zaid

The Prophet said, "After me I have not left any **affliction more harmful to men than women.**"

The most accurate appraisal of women in Muhammadan Islam is one found in *Mishkat al Masabih, Volume 2, Page 692,* by Waliuddin Abu Abdullah Mahmud Tabrizi as translated by Al Haj, Maulana Fazlul Karim's al Hadith:

"A woman is like a **PRIVATE PART.** When she goes out, the devil casts a glance at her"

That is why women in Muhammadan Islam have to be covered from head to toe because every square inch of their body is like a genital which would arouse the uncontrollable sexual desires of the Muhammadan males.

Sahih Al-Bukhari HadithHadith 3.826 "The Prophet said, 'Isn't the witness of a woman equal to half of that of a man?' The women said, 'Yes.' He said, 'This is because of the **deficiency of a woman's mind.'"**

Sahih Al-Bukhari Hadith 4.547 Narrated byAbu Huraira

The Prophet said, "But for the Israelis, meat would not decay and **but for Eve, wives would never betray their husbands."**

Bukhari:4.143/5.523

"When we reached Khaybar, Muhammad said that Allah had enabled him to conquer them. It was then that the beauty of Safiyah was described to him.

Her husband had been killed, so Allah's Apostle selected her for himself. He took her along with him till we reached a place called Sad where her menses were over and he took her for his wife, consummating his marriage to her, and forcing her to wear the veil.'"

*** In reality, after having murdered her husband, father, brother and others, he **RAPED** her.

The idea that he 'married' her is not only revolting under the circumstances of her capture, but utterly devoid of morality or logic. It is totally insane ***

Bukhari:6.28 "The Prophet said: **'I was shown the Hell Fire and the majority of its dwellers were women** who are disbelievers or ungrateful.' When asked what they were ungrateful for, the Prophet answered,

'All the favors done for them by their husbands.'"

Sahih Al-Bukhari Hadith 7.30/2 Narrated by Abdullah bin Umar

Allah's Apostle said, **"Bad omen is in the women, the house and the horse."**

Sahih Al-Bukhari Hadith 7.33 Narrated byUsama bin Zaid

The Prophet said, "After me I have not left any **affliction more harmful to men than women."**

Sahih Al-Bukhari Hadith 7.48 Narrated byHishams father

Khaula bint Hakim was one of those ladies who presented themselves to the Prophet for marriage. 'Aisha said, "Doesn't a lady feel ashamed for presenting herself to a man?" But when the Verse: "(O Muhammad) You may postpone (the turn of) any of them (your wives) that you please," (33.51) was revealed, 'Aisha said, **"O Allah's Apostle! I do not see, but that your Lord hurries in pleasing you."**

*** Even a **teenager** such as Aisha was at the time, realised that there was something very unusual in the manner that Muhammad received his conveniently 'descended' alleged 'revelations'.

They were all **'MADE TO ORDER'** revelations ***

The references that I have quoted so far are only a **fraction** of more to be found in the Quran and the Hadiths but I hope will suffice to demonstrate the reality of how women **actually** fare under Muhammadan Islam as compared to the lies and falsehoods repeatedly declared by invariably the male Muhammadan Muslims in the news media.

#6a. Quran contradictions: Peaceful and Warmongering Verses – Mecca Period

Q: It is a fact that most people are utterly confused about what they hear from various sources regarding the Quran as to whether or not it is peaceful.

We listen to Muhammadan Muslims reciting very conciliatory and peaceful verses from the Quran and then we hear others which are the exact opposite. Can you elaborate?

A: You are absolutely right of course, because it is extremely confusing.

The problem resides in the FACT that most people, whether they are followers of Muhammad or NOT, do not know, have not read and / or have not been told the facts about the history and background of the alleged 'revelations' of the Quran.

Q: With all due respect, I find this hard to believe. Take for example

Chapter 2: 256 *Let there be* **no compulsion in religion.** *Truth stands out clear from error;*

OR

Chapter 109 : 6 To you be **your religion** *and to* **me my religion.**

OR

Chapter 42: 15 …. Allah is our Lord and your Lord

Unto us our works and unto you your works; *no argument between us and you. Allah will bring us together, and unto Him is the journeying.*

Q: By no standard of morality or logic can any fair-minded person call the above Aggressive HAatemongering or Warmongering.

A: You are of course 100% correct but you haven't yet explained the background that would unravel these anomalies and misunderstandings. May I continue?

Q: Go on then

A: What I am about to explore with you is **NOT** anti Islamic propaganda because this information can be found by anyone interested in the subject either on the internet or in the relevant books as they were and are written by the Muhammadan Muslim scholars themselves.

Let me Explain

The alleged revelations of the Quran went through TWO very distinct periods with **irreconcilable** contents.

The first Period is called the **Meccan** period starting in the year 610AD and ending in **622/3AD.** During this period, Muhammad was **a man alone** against the whole of his own tribe the Quraysh as well as against every single other Pagan Arab, bar the few family friends and slaves who believed in his message.

Muhammad after all, was actually trying to **overthrow** and **overturn** all their centuries old beliefs.

He was attempting to **convert** them to Monotheism.

He was doing this by attacking, insulting and denigrating all the beliefs and traditions of the Arabs that had existed for centuries. He was obviously perceived as a devil obsessed or crazy person as the Quranic verses of that period duly report.

During this period, the verses were as passionate and as powerful as those of the Hebrew prophets of earlier times. They were also conciliatory and reasonable. The verses you quoted earlier, each one of them and several more, originated during the **Meccan** period, the first and conciliatory period.

After almost **thirteen years** of passionate preaching Muhammad was only able to convert an abysmally small number of people of less than **100 souls.** His tribe mocked and laughed at his antics and 'revelations'.

In the year, 622/3AD, Muhammad's fortunes changed dramatically when some men of the **Aus** tribe of the **Madina** PLEDGED to protect him and accepted him as their leader and in return, as the messenger of Allah to intercede on their behalf so that they end up in Paradise with unlimited Carnal, Sensual and Sexual pleasures when they die fighting for **"the cause of Allah"** that **is "Fi sabil Allah"**.

6b. Quran contradictions: Peaceful and Warmongering Verses Madina Period

Muhammad's migration from Mecca to Madina is the famously called **Hijra.**

Thus begins the **second period** of 'revelations' called the **Maina Period.**

Madina became the headquarters of the first **Organized Crime Syndicate** in history. Muhammad sent piratical raiding parties to slaughter, plunder, rape and enslave so called **Unbelieving** Arabs, the majority in the Arabian Peninsula.

He also attacked the Christian and Judaized Arabs. These attacks were conducted in ambush, without warning and **invariably** during the **Holy** and **forbidden** months of the Arabs.

To justify any and all of his criminal and unmerciful instructions to assassinate his opponents; to attack innocent and unsuspecting other Arabs, very convenient 'revelations' were descended upon him by Allah through the angel Gabriel, whenever and wherever he needed them, **sanctifying** his actions.

It was during the Madina period that the mantra **twinning** and invariably associating Muhammad with Allah was also, 'revealed':

"Allah and his messenger"

" Allah wa Rassoolahu"

It was also during this second period that almost all of the **Hatemongering & Warmongering** verses of the Quran were revealed.

The following verse, called the **abrogating verse** is the one that explains **ALL** the misunderstandings and contradictions that overwhelm and confuse people.

Surat al Baqara 2: 106 *"None of Our revelations do We **abrogate** or **cause to be forgotten** without substituting them with something better or simila...."*

Abrogation [Naskh] means that Muhammad's Allah 'revealed' verses that **over ruled and or overturned** previous ones.

Now let's take what is called the **'Fighting verse'** for example, which was revealed in Madina, it overturned or **over ruled 124** previous conciliatory verses of the Meccan period.

Surat al Tauba **9:** *5 "But when the forbidden months are past **then fight and slay** the pagans wherever ye find them and seize them **beleaguer** them and lie in wait for them in every stratagem (of war)..."*

Ibn 'Arabi said, "The verse of the *'sword'* 9:5, has abrogated 124 verses of the Quran" *(p. 69).*

According to **Ibn Kathir** (the verse of the **Sword)** abrogated every **peace treaty** that had been made with the idolaters – The Pagan Arabs

Previously, you our listeners, heard three conciliatory examples from the Meccan period. Now you will hear the verses which abrogated or overruled them:

Al Baqara 2: 256 *" Let there be **no compulsion in religion.** Truth stands out clear from error..."(Mecca)*

Al Imran 3: 85 *"If anyone desires a religion **other than Islam** (submission to Allah) never will it be accepted of him...";*

Al Saff 61: 9 *"It is He Who has sent His Apostle with Guidance and the Religion of Truth that he **may proclaim it over all religion** even though the Pagans may detest it..."*

Al Kafrun 109 : 6 *"To **you your religion** and to me **my religion....**" (Mecca)*

Al Hijr 15: 42 *" Allah is **our Lord and your Lord.***

Unto us our works and unto you your works; *no*

argument between us and you. Allah will bring us together, and unto Him is the journeying....."(Mecca)

Al Tauba 9: 29 *"**Fight those who believe not in Allah** nor the Last Day nor hold that forbidden which hath been forbidden by Allah and His apostle nor acknowledge the religion of truth (even if they are) of the **People of the Book** (Jews & Christians) until they pay the **Jizya** with willing **submission and feel themselves humiliated"***

These three examples are but a few of the hundreds of Abrogating and Abrogated verses in the Quran that constitute the core beliefs that have to be followed by **Fundamentalist Muhammadan Muslims.**

In fact, according to the Muhammadan exegetes, these verses appear in 71 out of 114 suras comprising **62.28%** of the Quran.

7. Jihad in Islam

Q: Muslims and Arabists often inform us that Jihad means Spiritual Struggle; is this true?

A: The word **Jihad** in the **Arabic** language has its root in **jahada** which does mean **Struggle/ Endeavour/ Strive.**

Unfortunately, those who explain it in **spiritual** terms are **deliberately** deceiving and misleading the public about its actual meaning based entirely upon the Arabic language of the Quran and the Hadiths.

In innumerable verses in the Quran and the Hadiths **Jihad** means only **ONE** thing:

"**Physical Warfare** in the cause of **Allah**" which in **Arabic** it is:

"Jihad fi Sabil^Allah"

Most people, whether followers of Muhammad or not, **do not know** that Muhammad **unilaterally** declared **total** and **eternal** war, **1400** years ago, against **ALL** unsuspecting Human Beings **who do not believe as he does.**

Contrary to all the falsified assertions by politically correct westerners and aided and abetted by Muhammadans who have every reason to hide the truth, Jihad is not a **spiritual struggle** for excellence but **continuous and relentless warfare** against all so called **Unbelievers** until all of humanity is either converted to Muhammadan Islam, is subject to it or is **slaughtered.**

In fact, among Muslim scholars, it constitutes the unwritten **Sixth Pillar of Muhammadan Islam.**

The Quran and the Hadiths are crystal clear in affirming this. The Quran and Ahadith contain hundreds of verses attesting to and asserting this **dogma.**

Not even **once** in the Quran can anyone find the word **jihad** mentioned by itself and meaning **spiritual struggle.**

All the derivatives of the word jihad in the Quran and Hadiths represent **acts of war** and **aggression** to spread the belief in Allah **and** in Muhammad as the messenger of Allah.

To be able to **indoctrinate** any human being, to be so prepared as to willingly die for a faith, thus becoming a martyr [shaheed] who would be rewarded with **eternal sexual, sensual & carnal pleasures** in the **after life** than in life on earth, should be considered among the most **Diabolical** weapons of war ever conceived.

In such a war, very little mercy could be shown to the enemy – the **Unbelievers** - until it is totally subdued, converted or exterminated.

This ideological 'weapon' has been used throughout 'Islamic' history both against the 'infidels' as well as against other 'unbelieving' sects of Islam.

In all of the Quranic verses - as well as in the Ahadith - Jihad is invariably associated with **physical warfare** and **fighting** and not as a **spiritual striving** for a **higher morality** and or **discovery** of **self.**

In the tradition of Muhammadan Islam, the world is divided into **two** major parts:

1 Dar Al Salam: (Territory of Peace)-

They comprise territories completely under the control of **Muhammadan (Muslims); al (Mu'mineen/Believers)** which is made up of two components:

(a) Dar Al Islam: Territories with a majority of Muslim peoples

(b) Dar al Sulh: Territories with a non- Muhammadan majority **(occupied)** and under the **'protection'** of the 'Muslims'

2 Dar al Harb: (Territory of war)-

All territories in the world that are not under the control of **Muhammadans** are considered to be in the hands of the alleged **(Kuffar/Unbelievers),** and consequently are fair game for attack, despoliation, rape and subjugation to **'Islam'.**

I.Q. Al Rassooli

In reality, there is no **secular war** in Muhammadan Islam because from the very beginning of the Muhammadan Islamic **polity**, war, plunder and aggression were the means by which the Muhammad and his followers built up their empire.

Jihad became a perpetual **holy duty** of warring against **All** infidels; that is a continuous war of aggression against **All** those who do not believe as they do; in

"Allah and his messenger, Muhammad"

These wars were not in defense of 'Islam' but to gain territory, economic wealth, slavery, booty, rape and plunder. Converting these peoples to '**Islam**' was last on the agenda of Muhammad's followers but became a very important by-product of these wars of aggression.

It is a cruel irony - if not actually divine justice - that among the largest victims of Jihadi terror were, are and continue to be **other** Muhammadans.

Each side of the conflict between two or more of the warring 'Muslim' factions or sects, accuses their opponents of Kufr and or Unbelief, turning them into *'**Enemies of Allah**'* and hence subject to 'divinely' sanctioned destruction.

In this manner and according to the Quran, their holy book, since all are Muslims killing other Muslims, none will ever be received in Paradise but will assuredly end up in Allah's Hell.

For the listeners who doubt all the above, the following very few sample verses and Hadiths should easily and conclusively sober them up:

Al Tauba 9: 5 *"But when the forbidden months are past then **fight and slay [fa'qtuloo]** the pagans wherever ye find them and seize them beleaguer them and lie in wait for them in every stratagem of war..."*

Al Tauba 9: 29 *"**Slaughter [qatiloo]** those who believe not in Allah nor the Last Day nor hold that forbidden which hath been forbidden by Allah and His apostle nor acknowledge the religion of truth [ISLAM] (even if they are) of the **People of the Book** until they pay the **Jizya with willing submission and feel themselves humiliated...**"*

Sahih Al-Bukhari Hadith 4.50 Narrated byAnas bin Malik

"The Prophet said, 'A single endeavor of fighting in Allah's Cause **(jihad) is better than the world and whatever is in it.**'"

Sahih Muslim Hadith 4631 & 4626 Abu Huraira

"I heard Muhammad say: ... **I love that I should be killed in Allah's Cause [Jihad]; then I should be brought back to life and be killed again.**'"

Sahih Al-Bukhari Hadith 4.73 Narrated by Abdullah bin Abi Aufa

Allah's Apostle said, **"Know that Paradise is under the shades of swords."**

There are **hundreds** more of similar verses in the Quran and the Hadiths for those who have **the appetite for more.**

We rest our case.

#8. ISLAMOPHOBIA

Islamophobia is a neologism used to refer to an irrational fear or prejudice towards Muslims and the religion of Islam.

The term has achieved a degree of linguistic and political acceptance which is utterly at odds with facts and reality.

Let us firstly deal with the **Facts:**

1. Muhammadan Muslims are the only group on the face of planet Earth who show their anger, their destructiveness, their Hatemongering and their Warmongering on TV, in Print, in their Educational System and in their Speech against ALL other belief systems be they Christian, Buddhist, Jewish, Hindu or Animists.

2. They are the only group who manifestation their Hate and Anger while holding their holy book the Quran in one hand and Guns, grenade launchers, swords and daggers in the other.

3. They are the only group who while demonstrating their hatred and anger shout and call upon the name of their god with their **Terror Verse**
   " Allahu Akbar"

4. They are the only group who in the *"name of Allah"* slaughter **unarmed** and innocent civilians by the sword, suicide bombings, beheadings, blowing up planes, buses, trains etc etc

5. Of all the acts of terror and **aggression** in the world today, Muhammadan Muslims have the pride of being the number one in at least **55 countries** in the world on **four continents.**

6. Muhammadan Muslim law, called the Sharia', discriminates unreservedly against the following:

a) All females (even be they followers of Muhammad

b) All **Unbelievers** such as Christians, Buddhists, Hindus, Jews etc

c) All Homosexuals

d) All sects of Muhammadan Muslims who do not follow their methods

7   Muhammadan Muslims **burn** and destroy the holy places of other religious groups such as Churches, Buddhist temples, Hindu shrines and synagogues without remorse.

8   Muhammadan Muslims show nothing but **utter contempt** for the beliefs, property and lives of all those who do not believe as they do.

9   Muhammadan Muslims massacre, mutilate, rape and destroy the lives and holy places of other Muhammadan Muslims who do not follow the same path.

10 Muhammadan Muslims in the Western Democracies, while hiding behind their Freedoms of Speech and Belief, declare in public and in the media that they intend to turn the Christian Democracies into replicas of their **depraved** belief systems.

11 Most Muhammadan Muslims in the world – the so called 'Silent Majority' – rarely if ever demonstrate against these inhumane, depraved and sickening acts and behaviour conducted daily in their name and in the name of 'Islam'.

12 One can understand and sympathize with those Muhammadan Muslims who live under Islamic governments and live in fear of being in the opposition, but those who live in Democracies **have no excuse whatsoever** in showing their disapproval, disgust and anger at those who are allegedly bringing Muhammadan

Islam in DISREPUTE.

13 It is one of the great ironies of history that it was Muhammad himself who said :

"Silence Means Consent", hence the silence of the followers of Muhammad in the West does mean that they **consent** to what others are committing in their name, in the name of Muhammadan Islam & Allah.

In fact and in reality, they have no choice since those that the media **erroneously** call 'Islamic Radicals' are actually the **truest believers** in the faith of Muhammadan Islam since they are **only** following what the **Quran** itself commands them to do in hundreds upon hundreds of verses:

To force into **Conversion,** to **Hate,** to **War,** to **Subjugate,** to **Slaughter,** to **Plunder,** to **Rape** and to **Enslave ALL** those human beings who **do not believe as they do.** That is the remaining **80%** of Humanity.

If all the above items, which any and all sane human beings are watching on TV, reading in the newspapers or listening to on the Radio **do not justify** being **afraid of Muhammadan Islam,** what does?

Muhammadan Islam **is so radical,** it has no shades.

#9. Was Muhammad a Prophet?

Q: Is a question that is repeatedly put to me by hundreds of people who do not know the facts; hence, I am putting up this chapter to enlighten them.

A: The Oxford dictionary, explains-

Prophet: A person who **predicts,** or claims to be able to **predict,** what will happen in the **future.**

From this root comes **Prophecy, Prophesy & Prophetic,** all of which are associated with **foretelling future events.**

From **Moses** to most of the **Jewish Prophets,** they were not only **warners** of their people, but actually **predicted** what would happen in the future.

Not once in the **Quran,** did **Muhammad** predict a future event that actually came true. In fact, **Aisha,** in the **Ahadith** insisted that he **could not** tell future events.

Al Imran 3: 179 Allah will not leave the believers in the state in which ye are now until He separates what is evil from what is good. Nor will He *disclose to you the secrets of the Unseen.* But He chooses of his Apostles (for the purpose) whom He pleases. So believe in Allah and His Apostles: and if ye believe and do right ye have a reward without measure.

Al A'araf 7:188 Say: "I have no power over any good or harm to myself except as Allah willeth. *If I had knowledge of the unseen* I should have multiplied all good and no evil should have touched me *I am but a warner* and a bringer of glad tidings to those who have faith."

Yusuf 10:20 They say: "Why is not a Sign sent down to him from his Lord?" Say: *"The Unseen is only for Allah (to know). Then wait ye: I too will wait with you."*

Al Jinn 72:26 He (alone) knows the Unseen nor does He make any one acquainted with His Mysteries

In none of the above verses does Muhammad claim any knowledge of the future. On the contrary, **he insists that he is incapable of doing so.**

Sahih Al-Bukhari Hadith 9.477 Narrated by Masruq

'Aisha said, "If anyone tells you that Muhammad has seen his Lord, he is a liar, for Allah says: 'No vision can grasp Him.' (6.103) And if anyone tells you that Muhammad has seen the Unseen **(can tell the future)** is a liar, for Allah says: "None has the knowledge of the Unseen but Allah."

*** In many of the verses of the Quran and stories of the Ahadith, Muhammad did his best to portray himself as an Arabian version following in the footsteps of the Hebrew prophets.

He actually fancied himself to be, the fulfillment of the Jewish tradition of the **Messiah;** that he, Muhammad, was the promised Messiah for whom the Jews & Christians had been waiting***

*Al Saf 61:6 And remember Jesus the son of Mary said: "O Children of Israel! I am the apostle of Allah (sent) to you confirming the Law (which came) before me and **giving glad Tidings of an Apostle to come after me whose name shall be Ahmad.**" But when he came to them with Clear Signs they said "This is evident sorcery!"*

*** Any reader of the Hebrew Bible and the New Testament would know that neither **Muhammad nor Ahmad** are either mentioned or predicted in these Scriptures.

Of course, being totally ignorant of the required attributes of the Jewish Messiah, he none the less, unilaterally claimed this position, and became full of hate towards the Arabians of the faith of the Jews because they derided his claims, and refused to follow his **cult.**

This enraged him to such an extent, as to have had their men massacred, and their women and children enslaved, raped or sold and their wealth distributed among his plundering followers **while he kept his 20% share of the booty and loot.**

Not a single one of the Hebrew prophets behaved in such an **ungodly, selfish** and **morally** as well as **religiously depraved** manner ***

Al Baqara 2: 204 *"There is the type of man whose speech about this world's life may dazzle thee and he calls Allah to witness about what is in his heart;* ***yet he is the most contentious of enemies.***

*** Ladies & gentlemen, this verse is the most incredibly truthful one in the Quran since it fits Muhammad **perfectly** ***

#10. The £10,000.00 Challenge to Muhammadan Muslims

We would like to point out especcially the obvious to any and all surfers of the Web or explorers of U Tube as well as those who read and watch the news, the following:

1. That although the followers of Muhammad are never inhibited from insulting, denigrating, demonizing and or dehumanizing the beliefs and characters of others, called **Unbelievers,** they do not tolerate and go into paroxysms of rage and violence against any and all those who subject their beliefs to scrutiny, comment or investigation.

2. The reason for this depraved behaviour is very simple: Since they cannot **ever** contradict the **facts** about their **Cult Belief System**, they resort to **exactly** the same reaction and methodology that Muhammad used against any and all those who **questioned** his veracity, **challenged** his claims to prophet-hood, or satirized him, be they **male** or **female,** Young or Old, Free or Slave. According to the Muhammadan Muslim records themselves in the **Ahadith**, they were invariably **assassinated** by treachery or **ambush.**

3. When Muhammad's veracity was questioned regarding his **alleged** Quranic revelations by his people the Quraysh or by the Arabian Jews and Christians, he resorted to the violence of the ignorant thug because he could not extricate himself from the **fact** that he was a deceiver, a liar and a charlatan who was **pretending** to be the Messenger of Allah.

4. Since any and all **true** Muhammadan Muslim Believers must follow the **Sunna al Nabawiya,** that is, they **must** emulate Muhammad's **deeds, behaviour, actions, thoughts** and **instructions,** as his **clones,** then they have no choice but to **murder, slaughter** and **destroy** any and all those **w**hom they perceive as

questioning the truthfulness of the Quran or **insulting** Muhammad, just as Muhammad did 1400 years ago.

5   Most people whether they are Muhammadan Muslims or **not**, truly believe and think that the Quran is a **holy** Scripture. In reality, when the subject of the Quran, its formation, its authorship & its compilation are **studied** based **entirely** on the Arabic of the Muhammadan Muslim sources, the readers will have absolutely no choice but to conclude that the Quran is neither **holy** nor is it a **scripture.**

6   It is obvious that any one who unquestioningly believes in a certain system will not accept any insults to his or her beliefs. That is why we receive a great number of deadly threats, obscene insults and accusations of being ignorant, stupid or **Islamophobic.**

7   You who are listening to this series of Questions & Answers, I would like to point out to you, again and again, that **contrary** to what the Politically Correct and invariably **ignorant** Media, Politicians & Religious Leaders of the Western Democracies tell you about the subject of Muhammadan Islam, the **facts** are the following:

    a)   The most **perfect** Muhammadan Muslim state was that of the **Taliban** in Afghanistan.

    b)   The most **perfect** follower of Muhammad is a **Jihadi** – so called Holy Warrior - like Osama bin Ladin.

    c)   The most reviled and unacceptable Muhammadan Muslims are those who disagree with the above & who would like to have decent relationships with all other human beings, the so called Unbelievers

    d)   The best allies and succour of Muhammadan Islam are **ignorance & stupidity.**

I.Q. Al Rassooli

e) The worst **enemies** of Muhammadan Islam are **knowledge** and **understanding** of the Quran & Ahadith as well as Arab and Islamic histories.

8   To counter the accusations made against us, we have put up a challenge on our web

www. inthenameofallah.org,

not only to the followers of Muhammad but actually

to **every** human being on the face of planet Earth.

It goes like this:

QUESTION:

WHY, THE READER OR LISTENER MAY ASK, SHOULD I INVESTIGATE THIS SITE AND NOT THE HUNDREDS OF OTHERS OF SIMILAR CONTENT ?

ANSWER:

BECAUSE THIS SITE MAKES AN OFFER UNHEARD OF IN THE ENTIRE INTERNET OF A REWARD WORTH

£10,000.00 (TEN THOUSAND POUNDS STERLING)

TO BE PAID FOR EVERY VERSE IN THE QURAN,

NO MATTER HOW MANY TIMES IT IS REPEATED,

THAT ANYONE ON THE FACE OF THE EARTH CAN PROVE THAT IT REPRESENTS

A NEW, PRACTICAL, SPIRITUAL AND INTELLECTUAL, CONCEPT, PRECEPT, THOUGHT OR IDEA,

WHICH, IN ANY WAY SHAPE OR FORM, IS EQUAL TO, OR SUPERIOR

TO ANYTHING THAT THE QURAN ITSELF, HAS

PLAGIARISED, PLUNDERED, PIRATED AND OR PERVERTED

FROM THE BIBLE, THE NEW TESTAMENT, ZOROASTERIAN AND PAGAN ARABIAN RELIGIONS,

THEIR TRADITIONS, THEIR FETISHES AND THEIR SCRIPTURES.

WHOEVER TAKES UP THIS CHALLENGE MUST ALSO ACCEPT

TO PAY AN EQUAL SUM OF

£10,000.00 (TEN THOUSAND POUNDS STERLING)

FOR EVERY VERSE IN THE QURAN,

NO MATTER HOW MANY TIMES IT IS REPEATED

THAT THE AUTHOR CAN SHOW BEYOND A REASONABLE DOUBT

AND WITHOUT A SHADOW OF A DOUBT

THAT IT HAD TO HAVE BEEN

PLAGIARISED, PLUNDERED, PIRATED AND OR PERVERTED

FROM THE BIBLE, THE NEW TESTAMENT, ZOROASTERIAN AND PAGAN ARABIAN RELIGIONS,

THEIR TRADITIONS, THEIR FETISHES AND THEIR SCRIPTURES.

We have absolutely no doubt that **no** follower or followers of Muhammad would take up this challenge since their arguments would have to be backed up with **facts, reality** and **intellect** and hope to win.

In **fact**, we know that the probability of such a person existing on Earth is equal to the probability of finding a **Snowflake** in Muhammad's **Inferno**.

11. What is the BLACK STONE?

A: The **Black Stone** or **al Hajar al Aswad** in **Arabic,** is the name given to the meteorite embedded in the corner wall of the **Ka'ba** that was venerated by the **Pagan Arabs centuries before Muhammad** and has become the prime centre of veneration of **Muhammadan Islam** by subsuming all the traditions and fetishes of the **Pagan Arabs** into the new wrapping of **'Islam'**.

By the way, the **Black Stone (al Hajar al Aswad)** is **never** mentioned in the Quran.

According to the **mythical traditions** of the **Arabs,** this stone was given to **Abraham** and **Ishmael** by the angel **Gabriel** to be the **corner stone** of the **Ka'ba.**

Al Baqara 2: 127 "*And remember Abraham and Isma`il raised the foundations of the House : "Our Lord! accept (this service) from us for thou art the All-Hearing the All-Knowing* "

Tirmidi Hadith 2577: This stone was originally **white in colour,** but became **black** because it was **touched by menstruating women** over the centuries.

One should ask the question as to why would **Abraham,** the first **monotheist** and friend of **God, allow the veneration of a stone?**

It was he after all who, according to the tradition of the **Jews** and the **Muhammadan Muslims,** destroyed all the figures of gods and goddesses that were venerated by his tribe, why would he now accept another symbol of paganism, a mere un-sculpted stone, after all?

The **Black Stone** is a comparatively small meteorite, being roughly 30 cm (12 in.) in diameter.

When pilgrims circle the **Ka'ba** as part of the ritual of the **Hajj,** many of them try, if possible, to stop and kiss the **Black Stone.**

The **Stone** is actually broken into several pieces, damage which occurred when it was stolen in 930AD by the **Muslim Qarmatian** warriors who sacked **Mecca** and carried the **Black Stone** away to their base in **Bahrain.**

It was returned twenty-two years later. In the process, the **Black Stone** was cracked. It is now held together by a silver band, which is fastened by silver nails to the **Stone.**

I would like to point out, however, that even though the Ka'ba contained 360 idols that were worshipped before **Muhammad,** the **Black Stone** was never kissed or made an idol of worship by the **Pagan Arabs.**

In fact, the **Ka'ba** was never worshipped by the idolaters prior to **Muhammad.** The building contained idols of worship but the building itself was never an object of worship.

The single most important reason for kissing the **Stone** is because **Muhammad did so.** No devotional significance whatsoever is attached to the stone.

Bukhari, Muslim and Abu Daw'ud Hadiths report that **'Umar ibn al Khattab** approached the **Black Stone** and kissed it. Then he said:

"By Allah! I know that you are a mere stone that can neither harm nor do any good. If I had not seen the Prophet kissing you, I would have never kissed you."

*** This is an extremely interesting statement from one who used to be a pagan. His conversion to Monotheism was so complete that he was able to make the above statement while his Muhammad was actually **venerating** an **idol** ***

Al-Khatabi said: "This shows that abiding by the **Sunnah of the Prophet** is binding, regardless of whether or not **we understand its reason or the wisdom behind it."**

Such information devolves obligation on all those whom it reaches, even if they may not fully comprehend its significance.

Sowayd bin Ghaflah said: "I have seen 'Umar kissing the **Black Stone** and touching it." He further said: **"I know that the Prophet was especially very particular about it."**

*** I would like to point out to our listeners that during the whole of his life, **Muhammad venerated, prayed in and circumambulated the Ka,ba** while it was **still** a place of **idolatry** containing **360 rock gods** and **goddesses** ***

Furthermore, our listeners should be made aware of the following facts:

1. No where in the **Bible** is the name of **Allah** mentioned.

2. No where in the Torah or the **New Testament** is there any mention of **Arabia, Mecca or the Ka'ba.**

3. No where in the **Bible** is there mention that **Abraham, Hagar or Ishmael** having ever set foot in **Arabia** especially in the area of **Mecca**, almost **1000 desert miles** away from **Canaan.**

4. Before **Muhammad**, no pagan **Arab** was called **Abraham/ Ibrahim or Ishmael/Ismail.** This is based on the study of the names of **all** the men mentioned in the **Ahadith** who belonged to the **Pagan Arab** tribes.

If **Abraham and Ishmael** were **truly** the **forefathers** of the **Arabs**, it stands to reason that at least **some** Arabs would have carried their name. **None did. Muhammad's** name on the other hand, appears among almost **50%** of his male followers.

5. One can understand that it was possible for the **Arabs** to have lost their **'original' Monotheism** and returned to **Paganism**; but it would be beyond logic or comprehension to assume that they **also** forgot the names of their most illustrios **'fathers'**.

6. No where in all the **oral traditions** of **Arabia**, the poems of the **Jahiliyah (before Muhammad)**, is there mention of **Abraham or Ishmael**, of Hagar (she is not even mentioned in the Quran), of **Maqam Ibrahim** in the **Ka'ba**, or anything about the **Black Stone.**

All these mythical traditions were **concocted** and put together by the followers of **Muhammad** over a period of almost **300 years** after his death.

7. The Quran **repeatedly** asserts that the **Pagan Arabs** had no *"knowledge of previous revelations"*. If so, how pray tell, could they have known about the **Hebrew Patriarchs** that they claim relationship to?

8. All the so called 'traditions' of 'Islam' regarding the origins of the **Black Stone,** the **Ka'ba, Abraham, Hagar, Ishmael, Adam & Eve** (she is not mentioned in the Quran either) were **concocted** and put together over a period of almost **300 years** after the death of **Muhammad.**

9. No where does the Quran even intimate that the Arabs are descended from Abraham and Ishmael but only that they were the first 'Muslims' and the alleged builders of the foundation of the Ka'ba.

10. Muhammad had to create for himself and his followers a **worthy** ancestry befitting *'the prophet of Allah'*. He had the genius to Plagiarise, Plunder, Pirate and or Pervert from the Bible the Hebrew characters, precepts, concepts, thoughts and ideas as a foundation for his new 'scripture'.

11. All these alleged 'traditions' are only **wishful** thinking that have been fostered upon the human intellect for the last **1400 years.**

Fiqh-us-Sunnah   Fiqh 5.74b

Sunnah of Tawaf

It is Sunnah to perform certain acts in tawaf as given below:

1. Facing the **Black Stone** at the start of the **tawaf** while uttering a **takbir (Allahu-Akbar),** and a **tahlil (La ilaha illahlah),** and raising one's hands as they are raised in prayers, **and if possible touching it with both hands and kissing it quietly, or placing one's cheek on it.**

Ibn 'Umar said: "Allah's Messenger (peace be upon him) faced the **Black Stone, touched it, and then placed his lips on it**

and wept for a long time." 'Umar also wept for a long time. The Prophet (peace be upon him) said: 'O 'Umar, this is the place where one should shed tears.'" (Reported by Al-Hakim, who considers it a sound hadith with a sound chain of authorities)

Al-Tirmidhi Hadith 2577 Narrated byAbdullah ibn Abbas

Allah's Messenger (peace be upon him) said, "The **black stone** descended from **Paradise** whiter than milk, but the sins of the descendants of Adam made it black."

Ahmad and Tirmidhi transmitted it, the latter saying that his is a hasan sahih tradition.

Al Nisa 4:113 "... *For Allah hath sent down to thee the Book and wisdom* **and taught thee what thou knewest not (before) [ma lam takoonoo ta'alamu ...]**".

Al Shura 42:52 "*And thus have We by Our command sent inspiration to thee:* **thou knowest not (before) what was Revelation and what was Faith...**"

Al Jumu'ah 62:2 "*It is He Who has sent amongst the Unlettered (Ummyeen) an apostle from among themselves to rehearse to them His Signs to sanctify them and* **to instruct** *them in Scripture and Wisdom* **although they had been before in manifest error**

In the **Qarawiyun Manuscript in Fez *(MS fos.8a-9b)* Umar ibn al Khattab** was being regaled by stories about the potency of invocation and the narrator told him that in the **Jahiliyah,** the **pagan Arabs knew nothing of a One and only God, the sending of prophets, resurrection, paradise or hell.**

Also in *(MS fos. 22b-23b)* where it states the following "**... The Arabs were illiterate. They did not study writing. All they knew of heaven and hell, the resurrection, the mission of prophets and so on was the little they heard from the Jews and Christians. This teaching had no effect on their lives**"

Before Muhammad, the Pagan Arabs did not know that they were related to Abraham or Ishmael.

12. What is the Ka'ba?

Q: Millions of people regard the Ka,ba as the holiest place in Muhammadan Islam. What in reality is the Ka'ba?

A: In **Arabic,** it means a **Cube/Stele/Beth-el.** The historical records show no evidence whatsoever that it was at any time but a **House of Idolatory** and was never associated with monotheism till the advent of **Muhammad.**

It was a primitively structured shrine built by the **Pagan Arabs** as a simple cube like structure, without a roof, which sheltered a **12 inch diameter meteorite in the eastern corner of its wall**.

According to ***Ibn Ishaq (p 84)*** "...it was made of loose stones above a man's height, and they wanted to raise it and roof it because men had stolen part of the treasure of the Ka'ba which used to be in a well in the middle of it..."

This stone can be kissed by the pilgrims during the perambulation (the circulation of the faithful around the **Ka'ba**). It was one of **pagan Arabia's** holiest shrines with **360 idols** around it and an object of pilgrimage.

Being a site of pilgrimage, brought to **Mecca** trade and wealth in the same way that all such sites of pilgrimage do - and as it continues to do so up to this time in **Saudi Arabia.**

It is an astounding **fact** that the name of **Mecca** – nor that of Jerusalem - are ever mentioned in the Quran while in the **Bible** the name of **Jerusalem** is mentioned **667** times.

It is also a fact that little is known about the history of the Ka'ba apart from the myths and the totally unsubstantiated Muhammadan traditions which are **full of contradiction**s that maintain the following:

that the Ka'ba was originally built by Adam to a celestial prototype.

This story is neither found in the Quran nor in the Bible. That after the Deluge, it was allegedly rebuilt by Abraham and Ishmael *(2:125/7)* as a place of worship.

Al Baqara 2: 127 *" And remember **Abraham and Isma'il raised the foundations of the house...**"*

The Quran - the presumed word of Allah - **contradicts** all the Ahadith stories by **denying Adam** any involvement whatsoever with the Ka'ba as it asserts that only Abraham & Ishmael were the builders of its foundation as the first House of Worship dedicated to the **One and Only Allah. *(2:126-7)***

While engaged in rebuilding, **Ishmael** received the **Black Stone** from the **Angel Gabriel.** This of course makes absolutely no sense, since Ishmael would have needed to build the foundations of the **Ka'ba** to **protect something special,** the **Black Stone** for example, and certainly not if it were empty.

Why else did he need to build foundations to a flimsy structure not worthy of any (god)? The Black Stone had to be there in the first place as a fetish and object of veneration.

Since **Abraham and Ishmael** were monotheists, and **Abraham** already, according to **Muhammadan** traditions, destroyed the idols of his father, **why would he and Ishmael build a shrine for another idol such as a meteorite?**

If the **Arab** tradition already knew of **Abraham,** why then did they lapse into idolatry for at least **twenty- five centuries** that followed, while the **Israelites** and the **Jews** carried forth the torch of **Monotheism** that **inspired Muhammad** to create the Quran?

How was it possible that not a single pagan Arab was called **Ibrahim or Ismail,** if they actually were **the *'fathers'* of the Arabs?**

In contrast, after **Muhammad,** his name is carried by an enormous number of his followers.

If the traditions are true, why then, do repeated Quranic verses insist, in clear terms, that they - the Arabs - were actually totally ignorant of previous revelations? *S2:151, 11:49; 12:3; 16:43 etc.*

It is imperative that we make clear even the **obvious**, that the alleged Arabian traditions **contradict** everything written in the Bible regarding Abraham and Ishmael since according to the Bible **neither Abraham nor Ishmael knew a god called Allah**

They **never** traveled south to Arabia

They **never** knew any place called Mecca or a structure called the Ka'ba.

They **never** built the foundation of any structure

They **never** heard of or knew any messenger called **Gabriel**

Every single item in both the Quran and Hadiths regarding Abraham & Ishmael are lies and deceptions.

Centuries before Muhammad, most of the rituals of Muhammadan Islam were already practiced by the pagan Arabs, such as:

Pilgrimage, circumambulating the Ka'ba, calling the names of their idols, touching the Black Stone, prostrating, running between the two hills Safa & Marwa, venerating ZamZam, fasting, wearing white clothing, etc. etc.

In reality, **Muhammad** simply incorporated all the pagan rituals, traditions and fetishes of the **Pagan Arabs** and **'Islamised'** them to give his cult legitimacy, a sense of identity and an image of uniqueness so that he made it easier and less stressful for his brother **Arabs** to move from idolatry and paganism to his brand of **Monotheism** by continuing the practices of their **pagan fathers.**

In short, all Muhammad did, was merely to obliterate the pagan representations of the idols without abolishing the pagan practices.

Muhammad's quarrel with his Quraysh tribe was not because they did not believe in Allah - which they obviously did - but because they **associated other gods and goddesses with him.**

The same **Muhammad,** who went into paroxysms of rage and disgust that fill the **Quran,** at the idol worshipping of his tribe the **Quraysh,** did not hesitate for one moment to **incorporate** every facet of their traditions and fetishes into his new cult without shame or remorse.

During the whole period of 23 years that he used to fulminate and attack his idol worshipping Quraysh tribe, **Muhammad** prayed in the Ka'ba with them, **while it was full of pagan gods and goddesses.** His **hypocrisy** knew no bounds.

To gain favour with the pagan Arab tribes, he actually joined them wholeheartedly but for the single and very simple amendment to the whole of their religion; that was, to believe in **ONE Allah,** instead of Allah and 360 other idols.

It is extremely relevant to relate the story that **Umar ibn al Khattab** reluctantly but very intelligently remarked about the kissing of the **Black Stone** in-

Bukhari Hadith 2:667

He very astutely remarked: **" I know that you are only a stone, that neither helps nor hurts, and if the messenger of Allah had not kissed you, I would not kiss you"**; he then kissed it.

It is very revealing, that although **Umar** knew that the gesture was empty and false, he nonetheless copied **Muhammad** in kissing the stone. Just like **Umar, billions of Muhammadans** had followed - and continue to follow - their **'spiritual'** leaders in this **shameful** practice of venerating what was and continues to be a **pagan ritual.**

Hence every Muhammadan who makes the Hajj, who runs between the hills, who kisses the Black Stone, etc, **is performing pagan rituals, founded on pagan superstitions and sanctioned by Muhammad himself.**

What is important to point out is that most of the same Muhammadans, who incessantly assail and assault the *'paganism'* of the **Christians,** do not even know that the entirety of their **'traditions and fetishes'** are based upon the **paganasim** of the ancestors of the **Arabs.**

It is always a pity and with great frustration that we cannot mention all the verses in the Quran and Hadiths regarding any of the subjects that we are exploring with you for lack of time.

It is up to you, the listeners, who are inquisitive and want to know more, to read the relevant books or visit the **DEFINITIONS** section in our website.

#13. The Hijab and Muhammadan Islam

Q: In the last few years, the Muhammadan Muslims have been asserting their religious right to have their women wear the Hijab in the western democracies. Is it really mandated in their religion?

A: Like all the answers and statements that I give in this series, no matter how unbelievable or even offensive they may sound, are nontheless, based entirely upon the Arabic language of the Quran and of the Hadiths with all the corresponding references.

The **Arabic** word **'Hijab'** is sometimes translated as **veil**, but it can also signify anything that prevents something from being seen, such as a **screen**, a **curtain**, a **wall** or even a **hymen**. The root of the verb is **'Hajaba'** meaning to **'Hide'**.

In the **Quran** the term was originally used to mean a **(Screen/Curtain/Divide from cloth)** to separate especially the guests from the females of **Muhammad's** household.

The story that explains the reason for the particular alleged revelation of **Aya/verse 33:53** is mentioned in detail in **Bukhari Hadith 8:255/7**.

Sahih Al-Bukhari Hadith 8.255 Narrated by Anas bin Malik

that he was a boy of ten at the time when **Muhammad** emigrated to **Medina**. He added: I served Allah's Apostle for ten years and I know more than the people about the occasion whereupon **the order of Al-Hijab was revealed**

It was first revealed during the marriage of Allah's Apostle with **Zainab bint Jahsh.** In the morning, the Prophet was a bridegroom of her and he invited the people, who took their meals and went away, but a group of them remained with Allah's Apostle and they prolonged their stay.

Allah's Apostle got up and went out, and I too, went out along with him till he came to the lintel of 'Aisha's dwelling place.

Allah's Apostle thought that those people had left by then, so he returned, and I too, returned with him till he entered upon Zainab and found that they were still sitting there and had not yet gone. The Prophet went out again, and so did I with him till he reached the lintel of 'Aisha's dwelling place, and then he thought that those people must have left by then, so he returned, and so did I with him, and found those people had gone.

At that time, the Divine Verse of Al-Hijab was revealed, and the Prophet set a screen between me and him (his family).

Al Ahzab 33: 53 "O ye who Believe! enter not the Prophet's houses until leave is given you for a meal (and then) not (so early as) to wait for its preparation: but when ye are invited enter; and when ye have taken your meal disperse without seeking familiar talk. Such (behavior) annoys the Prophet: He is ashamed to dismiss you **but Allah is not ashamed (to tell you) the truth. And when ye ask (his ladies) for anything ye mustask them from before a screen/ (Hijabi) that makes for greater purity for your hearts and for theirs.** *Nor is it right for you that ye should annoy Allah's Apostle or that ye should marry his widows after him at any time. Truly such a thing is in Allah's sight an enormity"*

*** It is crystal clear from the verse above, that all of its 'instructions' are to do with Muhammad's personal annoyance at the behaviour of his guests. As usual with Muhammad and his Quran, an instant **Made to Order** 'revelation' was descended to turn his personal objections into unchallengeable 'divine sanctions' emanating from the unsuspecting mouth of Allah the rock god of the Ka'ba ***

In fact, the actual Arabic words used in the verse above are

"...min warai hijabi..." which should have been translated instead to *"...from behind a screen...".*

By no stretch of the imagination can any intelligent being construe, that the verse implies or means 'to cover the body of the female believer with any special clothing'.

All it instructs, is that there should be a separation between the guests area of the home of the believers from the private areas.

While the idea of the **Hijab** was to create an atmosphere of modesty vis a vis the females of the believers, **the male Muhammadan exgetes created an incredible set of lies to control women in body, in mind and in soul thus making them totally subservient to their will.**

By what kind of twisted logic can anyone accuse the women of Muhammadan Islam of tempting the men if these men are too weak or stupid to control their sexual predatory appetites and emotions?

Using exactly the same perverted logic, one can also accuse Muhammadan men of tempting women and have them wear the Hijab instead, especially since the Quran instructs both the men & the women believers to be chaste and modest.

Sahih Al-Bukhari Hadith 8.257 Narrated by Aisha

(the wife of the Prophet) **'Umar bin Al-Khattab** used to say to Allah's Apostle *"Let your wives be veiled."* **But he did not do so.** ...Umar was anxious for some Divine orders regarding the veiling of women. So Allah revealed the Verse of veiling. Al-Hijab.

*** Although both the Quran and Hadiths clearly explain the meaning and reason for the Hijab, none the less, the male chauvinist followers of Muhammad deliberately misinterpreted and or misrepresented it to mean that the female followers should be covered from head to toe with a garment from which only their eyes can be seen.

This is a method to control Muhammadan Muslim women physically, intellectually and spiritually so as to have them totally subservient to the will of the men as if they were domesticated animals.

They want to cover the female followers of Muhammad - hundreds of millions of God's human creatures - as if they are an offense to the Almighty***

Al Haj Maulana Fazlul Karim, in *'Mishkat al Masabih'*, **Volume 2, P692 says:**

> " A woman is like a private part. When she goes out, the devil casts a glance at her"

That is why the male Muhammadan Muslims want their women covered, as if they were genitals.

The **Arabic** word **Hijab** is used in the **Quran** - four times ONLY - as in the following *verses 7:46; 17:45; 38:32; 42:51* to describe a screen, a divide, a separator, a curtain, a veil of separation.

In none of them, is the word associated with any kind of dress or costume covering the whole body of anyone or anything.

What is being enforced upon the Europeans and other Democracies today is a **politocised** form of **hijab** so that slowly but surely, more and more **Shari'a** based rules are insinuated into the consciousness of our democracies acting as a slow poisoning of our values.

The **Hijab** is **NOT** in the **Quran** or in the **Hadiths** as a total covering of the women of **Muhammadan Islam and no Muhammadan Muslim can prove otherwise.**

Muhammadan Muslims depend **entirely** upon the **ignorance** of humanity in general regarding the Arabic language and the **actual** meaning of the Quranic verses to **fool, to deceive** and to deliberately **misinform** them so that they can insinuate their agenda into our democracies.

#14. Quran Against the Christians

Q: According to the Hadiths, the Christian ruler of Abyssinia protected the followers of Muhammad who escaped alleged persecution at the hands of the pagan Arabs.

Also according to the Hadiths, Muhammad met with the priest Bahira who allegedly recognized him as a prophet.

Furthermore Muhamnmad was married to his first and wealthy wife Khadijah who had a very Christian background. Why then does the Quran attack Christianity and the Christians?

A: Muhammad's knowledge and understanding of **Christianity** was even more abysmal than that of his understanding of the **Hebrew Bible**, as we shall reveal.

The words **Christian & Christians** appears **14 times** in the **Quran:**

In positive form Three times

In negative form Seven times

In neutral mode four times

As we explain in our series numbers **6a & 6b** regarding the two periods of alleged revelations of the **Quran** as well as in number **18** regarding the cases of **Abrogating & Abrogated** verses, at the beginning of **Muhammad's** so called revelations in **Mecca,** he was conciliatory and accommodating towards both the **Christians** and the **Jews.**

His attitude changed when he went to **Medina** and was rejected by both the Christians and the Jews as a prophet and as a messenger of Allah. It was during this period that he started attacking **both** the **Christians** and the **Jews** with an avalanche of ignorant and ignoramus hatemongering and warmongering verses as well as with acts of terror against them.

Muhammad in his **Quran** made it clear to his followers that he was the awaited for **Messiah of** the **Jews and the Christians.**

Al Saf 61:6 "*And Jesus, the son of [Miriam], said: 'Children of Israel, I am the Messenger of Allah (sent) to you, confirming that (which was revealed) before me in the Torah, and giving Glad Tidings of a Messenger to come after me, whose name shall be Ahmad (the Praised One)' But when he came to them with Clear Signs, they said, 'this is sorcery!'"*

*** Not a single follower of Muhammad, past, present or in the future can point out such a prediction in the New Testament without **perverting, contorting & twisting, language, religion, reality and facts** ***

Al Baqara 2:116 "*They say: '**Allah hath begotten a son:** glory be to Him.' Nay, to Him belongs all that is in heavens and on earth: All are subservient and obedient to Him.*"

Muhammad's attacks on the **Christians** centered exclusively on the fact that Christians believe in the Trinity and that Jesus is the son of God. This, according to **Muhammad's** Monotheism is **shirk,** meaning associating other gods with God rendering such believers **Kuffar** subject to Conversion to **Muhammadan Islam** or to **death and destruction.**

No matter how sweet **Muhammadan scholars** try to sugarcoat these diametrically opposite beliefs, the bottom line is that **Christianity** is synonymous with **Paganism.**

Al Imran 3:56 "*As for those **disbelieving infidels [Jews, Christians & pagans]**, I will punish them with a terrible agony in this world and the next. They have no one to help or save them.*"

61 "*If anyone disputes with you about **Jesus being divine,** flee them and pray that Allah will curse them.*"

69 "*It is the wish of the followers of the **People of the Book [Jews & Christians]** to lead you astray. But they make none to go astray except themselves, but they perceive not. ...*"

I.Q. Al Rassooli

*** Since the People of the Book already had the **original** and **uncorrupted revelations,** Muhammad's Plagiarised, Plundered, Pirated and /or Perverted version of their scriptures was and still is no match to theirs.

That is why Muhammad's Quran **rants** incessantly about their **disbelief.** Of course they were and still are in **disbelief** about the **mendacity, perversity** and **unholiness** of Muhammad's Quran ***

Al Imran 3:118 "O you who believe! ***Take not into your intimacy those outside your religion [pagans, Jews, and Christians].*** *They will not fail to corrupt you. They only desire your ruin. Rank hatred has already appeared from their mouths. What their hearts conceal is far worse. ...*

*** This verse is one among hundreds that **discriminate, incite hatred** and **villify** all humans who do not believe as the Muhammadans do, in 'Allah and in Muhammad as his messenger' ***

*Al Nisa 4:157 "'****We killed the Messiah, Jesus,' but they killed him not, nor crucified him.*** *It appeared so to them (as the resemblance of Jesus was put over another man and they killed that man). Nay, Allah raised him up unto Himself. Those who differ with this version are full of doubts. They have no knowledge and follow nothing but conjecture.* ***For surely they killed him not.****"*

*** With this single verse, the Quran **obliterates** the whole of the Christian religion, because if Jesus did not **die** on the **cross,** then there would have been **no resurrection** from the **dead.**

Without **death & resurrection,** Jesus could not have been the Messiah, the **redeemer** of humanity, and hence there can be no Christianity.

Another obvious 'divinely revealed' error in the above is the fact that the Jews **never** accepted that Jesus was their Messiah and hence did not and could not have called him

'the Messiah, Jesus' ***

Al Ma'ida 5:17 "In ***blasphemy [kafara]*** *indeed are those that say that* ***Allah***

***is Christ the son of Mary.** Say: "Who then hath the least power against Allah if His Will were to destroy **Christ the son of Mary his mother** and all everyone that is on the earth....*

18 *"The **Jews and the Christians** say: '**We are sons of Allah,** and his beloved.' Say: 'Why then does He punish you for your sins? Nay, you are but men. He forgives whom He wishes and punishes whom He pleases.'"*

*** Muhammad's understanding of the words of the Bible - as repeatedly shown in his Quran - was **utterly abysmal to say the least.**

When the Bible mentions sonship, it is never meant as a biological one but only that god **not allah - is the father of all of His creation** ***

Al Ma'ida 5: 51 *" O ye who believe!* **take not the Jews and the Christians for your friends and protectors:** *they are but friends and protectors to each other. And he amongst you that turns to them (for friendship) is of them. Verily Allah guideth not a people unjust*

The listeners should not require many more such **Vile** verses to be convinced of the Quran's **Racism, Hatemongering** and **Discriminatory** attributes.

Incessantly throughout its verses and chapters as in this verse alone, there are **several** extremely important mistakes rendering its alleged origin as divine, **Null & Void.**

In this verse - as well as in all the other verses of the Quran - his mother is called **Miriam** and **not Mary.**

The title **Messiah** was given to Jesus by his much later followers from among the Greeks and Romans but not by the Jews. Furthermore Messiah is Hebrew for **Annointed** which is **Christ** in Greek.

Neither Jesus nor his mother knew any god by the name **Allah** especially since the God of Israel and Jesus, has **NO Name.**

It is thus, in summation, **impossible** that the angel Gabriel who had, 610 years earlier predicted the birth of Jesus as the **Redeemer** of humanity, could have 'revealed' to Muhammad such **Lies, Errors, Inconsistencies** and **Mendacities.**

All these **abnormalities** are easily explained when and if the listeners come to the only possible conclusion:

That all these verses emanated from the mind of Muhammad and were never **'revealed'** by Allah or by any **Omniscient, Compassionate & Merciful divinity.**

#15. Night Journey/ Laylat al Isra

Q: The claim by the followers of Muhammad for Jerusalem as their third holiest place is founded on the interpretation of this verse. Are these interpretations true? Factual? Historical?

A: The story of the **Night Journey** is copied - **like most of the important stories in the Quran** - from the traditions of the **Jews** regarding the **Ascent of Moses** to the **Seven Heavens** and visiting **Paradise and Hell** from **Midrash Gedullat Mosheh.**

There is in fact an Arabic translation of this Midrash in the Berlin library.

Muhammad in his Quran changed several items to suit the Arabian mind.

Isra is the name of **Surah 17** which is also called **Bani Isra'il, (The Children of Israel).** It is the alleged **Nocturnal Journey** from **Mecca** to the **Farthest Mosque** mentioned in:

*17:1 "Glory to (Allah) Who did take His Servant for **journey** [Asra/Travel] by night from the **Sacred Mosque [Masjid al Haram]** to the **Farthest Mosque [Masjid al Aqsa]** whose precincts We did Bless in order that We might show him some of Our Signs: for He is the one Who heareth and seeth (all things)"*

Even the obvious should be pointed out to the listener, that the name of **Jerusalem is Not Even Once** mentioned anywhere in the **Quran.**

Jerusalem, on the other hand, is mentioned **667** times in the **Bible.**

This alleged **'event'**, is described in

Bukhari Hadith 1:345 [Gabriel took Muhammad by hand to the first Heaven]

There is no mention of **Jerusalem**

Bukhari Hadith 5:227 & 4:429 [Gabriel & Buraq go to first Heaven]

Again, there is no mention of **Jerusalem**

Bukhari Hadith 9:608 [Gabriel took Muhammad by hand to first Heaven]

Yet once more, there is no mention of **Jerusalem**

The explanation of this **Aya/Verse** is found first and foremost in the **ONLY** biography of **Muhammad** written by **Muhammad Ibn Ishaq** in his book *Sirat Rassoul Allah.*

He informs us with great honesty, on the authority of Muhammad's premier wife Aisha, **that his body never left her side and that he was only transported spiritually.**

This is further corroborated by the **Qarawiyun Library Manuscript in Fez, Morocco,** where it repeats that **Aisha** the Prophet's wife and most intimate companion of his later years, declared emphatically that

"he was transported in his spirit (bi-ruhihi), while his body did not leave its place"

Also, the great **Al-Hasan al-Basri,** who belonged to the next generation, held **uncompromisingly** to the same view.

In another version in **(section 267 p 184),** it is Hind, Umm Hani d. of Abu Talib, Muhammad's cousin and sister of Ali that relates concerning the **Night Journey:**

"The apostle went on **NO Night Journey** except while he was in my house. **He slept that night in my house.**

He prayed the final night prayer and he slept and we slept there. ....."

A few traditions assert that this may have been a **physical** ascent, as affirmed by:

Sahih Al-Bukhari Hadith 5.228 Narrated by Ibn Abbas

The sights which Allah's Apostle was shown on the **Night Journey** when he was taken to **Bait-ul-Maqdis (i.e. Jerusalem)** were actual sights, (not dreams). And the Cursed Tree (mentioned) in the Qur'an is the tree of Zaqqum (itself).

Whose version should one trust, **that of the wife who slept with him or of his companions who were not present?**

Neither the Quran - which did not allow for a single miracle to be performed - nor Muhammad, ever declared that it was a miracle.

The most damning and damaging evidence against this concocted story is the historical and incontrovertible fact, that **there was no Masjid (Mosque) or Temple of Solomon in Jerusalem at the time of Muhammad,** since this Temple had already been destroyed by the Romans at least 580 years earlier; hence the verse could not possibly and realistically have meant Jerusalem.

It was the companions of Muhammad who, after his death, expressed the **erroneous, falsified and unsubstantiated opinion,** and later the **dogma** by creating a **Mythology** assuming a real **physical** transport to **Jerusalem,** in spite of the fact, that not one of the **Ahadith** above, mentions any **intermediate 'landing'** at **Jerusalem** but a **direct 'flight'** from **Mecca** to the **first Heaven** only.

On the other hand, it makes more sense to assume, that this was a **spiritual** transport to the Temple of Allah in Heaven.

This 'tradition' too, would have been a copy from the Jewish traditions regarding Jacob and Moses visiting the Seven Heavens.

It should further be pointed out, that according to all the Hadith records as well as from the Quran, one can discern a pattern of behaviour as well as of relaying a message which shows that Muhammad was obsessed with doing all his deeds - or alleged deeds/events - at **night, when there are no witnesses.**

Take for example, the following alleged most momentous events:

I.Q. Al Rassooli

Al 'Alaq 96:1 "Proclaim! in the name of thy Lord and Cherisher Who created 2 Created man out of a (mere) **clot of congealed blood...**"

Al Isra 17:1 " Glory to (Allah) Who did take His Servant for **journey by night** *[Asra/Travel]* from the **Sacred Mosque** to the **Farthest Mosque** whose precincts We did Bless in order that We might show him some of Our Signs: for He is the one Who heareth and seeth (all things)"

The first verse, represents Muhammad's alleged **first Quranic** revelation from the angel **Gabriel.**

Muhammad, the **purported 'greatest prophet'**, amazingly **forgot** on which **night** of the month of **Ramadan,** it took place.

The second verse, represents the alleged **Night Journey.**

In both cases, the **'miraculous events'** occurred in the **Dead Of Night** without **Witnesses,** and only the words of Muhammad as evidence.

These presumed **'miracles'** are in contrast to those stupendous ones performed by **Moses** in **daylight** and in front of the whole of the **Egyptian People** and the **Israelites.**

Muhammadan scholars have an incredibly difficult task explaining away the following abnormalities, inconsistencies' and illogical conclusions that emanate from all the stories about the Night Journey if it were really a physical one:

1 On his **'flight'** to **'Jerusalem'**, how could he have possibly observed **Moses** praying in his grave?

Since **Muhammad** was only an ordinary mortal, which of his senses could have been able to penetrate the earth of the grave to see **Moses?**

Even in the dark of night?

Was **Moses** physically intact?

Was he standing or horizontal?

Was it his spirit that Muhammad saw or his actual body which had not disintegrated after 2100 years?

According to the Bible, Moses did **not** have a **grave** how then could Muhammad declare that he saw him in one?

2 Muhammad led the previous prophets in prayers at the **'Temple'/Masjid** in **Jerusalem.**

There was no Temple at Jerusalem when Muhammad was alive since it had already been destroyed at least 550 years earlier.

There was only a **Christian cathedral** containing statues of **Jesus and Mary;** so where and what was this temple?

Accordingly this was a **pagan precinct** and Allah would not have considered it either holy or pure to *'bless'* it.

3 Among the prophets at prayer, yet once more was **Moses** present. He had just been observed in his grave but had now somehow, been transported to **'Jerusalem'** arriving even before Muhammad.

4 How did all the other prophets arrive at **'Jerusalem'**?

Muhammad allegedly had **Buraq.** What did the others have as transport? Which prophets were present?

5 Were the prophets in a spiritual or physical form?

6 If the prophets were there physically - like Muhammad allegedly was - then they must have been **resurrected before the arrival of the Messiah** and contrary to the assertions of the **Quran** that the **Qiyama/Resurrection** would occur at the **End of Days.**

7 If Muhammad led all these multitudes of people in prayers, who called for the prayers?

Where in **Jerusalem** was it conducted especially since there was no **Masjid** to pray in?

What did all of them recite?

How was it that no one in **Jerusalem** became aware of what should have been a great commotion especially in the dead of night.

8 Come to think of it, why did this journey occur **at night?**

Jerusalem was not lit by electricity and could not have been a glowing beacon, so how were all these **'prophets'** able to recognise each other in the darkness?

Why did Muhammad not visit it in daytime instead so that this **'miracle'** would have been infinitely more impressive and effective?

Why at night when there were **no other independent witnesses** to corroborate such a miraculous and unbelievable event?

How could have Muhammad possibly seen any and all of Allah's ayat/miracles **in the depth of darkness?**

9 If **Mecca were superior to Jerusalem,** as Muhammad later asserted, why then did not **all those** prophets meet at the **Ka'ba** in **Mecca instead,** whether spiritually or physically, and pay homage to Muhammad at his birthplace, as well as save him the inconvenience of a Night Journey?

10 Why did Buraq feel reluctant to carry Muhammad if it were sent by Allah? It should have **'known'** not to be afraid.

11 Why does not the word **Mi'raj appear in the Quran** to denote this miraculous event if it actually occurred?

12 Buraq would have definitely needed his wings to fly while in the earth's atmosphere; but to get to the Heavens it would have had to cross into outer space. How did Buraq and Muhammad survive such a trip if it were really physical?

13 How far is **Heaven** away from **Earth** that we have not been able to see or find it with the most incredibly powerful telescopes observing the beginning of creation at least **12 billion Light years away?**

14 Did Muhammad, Buraq and Gabriel travel at the speed of light?

More than the speed of light?

Time warped Space?

How was Muhammad able to do all these 'miracles' and return home within a few hours when the nearest star, Alpha Centaur of 4.2 light years would require so many years to get there?

Of course, **the only 'logical'** answer would be that Allah is capable of anything and everything and close the subject.

15 Since Gabriel was Muhammad's guide, why did he need to get permission for the gates to be opened at every Heaven?

After all, he was Allah's foremost angel/messenger and should not have needed the degrading and insulting process of identifying himself to any lower level angels. As a guest of Allah, Muhammad should not have needed all these unnecessary **'bureaucratic'** questions and delays.

16 How did the same prophets who were praying with him earlier get to the seven heavens so fast ahead of him without any delays or Gabriel as a guide and a **'pass-par-tous'**, nor Buraq to transport them?

17 Muhammad's wives assert that Muhammad never left their side.

Who could possibly be more knowledgeable about Muhammad's where abouts than especially his most jealous wife **Aisha**?

After all, **it was she who shared his bed and not the companions** nor the later Muhammadan scholars who created the myth of a physical transport.

18 Since this event was physical, it should have been one of the **most astounding** in the life of Muhammad.

How was it possible that Muhammad **forgot** what the alleged **Jerusalem Temple** looked like only **a few hours** after having supposedly visited it?

Only in dreams can one forget the most incredible 'vision' experiences.

How could an alleged prophet, who should have been able to foretell the future, forget the very recent past and the present?

19 Why did not Buraq remain with Muhammad after the **'miracle'** if it were real?

None of the **Ahadith** mention what transpired to it after **Muhammad** was 'returned' to **Mecca**.

If only the **Quraysh** were able to see this animal, they would have been turned with the whole of the **Arabian tribes** into perfect believers **without the need later on to slaughter them into submission and belief.**

20 The verse *17: 60 Behold! We told thee that thy Lord doth encompass mankind round about:* **We granted the Vision [al rou^aia]** *which* **We showed thee [araynaka]** *but as a trial for men as also the Cursed Tree (mentioned) in the Qur'an: We put terror (and warning) into them but it only increases their inordinate transgression! ...*

*** This asserts in the language of the Arabs that it was just a **vision** and not a **physical transport** ***

21 If all the above unbelievable miracles had transpired as some of the **Ahadith** allege, **how is it possible that the Quran neither mentions any of them, names them or even alludes to them?**

Why would **Allah 'reveal'** in hundreds of verses, the most mundane conversations, events and deeds, but **NOT ONCE** any of the **'most momentous events'** if they did actually occur?

Moreover, **pre-Islamic pagan Arabs** had no tradition or knowledge of **Jerusalem**.

Surah 17:1 is a single verse **which does not describe a miraculous journey at all** since if it were so, then it would have given us much greater details of such a wonderous and unusual event.

In fact, the next verse *17:2* discusses **Moses** and the subsequent verses other subjects, all of which have absolutely **no relevance** to the first alleged **momentous and miraculous event.**

#16. Quran Against the Jews

Q: Why was Muhammad's hatred of the Jews more virulent that that of the Christians?

A: The facts are borne out especially in the biography of Muhammad by **Ibn Ishaq** called **'Sirat Rassool ^Allah'** where in he shows that the **Judaised Arabs** of **Madina** especially, knew very well, that Muhammad was only a **Pretender, a Charlatan, a Liar and a Terrorist.**

He was **not** revealing to them a **single Precept, concept, Thought or Idea** that in any way shape or form was either **Equal to or Superior** to what he was **Plagiarizing, Pirating, Plundering and or Perverting** from their own Scriptures, traditions and fetishes as well as from others.

They were capable of questioning and challenging his alleged revelations and nefarious deeds so much, that he had no choice but to destroy them as witnesses to his Mendacity.

Al Imran 3:118 "O you who believe! **Take not into your intimacy those outside your religion (pagans, Jews, and Christians)**. They will not fail to corrupt you. They only desire your ruin. Rank hatred has already appeared from their mouths. What their hearts conceal is far worse.*

Al Nisa 4: 46 Of the Jews there are those who displace words from their (right) places and say: **"We hear and we disobey"**

160 For the iniquity of the Jews *We made unlawful for them certain (foods) good and wholesome which had been lawful for them; in that they hindered many from Allah's way.*

*** Muhammad and his Quran are wrong as usual, since the food prohibitions were mandated by God upon the Israelites - there were **no Jews** at that time - and not, as the Quran asserts, that they did it upon themselves.

The listener can verify and satisfy his/her intellectual curiosity by studying the list of forbidden foods in **Leviticus 11: 1--46*****

Al Ma'ida 5: 51 " O ye who believe! ***take not the Jews and the Christians for your friends and protectors:*** *they are but friends and protectors to each other. And he amongst you that turns to them (for friendship) is of them. Verily Allah guideth not a people unjust.*

64 The Jews say: "Allah's hand is tied up."
*** **No one on the face of planet Earth** can show a single such blasphemous verse anywhere in the Scripture of the Jews.

Muhammad's Quran is again deceiving its audience by perverting and twisting history, theology and facts.

The historical records speak volumes regarding the actions of the Jews and those of Muhammad and his followers.

The Jews did not conquer, mass murder, enslave, plunder, rape, destroy and dehumanize millions of peoples; the Arabs and Muhammadan Muslims, did.

They did so on a colossal scale, on three continents covering almost **ten** million square miles, slaughtering and enslaving hundreds of millions of people,

In The Name of Allah ***

Al Ma'ida 5:82"Strongest among men in enmity to the believers wilt thou find the Jews and Pagans

*** The hatred emanating from Muhammad's Quran can be cut **only** with a **chain saw.**

Here, the verse above, associates the Jews with the pagans; as if they too, are unbelievers.

In reality, this verse was **'revealed'** to justify Muhammad's slaughter and plunder of the produce and wealth of the Judaized Arabs that he, **an unemployable and unemployed** person, coveted ***

Al Tauba 9: 29 " *Fight those who believe not in Allah nor the Last Day nor hold that forbidden which hath been forbidden by Allah and His apostle nor acknowledge the religion of truth (even if they are) of the* **People of the Book** *until they pay the* **Jizya** *with willing* **Submission** *and feel themselves* **Humiliated.**

*** For those **ignorant** people among the followers of Muhammad, who have not read, let alone studied the Quran, this verse alone, was and is, a **unilateral declaration of war** by Muhammad, against the **Jews and Christians** as well as all other human beings who do not believe as he does***

30 " The Jews call **Uzair a son of Allah** *and the Christians call Christ the son of Allah. That is a saying from their mouths; (in this) they but imitate what the unbelievers of old used to say. Allah's curse be on them: how they are deluded away from the truth!*

*** Muhammad, **Falsely** but deliberately accuses the Jews - the first and most ardent **Monotheists** in the world - of saying that the **Uzair** is the **Son Of God.**

No follower of Muhammad - or any other human being on the face of this planet - can point to a single verse in the whole Scripture of the Jews, proving any of the egregious accusations made by Muhammad in his Quran***

Sahih Al-Bukhari Hadith 4.791 Narrated byAbdullah bin Umar

I heard Allah's Apostle saying, "The Jews will fight with you, and you will be given victory over them so that a stone will say, **'O Muslim! There is a Jew behind me; kill him!'** "

Sahih Al-Bukhari Hadith 6.252 Narrated byMusab

I asked my father, "Was the Verse: 'Say: (O Muhammad) Shall We tell you the greatest losers in respect of their deeds?'...... He said, "... regarding the Jews and the Christians, for the **Jews disbelieved Muhammad** and the **Christians disbelieved in Paradise** and say that there are neither meals nor drinks therein..

*** The above hadith shows that Muhammad's hatred of the Jews was because they denied his pretence for prophet-hood and alleged revelations.

Muhammad's polemic against the Christians was because they believe in a **Spiritual Afterlife** and **not** in Muhammad's **Physical Paradise** where his followers who died and die murdering so called Unbelievers aspire to.

Muhammad turned paradise into a house full of sensual and sexual pleasures for his utterly gullible and simple minded followers; a veritable **Whorehouse** of unlimited numbers of permanent and eternal virgins ***

To sum up, there are hundreds upon hundreds of such vile, loathsome, ignorant and stupid verses in both the Quran and Hadiths that we cannot possibly recite.

Many of the modern followers of Muhammad assert that the Christians are descended from PIGS while the Jews are from APES. They declare this repeatedly on their TV and Newsprint.

Let us, as usual, explore the following most staggering statistical **facts.**

There are approximately **6500 million human** beings in the world today.

There are approximately **14 million Jews** today compared with **1400 million followers of Muhammad.**

The Jews hence represent **0.2 %** of the human population while the Muhammadan Muslims are **21.5%.**

Yet, the Jews, the alleged descendants from **APES,** constitute **20%** of all **Nobel Prize** winners in history while **79%** of all the other Nobel Prize winners are **NOT** followers of Muhammad.

The Christians, the alleged descendants from **PIGS,** are the ones who brought electricity, running water, cars, paved roads, railways, hospitals, schools, sciences, art, planes, metal ships etc etc which the followers of Muhammad enjoy without ever giving them credit.

Lifting the Veil

In the **500 years** from 1450 to 1950, **not a single follower of Muhammad** from among the hundreds of millions can be named who has contributed anything of value to human progress.

The same can be said for the last 1400 years in the Arabian Peninsula.

The followers of Muhammad excel in Terror, Hatemongering, Warmongering, Deception, Mendacity, Hypocrisy, Disloyalty and Denial of Reality and facts.

It is interesting to note that the people who have been pagans for the previous 2300 years, have become, instantly, knowledgeable and great authorities on the Bible and Scripture, to such an extent as to challenge the veracity and beliefs of the People of the Book based **only** on the hearsay and the say so of the unlettered and ignorant Muhammad.

The same Muhammad has turned paradise into a house full of sensual and sexual pleasures for his utterly gullible and simple minded followers; a veritable WHOREHOUSE of unlimited numbers of permanent and eternal virgins.

Muhammad, had no concept or understanding of the **Spirit** world. His followers who die in **Jihad/Holy War** - all men - were to go **Bodily** to paradise to enjoy its carnal and sensual pleasures: eating, drinking, fornicating, without defecation or pregnancy ***

17. Quran & Pre-Destination

Q: On numerous occasions, I read about or heard Muhammadan Muslims speak of, and believe in, what they consider a FACT, which is PRE-DESTINATION; al QADAR; that is, that everything in the universe has already been Pre Ordained by Allah to happen or to be.

A: Muahmmad in his Quran makes it absolutely clear his belief in the **Pre-Destination** of all of **Life** as well as of everything else, whether animate or inanimate in this Universe.

All living creatures have been **Pre-Ordained** by Allah, even before their creation.

There is and can never be **Free Will** and/or **Freedom Of Choice** under the **Cult Of Muhammadan Islam.**

The study of the Quran and the Ahadith shows very clearly and unambiguously that they have not been able to bridge the diametrically opposite views of human free will and pre-destiny.

This condition is untenable and no amount of intellectual or theological contortions thought out by the followers of Muhammad can rectify or change the situation.

This dichotomy, renders most of the Quranic verses utterly meaningless from both the logical and the theological points of view as will be shown.

*Al Imran 3: 145 Nor can a soul die **except by Allah's leave** the term being fixed as by writing. [Wala cana li-nafssin an tamoota illa be ithni^Allah kitaba mouajjala]*

*** It is upon such repeated verses that the followers of Muhammad deny the concept of human free will. Their Allah had pre destined their entire **Life** for **GOOD** or for **Evil** ***

Al Nisa 4: 52 .... and those whom Allah hath cursed thou wilt find have no one to help...[oula^ika allatheena aoutoo nassiban mina^l kitabi you'^minoona bil jibti]

*** Again and again, the Quran alleges that Allah - the Merciful and Compassionate - predestines many of his own creations to Hellfire without any fault of their own.

The **God of Israel** on the one hand is very clear in the Bible in allowing Mankind to have the Free Will to choose between Good or Evil and be judged accordingly.

The Quran, on the other hand, has changed the rules without justification or justice to the detriment of most humans ***

*Al An'am 6: 59 ... **Not a leaf doth fall but with His knowledge:** there is not a grain in the darkness (or depths) of the earth nor anything fresh or dry (green or withered) but is (inscribed) in a Record Clear (to those who can read) [illa fi kitabin mubeenin]*

*** This verse, represents one of the clearest declarations of the concept of **Pre-Destination** in the Quran.

This concept degrades the human faculty and spirit by straight jacketing it into whatever status it is borne to.

Neither intellectually, nor morally, can this be acceptable since it makes Allah guilty of being unjust, immoral and full of hate as he condemns many of humanity to punishments for committing crimes that they were 'forced' to do because they were already 'pre-destined' to commit them by him [Allah] ***

Al A'araf 7: 34 To every people is a term appointed: when their term is reached not an hour can they cause delay nor (an hour) can they advance (it in anticipation).

Yunus 10: 100 *No soul can believe except by the Will of Allah and He will place Doubt (or obscurity) on those who will not understand.*

Al Hadid 57:22 *No misfortune can happen on earth or in your souls but is recorded in a decree before We bring it into existence: that is truly easy for Allah:*

We do not have time to recite many more such verses in the Quran and Hadiths that the listeners can read at their leisure on our advertised website.

I would like to end with **Two** of the most **Remarkable** and **Revealing** Hadiths:

Sahih Al-Bukhari Hadith 6.473 Narrated by Ali

...Muhammad said, "There is none among you, and no created soul but has his place written for him either in Paradise or in the Hell-Fire, and also has his happy or miserable fate (in the Hereafter) written for him."

*** This Hadith clearly states, from Muhammad's mouth the **Dogma Of Pre-Destination** ***

Al-Tirmidhi Hadith 96 Narrated by Abdullah ibn Amr

Allah's Messenger went out and he had in his hand two books. He said: Do you know what these two books are?

We said: Allah's Messenger, we do not know but only that you inform us. Thereupon he said: This one which my right hand possesses is a Book from the Lord of the worlds.

It contains the names of the inmates of Paradise and the name of their forefathers and those of their tribes.

It is most exhaustive and nothing will be added to it nor anything eliminated from it up to eternity.

He then said: This one in my left hand is a Book from the Lord of the worlds. It contains the names of the denizens of Hell and the names of their forefathers and their tribes. It is also exhaustive to the end and nothing will be added to it nor anything will be eliminated from it.

The Companions said: Allah's Messenger, (if this is the case)

then where lies the use of doing a deed if the affair is already decided?

Thereupon Muhammad said: Stick to the right course and remain as close to it as possible…

*** Ladies & Gentlemen, even his mostly illiterate, gullible and unlearned followers, were able to ask the most important and pertinent question regarding Muhammad's **concept** of

Pre destination, for which they did not get a satisfactory answer, because in reality, only the following conclusions can possibly make sense:

1. If people are **Pre Destined,** then there is absolutely no need for **Religion.**

Without the need for Religion, then there is definitely no need for **Prophets.**

Without the need for Prophets, then there is no need for **Muhammad.**

Without the need for Muhammad, then there is no need for his Quran.

2. With Pre destination, even **Satan** is made **Redundant** since he cannot possibly **Deceive** any human being whom Allah had already pre ordained to be good.

3. Another very important conclusion based upon this Hadith is that the only way possible for Muhammad to have known what was written in the two books and to differentiate between their contents, is if he could **Read & Write** especially since there is no record anywhere showing that either Gabriel or Allah had 'revealed' this knowledge to him.

This Hadith destroys completely the assertions by the followers of Muhammad that he was **Illiterate*****

#18. Abrogation or Naskh

Q: What are the Abrogating and Abrogated Verses of the Quran ?

A: The Quran is unique among all the holy Scriptures of other peoples since it is the ONLY one that allows the god of Muhammad, Allah, to keep changing his mind regarding his alleged revelations to Muhammad.

Q: Sorry to interrupt, do you mean that Allah revealed something to Muhammad and later on he changed the revelation? How is it conceivable for any Omniscient God not to know beforehand everything?

A: As shocking a realization as this is, the **fact** is none the less, that Muhammad's Quran contains Abrogated and Abrogating verses in **71 Suras - out of 114** - comprising **62.28%** of all the suras of the Quran that have had verses changed, over ruled or deleted.

This shows Muhammad's Allah as bereft of foresight, with a fickle mind and incapable of assessing the weaknesses and strengths of Muhammad or his followers; this is of course a blasphemous characterization of any Omniscient divinity.

Neither in the Hebrew Bible nor in the New Testament are there such verses. The God of Israel is not shown to give one command one instance and then changes it either immediately, shortly afterwards or much later because He did not realize that it was too onerous to be fulfilled by mere humans.

The verse that allows Allah to Abrogate was revealed in:

Al Baqara 2:106 *None of Our revelations do* **We abrogate** *or cause to be forgotten but We substitute something* **better or similar;** *knowest thou not that Allah hath power over all things?*

*** Why would any omniscient God not know beforehand the weaknesses or strengths of His creation?

It is unadulterated **blasphemy** to impugn to the Almighty human weaknesses and vulnerabilities.

Why would any almighty God change His 'mind' and replace earlier ordinances with others?

Why would such a God especially replace earlier ones with **similar** ones?

Why similar?

Why not *'reveal'* the better ones from the very beginning?

The reader is entitled to ask such questions that require intelligent and logical answers.

Can any Muhammadan Muslim provide any logical answers? ***

Al Nisa 4:82 *"Do they not ponder over the Qur'an? Had it been the word of any other but Allah they would surely have found a **good deal of variation in it,** much discrepancy and incongruity... those who check and scrutinize will know it."*

*** The Quran is challenging the readers' intellect.

The answers to the challenge are, incredibly, provided by the Quran and Hadiths themselves:

An enormous deal of variations is exactly what is found in the Quranic verses.

There is also of course the issue of the Satanic Verses which were repeated by Muhamnmad who did not recognize them as coming from Satan.

It is by **Divine Justice,** that the Quranic challenge has been met and our case against the veracity and alleged divine origin of the Quran is rested ***

Al Ra'd 13:38 *"It was not for any Apostle to come up with a miracle or sign unless it was granted by Our permission. For every age there is a Book revealed.*

Ar-Rahman abrogates, blots out, or confirms (whatever He wants)."

Al Nahl 16:101 And when We exchange a verse in place of another verse and Allah knows very well what He is sending down they say, 'Thou art a mere forger! Nay, but the most of them have no knowledge.

*** The reader should be aware of the incredibly unusual **transition** in the verse above from *'We exchange....another verse'* to *'and Allah knows...down'*

Why and how could Allah *'speak'* in the first person *[We]* at the beginning of the verse and then moving immediately and without any logical or grammatical reason to the impersonal *[and Allah]* in the second part of the same verse?

It is precisely because Allah **"knows very well what he is sending down"** that he has absolutely no reason to change his mind and abrogate or make forgotten an earlier *'revelation'*.

Even the illiterate and unlearned Arabs of Mecca found it intellectually and theologically fraudulent to believe in such a fickle, indecisive and fallible Allah.

Since the Quran and its interpreters, repeatedly mention the inviolability and eternal character of Allah's rules and regulations, how can they at the same time explain away the most controversial cases of the abrogated and abrogating *Suras* which number 71, that is 62.28% of the Quran?

In addition to the above anomaly, the reader should also be aware of the missing and forgotten verses that are mentioned in the Ahadith.

Why and what for would Allah, the Omniscient, the All Knowing, change his mind at what he had already announced and *'replace'* it with one *'equal'* or *'better'* than the first?

What would the purpose be of changing one for an **Equal**?

Why change it if it is only for an **Equal**?

Does Allah break his own promises and instructions?

Does Allah hence have more than **One Preserved Tablet** in **Heaven**?

If so, which one of them is the correct one?

It all sounds more than just blasphemy and mumbo jumbo.

It is all an insult to the Almighty and to the intelligence of all human beings who accept such profanity and idiocy of a concept or dogma
***

All the **abnormalities, ambiguities, stupidities** and **contradictions** in the Quran are instantly and summarily resolved when the listeners/ readers absorb and accept the simple and unchallengeable following conclusions:

That there is not a single letter, let alone a word, a verse or a chapter in the Quran that could have been revealed by any Omniscient, Merciful or Compassionate divinity because in reality, every letter, word, verse and chapter in the Quran is the product of Muhammad's imagination, his own personal **ALTER EGO,** cleverly projected into the unsuspecting mouth of Allah, the supreme pagan rock god of Mecca, imbedded into the corner wall of the Ka'ba called the **Black Stone.**

Allah, Gabriel and Muhammad are one and the same. Muhammad used Allah and Gabriel as props to give his alleged revelations a cloak of sanctity and divinity but in reality it is all otherwise **Satanic** and totally Muhammad's .

Those who doubt what is being revealed here can read much more on our website as well as when they read the following books written by the followers of Muhammad :

Al Suyuti's *Al Itqan fi Ulum al Quran*

Jamal al Din al Juzi in his *'Nawasikh al Quran'*

Abu Ja'afar al Nakhass ' *al Nasikh wal Mansukh'.*

#19. Quran Against All Unbelievers

Q: When reading the Quran, the translators use the terms UNBELIEVERS & DISBELIEVERS. Will you please clarify the distinction between these two groups of people.

A: **Unbelievers** are all those who do not believe in Allah **and** in his messenger Muhammad. It is used invariably against Pagans, Hindus, Buddhists and Animists.

This in reality, includes all members of the human race who are not believers in Allah, the Muhammadan Arabian version of the

God of Israel.

Disbelievers on the other hand, are the Jews and Christians who did not and do not accept Muhammad's **Cult Belief System** but who already know the One and Only God of Israel and Jesus.

Muhammad and his Quran had declared total and unremitting war,

1400 years ago, against all of humanity unless and until they are all converted, subjugated or slaughtered.

The Quranic verses are very clear, precise, unambiguous, deadly and totally immoral and disgusting.

If the Almighty wanted humanity to believe in Him and only Him, he would have easily programmed them to grovel to Him for ever.

The Almighty does not need either Muhammad and or his ignorant and murderous followers to force humanity to believe in Him.

To suggest that He does, is the ultimate profanity and blasphemy.

Al Baqara 2: 190 Fight in the cause of Allah [Wa qatiloo fi sabil^allah] those who fight you but do not transgress limits; for Allah loveth not transgressors.

191 And slay them [wa^ qtuloohum] *wherever ye catch them and turn them out from where they have turned you out*

193 And fight them [Wa^ qatiloohum] *on until there is no more tumult or oppression and there prevail justice and faith in Allah; but if they cease let there be no hostility except to those who practice oppression.*

*** Many Muhammadan scholars do their best to hide the actual message of the Quran of **Universal Subjugation** to the will of Allah by misleading people who are ignorant of the Arabic language of the Quran and Hadiths, as well as of the historical record of Muhammad into believing that these Quranic messages pertained **Only** to the time of Muhammad in his struggle against the Pagan Arabs whose beliefs, religion and traditions he was insulting, denigrating and attacking.

This is of course an incredible and demonstrable lie since his followers conquered, subjugated, slaughtered and enslaved, millions of people on three continents who never heard of Arabs or had any aggression against them.

Therefore, slaughtering the **Unbelievers** is not restricted to the pagan Arabs but also to **All** those who do not believe in the message of Muhammad:

All Hindus, Zoroasterians, Animists, Christians, Polytheists, Buddhists, Jews etc anywhere and every where on Earth ***

Al Nisa 4:76 *Those who believe* **fight in the cause of Allah** *[youqatiloona fi sabil^Allah] and those who reject faith fight in the cause of evil [youqatiloona fi sabil^al Taghooti]: so fight ye [fa qatiloo] against the friends of Satan*

*** Those who reject faith are obviously all humans who do not follow Muhammad or his message ***

Al Ma'ida 5: 51 *O ye who believe! take not the* **Jews [Yahood]** *and the* **Christians [Nassara]** *for your friends and protectors: they are but friends and protectors to each other. And he amongst you, that turns to them (for friendship), is of them. Verily Allah guideth not a people unjust.*

Al Anfal 8: 55 For the worst of beasts in the sight of Allah are those who reject Him: They will not believe [la you^minoona]

67 It is not fitting for an apostle that he should have prisoners of war until he hath thoroughly subdued the land.

*** Allah, the god of Muhammad, the Most Merciful and Compassionate, forbids Muhammad from taking prisoners of war from among the **Unbelievers**.

Allah, would rather have them slaughtered by Muhammad and his thugs ***

Al Tauba 9: 5 But when the forbidden months are past, then fight and slay [fa^qtuloo] the pagans [mushrikeena] wherever ye find them and seize them, beleaguer them, and lie in wait for them, in every stratagem (of war

29 Slaughter [qatiloo] those who believe not in Allah nor the Last Day, nor hold that forbidden which hath been forbidden by Allah and His apostle, nor acknowledge the religion of truth [that is Islam] (even if they are) of the **People of the Book,** until they pay the **Jizya** with willing **submission**, and feel themselves **humiliated.**

*** **Al Tabari 9:86** explains "Don't seduce the Jews or Christians for incumbent on them is to pay the **jizyah protection tax.**"

The Muhammadan conquerors needed to levy taxes on their victims and did not want them to convert and hence be absolved ***

Al Tauba 30 The Jews call Uzair a son of Allah and the Christians call Christ the son of Allah. That is a saying from their mouths; (in this) they but imitate what the unbelievers [al latheena kafaroo] of old used to say. Allah's curse be on them: how they are deluded away from the truth! **73** O Prophet! **strive hard [Jahid]** against the **unbelievers [al kuffara]** and the **Hypocrites [Munafiqeen]** and be firm against them. Their abode is hell an evil refuge indeed.

Muhammad 47: 4 Therefore when ye meet the **Unbelievers [al latheena kafaroo]** smite at their necks...

Nuh 71: 26 And Noah said: "O my Lord! Leave not of the **Unbelievers [kafireena]** a single one on earth!

*** Ladies and Gentlemen be aware that there is not a single verse in the whole of the Quran, that prescribes mercy towards the unbelievers. ***

Al Muzammil 72:15 `But those who swerve (unbelievers) they are (but) fuel for Hell Fire `

*** There are of course many more of such evil, blood-curdling, hatemongering and warmongering verses if the reader has the stomach to look for them, especially in the **'TotalWar' Section** of our Website.

The Quran is NOT a 'holy' book.

The Quran is a Roadmap to TOTAL WAR.

The Quran is Muhammad's early version of Hitler's Mein Kampf ***

#20 Islam & African Slavery

Q: I must admit, that I too, among hundreds of millions of educated people, was under the impression that the African Slave Trade was the sole responsibility of the Christian Europeans, the White Race.

That is, until I started exploring the subject in greater depth and especially after reading an incredibly enlightening book called

" *The Legacy of Arab-Islam in Africa*" by John Alembillah Azumah.

My whole perspective and understanding of the subject has changed dramatically and I would like you to tell us more about this subject.

A: The **success** of Muhammadan Islam in **Deceiving, Misinforming, Deforming** and **Contorting** both History & Reality over a period of almost **1400 years** has been **Astounding. That is, until NOW.**

The Greatest Tragedy About This Particular Subject, Is that most of the descendants of African Slavery, the Black People in the Americas, around the world as well as among the African Blacks, are totally **Ignorant** of the actual facts.

Before we loose the concentration of our listeners, I would like to make the following statement and **then** prove it:

That the worst, most inhumane and most diabolical institution of the **Black African Slave Trade,** was initiated, refined, perpetrated and implemented by the **Muhammadan Arabs** and later aided and abetted by the **Black** converts to **Muhammadan Islam.**

I predict that as usual, the **two Sub Cultures,** those of: **Denial of Facts & of Political Correctness** will attack us without **Once Disproving** a **Single** statement and or conclusion that we make.

Slavery was **Not** created by the **White races,** because it has existed throughout human history and practiced by EVERY tribe, culture, civilization, racial group and religion.

In fact, the very word **Slavery** has its root in the name **Slav** based upon the **Slavic** peoples of Europe who were subjugated by other Europeans

It is not common knowledge that the **Arabic** word 'ABD' is synonymous with the meaning of **Slave;** for example, **Abd Allah** means literally the **Slave of Allah** and **that in the language of the Arabs-**

All Black Peoples are called **'Abeed'** plural for **'Slaves'.**

While much has been written concerning the **Trans-Atlantic** slave trade, surprisingly little attention has been given to the **Islamic** slave trade across the Sahara, the Red Sea and the Indian Ocean.

While the European involvement in the African Trans Atlantic slave trade to the Americas lasted for just over three centuries, the Arab involvement in the African slave trade has lasted fourteen centuries, and in some parts of the Muhammadan world is still continuing to this day.

The birth of **Muhammadan Islam** and its conquests, brought about the birth of **Institutionalized, Systematized and Religiously Sanctioned Slave Trade, on a Massive & Global Scale.**

In fact, the **Quran** allows the taking of slaves as **'booty',** or **'reward'** for wars of aggression against any and all **Unbelievers (most of the human population).**

This has led to an enormous number of so called **'Holy Wars'** , **'Jihad' in Arabic.** There was, and is, absolutely nothing **'holy'** about these wars which are primarily

to **plunder, slaughter, rape, subjugate** and **rob** other human beings of their wealth, produce, freedom and dignity.

Muhammadan Muslim states and tribes, attacked other **non-Muslim** groups to achieve these objectives. Although **Islamic**

jurisprudence laid down regulations for the treatment of slaves; **however, incredible and heinous abuses have occurred throughout the history of Muhammadan Islam.**

By the **Middle Ages,** the **Arabic** word **"Abd"** was in general use to denote a **black slave** while the word **"Mamluk"** referred to a **white slave.**

Ibn Khaldun (1332 - 1406) the pre-eminent **Islamic** medieval historian and social thinker wrote: "The **Negro nations are as a** rule **submissive** to **slavery,** because they have **attributes** that are quite similar to **dumb animals."**

It should also be noted, that **black slaves were castrated** "based on the assumption that the blacks had an **ungovernable sexual appetite."**

When the **Fatimid Caliphate** came to power in Egypt, **they slaughtered all the tens of thousands** of black military slaves and raised an entirely new slave army. Some of these slaves were conscripted into the army **at age ten.** From Persia to Egypt to Morocco, **slave armies from 30,000 to up to 250,000** became common-place.

The **Islamic slave trade** took place across the **Sahara Desert,** from the coast of the **Red Sea,** and from **East Africa** across the **Indian Ocean.** The **Trans Sahara** trade was conducted along **six major slave routes.**

Just in the 19th Century, for which we have more accurate records, **1.2 million slaves** were brought across the **Sahara** into the **Middle East,** as well as a further **450,000** down the **Red Sea** and **442,000** from **East African** coastal ports.

That is a total of **2 million black slaves** - just in the 1800's. At least **8 million more were calculated to have died before reaching the Muslim slave markets.**

A comparison of the **Islamic slave** trade to the **American slave** trade reveals some extremely interesting contrasts.

While two out of every three slaves shipped across the Atlantic were men, the proportions were reversed in the Islamic slave trade. Two women for every man were enslaved by the Muslims.

While the mortality rate for slaves being transported across the **Atlantic** was as high as **10%,** the percentage of slaves dying in transit in the **Trans Sahara and East African** slave trade was a staggering **80 to 90%.**

While almost all the slaves shipped across the Atlantic were for agricultural work, most of the slaves destined for the **Muslim Middle East** were for **sexual exploitation as concubines, in harems,** and for military service.

While many children were born to slaves in the **Americas,** and millions of their descendants are citizens in **Brazil** and the **USA** to this day, very few descendants of the slaves that ended up in the **Middle East** survive.

While most slaves who went to the **Americas** could marry and have families, most of the **male slaves** destined for the **Middle East were castrated,** and most of the children born to the women were **killed at birth.**

It is estimated that possibly as many as **11 million Africans** were transported across the **Atlantic (95% of** which went to **South and Central America,** mainly to **Portuguese, Spanish and French** possessions. **Only 5%** of the slaves ended up in the **United States).**

However, a minimum of **28 million Africans** were enslaved in the **Muslim Middle East.** Since at least **80%** of those captured by **Muslim slave traders** were calculated **to have died before reaching the slave markets,** it is believed that the **death toll** from **1400 years** of **Arab & Muslim slave raids** into **Africa** could have been over **112 millions.**

When added to the number of those sold in the slave markets, the total number of **African victims** of the **Trans Saharan and East African** slave trade could be significantly higher than **140 million people.**

What is **obscene** about this whole subject is the **Muhammadan Muslim and Arab culture of denial** regarding their complicity in the **African Slave Trade** as well as the **ignorance of Black Muslims** about the reality of their past & present conditions.

The statistics and reports above are based upon the log books kept at the African Slave ports, ship logs, travelers' reports, eyewitness accounts etc etc.

Ladies and gentlemen, the **Facts** and **Reality** of **Muhammadan Islam's Complicity** in the Slave Trade and their inhuman depravity are **infinitely** more devastating, more staggering and more incomprehensible than all the nightmare **Fictions** in the world

#21. Myth of Islamic Civilization

Q: The Muhammadan Muslim media and individuals as well as so called Arabists incessantly speak in invariably glowing terms, of the contribution of the Muhammadan Muslims to human civilization. What is the reality?

A: Before I address this question, there is an extremely important word that has to be defined first, which is at the root of this discussion, this word is **civ·i·li·za·tion.**

According to the English language, it comprises a society which is in an advanced state of social development, with complex legal, political and religious organizations; that is, in an advanced state of intellectual, cultural, and material development in human society, marked by progress in the arts and sciences, the extensive use of record-keeping, including writing, and the appearance of complex political and social institutions.

Like everything else about **Muhammadan Islam, Facts and Reality are Contrary to ALL** their exaggerated and invariably false and wishful thinking declarations.

Let us examine the historical facts as recorded by the Muhammadan Muslims themselves and their contemporaries.

In the Arabian Peninsula where Muhammad was born, the Arabs were among the most **illiterate, superstitious and unlearned nomadic and semi nomadic people** in what we call the Middle East today.

Although surrounded by other truly advanced cultures, they had not even the semblance of a **Civilization** to speak of: they had no central authority such as a king or a Priest/king, no government, no army, no civil service, no arts, no sciences and no record keeping.

The Arabs, under the banner of so called Islam, conquered several civilizations on three continents:

such as the Zoroasterian Sassanid Persian Empire, the Byzantine Christian Empire, the Coptic Christian Egyptians, the Hindu Indians, the Buddhist Chinese, etc. These were truly advanced civilizations.

It is therefore **inconceivable** to suggest, that the Arabs could have imparted **anything** of value to the subjugated peoples of these conquered civilizations.

In Arabic, the subject people who converted to Muhammadan Islam are called **Mawali,** meaning **Clients/Followers/Supporters.** This is an extremely relevant and important word **Because** it is from among the conquered people of these **Civilizations,** that the Arab Imperialists were able to build their mosques, their palaces, run their trade and economies, collect taxes and take census.

It was from among the Mawali and the Jews and Christians of the conquered territories that Greek, Roman and Hebrew literature, philosophies and sciences were translated to Arabic.

From 701 to 1424, a period of about 700 years, a maximum of **80 scientists** and scholars under the sword of Muhammadan Islam – mostly from among the Mawali - contributed a wealth of advancement in many branches of knowledge.

It is vitally important for the readers to realize, that these scholars, based **ALL their knowledge** on foundations first set by others, centuries before them:

Egyptian, Hebrew, Persian, Greek, Roman, Byzantine, Indian , etc whose knowledge and writings were translated into Arabic by men from the conquered peoples, by converts to Muhammadan Islam (Mawali) as well as by Jews, Christians and others.

The so called Islamic Science and or Islamic Civilization had absolutely nothing whatsoever to do with Muhammadan Islam. Almost the entirety of these scholars and scientists **excelled** not because of Muhammadan Islam but **in spite** of Muhammadan Islam since they were invariably **secular** thinkers.

No knowledge whatsoever, in the sciences, arts, engineering, architecture, philosophy etc, etc can possibly sprout under

Fundamentalist Muhammadan Islam, because the **only** knowledge that Fundamentalist Muhammadan Islam can recognize as valid and worthy, is knowledge of the Quran which they call **ILM**.

Out of the eighty or so scientists and scholars mentioned above only a **handful** were pure Arabs. The remainder were Persian, Turk, Jews, Christians, Kurds, Sabians, Spaniards, North African, etc.

In reality, this science and this civilization should be, and must be called **MAWALI** Science and or Mawali Civilization because Muhammadan Islam contributed absolutely nothing to its evolution, propagation and or establishment.

Nothing of value in human intellectual endeavours can possibly be created or grow under Fundamentalist Muhammadan Islam.

Muhammadan Muslims listening to this chapter of our series, will be outraged at such statements. Well, let them think about the following facts and find out the common denominator that underlines them:

1. Can any follower of Muhammad name **FIVE** Muhammadan Muslims who had contributed anything whatsoever to human intellectual, artistic and philosophical advancement from among the tens of millions in the Arabian Peninsula in the last 1372 years between 635 to 2007?

2. Can any follower of Muhammad name **FIVE** Muhammadan Muslims who have contributed anything whatsoever to the advancement of human knowledge in the sciences, arts, philosophy, theological discourse etc, from among the Hundreds of Millions of Muhammadan Muslims in the world during the **500 years** from 1450 to 1950 AD?

The only reason that they cannot find these scientists or scholars is because **Fundamentalist Muhammadan Islam** cannot survive under the bright light of knowledge, freedom of thought, freedom of expression, freedom of religious belief and or freedom of intellectual dialogue and debate, because the best and most perfect system of Fundamentalist Muhammadan Islam is that of the **Taliban** in

Afghanistan: a state of mind-boggling **Ignorance, Religious Intolerance, Hate, Terror** and **Utter Stupidity.**

Fundamentalist Muhammadan Islam can only survive in **Darkness** and as we know, very little if anything can bloom and prosper in the dark without sunshine.

That is why, very little knowledge, if any, emanates from over 50 Muhammadan Muslim states in the world today of over 1.4 billion souls.

The above statements and **facts** are available for all to read and no amount of Muhammadan Muslim anger, diatribes, hatemongering threats and terror can change an iota of them.

Muhammadan Muslims thrive in the **Twilight Zone** of **Denial** and of blaming all others. The **Denial** of **Facts;** the denial of **Reality;** the **Blame Others Syndrome.**

For as long as they are not willing or able to face facts, Muhammadan Islam and Muhammadan Muslims will continue to remain forever fixed in the **Time Warp** of the **Seventh Century,** the time of Muhammad and his Quran.

#22. Quran Against the Arabs

**Q: It was interesting that some of the Quranic verses that I read, attack the Arabs of the Peninsula in a similar fashion to those used against the Christians, the Jews and the Pagans.
Will you explain why?**

A: Muhammad's Quran is an equal opportunity hatemongering book; not only does it attack and insult the Jews and Christians, but does the same to his own brother & sister Arabs who are supposedly of the **Umma** of Muhammad and whom he was attempting to convert by **Bribery, Terror** or **Slaughter.**

The verses that I shall quote from the **Quran** will not make sense to **any** listeners unless and until they also read about the actual background of each event.

I shall try my best to explain them and those among the listeners who may think I am deceiving them can read them in any **Quran** that also contains explanations.

*Al Tauba 9: 90 And there were among the **desert Arabs** Men who made excuses and came to claim exemption; and those who were false to Allah and His apostle sat inactive. Soon will a grievous penalty seize the unbelievers among them.*

*** The interpreters of the Quran, as usual, do their best to whitewash a very treacherous and bloody event called the Tabuk expedition when many of the followers of Muhammad refused to go to war against the Byzantines ***

97 *The Arabs of the desert are the worst in unbelief and hypocrisy and most fitted to be in ignorance* *of the command which Allah hath sent down to his apostle...*

98 *Some of the **desert Arabs** Look upon their payments as a fine and watch for disasters for you:* **on them be the disaster of evil..**

*** The *'payments'* alluded to above is called **Zakat** and was **Imposed** upon his followers by Muhammad and hence cannot be called charity especially since it was a form of taxation to increase the purse of Muhammad so that he can buy more arms to conduct his acts of terror against all other Arabs, the so called **'Unbelievers'** as well as a means to **Bribe** others into the 'new faith'. Nothing of the above is sacred ***

101 Certain of the desert Arabs round about you are hypocrites as well as (desert Arabs) among the Medina folk: **they are obstinate in hypocrisy:** *thou knowest them not: We know them: twice shall We punish them and in addition shall they be sent to a grievous penalty.*

*** Contrary to all the allegations and contumacy made against the ordinarily peaceable desert Arabs, the facts are, that it was Muhammad and his followers who forced most of them to turn to piracy and terror against their own kith and kin as well as against all those who did not believe in Muhammad as Allah's messenger.

It is typical of most criminal minds to **Project** upon their victims their own criminalities and demented characteristics.

More over, all the reports that we have available about the pagan Arabs were propagated and later written by the victorious Muhammad and his followers who made them look as if they were evil, bloodthirsty, treacherous, treasonable and wily people who sacrificed humans and especially little girls.

Nothing could be further from the truth since when one studies, and I always repeat the word **Studies,** in detail, their poetry, the Ahadith and many unbiased reports, they turn out to have been far **Superior** to any followers of Muhammad.

The historical records of Muhammadan Islam, as written by his followers show very clearly, that it was a movement that started with the **shedding of a sea of Arab blood** to start with; then it was propagated through the **shedding of an ocean of innocent blood** on three continents and continues even today by the shedding of more blood without discrimination between believers or unbelievers ***

*Al Tauba 9: 120 It was not fitting for the people of Medina and the **bedouin Arabs** of the neighborhood **to refuse to follow Allah's Apostle** nor to prefer their own lives to his...*

*** Since every verse in the Quran actually represents

MUHAMMAD'S own ALTER EGO,

it is then no wonder, that almost all of them reflect his own state of mind at that moment of time and are conveniently **'revealed'** at his own beck and call to **'command'** his followers to whatever he wanted them to do in the name of the unsuspecting Allah, the pagan supreme rock god of the Ka'ba***

*Al Fath 48: 11 **The desert Arabs** who lagged behind will say to thee: "We were engaged in (looking after) our flocks and herds and our families; do thou then ask forgiveness for us." ....*

*16 **Say to the desert Arabs** who lagged behind: "Ye shall be summoned (to fight) against a people given to vehement war: then shall ye fight or they shall submit. ....*

*Al Hujurat 49: 14 **The desert Arabs say** "We believe." Say "**Ye have no faith**; but ye (only) say `We have submitted our wills to Allah.' For not yet has Faith entered your hearts. ....*

*** If the desert Arabs **'loved fighting and plunder'**, then there would have been no reason to have all the above verses allegedly revealed.

The Desert Arabs usually fought to defend themselves, their animals and their grazing lands. They were not **wanton war-mongerers** like Muhammad and his followers.

Of course, these illiterate Arabs did not, in the end win the wars of aggression conducted by Muhammad and his thugs against them, who became the victors and hence **re-wrote history** to suit their agenda.

Not a single verse above nor any of the 'explanations' given by the later followers of Muhammad, fit neither the **truth,** logic or reality.

All of them are used to 'criminalize' their innocent victims so that the actual perpetrators of all evil get away with murder by contorting, perverting and twisting both History and **facts.**

For the last 1400 years, Muhammad and his followers have been able to deceive and fool people who are ignorant of the Arabic language of the Quran and Hadiths into believing that Muhammad was a prophet and that Allah is God.

Slowly but most assuredly, more and more people around the world are realizing the Falsity and Mendacity of what they have been and are being taught.

#23. Quran vs Bible Contradictions

Q: In numerous and extremely important instances, I found that the Quranic version of the Biblical events, invariably contradict or are utterly different from their originals in the Bible.

If Allah is the same as the God of Israel and Jesus, how is it possible and logical that he could have revealed TWO or more irreconcilable and/ or dissimilar versions of the same events?

A: Among all the chapters of this series, this is actually one of the **most important** questions since it hits at the very foundations of who **Allah** really is.

It is common knowledge that the **Almighty**, by whatever name we may give Him, has to be **all knowing** and **infallible.**

Blasphemously, the Quran proves that **Allah** is otherwise: **uncertain, vacillating and extremely fallible:**

Item 1:-

Let us start with the first verse allegedly revealed to Muhammad in *Surat al Alaq* **96** about the creation of mankind.

> 1 *Proclaim! (or Read!) in the name of thy Lord and Cherisher Who created*
>
> 2 ***Created man out of a (mere) clot of congealed blood:***
>
> *In Arabic, it says : "Iqraa bismi rabbica al llathi khalaqa,* ***Khalaqa al inssana min alaq"***
>
> Well, anyone who has read the Bible would remember or know that of all of God's creations, **Adam** was formed from **dust,** by the hand of God and then God **breathed** into its nostrils and made it alive.

The Quranic version is utterly illogical and contradicts the **only** and original Biblical version

Item 2:-

> *Al Baqara 2: 127 And remember **Abraham and Isma`il raised the foundations of the House** (with this prayer): "Our Lord! accept (this service) from us for thou art the All-Hearing the All-Knowing.*

Once more, it has to be pointed out that the Bible has no knowledge of a god called Allah, nor of a village called Mecca or of a temple called Ka'ba.

Moreover, neither Abraham nor Ishmael ever set foot in Mecca or the Arabian Peninsula to build the foundations of a **Pagan Temple** called the Ka'ba.

Item 3:-

> *Al Qasaa 28: 48 "Pharaoh said: "O Chiefs! no god do I know for you but myself: **therefore O Haman!** light me a (kiln to bake bricks) out of clay and build me a lofty palace that I may mount up to the god of Moses: but as far as I am concerned I think (Moses) is a liar!"*

The name of **Haman** appears **ONLY** in the **Bible** in the story of Esther in the years 400 BC in Persia; while Moses and the Exodus were in the year 1450 BC in Egypt; Pharaoh had no one called Haman as his prime minister. The Quranic version is once more in error not only in location but also in a time **dislocation of 1000 years.**

Item 4:-

> *Maryam19: 23 And the pains of childbirth drove her to the trunk of a palm-tree: she cried (in her anguish): "Ah! would that I had died before this! Would that I had been a thing forgotten and out of sight!"*

This verse actually describes the birth of Jesus while Mary is alone and under a **palm tree**. Unfortunately for the Quran, the original story in the Gospels disagrees completely.

It appears, that the angel Gabriel, who had, 610 years earlier, revealed the birth of Jesus to Mary, had become so senile and stupid that he gave the wrong information to Muhammad.

Maryam, 19: 27 *At length she brought the (babe) to her people carrying him (in her arms). They said: "O Mary! truly an amazing thing hast thou brought!*

28 O sister of Aaron! *thy father was not a man of evil nor thy mother a woman unchaste!"*

*** WOW! Mary is now the **sister** of Aaron & Moses of a **1450 years** earlier period.

This error is more understandable since in the Quran Mary's name in Arabic is rendered **Mariam**

Those who know the Bible, would also know, that the sister of Moses and Aaron **is** called Mariam, hence this explains Allah's very **simple** but understandable confusion ***

Item 5:-

Al Nisa 4: 157 *That they said (in boast) "We killed Christ Jesus the son of Mary the Apostle of Allah";* **but they killed him not, nor crucified him,** *but so it was made to appear to them, and those who differ therein are full of doubts with no (certain) knowledge but only conjecture to follow for of a surety they killed him not.*

158 *Nay* ***Allah raised him up unto Himself;*** *and Allah is Exalted in Power Wise.*

Once again do the Gospels vehemently **disagree** with Allah and Gabriel's version of events.

Most important of all, this **single** verse **destroys** the whole concept of Christian Belief since without Crucifixion, there is no Death; without Death, there is no Resurrection, and **without death and resurrection, there is no Christianity.**

There are hundreds more of such differences between the Quran and the Bible.

The readers have very limited choices in trying to understand how this is possible; how the divine who allegedly revealed the Quran can be so wrong.

In our opinion, the answer is very simple and goes like this:

Since it is **Illogical** to believe that **any Omniscient, Merciful and Compassionate God** would have revealed all the Discrepancies, Hatemongering, Warmongering, Discrimination, Grammatical Errors, as well as the Historical and Character dislocations, Mendacities, Abnormalities, Inconsistencies, Time and Space Displacements that permeate the Quranic versions of the Biblical events, then only **one** conclusion can be possible.

Every letter, every word, every verse and every chapter in the Quran are the product of Muhammad's personal thoughts and imaginings, the secretions of his mind based upon his distorted recollections of stories and tales he had heard in earlier times from Jewish and Christian individuals.

They actually represent his own **ALTER EGO,** cleverly projected into the unsuspecting mouth of **Allah,** the **name** of the supreme pagan rock god of Mecca embedded into the corner wall of the Ka'ba, called the **Black Stone.**

The authors of the Quran: Muhammad, Allah and Gabriel are one and the same. They are **ALL Muhammad** himself, while **Allah, Gabriel and Satan** are mere props required to give his alleged revelations sanctity and divine authority.

After **13 years** of preaching to a pagan Arab audience consisting of illiterate, superstitious, unlearned and gullible people, **less than one hundred people** swallowed Muhammad's claims and posturing for prophet-hood.

Muhammad was not even able to convince his own kith and kin of his claims as the messenger of Allah let alone the Jews and Christians of Arabia.

In the end, he had to use **Terror, Bribery and Slaughter** to bring them **all** under his control and **force** them to believe in him.

There is, in the final analysis, absolutely nothing **Divine** about the Quran and any follower of Muhammad, anywhere on this planet, who would attempt to challenge these statements and conclusions based entirely on the Muhammadan records themselves, will have the same probability of success, as finding a snowflake in Muhammad's **inferno**.

#24. Satanic Quran

Q: We have so far explored many and varied subjects regarding the Quran and Hadiths, based entirely upon the Muhammadan Muslim records.

We shall be dealing with a great many more subjects especially regarding the compilation, collection and formation of the Quran in the 300 years after the death of Muhammad. All of which will be based entirely upon the Muhammadan records themselves.

Can you, none the less, give us your conclusions about the Quran?

A: Before I answer your question, I would like to repeat once more the following facts:

No human being is born evil.

Young children, toddlers' age, before they have had their minds corrupted, indoctrinated and programmed, do **not** distinguish between colour, race, gender, ethnicity, religion or political affiliations.

They are all totally INNOCENT.

Every human being is a **product of indoctrination** by their parents, their siblings, their family and their culture.

Not a single one of us has had the free will to choose our parents, our race, our nationality or our beliefs.

The followers of Muhammad are not born **evil**. They are **programmed** to be **evil**: to **hate** and to **discriminate** against all those who do not believe as they do.

The male followers of Muhammad treat their females as if they were **domestic animals** without individual rights, without respect and dominate them through terror, fear and violence.

Muhammadan Islam is **theocratic** and hence does not allow for freedoms of conscience, of political rights, of religious rights, of democracy, of individual human rights and dignity etc etc.

All you have to do is look at the **55 so called Muslim states** in the world today and you already have your answer.

It is the **Quran** which instructs them to **HATE 80% of** humanity because they do not believe in **Allah and in Muhammad as his messenger.**

It is the **Quran** which discriminates against the women followers of Muhammad and treats them like chattel.

It is the **Quran** which forbids the followers of Muhammad from reading and exploring the beliefs and religions of other people, lest they find out the facts and reality about itself.

It is the **Quran** which divides humanity into **TWO** camps: that of the **Believers 'Dar al Salam'/ Territory of Peace** against that of the **Unbelievers 'Dar al Harb'/ territory of War.**

It is the **Quran** which mandates that the whole of humanity has to become Muhammadan Muslim or under Muhammadan Islam **by Conversion, by Submission or by Slaughter.**

It is the Quran which mandates that Muhammadan Islam should be at **war**, to **aggress**, to **expand, enslave** and to **plunder** all so called Unbelievers.

Muhammadan Islam's own historical record is a **Testament** to the above.

It was Muhammad, in his Quran who, **1400 years ago, unilaterally declared war** against all other human beings on earth who do not believe as he does.

It is the clear and declared intention of the followers of Muhammad, in all forms of media, especially in the Western Democracies, that their objective is to **Islamize** Christian Europe, Hindu India, Buddhist China and all others.

One cannot find a **single** applicable merciful or compassionate verse in the **Quran** towards any and all unbelievers.

Muhammadan Islam, and its male followers, exhibit an **obscene degree** of **Hypocrisy,** of **Mendacity** and of **Racism, compounded** with a **Pathological** and **Depraved Indifference** to **Reality,** to **Facts,** to **Mercy,** to **Compassion,** to **Veracity,** to **Feelings,** to **Loyalty,** to **Friendship** and to **Language.**

While Muhammadan Muslims in our democracies demand their rights of religious traditions, **they forbid the same rights to** Christians, Buddhists, Hindus, Jews and Animists among them.

While they are allowed to build many of the most gigantic mosques in the democracies, **they forbid the building of any holy places to others.**

While they demand equal rights under the law in the democracies, **they give none to others.**

While they are allowed and take advantage of proselytizing in the democracies, **they would slaughter anyone** from another religion from doing the same in their states.

While they are allowed to preach and flaunt the Quran in public in the democracies **they forbid** the same to any others under penalty of death.

While they welcome converts to Muhammadan Islam, **they would butcher** them if they change their mind to opt out.

They are explicitly forbidden in the Quran from befriending any Christians and Jews as well as any **Unbelievers.**

In most Muhammadan Muslim states they attack, burn, rape, abduct, force into conversion, Christians, Hindus, Buddhists and others.

98% of all acts of **terror** in the world today, such as hijackings, suicide bombings, blowing up trains, cars, buildings, etc – **invariably** against defenseless and innocent civilians, in Europe, Asia, America and Africa, are conducted by the 'peace loving' followers of Muhammad.

Islam does **not** mean peace. In Arabic, Islam means only **submission.** Submission to Allah.

That is why they want the whole of humanity to Submit either to Allah or to themselves.

They want to drag the whole of humanity down to their level, the **abyss** of Ignorance, of Stupidity, of Hate and of Discrimination.

Muhammadan Muslims are the **Clones** of Muhammad even after 1400 years.

The **Common Denominator** in all of the above has its roots in the **Quran.**

The **disease** is called **Muhammadan Islam.**

The **symptoms** of this disease are: Hatemongering, Warmongering, Ignorance, Stupidity, Discrimination, Racism etc.

This **disease** is propagated through the so called 'religious' leaders such as Mullahs, Imams, Ayatullahs etc in their Madrasahs, the religious schools, their education system and their media.

This disease attacks the brain centers of the followers of Muhammad especially the areas of **Logic,** mercy and compassion, turning the victims into **Zombies,** the Living Dead.

The source of this disease is a **Virulent Virus** called the **Quran.**

No Compassionate and Merciful divinity would have produced the **Discrepancies, Hatemongering, Warmongering, Discrimination, Historical and Character dislocations, Mendacities, Abnormalities, Inconsistencies, Time and Space Displacements and Grammatical errors** that permeate the **Quranic** verses.

In **fact,** every letter, every word, every verse/ aya and every chapter/ sura in the **Quran** is the product of **Muhammad's** personal thoughts and imaginings, his own **ALTER EGO,** cleverly projected into the unsuspecting mouth of **Allah,** the **name** of the supreme pagan rock god of **Mecca** embedded into the corner wall of the **Ka'ba,** called the **Black Stone.**

There is, in the final analysis, absolutely nothing DIVINE about the **Quran** and any follower of Muhammad who would attempt to challenge these statements and conclusions based entirely on the records authored by the **Muhammadans** themselves, will have the same probability of success as finding a **snowflake** in **Muhammad's Inferno.**

The Quran is SATANIC.

Its Fundamentalist followers have no choice but to be the same.

#25. Suicide in Islam

Q: In the last few years, Muhammadan Muslims have been conducting a reign of terror all over the world by the use of Human Suicide Bombers to try and achieve their goal of Islamizing the world.

The so called SHAHEEDS/ MARTYRS have been promised by their Mullahs or so called religious leaders, that they would end up in Muhammad's version of Paradise with Sexual, Sensual and Carnal pleasures for eternity.

Does the Quran sanction suicide?

Are these promises factual?

Can you please elaborate?

A: It is of vital importance to **first** understand the actual meaning of words. For example, in the Quran and Hadiths a **martyr** or **shaheed** is one who dies in **battle** against an **armed** enemy, in combat, and **definitely not** as a Suicide against civilian targets.

Although the **Quran** in fact is full of references to superb pleasures of the flesh, both male and female, of unlimited drinking of wine and all types of food and so on and so forth *such as in 56:15-24* **to the Shaheed/Martyr,** it also clearly **prohobits** committing **suicide** by any manner or means.

*Al Baqara 2: 195 And spend of your substance in the cause of Allah **and make not your own hands contribute to your destruction** but do good; for Allah loveth those who do good.*

Al Nisaa 4: 29 O ye who believe! *eat not up your property among yourselves in vanities: but let there be amongst you traffic and trade by mutual good-will:* **nor kill (or destroy) yourselves: [wa la taqtuloo anfusakum]** *for verily Allah hath been to you Most Merciful.*

The Ahadith also, prove that Muhammad considered committing suicide a cardinal sin.

Despite the Quran's and Muhammad's prohibitions, Muhammadan scholars are justifying acts of wanton murder by suicide bombings and hijackings as true to *'Islam'*. They promise those *'martyrs'* unlimited pleasures of the flesh with seventy two beautiful virgins in paradise.

Sahih Al-Bukhari Hadith 2.445 Narrated by Thabit bin Ad Dahhak

The Prophet said, "Whoever intentionally swears falsely by a religion other than Islam, then he is what he has said, (e.g. if he says, 'If such thing is not true then I am a Jew,' he is really a Jew).

Whoever commits suicide with a piece of iron will be punished with the same piece of iron in the Hell Fire."

Narrated Jundab the Prophet said, "A man was inflicted with wounds and **he committed suicide,** and so Allah said: My slave has caused death on himself hurriedly, so **I forbid Paradise for him."**

Sahih Al-Bukhari Hadith 2.446 Narrated by Abu Huraira

The Prophet said, "**He who commits suicide** by throttling, shall keep on throttling himself in the Hell Fire (forever) and he who commits suicide by stabbing himself shall keep on stabbing himself in the Hell-Fire."

Sahih Al-Bukhari Hadith 8.73/126/647 Narrated by Thabit bin Ad Dahhak

And if somebody **commits suicide** with anything in this world, **he will be tortured with that very thing on the Day of Resurrection.**

Hadith Qudsi Hadith Qudsi 28

There was amongst those before you a man who had a wound. He was in [such] anguish that he took a knife and made with it a cut in his hand, and the blood did not cease to flow till he died.

Allah the Almighty said: My servant has himself forestalled Me; **I have forbidden him Paradise.**

*** It is obvious from all of the above, that the modern **'suicide bombers'** among the Muhammadans have been deliberately and maliciously brainwashed - by so called Quranic teachers who have a political and not a spiritual agenda to fulfill - into believing that they will go to **Paradise** with unlimited **pleasures with 72 virgins.**

It is crystal clear from the above Quran & Hadith verses, that **martyrdom** requires dying or getting killed in **battle** and not by **committing suicide.**

If only these would be suicides actually realized, that they will end up in **Hell** blowing themselves up repeatedly till the Last Days, none of them would have committed these insane and depraved acts ***

#26. Charter of Umar

It is vitally important that the listeners realise the following:

99.99% of **Unbelievers** as well as **Muhammadans**, have no idea or have never heard of the **Charter of Umar.**

After the rapid expansion of the Arabian Muhammadan dominion in the 7th century, Muhammadan leaders were required to work out a way of dealing with **Non-Muslims,** who remained in the majority in many areas for centuries. The solution was to develop the notion of the **"dhimma",** or **"protected person".** The Dhimmi were required to pay an extra tax, the **Jizzya,** many times onerous with humiliation and were unmolested until such time as a distraction was needed for the populace.

The Pact of Umar is supposed to have been the peace accord offered by the **Caliph Umar** to the Christians of Syria, a "pact" which formed the pattern of later interaction.

Historians are **not** unanimous as to which Umar this **Charter / Pact or Covenant** is actually attributed, whether **Umar ibn al Khattab,** the second **Khalifa** or the **Ummayad Umar the II.**

In the final analysis, it is **not** important to whom it should be attributed since the **Conquering Muhammadan Muslims implemented** it and have been doing so for the last **1400 years** and continue to do so in the 21st century in most Muhammadan states.

The following is from Al-Turtushi, , pp. 229-230.

We heard from 'Abd al-Rahman ibn Ghanam [died 78/697] as follows:

When Umar ibn al-Khattab, may Allah be pleased with him, accorded a peace to the Christians of Syria, we wrote to him as follows:

In the name of Allah, the Merciful and Compassionate. This is a letter to the servant of Allah Umar [ibn al-Khattab], Commander of the Faithful, from the Christians of such-and-such a city. When you came against us, we asked you for safe-conduct (aman) for ourselves, our descendants, our property, and the people of our community, and we undertook the following obligations toward you:

We shall not build, in our cities or in their neighborhood, new monasteries, Churches, convents, or monks' cells, nor shall we repair, by day or by night, such of them as fall in ruins or are situated in the quarters of the Muslims.

We shall keep our gates wide open for passersby and travelers.

We shall give board and lodging to all Muslims who pass our way for three days.

We shall not give shelter in our churches or in our dwellings to any spy, nor bide him from the Muslims.

We shall not teach the Qur'an to our children.

We shall not manifest our religion publicly nor convert anyone to it.

We shall not prevent any of our kin from entering Islam if they wish it.

We shall show respect toward the Muslims, and we shall rise from our seats when they wish to sit.

We shall not seek to resemble the Muslims by imitating any of their garments, the qalansuwa, the turban, footwear, or the parting of the hair.

We shall not speak as they do, nor shall we adopt their kunyas.

We shall not mount on saddles, nor shall we gird swords nor bear any kind of arms nor carry them on our- persons.

We shall not engrave Arabic inscriptions on our seals.

We shall not sell fermented drinks.

We shall clip the fronts of our heads.

We shall always dress in the same way wherever we may be, and we shall bind the zunar round our waists

We shall not display our crosses or our books in the roads or markets of the Muslims. We shall use only clappers in our churches very softly.

We shall not raise our voices when following our dead.

We shall not show lights on any of the roads of the Muslims or in their markets.

We shall not bury our dead near the Muslims.

We shall not take slaves who have been allotted to Muslims.

We shall not build houses overtopping the houses of the Muslims.

(When I brought the letter to Umar, may Allah be pleased with him, he added, "We shall not strike a Muslim.")

We accept these conditions for ourselves and for the people of our community, and in return we receive safe-conduct.

If we in any way violate these undertakings for which we ourselves stand surety, we forfeit our covenant [dhimma], and we become liable to the penalties for contumacy and sedition.

Umar ibn al-Khittab replied: Sign what they ask, but add two clauses and impose them in addition to those which they have undertaken.

They are: "They shall not buy anyone made prisoner by the Muslims," and "Whoever strikes a Muslim with deliberate intent shall forfeit the protection of this pact."

It is imperative that our readers comprehend the following:

1. The Muhammadans were imposing **degrading** and **discrimnatory** rules on the conquered peoples in **their own homeland** by the **aggressors.**

2. The Muhammadan Muslims were **protecting** the

natives from **whom?**

3   Every condition above represents utter **contempt** for the religious beliefs and feelings of the subjugated peoples, for their culture, their heritage and their dignity in their own land.

4   Although generally they were unmolested, it did not stop the leaders to have them massacred whenever they needed to distract the Muhammadans in times of stress.

5   While the Muhammadan Muslims in the majority of their countries continue to implement many of the above against all **Unbelievers,** they, with an obscene degree of **hypocrisy, demand** all human rights in the **democracies** and at the same time, **disloyally**, intend to bring down the institutions of the host countries to their abysmal level of **intolerance, ignorance** and **stupidity.**

I would like to leave any further conclusions or comments to our readers regarding the mercy and compassion of **Muhammadan Islam** vis a vis the **People of the Book.**

#27. Foreign Words in Quran

Q: The Quran in several verses asserts that it is in pure Arabic, by an Arab, Muhammad, to Arabs. Yet according to my own studies, I was surprised at the fact that many of the Muhammadan linguists had great difficulty in finding the Arabic origins or roots of many of the most important words in the Quran.
Can you elaborate?

A: Contrary to what many Muhammadan Muslim authors have us believe, Muhammad and Arabia were surrounded by higher religions and civilizations with whom they had constant and full contact and from whom they borrowed numerous religious and cultural terms.

This fact was fully recognized by the earliest Muslim exegetes, who showed no hesitation in noting words as Christian, Iranian or Jewish in origin as were compiled by Al Suyuti in his *Itqan*, al Tabari, al Baghawi, al Razi and many more.

It was under the later scholars such as **al Shafi'I** that this fact, for obvious sectarian reasons, was pushed into the background and an orthodox doctrine was elaborated - later turned into a **dogma** - to the effect, that the Quran is a unique product of the Arabic language.

The modern Muhammadan scholar is seriously distressed by any discussion of the foreign origin of words in the Quran.

It is extremely rare, based on proven historical and linguistic grounds, that an uncivilized people, such as the pagan Arabs were, would not be enormously influenced by the surrounding more superior civilizations, religions and cultures.

For the Muhammadan Arabs to pretend, that the Arabic language per se, prior to the Arabian conquests of the surrounding civilizations contained all the words used in the Quran is totally absurd, contrary to facts, unsubstantiated and desperate wishful thinking.

It is invariably, the more dominant powers or civilizations that impose their language upon the lesser ones as actually happened initially by the Greeks, the Romans and finally by the Arabs in their turn.

Anyone dispassionately studying the Quran will realize that Muhammad drew his inspiration not from his own primitive & arid pagan religious background but most certainly from the vocabulary and religious terms of the great monotheistic religions that had already found root in the spiritual soil of Arabia, especially the Jews and Christians.

It is extremely important to point out that there were very powerful Arabian Christian tribes who were dominant both in Syria and Iraq and who wrote and spoke **Syriac.**

Vocabulary of Syriac origin was already coming into use in Arabia long before Muhammad and his Quran. The court of al Hira in Iraq was a rendezvous of the poets and literature of the day. Many of the most prominent poets of **pre-Islamic Arabia such as Imru'l Qays, Mutalammis and Abdi b. Zaid** were **Christians** and their poetry was naturally impregnated with Christian words and ideas.

Even in the extant poetry of such non-Christians as **Al Nabigha and Al Ash'a,** one finds the strong influences of Syrian Christianity because they spent time at the court of **al Hira.**

The Ahadith and the biography of Muhammad assert that he traveled to **Syria (al Sham)** both as a child and later as a merchant on behalf of his wife **Khadija** who was not only a Hanif but also associated with Christianity through her uncle **Waraqa bin Naufal.**

Muhammad was surrounded by enormously powerful non Arabian influences that shaped his thoughts, his inspirations and his Quranic prose and to pretend that he was not affected by them is contrary to logic, to reality to veracity and to history.

*Yusuf 12: 2 We have sent it down as an **Arabic Qur'an** in order that ye may learn wisdom.*

*Ta Ha 20: 113 Thus have we sent this down an **Arabic Qur'an***

*Al Shu'ara 26:195 In the perspicuous **Arabic tongue**.*

*Al Zumar 39: 28 (It is) a **Qur'an in Arabic** without any crookedness (therein): in order that they may guard against Evil.*

*Fussilat 41:3 A Book whereof the verses are explained in detail a **Qur'an in Arabic** for people who understand*

*** According to the Ahadith, the Quran was 'revealed' to Muhammad in **seven** modes.

Why were so many modes necessary if it were such a pure form of Arabic in the first place?***

Al-Tirmidhi Hadith 2215 Narrated by Ubayy ibn Ka'b

Ubayy told of Allah's Messenger meeting Gabriel and saying, "I have been sent, Gabriel, **to a people who are unlettered,** among whom are old women and old men, boys and girls, and men who have never read a book."

He replied, "The Qur'an, Muhammad, has been sent down in **seven modes.**"

Tirmidhi transmitted it.

Al Suyuti cites in his ***al-Itqan*** (Cairo 1925), vol.1, ch. 38 pp (135/41) about **118 words** which are not of Arabic origin but from Hebrew, Persian, Abyssinian, Aramaic, Syriac etc. most of which are among the most important, without which, the Quran could not possibly make sense.

The following are a few samples:

Hebrew/Aramaic: Madrassah (School)/Beit ha Midrash, Sadaqah (Charity), Surah (Chapter, Revelation), Mus'haf (Holy Book), Malak (Angel)/Mal^akh, Ma'idah (table), Sakinah (Holy Spirit)/ Shekhina; Tahara (Purity); Jahannam/Hell (Gehinnom); Medina/

Town (Medinah); Shaytan/Satan (Satan); Jibril/Gabriel (Gibbor-El); Kanisah/Church (Kinnesset); Nabi/prophet (Nabi); Zakah/Charity (Zakah); Deen/Religion (Din); Misr(Egypt)/Misra^im; Furat(Euphrates)/Prat; Dijlah(Tigris)/ Hiddekkel; Ahbar(Jewish Doctor)/ Haber; Asbat(tribes of Israel)/Sabt; Allahumma/Elohim;

Christian Abyssinian: Mirhab (Niche), Minbar (Pulpit), Burhan (Proof), Hawariyoun (Apostles/Jesus' disciples); Mi'raj/Ladder; Mushaf/Holy Book);

Persian: Barzakh (Obstacle) (S23:102; 55:20; 25:55), Firdaws (Paradise) (S18:107; 23:11); Zanjabil (Ginger) (S76:17); Sijjil (Stones) (S105:4);, Firind (Sword), Khandaq (To Dig/Ditch); Zandaqah (Zandiq=Fire Worshipper)

Syriac: (Dawud/David; Sulayman/Solomon; Isa/Jesus; Nuh/Noah; Bi'ah/Church; Salah/Prayer; and all the Biblical names in the Quran

Greek: Kharaj (Land Tax)/Choregia; Dinar (Currency)/Denarius;Iblis(Devil)/Diabolos; Injil(Gospel)

The Quran asserts repeatedly that it is a **new scripture** for the Arabs hence it would have been impossible for the native Arabic vocabulary and language to, all of a sudden, create and invent new words and terminology to express all its new ideas to fit the occasion.

In fact, many of the words, terms and concepts were already available - off the shelf, so to speak - to Muhammad to **plagiarise, plunder, pirate and or pervert** to suit his agenda.

*** When one studies the subjects above, based upon the works of the Muhammadan exegetes who had dealt with this very difficult but important matter, one will find out that they were themselves at a loss as to the roots of many of the words, especially since they were not linguists in the four, five or six languages that the Quran had copied words from.

They actually had the most meager philological resources at their disposal; so much so, that al Suyuti and those who preceded him completely missed the fact that several of the words that they alleged to have been foreign were in fact Arabic in origin.

The Quran cannot possibly exist without the foreign words that permeate its verses and chapters.

Al Suyuti's *Al Muhadhdhab* has the most complete classification of borrowed words in the **Quran** that have survived the centuries. He divides them in his ***Mutawakkili*** into the following classes:

1	Ethiopic	Habashi
2	Persian	Farisiya
3	Greek	Roumiya
4	Indian	Hindiya
5	Syriac	Syriyaniya
6	Hebrew	Ibraniya
7	Nabatean	Nabatiya
8	Coptic	Coptiya
9	Turkish	Turkiya
10	Negro	Zinjiya
11	Berber	Barbariya

Other words:

Taht 19:24 (Nabataean);

Hayt laka 12:23 (Coptic);

Sayidha 12:25 (Coptic);

Mazjat and Bidtha'a 12:88 (Coptic);

Abadta 26:21 (Nabataean);

Abla'a 11:46 (Nabataean);

Akhlad 7:175 (Hebrew) etc etc are actually all Arabic ***

#28. Last of the Prophets

Q: We are constantly told by the followers of Muhammad that he was the last prophet.
That no other prophet will come after him.

Was Muhammad a prophet?

On what basis do they form such a dogma ?

A: In the Quran there is only **one** verse upon which the followers of Muhammad secure their argument above.

As usual with Muhammadan Muslims, their argument is spurious, without foundation and based on erroneous or deliberate mistranslation and misinterpretation of the verse.

This singular verse is in chapter Al Ahzab

Al Ahzab 33:40 "*Muhammad is not the father of any of your men but (he is) the Apostle of Allah and the*

Seal [Khatim] of the Prophets [al Nabiyyna]: *and Allah has full knowledge of all things*"

In **Arabic** this is read as " ***Khatim al Nabiyyna***", allegedly meaning the

"the Last of the Prophets".

When this verse and the Ahadith stories are scrutinized, this interpretation is shown to have been purposely falsified to fit the agenda of Muhammad's followers.

Sahih Al-Bukhari Hadith 4.189 Narrated by Anas

When the Prophet intended to write a letter to the ruler of the Byzantines, he was told that those people did not read any letter unless it was stamped with a SEAL [Khatim]. So, the Prophet got a silver ring-as if I were just looking at its white glitter on his hand- and stamped on it the expression

Lifting the Veil

"Muhammad, Apostle of Allah" ------ " Muhammad Rasool'Allah"

The Hadith above produces two corollaries:

1 Muhammad did not know about the term and/or the word **Khatim** which means a **seal** of a letter to **authenticate** its origin and to render it protected from tampering.

It was only after this explanation that he used it in the verse above to mean that he was the authenticator of previous revelations and **not** as the **last** of the prophets.

God never put a limit to His prophets since they are always required to bring back people to the path of righteousness after having strayed

The Arabic word **(Khatim)**, is actually derived from the original **Hebrew (Khatima)** meaning **(Signiature/Inscription/Seal Ring)**.

2 Most important of all, even Muhammad's insignia was **'Apostle/ Messenger'** and **NOT** **'Prophet of Allah'**.

In the Arabic language there is an extremely important difference between Rassool/ Messenger and Nabi/Prophet because a Prophet can also be a Messenger but a Messenger cannot also be a Prophet.

According to both the Quranic verse and the Hadiths, Muhammad did **not** claim outright **prophethood.**

From the theological point of view alone, the reader must understand that the concept of the 'last prophet' resides in the arrival of the Messiah, which is after all, a Jewish concept.

Muhammad, not only did not fit this title, but the whole of the Quran has no record of a single prophesy.

Even those that were later concocted in the Ahadith, are proven to be untrue.

Sahih Al-Bukhari Hadith 9.477 Narrated byMasruq

'Aisha, The Mother of the Believers (Muhammad's wife) said,

"if anyone tells you that Muhammad has seen the Unseen (the **future**) he is a liar, for Allah says: "None has the knowledge of the Unseen (the **future**), but Allah."

The title **Prophet** must fit the deeds, and Muhammad was not one.

Based upon all the references shown, it is clear that had Muhammad wanted to assert that he was the last of the prophets, he would have had to use the following Arabic expression:

".. AKHER [LAST] al Nabiyyoun /Anbiyaa..." , neither of which are of course used.

Muhammad's actual intent, was to demonstrate that he was so much greater than **all** the previous prophets, that he was in a position to **authenticate** their revelations.

In similitude of a **teacher authenticating** or **grading** the level or degree of aptitude of a student's exam paper.

Furthermore, the Ahadith are replete with the expression

"Allah and his **messenger**" OR "Allah & his **messenger** know best". The word prophet is never used.

The term **khatim** also appears in different forms:

Al Baqara 2:7 [Khatama Allah ala qulubihim] which is translated to "...*Allah set a seal upon their hearts*...".

Al An'am 6:46 [Khatama ala qulubikum] ... "...*Sealedl up your hearts...*"

Ya Sin 36:65 [Al-yawm nakhtimu ala afwahihim] is "...*Today we put a seal on their mouths...*".

Al Shua'ra 42:24 [Allahu yakhtimu ala qalbika] "...*Allah put a seal upon your heart...*".

Al Jathiyah 45:23 [Wa khatama ala sam'ihi wa qalbihi] .. "...*and sealed up his heart and hearing...*".

Al Ahqaf 46:9 Say: "I am no bringer of new-fangled doctrine among the apostles nor do I know what will be done with me or with you. I follow but that which is revealed to me by inspiration: I am but a Warner open and clear."

Al Mutaffifin 83:25 Their thirst will be slaked with Pure Wine sealed *[Rahiqi Makhtoomin]*:

26 The seal *[khatamuhoo]* thereof will be Musk: ...

The term **seal** has had its actual meaning deliberately perverted by the Muhammadans to mean **last** for obvious theological and sectarian reasons.

The fact is that the word **Khatim** means only a seal - usually a signiature ring - which authenticates a document to prove its originality.

It does not mean, at all, that Muhammad is the **last** of the prophets since if that were what the Quran wanted to impart, it would have said

"..there will be no other prophets after me.."

#29. Satanic Verses

Q: Twenty years ago, the world was awash with reports about Salman Rushdie's book the ' *Satanic Verses*' for which he received the usual Muhammadan Muslim response to any criticism or investigation of Muhammadan Islam, a Fatwa, that is a religious decision, to have him assassinated.

Was there and is there a record of these verses in Muhammadan Islam?

A: Muhammadan Islam, basing its Monotheism on that of the Israelites and their Torah, strongly opposes idolatry, polytheism and associating anything or anyone with Allah.

This contrasts sharply with the contention by Muhammad's Pagan Arab contemporaries who believed that Allah had associates.

Some of these associates are mentioned in the Quran, among them are three female deities: **al-Lat, al-Uzza** and **Manat** who were, according to the religious beliefs of the pagan Arabs, the **DAUGHTERS** of Allah, the supreme deity of the Ka'ba. Each had a shrine in separate places not far from Mecca in Arabia, where Muhammad was born and began his mission.

Although the Quran, in its present form, obviously rejects these deities, **'Muslim'** history asserts otherwise.

The Muhammadan records assert that Muhammad actually spoke **Satan's** words as if they were the words of Allah. This event is documented by several early Muhammadan scholars and is referenced in the Hadith and the Quran.

Later Muhammadan scholars, **ashamed and embarrassed** that their self declared prophet spoke Satan's words, denied the event occurred. A myriad of excuses and contorted stories have been put forth by these later scholars to cover up **Muhammad's sinful error.**

It must be very clearly pointed out, that the **"Satanic Verses"** event is not something made up by non-Muslims.

The event is recorded by the earliest Muhammadan sources available reporting on Muhammad's life. No one should think that it is a story made up by people who are critical of 'Islam'. It is an episode directly found in the early Islamic records.

This subject is one of the most controversial in Muhammadan Islam because, allegedly, **Satan was able to deceive Muhammad** and thus insinuate himself in the Quran by causing Muhammad to recite his words as if they were Allah's words.

Muhammadans always use the mantra *"bring forth the proof"*. Well, the proof is as follows:

This event is actually documented by the four early biographical writers of Muhammad's life:

Ibn Ishaq's *"Sirat Rasulallah"*, Wakidi, Ibn Sa'd's *"Kitab al-Tabaqat al-Kabir"*, and Tabari's "History"

The Hadith and Quran also contain direct references. Additionally several other Islamic scholars on Hadith (traditions) support the event's occurrence such as:

Ibn Abi Hatim, Ibn al-Mundhir, Ibn Mardauyah, Musa ibn 'Uqba, and Abu Ma'shar.

It is all the more strange that Ibn Hajar, a recognized authority on traditions insists on the truth of this report and says,

"As we have mentioned above, three of its chains of narrators satisfy the conditions requisite for an authentic report."

*** Because of time constraints, we shall explore al Tabari's version of the events and those who need more detail should go to our Definitions Section in our Website ***

<u>Tabari VI.107</u> : SATAN CASTS A FALSE REVELATION ON THE MESSENGER OF ALLAH'S TONGUE

The messenger of Allah was eager for the welfare of his people and wished to effect a reconciliation with them in whatever ways he could. He longed in his soul that something would come to him from Allah which would reconcile him with his tribe. With his love for his tribe and his eagerness for their welfare it would have delighted him if some of the difficulties which they made for him could have been smoothed out, and he debated with himself and fervently desired such an outcome. Then Allah revealed:

Al Najm 53:19 *Have ye thought upon al-Lat and al-Uzza*

> **20** *And Manat, the third, the other?*
>
>> At this very moment, **Satan** allegedly cast on his tongue, because of his inner debates and what he desired to bring to his people, the words:
>
> **21** *These are the exalted cranes [Gharaniq] (intermediaries)*
>
> **22** *Whose intercession is to be hoped for.*

When the Quraysh heard this, they rejoiced and were happy and delighted at the way in which he spoke of their gods, and they listened to him, while the Muslims, having complete trust in their prophet in respect of the messages which he brought from Allah, did not suspect him of error, illusion, or mistake.

When he came to the prostration, having completed the surah, **he prostrated** himself and the Muslims did likewise, following their prophet, trusting in the message which he had brought and following his example.

Those polytheists of the Quraysh and others who were in the mosque likewise **prostrated themselves** because of the reference to their gods which they had heard, so that there was no one in the mosque, believer or unbeliever, who did not prostrate himself.

The Quraysh left delighted by the mention of their gods which they had heard, saying, "Muhammad has mentioned our gods in the most favorable way possible, stating in his recitation that they are

Lifting the Veil

the high **flying cranes *[Gharaniq]*** and that their intercession is received with approval."

*** It is very important to point out here and now, that Muhammad and his Muslim followers were prostrating themselves and praying in a purely **pagan mosque**, a House of **idolatry,** since they were surrounded by the rock gods of the Quraysh.

Muhammad should not have done so at all as an alleged **monotheist.**

This only shows that he was always willing to compromise his beliefs until such time as he could overcome or destroy all those who did not believe as he did, as in fact he eventually achieved ***

Then Gabriel came to the Messenger of Allah and said,

"Muhammad, what have you done? You have recited to the people that which I did not bring to you from Allah, and you have said that which was not said to you."

Then the messenger of Allah was much grieved and feared Allah greatly, but Allah sent down a revelation to him, for He was merciful to him, consoling him and making the matter light for him, informing him that there had never been a prophet or a messenger before him who desired as he desired and wished as he wished but that Satan had cast words into his recitation, as he had cast words on Muhammad's tongue.

Then Allah cancelled what Satan had thus cast, and established his verses by telling him that he was like other prophets and messengers,

and replaced the offending Satanic Verses with:

21   What! for you the male sex and for Him the female?

22   Behold such would be indeed a division most unfair!

I.Q. Al Rassooli

The question that any inquisitive mind will ask is:

How many other verses in the Quran were actually revealed to Muhammad by **SATAN** and **Not Gabriel?**

The **Satanic Verses** also destroy another challenge in the Quran:

Bani Israil 17: 88 *Say: "If the whole of mankind and Jinns were to gather together to produce the like of this Qur'an they* ***could not produce the like thereof*** *even if they backed up each other with help and support.*

*** Ladies and Gentlemen, it is clear from the above that in desperation, and in a moment of weakness, Muhammad was willing to compromise his Monotheism by conceding to allow the daughters of Allah to remain as intercessors in his 'Islam'; that is, he was willing to allow three other associates with Allah.

Muhammad actually **sinned** and all the excuses that we read and all the explanations are used to hide a very simple fact:

Muhammad **kafara** because he associated other gods with Allah.

When he realized the enormity of what he had done, he **repented** and to rectify his error he first accused the **innocent** SATAN of having tricked him and then **'revealed'** the very conveniently **descended abrogating** verses followed by others in which, Allah only **admonished** him and made **light banter** of his enormous **sin.**

Neither Satan, Gabriel nor Allah were involved; it was all Muhammad at his very best:

Deceitful, wily, beguiling and very much in control of his mostly very **superstitious, ignorant, fearful, illiterate** and totally **obedient flock.**

#30. Seventy Two Virgins

Q: Is it true that in the Quran or in the Hadiths, there are promises to whoever dies as a Martyr/ Shaheed for Muhammadan Islam that they would end up in Paradise with unlimited Sexual, Carnal and Sensual pleasures for eternity with 72 virgins?

A: The Quran is replete with verses promising the believers infinitely greater rewards in the **Afterlife** than in **Life**.

Al Baqara 2: 25 "*But give glad tidings to those who believe and work righteousness that their portion is Gardens beneath which rivers flow. ... they are fed with fruits ... and they have therein* **companions** *(pure and holy); and they abide therein (for ever).*

Al Najm 55: 70 " *In them will be* **fair (companions)** *good and beautiful*

72 Companions restrained (as to their glances) in (goodly) pavilions

74 Whom no **man or Jinn** *before them has touched*

*** The listeners should be made aware that in the Quran and in Sharia law, the **Jinn** (who are **Demons**) are a **Race** of **Fire** but are otherwise **Identical** to human beings:

They have intellect and can have intercourse with humans, they can be either Believing 'Muslims' or Unbelievers.

They too are pre destined by Allah to end up in his Hell or Paradise.

In the Bible, I would like to point out to our listeners, neither the Jinn/ Demons nor Satan are mentioned as part of God's creation.

They are in reality, purely the product of human imagination ***

*** Muhammad's Quran, promises his followers, that by dying while slaughtering unbelievers to spread Muhammadan Islam all over the world, their rewards in death, represent everything that they have lacked in life and more:

Gardens, flowing water, greenery and shade; unlimited food both in type and in quantity; unlimited sexual pleasures both for those who prefer boys or those who prefer females; wine and luxuries.

It should not be a great wonder then, that Muhammad's generally very gullible and ignorant followers would prefer to die than to live.

Who would not, if they believed all the above rewards? ***

Al-Tirmidhi Hadith3834 Narrated by Al-Miqdam ibn Ma'dikarib

Allah's Messenger said, "The martyr is married to **seventy-two wives** of the maidens with large dark eyes; and is made intercessor for seventy of his relatives."

Al-Tirmidhi Hadith 5648 Narrated by AbuSa'id

Allah's Messenger said, "The lowliest of the inhabitants of Paradise will be he who has **eighty thousand servants** and **seventy-two virgins ....**

*** Muhammadan scholars indoctrinate their acolytes to commit slaughter and murder of all **Unbelievers** in *"The Name of Allah"* with promises of seventy two virgins based upon the above Ahadith.

The same followers of Muhammad, who when alive and in the physical world, are allowed a maximum of four wives, and a minimum of pleasures since they are prohibited from:

Gambling, Drinking Wine, Singing, Dancing, Painting, wearing Gold or Silk, reciting poetry, playing chess, etc, etc, are allowed in death, seventy two virgins with unlimited Sexual, Carnal and Sensual Pleasures.

Muhammad's version of Paradise becomes a WHOREHOUSE for those who commit atrocities against all humans who do not believe in 'Allah and in his messenger Muhammad'.

All those murdered human beings are unbelievers in the first place because Allah pre ordained that they should be so.

Hence the Merciful and Compassionate Allah of Muhammad, who programmed them to be unbelievers in the first place, none the less, consigns them to a pre destined Hell Fire through no fault of their own, so that they would be slaughtered by the followers of Muhammad who are then rewarded to Paradise when killed during their missions of extermination.

It should be pointed out that not once in the Quran nor in the Ahadith is there any mention that it was the angel Gabriel who informed Muhammad of such a reward (of seventy two virgins).

It was Muhammad alone who promised his gullible and believing followers of them ***

Sahih Al-Bukhari Hadith 4.544 Narrated byAbu Huraira

They will not urinate, relieve nature, spit, or have any nasal secretions.

*** The **Cult** of Muhammad has no concept of the **Spiritual** world. Those of his followers who die while attempting to slaughter **Unbelievers,** end up in a **Physical** whorehouse type of paradise with unlimited sex, food and other carnal and sensual pleasures.

With promises of such **eternal rewards**, one should not be surprised, that the **believing** followers of Muhammad would commit **murder, slaughter,** Death & **destruction** upon all **unbelievers** to attain these unenviable **incentives.**

These believers are **never** informed, that in the Quran and in other Hadiths, Muhammad utterly **forbids** committing **suicide** and the penalty is to suffer in Hell for eternity.

Those who do so, are generally **ignorant** believers, who are brainwashed by totally **Immoral** and **evil** 'Muslim' leaders who **indoctrinate** them so as to fulfill their own political or sectarian agendas ***

Al Imran 3: 15 For the righteous are gardens in nearness to their Lord with rivers flowing beneath; therein is their eternal home; with companions pure (and holy) ...

Al Nisaa 4: 57 But those who believe and do deeds of righteousness We shall soon admit to gardens with rivers flowing beneath their eternal home: therein shall they have companions pure and holy: We shall admit them to shades cool and ever deepening

Al Dukhan 44: 51 As to the Righteous (they will be) in a position of Security

    52   Among Gardens and Springs;

    53   Dressed in fine silk and in rich brocade they will face each other;

    54   So; and We shall Join them to Companions with beautiful big and lustrous eyes.

    55   There can they call for every kind of fruit in peace and security;

Al Tur 52: 20 They will recline (with ease) on Thrones (of dignity) arranged in ranks; and We shall join them to Companions with beautiful big and lustrous eyes.

Al waqi'ah 56:22 And (there will be) Companions with beautiful big and lustrous eyes....

35 We have created (their Companions) of special creation.

36 And made them virgin-pure (and undefiled)

37 Beloved (by nature**) equal in age** .....

Al Saffat 38: 52 And beside them will be chaste women restraining their glances (companions) **of equal age.**

Al Naba' 78: 33 Companions of Equal Age;

*** These are very interesting verses since they imply that a **50 years old 'martyr'** will have a **fifty years old virgin companion** and so on ***

#31. Taqiyah/ Islamic Subterfuge

Q: Is it true that Muslims are allowed by the Quran to deceive any and all Unbelievers, that is all human beings who are not followers of Muhammad, when the Muslims are in a weaker position?

A: It was **Muhammad** who **1400 years ago,** unilaterally declared **total war** against all those who do not believe as he did, the **unbelievers.**

He asserted repeatedly, that the most important and fundamental **art** of war is, **deception.**

Hence **Taqiyah** - after a passage from the **Quran** - is the **Muhammadan Muslim doctrine** and practice of (Self Protection; Religious Dissimulation; Concealment; Disguise; Deception; Subterfuge) whereby it is considered acceptable to conceal one's **true beliefs** and even identity in the face of perceived adversity.

The above definition must be clearly explained

First, the **concealment** of one's beliefs does **not** mean an **abandonment** of these beliefs. The distinction between "concealment" and "abandonment" **must** be clearly understood.

Second, the word "beliefs" and/or "convictions" does **not** necessarily mean "religious" beliefs and/or convictions, **Only.**

Let us look at al-Taqiyya According to the Sunnis

===

Some Sunnis assert that **al-Taqiyya** is an act of **pure hypocrisy** that serves to conceal the truth and reveal that which is the exact opposite (of the truth). Furthermore, according to those Sunnis**, al-Taqiyya** constitutes a lack of faith and trust in **Allah** because the person who conceals his beliefs to spare himself from imminent danger is fearful of humans, when, in fact, he should be fearful of **Allah** only. As such, this person is a coward.

Let us now look at the Sunni Sources in Support of al-Taqiyya

==

The following exposition will demonstrate the existence of al-Taqiyya in the Quran, Hadith, Muhammad's as well as his companions' custom.

As usual, Sunni books will be used to further the argument. This is in keeping with our commitment to reveal the **truth** by showing that the Sunnis reject the Shia's arguments, while **their own** books are replete (full) with the **same** ideologies that the Shia uphold! It is in similitude of the

"Pot calling the Kettle, BLACK"

Although some Wahhabis staunchly argue their aforementioned statements, and aggressively defame the Shia and refute their doctrines, they have failed to explain the validity of their argument vis-a-vis the existence of these **same** doctrines in their own books.

Those who think that they are the true protectors of the **SUNNA** of **Muhammad** and the only guardians of the **Islamic Faith,** how can they explain their own rejection of that which they are supposed to protect?

Rejecting al-Taqiyya is rejecting the Quran, as will be shown.

Reference 1:

Jalal al-Din al-Suyuti in his book, *"al-Durr al-Manthoor Fi al-Tafsir al- Ma'athoor,"* narrates Ibn Abbas - who is the **most** renowned and trusted narrator of tradition in the sight of the Sunnis – regarding his opinion of al-Taqiyya in the Quranic verse:

Ali Imran 3:28 *Let not the believers take for friends or helpers* ***unbelievers*** *rather than* ***believers****; if any do that, in nothing will there be help from* ***Allah****; except by way of precaution that ye may* ***guard yourselves*** *from them* ***(tattaqoo)****. But Allah* ***cautions you*** *[touqatan] (to remember) Himself for the final goal* ***is to Allah****.*

that Ibn Abbas said:

"al-Taqiyya is with the tongue only; he who has been **coerced** into saying that which angers **Allah** and his heart is comfortable (i.e., his **true** faith has **not** been shaken.), then (saying that which he has been coerced to say) will **not** harm him (at all); (because) al-Taqiyya is with the tongue only, (**not** the heart)."

Reference 2:

Abu Bakr al-Razi in his book, *"Ahkam al-Quran," v2, p10,* has explained

the aforementioned verse by affirming that al-Taqiyya should be used when one is afraid for life and/or limb.

In addition, he has narrated that **Qutadah** said with regards to the above verse:

"It is permissible to speak words of unbelief when al-Taqiyya is mandatory."

Reference 3:

Ibn Abbas also commented on the above verse, as narrated in **Sunan al Bayhaqi** and **al Hakim's** *"Mustadrak",* by saying:

"al Taqiyya is the uttering of the **tongue,** while the **heart** is comfortable with **faith**"

Which means that the tongue is permitted to utter any untruth in a time of need, as long as the heart is not affected; and one is still a believer"

When the followers of Muhammad are in a weak position vis a vis the unbelievers or even other sects of 'Islam' or threatened and cannot defend themselves, they are then allowed to do whatever is expedient to survive even if it meant breaking every prohibition in the Quran

The doctrine of **Al Taqiyah** allows the followers of Muhammad to become short or long term **sleepers,** to use deception, misinformation, disinformation, plant seeds of discord and sedition **and all other manners of lies to** bring about the collapse of the entity being **subverted – which is of course the government of the Unbelievers -** so that the **'muslims'** can take over with minimum opposition or losses.

It saves them from having to become martyrs for their faith.

In today's terms for instance, the followers of **Muhammad** put forth the following **lies & misinformation:**

That **Jihad** is actually the **'struggle' of the spirit;** that the **'extremists'** are the **aberration** and not the norm;

that **'fundamentalists'** do not represent **'true Islam';**

that **'Islam' is a religion of 'peace'** even though almost **95%** of all of today's world conflicts and acts of terror are instigated and perpetrated by **'muslims;**

that **'Islam'** is a **'tolerant religion'** when in fact all **unbelievers** are not allowed to publicly and freely express their religious beliefs anywhere in almost **50 'islamic'** states in the world;

that **'Islam'** is **pro democratic** when neither the **women** in **'islam'** nor other **'non believers'** are allowed even a semblance of freedoms or the rights of the **dignity of 'man'** under the recognized and universal

'Human Rights Charter'..etc etc..

In the present day, just as they did in the past, **Fundamentalist Muhammadan Muslims** use this **'theological loophole'** as a means of infiltration and subterfuge to absolve **Muslim terrorists** and members of suicide squads from looking like **observant Muslims** so as to be able to blend among the populace of the nations they are targeting and not cause suspicion or attention to be paid to them.

This process allows the **Muhammadans** - who are absolved of all wrong doing - to **temporarily** bend to foreign authority, and are even allowed to **make terms** with it for as long as they are weak until such time that **they can overthrow or destroy it.**

The principle of **Taqiya** allows the ignorant **Western** and or **Unbeliever statesman** to fall into the deadly trap of trusting the words, the signature or any form of agreement made with a **'muslim'**.

He neither realizes nor conceives that all these procedures and agreements are totally meaningless since the signatory to the agreement, the **Muhammadan Muslim, has absolutely no intention of honouring them in the long term.**

They are only a **means to an end;** that is the **end** of the gullible non believer who signed them.

When dealing with a **'muslim'** statesman or diplomat, **the real issue** is **not** what he says or means but actually what he intends to do 'in his heart', which is of course unfathomable.

Muhammad repeatedly asserted that deception is one of the best strategies of waging war.

We in the **Western democracies,** and everywhere else in the world who are **Unbelievers,** are being Deceived, Subverted and slowly destroyed from within and without by the followers of **Muhammad** because our leaders do not **comprehend or understand** those they are dealing with.

#32. And Then it was Revealed

Q: While reading some of the commentaries explaining the Quranic verses both in the Quran and the Hadiths, I was struck by a sentence which was repeated innumerable times proclaiming that such and such an event happened and THEN a verse was revealed!
Can you explain this?

A: *"And then it was revealed.."* is a mantra that permeates Bukhari, Muslim, Abu Dawood & Tirmidi Hadiths as well as Ibn Ishaq's biography of Muhammad.

In hundreds upon hundreds of instances, an event had occurred or an action was taken or ordered by Muhammad, for which, afterwards, that is after the event, a convenient and very appropriate *'revelation'* was *'descended'*, justifying or explaining it by an indisputable *'divine decree'*.

In the cases of the Hebrew prophets, they predicted events beforehand and then these predictions came to be true.

This **IS** the essence of prophecy.

In Muhammad's case, almost none exist in such a manner, but are invariably 'prophesised' **AFTER** an event had occurred and in **HIND-sight**.

The most remarkable, astounding and disturbing realization that one faces, after studying the Ahadith, Ibn Ishaq's *'Sirat Rassul'Allah'* and most of the Maududi analysis of the *'revealed'* **verses and suras,** is the enormous number of repeated mantras such as

'..*and Allah revealed*...' or

'...*then it was revealed*...' or

' ....*then Gabriel revealed*....' that fill them.

In Bukhari Hadith alone, there are **more than 450** such Hadiths; here are a few of them to enlighten the listeners-

Sahih Al-Bukhari Hadith 3.546 Narrated by Abdullah (bin Masud)

The Prophet said, "Whoever takes a false oath to deprive somebody of his property will meet Allah while He will be angry with him.

Then **Allah revealed:** *'Verily those who purchase a little gain at the cost of Allah's covenant, and their oaths...'* **(3.77)**

Al-Ashath declared:

This verse was revealed concerning me.

I had a well in the land of a cousin of mine. The Prophet asked me to bring witnesses (to confirm my claim). I said, 'I don't have witnesses.' He said, 'Let the defendant take an oath then.' I said, 'O Allah's Apostle! He will take a (false) oath immediately.' Then the Prophet mentioned the above narration **and then Allah revealed the verse to confirm what he had said."**

(See Hadith No. 3692)

Sahih Al-Bukhari Hadith 6.38 Narrated by Sahl bin Sad:

The Verse

"And eat and drink until the white thread appears to you distinct from the black thread," was revealed, but: ***"... of dawn"*** was not revealed (along with it) so some men, when intending to fast, used to tie their legs, one with white thread and the other with black thread and would keep on eating till they could distinguish one thread from the other.

Then Allah revealed....

"... of dawn," whereupon they understood that meant the night and the day.

Sahih Al-Bukhari Hadith 6.175 Narrated by Ibn Abbas

When the Verse: *"If there are twenty steadfast amongst you, they will overcome two hundred." (8.65)* was revealed, then it became obligatory for the Muslims that **one (Muslim)** should not flee from **ten (non-Muslims).** Sufyan (the sub-narrator) once said, "Twenty (Muslims) should not flee before two hundred (non-Muslims)."

Then there was revealed:

"But now Allah has lightened your (task)..." (8.66)

So it became obligatory that one-hundred (Muslims) should not flee before two hundred (non-Muslims).

*** Allah it seems, did not realize that 20 of the followers of Muhammad could **NOT** possibly fight against 200 and win so he changed his mind to reduce the odds to the more realistic 2 to one ratio***

Sahih Al-Bukhari Hadith 6.443 Narrated by Ibn Abbas

Allah's Apostle was met by the **Jinns (Demons)** while he was offering the **Fajr prayer** with his companions. When they heard the **Holy Qur'an** being recited (by Allah's Apostle), they listened to it and said (to each other). This is the thing which has intervened between you and the news of the Heavens.**" Then they returned to their people** and said, "O our people! We have really heard a wonderful recital (Qur'an). It gives guidance to the right, and we have believed therein. We shall not join in worship, anybody with our Lord." (See 72.1-2)

Then Allah revealed to His Prophet (Surat al-Jinn):

"Say: It has been revealed to me that a group of Jinns listened (to the Qur'an)." (72.1)

*** **The Quran is the only 'holy book' which includes Jinn, Satans & Demons as an important part and parcel of its belief system, even to the extent that these 'enemies of Allah' are used as witnesses to the 'veracity' and 'authenticity' of the Quran ***

From Muslim Hadith, here are a few more-

Sahih Muslim Hadith 1212 Narrated by Aisha

The Prophet entered my house when a **Jewess** was with me and she was saying: Do you know that you would be put to trial in the grave? The Messenger of Allah trembled (on hearing this) and said: It is the **Jews** only who would be put to trial. Aisha said: We passed some nights and then the Messenger of Allah said:

Do you know that it has been revealed to me:

"You would be put to trial in the grave"?

Aisha said: I heard the Messenger of Allah seeking refuge from the torment of the grave **after this.**

Sahih Muslim Hadith 1317 Narrated by Al-Bara ibn Azib

This verse was revealed (in this way): *"Guard the prayers and the **Asr** prayer."* We recited it (in this very way) as long as Allah desired.

Allah then abrogated it and changed to:

*"Guard the prayers, and the **middle** prayer.*

Sahih Muslim Hadith 1877 Narrated by Jabir ibn Abdullah

The Apostle of Allah was delivering the sermon on Friday in a standing posture when a caravan from Syria arrived The people flocked towards it till no one was left (with the Prophet) but twelve persons,

and it was on this occasion that this verse in regard to Jumu'ah was revealed:

"And when they see merchandise or sport, they break away to it and leave thee standing."

Sahih Muslim Hadith 4328 Narrated by Sa'd ibn AbuWaqqas

Mus'ab ibn Sa'd said: My father took a sword from the **Khums** and brought it to the Prophet and said: Grant it to me. He refused.

At this Allah revealed (the Qur'anic verse):

*"They ask thee concerning the spoils of war. Say: The spoils of war are for **Allah** and the Apostle" (viii.1).*

Almost all such 'revelations' occurred **after** an event had transpired or because Muhammad needed a divine justification and **sanction** for any and **all** of his requirements, carnal or otherwise.

Allah it seems from these reports, was ready and waiting at all times, to be at Muhammad's beck and call, to fulfil any and all of his requests instantly and without any prevarications.

Of all the prophets so far recorded, Allah - the god of the pagan Arabs - was most and singularly mindful **only** of Muhammad's personal needs and requirements.

*** One does not have to be a scholar or a rocket scientist to realize, that there is something unusual and unsavoury about the fact, that Muhammad claimed that all his *'revelations'* were divinely inspired when in fact, based upon all the above stories alone, not one of them could have been.

Each one of these stories, and hundreds more in both the Quran and other Hadiths, prove beyond a reasonable doubt, that they were

MADE TO ORDER
'revelations' by Muhammad, as and when he needed them.

The whole of the Quran is nothing more than Muhammad's own

ALTER EGO
projected into the unsuspecting mouth of Allah, the supreme pagan rock god of the Quraysh tribe, embedded into the corner wall of the Ka'ba, called the **Black Stone.**

Muhammad, Gabriel, Allah & Satan are **ONE** & the **SAME** character:

Muhammad himself.

The most shocking and disturbing realization from all of the above, is the certainty that even among the most learned followers of Muhammad, it is **impossible** for any of them to admit this fact because it would destroy and completely discredit Muhammad, his Quran and the whole of Muhammadan **'Islam'** ***

#33. Muhammad's Compassion & Mercy

Q: We incessantly hear and read in the Arabic and Muhammadan Muslim media about Muhammad's unique characters of Mercy and Compassion. How true are these attributes?

A: I would like our listeners to share with us the knowledge that it is **only** by **divine justice,** that the Muhammadan records as written by their exegetes and historians **uncover** the facts, reality and truth about Muhammad's actual attributes.

We shall show, based entirely upon these – his own follower's records in the Hadiths and his biography – that Muhammad was the **exact** opposite of what his later and present followers want the world to believe by the use of the most abysmal levels of misinformation, disinformation, deception and utter and complete lies.

The following examples taken from different sources are only the **TIP** of an enormous Garbage Dump of Depraved and Obscene acts.

Ibn Ishaq:288 "The Quraysh said, 'Muhammad and his Companions have **violated the sacred month**, shed blood, seized property, and taken men captive.

It was **always** Muhammad who broke every Arabian rule and tradition to start with and then 'revealed' the appropriate **MADE to ORDER** verses **sanctifying** his **nefarious** deeds

Ishaq:535 "The women began to cry after learning about Ja'far's death. Disturbed, Muhammad told Abd-Rahman to silence them. When they wouldn't stop wailing, Allah's Apostle said, 'Go and tell them to be quiet, and if they refuse **throw dust in their mouths.'"**

Ishaq:596 "'Prophet, this group of Ansar have a grudge against you for what you did with the plunder and how you divided it among your own people.'

After due praise and exaltation of Allah, he addressed them. 'Ansar, what is this talk I hear from you? What is the grudge you harbor in your hearts against me? Do you think ill of me?

Did I not come to you when you were erring and needy, and then made you rich by Allah?' '

[They answered] "You came to **us discredited,** when your message was rejected by the Quraysh, and **we believed you.**

You were **forsaken** and deserted and we **assisted** you.

You were a **fugitive** and we took you in, **sheltering** you.

You were **poor and in need,** and we **comforted** you."

*** **His followers among the Ansar gave him the most truthful replies in the whole of the Hadiths** ***

Tabari VIII:97 "When I returned to Medina, the Prophet met me in the market and said, **'Give me the woman.'** I said, 'Holy Prophet of Allah, I like her, and I have not uncovered her garment.'

Muhammad said nothing to me until the next day. He again met me in the market and said, 'Salamah, **give me the woman.'** I said, 'Prophet, I have not uncovered her garment but she is yours.'"

Tabari IX:34 "Khuwaysirah came and stood by the Prophet as he was giving gifts to the people and said, 'Muhammad, I have seen what you have done today.'

'Well, what did you see?'

He said, 'I don't think you have been fair.'

Allah's Messenger became angry. 'Woe to you! If justice is not to be found with me, then with whom is it to be found?'"

"Umar ibn al Khattab said, 'Muhammad, allow me to **kill him.'**"

Ishaq:595 "The Apostle said, 'Get him away from me and **cut off his tongue.'**"

Lifting the Veil

Tabari VII:65 "When the Apostle was in Safra, Nadr was assassinated. When Muhammad reached Irq al-Zabyah he killed Uqbah.

When the Prophet ordered him to be killed, Uqbah said, 'Who will look after my children, Muhammad?'

"**Hellfire**,' the Apostle replied, and he was murdered"

*** Muhammad, as portrayed in both the Quran and the Ahadith, shows his usual mercy and compassion by slaughtering prisoners of war just because they satirized him ***

Tabari VIII:38 "The Messenger of Allah commanded that **all of the Jewish men and boys who had reached puberty should be beheaded.** Then the Prophet divided the wealth, wives, and children of the Banu Qurayza Jews among the Muslims."

*** The readers should be made aware that the Qurayza tribe was not a military organization but manufacturers in leather and metal and were not a threat to Muhammad or his followers except that they had wealth that Muhammad coveted and needed to acquire so that he could **bribe** even more pagans to his cause.

The **mass murder** of civilians and the **sea** of blood that Muhammad initiated in Arabia was later on continued by his followers against millions of other nationalities in an **ocean** of blood on three continents, by the Arab & Muhammadan Muslim conquerors ***

Ishaq:550 "Muhammad ordered that certain men should be **assassinated** even if they were found behind the **curtains of the Ka'aba.** Among them was Abdallah bin Sa'd

The reason that Allah's Messenger ordered that he should be slain was because he had become a Muslim and used to write down Qur'an Revelation. Then he apostatized [rejected Islam]."

*** Muhammadan Islam **welcomes all** converts with open arms **without** informing them that if they changed their mind and wanted to opt out, they would loose their **head** ***

ishaq: 676 [Asma bint Marwan said to the Aus & Khazraj] of the Madina

'You obey a stranger who encourages you to murder for booty. You are greedy men. Is there no honor among you?'

Upon hearing those lines Muhammad said, **'Will no one rid me of this woman?'** Umayr, a zealous Muslim, decided to execute the Prophet's wishes.

That very night he crept into the writer's home while she lay sleeping surrounded by her young children. **There was one at her breast.** Umayr removed the suckling babe and then plunged his sword into the poet. The next morning in the mosque, Muhammad, who was aware of the assassination, said, 'You have helped Allah and His Apostle.'

Umayr said. 'She had five sons; should I feel guilty?'

'No,' the Prophet answered. 'Killing her was as meaningless as two goats butting heads.'"

*** If killing her was so meaningless, then she could **not** possibly have been a threat to Muhammad. He had her **murdered** simply because she **opposed** him ***

Bukhari:4.256 "The Prophet passed by and was asked whether it was permissible to attack infidels at night with the probability of exposing their women and children to danger.

The Prophet replied, 'Their women and children are from them.'"

*** Muhammad was able to instill in his followers the most **debased** instincts that any human being could possibly carry:

deception, lying, cowardice, treachery, perfidy compounded with a **depraved indifference** to **morality, mercy** or **compassion.**

In fact, his followers became his Psychological and Intellectual **clones,** up to this day as witnessed by their deeds all around the world***

sahih al-bukhari hadithhadith 9.37   narrated   byabu qilaba

Anas bin Malik said: "Eight persons from the tribe of 'Ukl came to Allah's Apostle and gave the Pledge of allegiance for Islam (became Muslim).

The climate of the place (Medina) did not suit them, so they became sick and complained about that to Allah's Apostle. He said (to them), "Won't you go out with the shepherd of our camels and drink of the camels' milk and urine (as medicine)?" They said, "Yes." So they went out and drank the camels' milk and urine, and after they became healthy, they killed the shepherd of Allah's Apostle and took away all the camels.

This news reached Allah's Apostle, so he sent (men) to follow their traces and they were captured and brought (to the Prophet).

He then ordered to **cut their hands and feet, and their eyes were branded with heated pieces of iron, and then he threw them in the sun till they died.**"

In Conclusion :

*** No prophet in recorded human history had ever acted with such **depraved pathological indifference** towards other human beings.

Muhammad is the only alleged 'divinely inspired' messenger who acted in such a wanton manner.

#34. Khadijah & Islam

Q: According to my studies of Ibn Ishaq's "Sirat Rassol^Allah", the biography of Muhammad, I was struck by the fact that his first wife, Khadijah had an enormous and lasting influence on both his theological learning and his psychology.

Because she was a woman, the followers of Muhammad have purposefully neglected to high light her outstanding contributions to Muhammad's self perceived mission of creating the Quran as a scripture for his fellow pagan Arabs.

Will you elaborate?

A: Your conclusion is perfectly correct. In fact, and without the slightest exaggeration, neither **Muhammad** nor his **Quran** would have become part of history without **Khadijah's** singular contributions.

Let us, as usual, look at the **Muhammadan** records themselves.

It was **Ibn Ishaq's** *"Sirat"* that gave us the very earliest reports – as well as a great number of myths - about **Muhammad & Khadijah** on pages 82/83.

Khadijah bint Khuwaylid was a twice widowed very rich and powerful merchant woman in her forties when **Muhammad** was about 25 years of age. According to the so-called but unsupported 'Traditions', **Muhammad** was a decent, honest and intelligent man.

Because of his reputation, Khadijah employed him to take her goods to Syria and trade with them, in spite of the fact that the traditions also assert, that he was **illiterate.**

After he returned with the merchandize, she was able to sell them at a great profit. It was Khadijah - contrary to the male dominated traditions of the **Arabs** - who proposed marriage to **Muhammad,** and he accepted.

As usual in **Muhammadan Islam,** controversy surrounds **Khadijah's** children by her second husband and involves the other daughters or step-daughters of **Muhammad.** These daughters were **Zainab, Ruqayya, and Umm Kulthoom.** Some historians say that these were Khadijah's daughters by her second husband; whereas others insist they were her daughters by **Muhammad.** This is not probable considering **Khadijah's** advanced age at the time she married Muhammad.

Fatimah (605-632) may have been the daughter of Muhammad and Khadija. She was Muhammad's favourite. Two boys who died at an early age were **al Qasim** and **al Tahir**

According to the traditions also – depending on which one - , **Khadijah** was a **hanifiyyah,** that is one who was neither a **Christian** nor of the beliefs of the **Jews** but one who believed only in the **God of Abraham.**

Her uncle was **Waraqa bin Nawfal** who had converted from paganism to **Christianity.**

It is extremely important that the lreaders should be made aware that the **Christians** and the so called **Jews** of **Arabia** were **NOT** foreigners but actually Aboriginal and Indigenous natives of **Arabia** who had willingly- without coercion - converted to these beliefs, centuries **BEFORE Muhammad** & his **Quran** but were subsequently destroyed and or exiled by **Muhammad** and his followers.

One of the most revealing **Hadiths** regarding **Khadijah's** importance is part of the following when **Muhammad** allegedly encountered the angel **Gabriel** for the first time-

Sahih Al-Bukhari Hadith 1.3   Narrated by Aisha

Thereupon he caught me for the third time and pressed me, and then released me and said,

"Iqraa bismi rabbika^allathi khalaqa, khalaqa^al insane min alaq" 'Read in the name of your Lord, who has created , created man from a clot*

Then Allah's Apostle returned with the Inspiration and with his heart beating severely. Then he went to Khadija bint Khuwailid and said, **"Cover me! Cover me!"**

They covered him till his fear was over and after that he told her everything that had happened and said,

"I fear that something may happen to me."

Khadija replied, "Never! By Allah, Allah will never disgrace you. ...

Khadija then accompanied him to her cousin Waraqa bin Naufal who, during the **Pre-Islamic Period** became a **Christian** and used to write the writing with **Hebrew** letters. He would write from the **Gospel in Hebrew** as much as **Allah** wished him to write.

He was an old man and had lost his eyesight. Khadija said to Waraqa, "Listen to the story of your nephew, O my cousin!" Waraqa asked, "O my nephew! What have you seen?" Allah's Apostle described whatever he had seen. Waraqa said, "This is the same one who keeps the secrets (angel Gabriel) whom Allah had sent to **Moses.**

*** Our readers should know that the angel **Gabriel never** appeared to Moses but to Mary the mother of Jesus, and if Warqa was truly a learned Christian, he would not have uttered such incredible **drivel** ***

Al-Tirmidhi Hadith 117   Narrated by Ali ibn Abu Talib

Khadijah asked Allah's Apostle about her children who had died in the days of ignorance. Thereupon Allah's Messenger said: "They are in **Hell Fire" and when he saw the sign of disgust on her face,** he said: If you were to see their station you would hate them.

She said: Allah's Messenger, what about my child that was born of your loins?

He said: It is in Paradise.

Then Allah's Messenger said: Verily the believers and their children will be in Paradise and the unbelievers and their children in the **Hell Fire.**

*** Muhammad, Allah's messenger, showed his **usual** legendary **Compassion & Mercy** by consigning **innocent** children to Hell's Fires just because their parents were **unbelievers** ***

Al-Tirmidhi Hadith 6181 Narrated by Anas ibn Malik

The Prophet said, "Among the women of the universe, Mary, daughter of Imran, Khadijah, daughter of Khuwaylid, Fatimah, daughter of Muhammad, and Asiyah, the wife of Pharaoh are enough for you."

*** Our readers should be aware that **Mary** the mother of **Jesus** was **NOT** the daughter of **Imran** nor was **Asiyah** the wife of **Pharaoh.**

Neither the **Hebrew Bible** nor the **New Testament** mention these falsehoods

The above are the usual concocted stories that were created during the **300 years** after Muhammad's death.

Not a single one of them is based on **FACTS** or any kind of records that existed among the **Arabs. Just the usual** pure **Lies** and **Mendacities** ***

Almost all of the stories regarding Muhammad's wives are the product of centuries of later concoctions to create for Muhammad a family **identical** in its holiness and purity to that of Jesus & Mary

The most important conclusions regarding Khadijah's background show that **contrary** to the perverted picture painted about the **Jahiliah** Arabs – before Muhammad's Islam – regarding their women, are the following facts:

1. Khadijah was able to **inherit** her father's wealth without the interference of any males of her family

2. That she was able to act as a merchant without any **male's permission**

3   That she was a very successful merchant in her own right, independent of any male

4   It was she who **proposed** to Muhammad instead of the traditional other way round

5   It was she who **supported Muhammad** throughout his life with her, contrary to the prevailing traditions

6   She was a very independent and assertive woman

7   She calmed him when he was disturbed

8   She encouraged him when he was afraid

9   She comforted him when he was unsure

10 She knew about the one and only Allah long **before** Muhammad's alleged revelations

11 As a Hanifiyah, she was already a believer in the One & Only God of Abraham.

12 She exerted enormous influence upon him away from his original **paganism**

13 Her Christian relative Waraqa exposed Muhammad to both the Torah and the Gospels

14 Contrary to what the 'traditions' assert, he did not marry any other while she was alive **not** because he loved her so much but because she was financially much more powerful than he was

15 In the end, Muhammad, as was his wont, paid the women of Arabia back with his usual **ingratitude** by reducing them to the level of **sex slaves** and or Domestic Animals

Without Khadijah's moral, psychological and financial support, Muhammad would not have been able to compose his Quran or succeed in fooling hundreds of millions of people into believing that he was the messenger of Allah

In fact, the female followers of Muhammad should **revolt** against all the oppressive, terrorizing and humiliating **man made** rules and regulations especially those who live in the Western democracies and throw away the shackles of enslavement that have been put around them.

#35. Fifty Prayers a Day

Q: According to several versions of the Hadiths regarding the Night Journey, Muhammad was instructed by Allah to pray as well as his followers the staggering number of FIFTY prayers a day.

These were reduced to a more manageable FIVE prayers a day with the help of Moses.

Will you elaborate?

A: Let us start with a shortened version of the story first and then the explanations.

Sahih Al-Bukhari Hadith1.345 Narrated by Abu Dhar

Allah's Apostle said, "While I was at **Mecca the roof of my house** was opened and **Gabriel** descended, opened my chest, and washed it with Zam-zam water. Then he brought a golden tray full of wisdom and faith and having poured its contents into my chest, he closed it.

Then he took my hand and ascended with me to the nearest heaven, when I reached the nearest heaven, Gabriel said to the gatekeeper of the heaven, 'Open (the gate).' The gatekeeper asked, 'Who is it?' Gabriel answered: 'Gabriel.' He asked, 'Is there anyone with you?' Gabriel replied, 'Yes, Muhammad is with me.' He asked, 'Has he been called?' Gabriel said, 'Yes.' So the gate was opened and we went over the nearest heaven and there we saw a man sitting with some people on his right and some on his left.

I asked Gabriel, 'Who is he?' He replied, 'He is **Adam** and the people on his right and left are the souls of his offspring.

Then he ascended with me till we reached the **second heaven** and he (Gabriel) said to its gatekeeper, 'Open (the gate).' The gatekeeper said to him the same as the gatekeeper of the first heaven had said and he opened the gate.

Anas said: "Abu Dhar added that the Prophet met **Adam, Idris, Moses, Jesus and Abraham,** he (Abu Dhar) did not mention on which heaven they were but he mentioned that he (the Prophet) met Adam on the nearest heaven and **Abraham on the sixth heaven.**

The Prophet added, "Then Gabriel ascended with me to a place where I heard the creaking of the pens." Ibn Hazm and Anas bin Malik said: The Prophet said, **"Then Allah enjoined fifty prayers on my followers.**

When I returned with this order of Allah, I passed by **Moses** who asked me, 'What has Allah enjoined on your followers?' I replied, 'He has enjoined fifty prayers on them.'

Moses said, 'Go back to your Lord (and appeal for reduction) for your followers will not be able to bear it.' (So I went back to Allah and requested for reduction) and He reduced it to half.

When I passed by **Moses** again and informed him about it, he said, 'Go back to your Lord as your followers will not be able to bear it.' So I returned to Allah and requested for further reduction and half of it was reduced.

I again passed by **Moses** and he said to me: 'Return to your Lord, for your followers will not be able to bear it. So I returned to Allah and He said,

'These are five prayers and they are all (equal to) fifty for My Word does not change.' I returned to Moses and he told me to go back once again. I replied, 'Now I feel shy of asking my Lord again.

*** The story of Muhammad's 'Ascent' through the Seven Heavens is a variation upon the one Muhammad copied - and altered to suit himself - from the Midrash of the Jews regarding a similar but prior experience made by Moses

(Ginsberg: *Legends of the Jews* Vol:2, p:304).

The listeners should be made aware that there is no mention in this version of the 'traditions' of Muhammad riding **Buraq nor** any intermediary visit to the **Temple of Solomon at Jerusalem** to get from Mecca to the **seven heavens.**

If Allah really loved Muhammad as much as he claims in the Ahadith, then the Compassionate and Merciful Allah, could not and would not have ordered him and his followers to pray **fifty** times a day.

This would have meant that they would neither have time to work, trade, make a living or sleep since they would have had to pray every **28.8 minutes** of the day and night.

Muhammad slavishly and bereft of any thought or logic, accepted this utterly untenable and unmerciful instruction without any prevarication or objection.

Even as an allegorical story, it beggars belief in its stupidity and blasphemy for insulting Allah's wisdom, compassion, mercy and fairness, if Allah is the God of Israel & Jesus.

It was only due to the wisdom of Moses and his supreme advice to Muhammad that he, Muhammad, was able to have any followers whatsoever.

It was because Moses repeatedly insisted that Muhammad should ask Allah for a reduction of such an onerous and unreasonable demand that was **ultimately reduced from FIFTY to FIVE prayers a day,** that Muhammad could even have a 'religion'.

Both Muhammad and his followers owe Moses an incredible debt of gratitude.

Again and again, it can be shown that without a shadow of a doubt, the whole of the Cult Belief System of Muhammad is built upon the 'Islamized' precepts and foundations of the Bible as well as upon almost all the traditions and fetishes of the pagan Arabs ***

In a different version of the same story-

Sahih Al-Bukhari Hadith 4.429 Narrated by Malik bin Sasaa

Lifting the Veil

The Prophet said, **"While I was at the House** in a state midway between sleep and wakefulness, (an angel recognized me) as the man lying between two men. A golden tray full of **wisdom and belief** was brought to me and my body was cut open from the throat to the lower part of the abdomen and then my abdomen was washed with Zam-zam water and (my heart was) filled with wisdom and belief.

Al-Buraq, a white animal, smaller than a mule and bigger than a donkey was brought to me and I set out with **Gabriel**. When I reached the nearest heaven.

*** In this version, **al Buraq** was used to transport Muhammad from Mecca to the first heaven **without** any landing at Jerusalem.

It should be pointed out that in all the different sources including **BH5.227 & BH9.608** of the above story, the following extremely important observations should be taken into account:

1 In none of them did Muhammad go to **Jerusalem** but went directly from Mecca to the Heavens.

2 In none of them did he pray at **Jerusalem.**

3 There are important discrepancies between the various versions regarding the place where he was asleep, the number of angels who were present and whom he met in the different heavens.

4 In none of them was Buraq tied to or at the sacred rock or wall at Jerusalem.

5 In all of them, it was the advice of Moses which saved Muhammadan 'Islam' from complete and utter irrelevance.

6 In numerous Hadiths, Muhammad claimed he was the most **'BELOVED of Allahs'** apostles.

Based upon the Hadiths, it was **NOT** through an act of love that Allah demanded **50** prayers from Muhammad and his followers.

7 All of them attest that Muhammad's vital organs were washed and that he was filled with belief.

Why was he filled with belief if he was as sinless as his followers insist in their dogma?

Where, among all the above **discrepancies & mendacities** is the **TRUTH ?**

#36. Compilation of the Quran

Q: Every follower of Muhammad believes sincerely that the Quran that we have today is EXACTLY the same as the one left for them by Muhammad 1400 years ago.
How true is their perception ?

A: There is absolutely no doubting the sincerity of their belief. This is after all, exactly what their scholars have taught them throughout their life and without actually researching the subject with an open mind, they shall continue to believe this. But, let us investigate the records left to us by the scholars of **Muhammadan Islam** themselves.

At the very beginning of **'Islam'**, the **Quran** was being **memorized** and not yet **compiled into a written form** especially since as long as **Muhammad** was alive and receiving **'revelations'** - over a very long period of 23 years - new Suras were **being added** while others were **being revised, deleted** and/or **abrogated.**

*Al Ankabut 29: 45 Recite what is sent of the **Book** by inspiration to thee and establish Regular Prayer*

*Al Fatir 35: 31 That which We have revealed to thee of the **Book** is the Truth confirming what was (revealed) before it*

*** All verses in the Quran that speak of it as a Book are wrong and deceiving since the Quran was **NEVER** in book form while Muhammad was alive ***

When **Muhammad** died, there existed **no singular codex** of the **Quranic** text, that is, there was not in existence any collection of **'revelations'** in a **Final Review** form.

Also, there was not a single memorizer who knew all the verses of the **Quran;** all these verses were scattered in the memories of hundreds of **Huffaz, memorisers.**

Without a doubt, **Muhammad** failed utterly in his primary mission of giving his followers a **SINGLE Authorized Scripture** because in reality he died without authenticating a unified codex of the **Quran**. The fact that he left his followers with **SEVEN** modes/ versions of the **Quran**, speaks volumes about his failure.

The consequences of this failure became paramount when his followers were reciting different versions of the alleged **'words of Allah'**. This failure has endured- **and continues** - for the last **1400 years**.

All attempts by his present followers to gloss over this fact are doomed to fail since the records of the **Muhammadan scholars** in the centuries after his death attest to **otherwise**.

After his death and as the **memorizers (Huffath),** were becoming extinct through slaughter in battle or otherwise, **Umar ibn al Khattab,** recommended that it should be committed to writing. **Abu Bakr** entrusted the task to **Zayd ibn Thabit** of al **Madina** who used to be **Muhammad's** secretary.

Sahih Al-Bukhari Hadith 6.509 Narrated by Zaid bin Thabit

Abu Bakr As-Siddiq sent for me **when the people of Yamama had been killed** (i.e., a number of the Prophet's Companions who fought against **Musailama).** (I went to him) and found 'Umar bin Al-Khattab sitting with him. Abu Bakr then said (to me), "Umar has come to me and said:

'Casualties were heavy among the Qurra' of the Qur'an (i.e. those who knew the Quran by heart) on the day of the Battle of Yamama, and I am afraid that more heavy casualties may take place among the Qurra' on other battlefields, whereby a large part of **the Qur'an may be lost.** Therefore I suggest, you (Abu Bakr) order that the Qur'an be collected."

So I started looking for the Qur'an and collecting it from (what was written on) palmed stalks, thin white stones and also from the men who knew it by heart, till I found the last Verse of *Surat At-Tauba (Repentance)* with Abi Khuzaima Al-Ansari, and **I did not find it with anybody other than him.**

All were brought together and a text was constructed.

From the above quotes, it means that the **pagan Arabs** had not by then mastered the art of writing or the use of writing materials such as clay, papyrus, metal sheets or even skins of animals. The **Arabs** of the **Hijaz** - contrary to all the efforts of **Muhammadan** propaganda - were mostly illiterate and uneducated people.

Then the complete manuscripts of the **Qur'an** remained with Abu Bakr till he died, then with 'Umar till the end of his life, and then with Hafsa, the daughter of 'Umar.

In 651AD, **Uthman bin Affan**, canonized the **Madina** codex and ordered all others **(SIX** other versions of the **Quran) DESTROYED.** If it were true that there were many **'memorizers'** of the **Quran**, why then did they need to collect the **Quranic** verses from diverse and unrelated **'documents'** such as leafstalk, bone, parchments as well as the memories of men?

What is also blatantly problematic to the **Muhammadan scholars** are the variations in the several extant **Qurans** of the time making it impossible to tell which version is the alleged **'word of Allah'**, since **'his word'** should have been only **ONE** and not several.

In fact, there were several metropolitan codices in **Arabia, Syria** and **Iraq** with divergent readings blamed on the defective nature of **Kufic script** which contained no vowels, and so the consonants of verbs could be read as actives or passives, and, worse still, many of the consonants themselves could not be distinguished without diacritical dots which were added much later.

Sahih Al-Bukhari Hadith6.510 Narrated by Anas bin Malik

Hudhaifa bin Al-Yaman came to **Uthman** at the time when the people of **Sham** and the people of **Iraq** were waging war to conquer **Arminya** and **Adharbijan. Hudhaifa** was afraid of their (the people of Sham and Iraq) **differences in the recitation of the Qur'an,** so he said to 'Uthman, "O chief of the Believers! Save this nation before they differ about the **Book** as **Jews** and the **Christians** did before."

So 'Uthman sent a message to **Hafsa** saying, "Send us the manuscripts of the **Qur'an** so that we may compile the Qur'anic materials in perfect copies and return the manuscripts to you."

Hafsa sent it to 'Uthman. 'Uthman then ordered Zaid bin Thabit, 'Abdullah bin AzZubair, Said bin Al-As and 'Abdur-Rahman bin Harith bin Hisham to **rewrite** the manuscripts in perfect copies.

'Uthman said to the three Quraishi men, "In case you disagree with Zaid bin Thabit on any point in the Qur'an, **then write it in the dialect of Quraish,** the Qur'an was revealed in their tongue."

They did so, and when they had written many copies, 'Uthman returned the original manuscripts to Hafsa.

'Uthman sent to every Muslim province one copy of what they had copied, and ordered that all the other Qur'anic materials, whether written in fragmentary manuscripts or whole copies, be burnt.

Said bin Thabit added, "A Verse from **Surat Ahzab** was missed by me when we copied the Qur'an and I used to hear Allah's Apostle reciting it. So we searched for it and found it with Khuzaima bin Thabit Al-Ansari. (That Verse was):

'Among the Believers are men who have been true in their covenant with Allah.' **(33.23)**

A further serious impediment which complicated the correct compilation of the **Quran** is the fact that there were verses which were spoken in **Madina** but were included in suras which began in **Mecca,** and **vise versa.**

The problem that existed and persisted during the life-time of **Muhammad** for his followers is the fact, that for as long as he was alive, new *'revelations'* - **whereby the omniscient Allah was nonetheless allegedly changing his mind** - were very conveniently being added to and some subtracted from the earlier ones **(Abrogated** and **Abrogating** verses which affected **71** of the **114 Suras** of the Quran**).**

This is why at the time of **Muhammad's** death there existed no singular codex of the **'sacred text'**. It is also reported that some major parts of a **Sura were eaten by a domestic animal.**

Another **Sura**, that of **Al Rajm**, was asserted by **Umar ibn al Khattab** to have existed but is not included in the **Quran.**

The final text of the Quran was actually fixed in 933AD.

Since the **Quran** is supposed to be the word of **Allah** - who is the one who taught **Moses the Torah** - then the only and unmistakable conclusion for the enormous inconsistencies and differences between them must be because it was the **Muhammadans** who corrupted the **Quran** to suit their own agenda.

The criminal invariably projects upon his victim his own hatreds, shortcomings and lack of morality and justice; so do the **Arab and Muhammadan scholars.**

They have conspired over the centuries - **and even at the present** - to control all the information that they pass on to the **'believers'** by perpetuating the myth of the perfect and divine **Quran** contrary to the historical, philological and theological records that prove it to be otherwise.

In fact, the greatest threat to **Muhammadan 'Islam'** is the acquisition of knowledge, especially of the **Bible,** by the masses of **'believers'.**

Of **114 Suras** in the **Quran, only 43** were not changed. All the others had verses that were either **abrogated or abrogating;** this means that in the course of **23 years** of **Muhammad's** mission, the **omniscient Allah** changed his mind **at least 71 times.**

In summation, the following historical and theological facts are crystal clear and indisputable:

1) The greatest number of **'traditions'** and fetishes of the **'Muslims'** are nothing but a continuance, a re-packaging and **'Islamization'** of pagan rites and actions that pre-existed **Muhammad** and his **Quran.**

2) Almost all the precepts and concepts of importance in the

Quran have been **plagiarised, plundered, pirated and/or perverted from the Hebrew Bible and Scriptures, from the New Testament and Apocrypha,** from **pagan Arabian** religion and also from **Zoroasterian** religion and traditions.

Abu'l Fath Muhammad Shahrestani (479/1086-548/1153), in his valuable book on sects and religions *(al Melal wa'lNihal)* asserts that many of the rites and duties of **'Islam'** are continuations and practices which the **pagan Arabs** had adopted from the **Jews.**

3) Even if **Muhammad** were **illiterate** (not able to read or write), does not negate his ability **to compose and recite prose and or poetry.** Most of the poets of **Arabia** were **illiterate but masters of the spoken language.**

The oral poetic tradition of the Arabs was their greatest legacy since they left almost nothing in the form of writing thus proving beyond a shadow of a doubt that poetry and prose in Arabia was completely independent from literacy.

4) The **Quran** is only a tossed salad bowl of stories, concepts and precepts **plagiarized, plundered, pirated and or perverted at will from the beliefs of other peoples,** to suit **Muhammad's** agenda of inventing a suitable **Scripture** for his fellow **pagan Arabs** to equal if not rival those of the **People of the Book.**

'No copy of any masterpiece, no matter how well done it may be, can ever equal to, let alone surpass an original'.

5) The followers of **Muhammad** can try their best to **obfuscate, contort, pervert and twist the facts to 'prove' otherwise,** but it is a **Mission Impossible** to accomplish.

That is why when they cannot counter the **truth with facts or logic, they invariably resort to violence**

to silence their opponents just as was done earlier by **Muhammad.**

6) The so-called **Arabic Quran** contains at least **118 words** of paramount and vital importance that are actually **totally foreign** and are derived from **Hebrew, Aramaic, Ethiopic, Syriac, Greek, Persian and Sanskrit** to name just a few.

In conclusion, the followers of Muhammad, contrary to all proofs and logic, reject the universal record of history and the Bible, but assert and believe that ONLY the Quran is true.

#37. Biblical Corruption Allegations

Q: For centuries and even unto today, the scholars of Muhammadan Islam assert that BOTH the Hebrew Bible and the New Testament are NOT the originals revealed to Moses and Jesus but are the product of alterations and perversions by their later followers. On what basis can they prove their allegations?

A: It was **Ibn Khazem (1064)** who was the first Muhammadan to charge that the Bible has been corrupted and falsified by the followers of Moses and Jesus.

This charge was made in a last ditch and desperate effort to defend **'Islam'** against Christianity because he came upon the many serious and unexplainable contradictions and differences between the Quran and the Bible.

Believing by faith that the Quran is true and incorruptible, Ibn Khazem had absolutely no choice but to come to the conclusion that then it must be the **CURRENT Bible** that is false and untrue especially since Muhammad instructed his followers to respect the Bible in the first place.

Therefore, the present text must have been falsified by the **Christians** and the **Jews AFTER** the time of **Muhammad**. His conclusions and arguments are **not** based on any historical facts but entirely upon his **unshakable faith** in the truthfulness and divine origin of the **Quran.**

Many other exegetes, did not accept or agree with his conclusions among whom are many of the luminaries of 'Islam' such as:

1. **Ali al Tabari** (d 855) who accepted the Gospel texts

2. **Al Bukhari** (810-870)

3. **Al Mas'udi** (956)

4. **Abu Ali Husain bin Sina** (1037)

5. Al Ghazali (1111) who did not accept his teachings

6. Ibn Khaldun (1406) ditto.

In reality it is not up to the **People of the Book** to prove their **Book** is uncorrupted but up to the **Muhammadans** to do so based on any **'original'** book that would show these corruptions.

The interpreters of the **Quran** repeatedly denigrate and accuse both the **Jews** and **Christians** of having tampered with and or **'corrupted'** their **Holy Books** to suit their - with as yet unexplained and unidentified - nefarious purposes.

These evil, mendacious and unsubstantiated accusations are in fact introduced to cover up the incredibly huge number of unexplainable and irreconcilable differences in both the **Quran** and its interpretations with the same events as described in their original versions in the **Bible** and **Scriptures**.

Hence, with an extremely simple and general sentence they, the followers of **Muhammad,** attempt to dismiss and gloss over all these discrepancies as items that have been deliberately - and presumably with diabolical pre meditation- modified by the **Jews** and **Christians** to deprive **Muhammad** and his followers of their **'rightful'** place among the **Divinely** revealed scriptures.

Unfortunately for the **Muhammadan** accusers, it can be easily demonstrated that in all its relevant verses, the **Quran** declares the **Bible** to be a true revelation of **Allah** and demands faith in it such as can be shown in the following *Suras* which presuppose the availability of the true revelation of **Allah** to the **Arabs** at the time of **Muhammad:**

2:40/1,129,136,285; 3:3,71,93; 4:47/51,69,70; 5:44; 6:91/2; 10:37,94; 21:7; 29:45/51; 35:31/2; 46:12.

*Al Baqara 2:136 Say ye: "We believe in **Allah** and the revelation given to us and to Abraham Isma'il Isaac Jacob and the Tribes and that given to Moses and Jesus** and that given to (all) Prophets from their Lord we make no difference between one and another of them and we bow to **Allah** (in Islam)."*

285 *The Apostle believeth in what hath been revealed to him from his Lord as do the men of faith. Each one (of them) believeth in Allah His angels **His books and His Apostles "We make no distinction (they say) between one and another of His Apostles***

*** In the above verses the Quran makes no distinction between Allah's revelations; that is they are **ALL** true and uncorrupted ***

*Ali Imran 3: 3 It is He Who sent down to thee (step by step) in truth the Book **confirming what went before it;** and He sent down **Law (Of Moses)** and the **Gospel (of Jesus)** before this as a guide to mankind and He sent down the Criterion (of judgment between right and wrong).*

*** No where does the Quran even **IMPLY** that the **People of the Book** had **corrupted** the **Texts** of their Scriptures but only that some of them **misrepresented** the **meaning of some** Texts ***

*3: 93 All food was lawful to the **children of Israel except what Israel made unlawful for itself before the Law (of Moses) was revealed.** Say: "Bring ye the Law and study it if ye be men of truth."*

*** In the particular case above, the Quran implies that the Children of Israel 'corrupted' some of Allah's commands **BEFORE** the revelations to Moses and **not AFTER** ***

Al Nisaa 4: 47 O ye people of the Book! believe in what We have (now) revealed confirming what was (already) with you

*** If, as **al Khazem** and other **ignorant** followers of Muhammad insist that the **People of the Book** have corrupted their Books, they could have done this only **after** Muhammad's Quran and not **before** since this verse **clearly** shows, that the **Quran** is **confirming** these same previous revelations and would not have done so if they had already been corrupted ***

Al Ma^ida 5:44 It was We who revealed the law (to Moses); therein was guidance and light. By its standard have been judged the Jews by the Prophet who bowed (as in Islam) to Allah's will by the Rabbis and the doctors of Law: for to them was entrusted the protection of Allah's Book and they were witnesses thereto:

*** In the verse above, the Quran asserts that the Jews were entrusted with protecting and preserving Allah's Book, the Torah, and there is no indication given here that they failed that trust especially since it was because they had done so that Muhammad was able to bring about the Quran as a scripture to his own pagan people.

Since the followers of Muhammad are certain that the People of the Book had deliberately corrupted their Books, then the onus is on them to show the original uncorrupted ones upon which they base their puerile and unsubstantiated allegations ***

Al An'am 6: 91 ...... Say: "Who then sent down the **Book which Moses brought? a light and guidance to mankind:**

92 And this is a Book which We have revealed bringing blessings and confirming (the revelations) **which came before it**

*** It would defy logic and intellect to believe that the **Quran** would have **used 'corrupted' Books** as **confirmation of its own authenticity.**

No where does the Quran **ever** imply that the **texts** of the Scriptures of the People of the Book had been tampered with or **corrupted.**

Since this is the case, then any alleged corruptions would have happened **after** the Quranic 'revelations'. If so, then the Muhammadan accusers have an unenviable intellectual, theological and historical **magical act** to perform:

1. They have to prove the most STUPENDOUS and massive literary editing ever performed in the history of humanity; that the Jews and Christians were able to **alter** the **texts** of **every** single Book of theirs all over the world, in **every country,** in all the languages that the Bible was written in, with the consent, agreement and collusion of all the Jewish Rabbis as well as all the Christian priests, without leaving a single copy of any **original bible.**

2   To believe that the Jews and Christians were able to accomplish all the above without leaving a trace of such a **conspiracy,** requires a human mind and **intellect** that also believes in **flying** elephants and that the Moon is made of cheese.

3   The listeners should be aware that **every** commentary in every Quran attempting to explain the Quranic verses is based upon the very same allegedly **'corrupted'** Bibles.

4   The **onus** is upon the followers of Muhammad to prove their case by showing mankind a **single original uncorrupted bible** upon which they can rest their Fallacious, Insane, Contemptible and Ignoramus allegations.

It is the simple case of " PUT up or SHUT up " ***

#38. Muhammad & Knowledge

Q: I was astounded to learn that the Sunni Muhammadan scholars of Arabia teach their children in this 21st century, that the Earth is flat and that the Moon landing is a great deception by the Unbelievers.
Is this true ?

A:In the Quran, the word ILM/Knowledge has only one meaning:

Knowledge of RELIGION and NOT of anything else. It is a deliberate lie when Muhammadans point out the word knowledge as pertaining to the sciences, arts and independent thought

Muhammadan scholars have written an enormous number of books claiming that **Muhammad** was a **super genius** whose knowledge was stupendous and way ahead of his time.

The following are - a very small sample – of verses and Ahadith that show the true state of affairs and it is left to the reader to evaluate the veracity or lack there of, of such claims.

Al Hijr 15: 19 And the earth We have spread out (like a carpet); set thereon mountains firm and immovable;

Al Nahhal 16: 15 And He has set up on the earth mountains standing firm lest it should shake with you

Al Kahf 18: 47 One Day We shall remove the mountains and thou wilt see the earth as a level stretch

*** The Erath is flat and the mountains are what hold it in stretch ***

18: 86 Until when he reached the setting of the sun He found it set in a spring of murky water: near it he found a People:

We said: "O Zul-qarnain! (thou hast authority) either to punish them or to treat them with kindness."

*** The Sun which is at least **1,000,000** times bigger than the Earth, **sets in a puddle of muddied water** ***

Al Anbiyaa 21: 30 *Do not the Unbelievers see that the heavens and the earth were joined together before We clove them asunder?* ***We made from water every living thing***

*** Neither in the Bible nor in Biology, is there such an absurd and unrealistic idea.

Life, according to the theory of evolution, started **IN** water and **NOT** from water ***

Ya Sin 36: 40 *It is not permitted to the* **Sun to catch up the Moon nor can the Night outstrip the Day**: *each (just) swims along in (its own) orbit (according to Law).*

Al Saffat 37: 6 *We have indeed* ***decked the lower heaven*** *with beauty (in) the stars*

*** According to Astronomy, there is no heaven and the stars are definitely not for decorative purposes ***

Fussilat 41: 12 *So He completed them as* ***seven firmaments*** *in* ***two Days*** *and He assigned to each heaven its duty and command. And We adorned the lower heaven with lights and (provided it) with guard.*

*** Neither the Bible, which is the source of this version of creation, nor Astronomy, mention any **Seven Heavens** ***

'Abasa 80:17 *"....From what stuff did He create man?* ***From nutfa (male and female semen drops)*** *He created him and set him in due proportion."*

*** Neither Muhammad nor the translator of this verse got it right since the **woman** provides the **ovum** and not semen drops***

Sunan of Abu-DawoodHadith 4705 Narrated by Al-Abbas ibn AbdulMuttalib

I was sitting in al-Batha with a company among whom the Apostle of Allah was sitting..He asked: Do you know the distance between Heaven and Earth? They replied: We do not know. He then said: **The distance between them is seventy-one, seventy-two, or seventy-three years.** The heaven which is above it is at a similar distance. Above the seventh heaven **there is a sea,** the distance between whose surface and bottom is like that between one heaven and the next. Above that there are **eight mountain goats** the distance between whose hoofs and haunches is like the distance between one heaven and the next. **Then Allah**, the Blessed and the Exalted, **is above that.**

*** Muhammad being a **cameleer,** measures distances by **time;** that is, the time it takes him and his animal to get from point A to point B.

He of course applies the same methodology to describe astronomical distances without qualifying the rate of speed.

Moreover, according to all the knowledge that we have regarding Astronomy and Cosmology, Muhammad's concepts are, to put it mildly, **ignorant, stupid and infantile*****

Sunan of Abu-DawoodHadith 5222 Narrated byBuraydah ibn al-Hasib

I heard the Apostle of Allah say: **A human being has three hundred and sixty joints** for each of which he must give alms.

Bukhari: 1.510

"Allah's Apostle said, **'If it is very hot,** the severity of the heat is from the raging of the **Hell Fire.'"**

***According to human Anatomy, Muhammad is once again wrong.

His **obsession** with **Hell** is unrelenting and **Satanic** as revealed in so many verses of the Quran and Hadiths ***

Bukhari: 4.482

"Allah's Apostle said, 'The Hell Fire complained to its Lord saying, "O my Lord! My different parts are eating each other up." **So, He allowed it to take two breaths, one in winter, the other in summer**. This is the reason for the severe heat and bitter cold you find in weather.'"

Sahih Al-Bukhari Hadith 4.430 Narrated by Abdullah bin Musud

Allah's Apostle, the true and truly inspired said, "*(The matter of the Creation of)* a human being is put together in the womb of the mother **in forty days,** and then he becomes **a clot of thick blood** for a similar period, and then **a piece of flesh** for a similar period......

*** A **gestation** period of **three months** is of course contrary to biology. So much for Muhammad's knowledge and divine inspirations***

Sahih Al-Bukhari Hadith 4.494 Narrated by Ibn Umar

Allah's Apostle said:....you should not seek to pray at sunrise or sunset for **the sun rises between two sides of the head of the devil (or Satan)."**

*** Excellent Muhammadan science of Astronomy***

Sahih Al-Bukhari Hadith 4.537 Narrated by bu Huraira

The Prophet said "If a house fly falls in the drink of anyone of you, **he should dip it (in the drink),** for one of its wings has a **disease** and the other has the **cure** for the disease."

*** Muhammad's superb intellectual and hygienic analysis and conclusions are beyond measure***

Sahih Al-Bukhari Hadith 4.539 Narrated by Abu Talha

The Prophet said, **"Angels do not enter a house** which has either a **dog** or a **picture** in it."

Bukhari: 4.546

"Allah's Apostle said, **'Gabriel** has just now told me of the answer. If a man has sexual intercourse with his wife and **gets discharge first, the child will resemble him,** and if the **woman gets discharge first, the child will resemble her.'"**

*** Even the Archangel of Allah is made to look profoundly stupid ***

Tabari I:293 "When Allah cast Adam down from Paradise, Adam's feet were on earth while his head was in heaven.

Adam was **NOT** *'cast down'* from paradise; he was **'kicked out'** from the Garden of Eden, which was on Earth and **NOT** in Heaven.

There are hundreds more of similar Hadiths and Quranic verses, but I hope that the above are sufficient for the listeners to have learned a great deal of correct and truthful facts and knowledge from the mouth of Muhammad.

#39 Arab & Islamic Imperialism

Q: Almost every book, newspaper or thesis written by the scholars of Muhammadan Islam rebuke, defame and insult the West especially for their Imperialism and occupation of Arab and Muhammadan lands but at the same time glorify their own conquests and find nothing hypocritical with such logic.
What about their conquests?

A: You are absolutely right in labeling their behaviour as Hypocritical.

I must point out to our listeners the following **irrefutable** facts:

It was **because** of **Western Imperialism** that **Arab** and **Muhammadan** lands were introduced to Education; Sanitation; Electricity; Running Water; Democracy; Roads; Trains; Cars; Planes; Medicines; Inoculation; etc. etc.

It was also **because** of **Western Imperialism** that the **Arabs** were **liberated** from the yoke of the **Muhmmadan Muslim Ottoman Empire** and **22 Arab** countries that **did not exist** before were created.

It was due to **Western Imperialism** that these peoples re-discovered their past history due **exclusively** to the Archaeological discoveries and research financed and conducted **entirely** by the **West**.

Now let me compare these positive achievements of the **West**, with what the **Muhammadan Muslims** contributed towards their conquered peoples and lands.

Let us first set the **record** straight: The **Arab** conquests during and after the death of **Muhammad** were not **only** motivated by the desire to spread **Islam** but mainly to acquire territory and wealth. In fact, the spread of **Islam** was just a byproduct of the conquests.

As was true throughout human history, enormous wealth brought with it enormous power. Wealth and power are synonymous. But, enormous power also engendered enormous corruption.

The **Arabs** were just as greedy and just as weak as anyone else when faced between the choice of acquiring wealth or staying as good observant poor **Muslims** in the **Arabian desert**. The **Arabs** conquered and subjugated other peoples and lands and became just another **imperialist** power.

The same modern **Arabs** and **Muhammadans** who condemn **European** and **American imperialism** have very conveniently forgotten their own conquests. Unlike all other **Imperial powers** that have ceased to exist, **Arab** imperialism continues to this day - **1400 years later** - in control and in subjugation of peoples and lands that **never** belonged to them except through conquest and enslavement.

The speed with which the **Arabs** were able to conquer was astounding and the main reason - especially in what we call today **Syria, Iraq, Lebanon, Israel and Egypt** – was because most of these peoples welcomed them as would be deliverers from the intolerance and subjugation of the **Byzantine Christian Empire.**

Very few of the **Arab** victories would have been possible had the populace been hostile to them. It is a fact that the **Arabs** had absolutely no instruments of siege nor were they adept at such warfare at the very beginning of their conquests.

Muhammad started the **Arabs** on the path of imperialism from the time of the **Hijra** in **622CE** with the following allegedly *'revealed'* verses:

*Al Tauba 9: 5 But when the forbidden months are past then **fight** **and slay the pagans wherever ye find them** and seize them beleaguer them and lie in wait for them in every stratagem (of war);*

*9: 29 Fight those who believe **NOT** in **Allah** nor the Last Day, nor hold that forbidden which hath been forbidden by **Allah** and His apostle, nor acknowledge the religion of truth **[Islam] (even if** **they are) of the People of the Book [Jews and Christians]*** *until they pay the **Jizya [Poll Tax]** with willing **submission** and feel themselves **humiliated.***

Ali Imran 3: 19 The **Religion before Allah is Islam** (submission to His will):

85 *If anyone desires a religion other than Islam (submission to Allah) never will it be accepted of him*

Muhammad started his **Jihad (Plunder** and **Slaughter sanctified by Allah)** first against his own tribe of **Quraysh** then followed with the forced conversion or destruction of other **Arab** tribes, then the **Arabian Jews** and **Christians.**

Based upon the above alleged *'divine revelations'*, the forcibly converted - illiterate and uncivilized **Arab Bedouins** - led by the **Caliphs** who succeeded **Muhammad**, conducted wars of extermination and or subjugation against all of humanity from Iraq and Syria to Iran; from India to China; from Egypt to the Atlantic and from Cyprus to Italy, Spain and France.

In about **100 years,** the **Arabs** and their forced converts achieved an empire greater in size than that of **Rome's** of **1000 years.**

This **Arab Empire** caused the destruction, plunder of wealth and enslavement, not only of millions of human beings, but also of temples, religions, civilizations, traditions, cultures, art and languages of the subjugated peoples and nations.

The so called **Islamic Arts,** were and are only copies of those of the **Byzantine, Sassanid** and **Indian Civilizations.**

The so called **'Islamic Civilization'**, is a first class **misnomer** because in reality it should be called the **'Mawali Civilization'**, since the **Arabs** had no civilization to contribute to the enslaved peoples.

On the **contrary**, it was the **subjugated civilizations** that gave the **Arabs** the foundations upon which to continue – with fits and starts and against all the **Islamic Shari'a** laws and **Arab** traditions – on the path that led them to greater enlightenment.

Converse to all the lies and propaganda of the **Arabs,** past and present, most of the scientists and luminaries of **'Islam'** were actually from among the **Mawali (the converted subject people to Islam)** such as the **Persians, Syrians, Jews, Christians, Hindus etc.** as the **'Islamic'** records themselves assert.

Without a shadow of a doubt, **Arab Imperialism** has been the **most enduring**, the **most destructive** and the **least useful** in the **history of the world.** This assertion is based entirely on the following indisputable facts:

1 There was no **Arab civilization** in the **area and era** of **Muhammad.** His followers were mostly illiterate and very simple and superstitious nomadic and semi nomadic people.

2 The **Arabs** conquered several of the **most ancient and established civilizations in the world;** plundered them, massacred many and enslaved and subjugated the remainder. This applies particularly to the **Byzantine Empire** which fell more due to **Christian** infighting than to **Arab** military prowess.

Arab and **Isalmic Imperialism** was so **total** that they **forced** the conquered peoples to convert to **Muhammadan Islam,** to loose their religious and cultural identities as well as their language.

The Arabs could not, and did not, contribute anything to them, since they themselves were far inferior culturally, theologically and intellectually.

Arab imperialism, unlike that of the **Persians, Greeks, Romans** and the recent so called **Western imperialism,** is almost totally **parasitic.**

3 Nearly **95%** of all so called **Muslim scientists,** were from among the **Mawalis** - converts from among the conquered peoples - and not pure **Arabs.**

All of them excelled, **not because of Muhammadan Islam, but in spite of it,** and invariably, during periods of history, when the conditions were of toleration that allowed **Christians, Jews** and others, to contribute and cross fertilize knowledge.

It is a given, that **human intellect can only thrive under conditions of freedom of thought** and the ability to exchange ideas and communication.

It can **never** excel under conditions of **theocratic terror**, as invariably exists under the **Sharia law** of **Muhammadan Islam**.

4 Most of so called '**Islamic science**', was only built upon the foundations of **Greek, Roman, Hebrew, Byzantine, Persian and Indian knowledge,** and had it not been for the translations of these ideas and thoughts, by **Christians** and **Jews** of the **Arabian Empire, 'Islamic science'** would not have existed.

In **fact,** nothing of value, intellectual, artistic, spiritual or literary can ever sprout in the darkness cast by Fundamentalist Muhammadan Islam upon all the peoples and lands that it occupies.

Ladies and gentlemen, the most **perfect** example of the Fundamentalist Muhammadan State was that of the **taliban** in Afghanistan:

A nation of Mind-boggling Ignorance, of Depraved Injustice and Inhumanity.

Human intellect and achievements can only **excel in the sunshine of freedoms of:**

thought, religion, politics, literature, art and **expression** which Muhammadan Islam abhors, avoids and detests ***

#40 Allah's Share of the Plunder

Q: From my research of the Quran and Hadiths, I found a great number of verses that mention how Allah and Muhammad had a 20% share of ALL the Plunder, Booty, Loot and slaves taken by Muhammad and his followers in their piratical raids.

I am embarrassed to ask why would Allah, if he is the Almighty Creator of the Universe, need any share of the plunder of his own creation?

What kind of Logic, Morality or Intellect would attribute such blasphemy to any divine entity?

A: In Arabic, the **Fifth of the plunder is called al Khums or (20%)**, which is the portion of all **booty, plunder** and **loot** taken in **piratical raids** upon innocent and unsuspecting tribes and people that is the **share** of **Allah and Muhammad.**

The **Quran** and **Ahadith** do not tell us the percentage proportion of the **Khums** that belongs to **Allah** and what to **Muhammad.** One must come to the conclusion after studying the subject, that it really is irrelevant, **since Allah never** claimed his share, all of which hence belonged to **Muhammad.**

Why would Allah, the alleged creator of the universe, need a share from the booty and plunder of his own creation, as perpetrated by Muhammad and his thugs?

Neither **Muhammad** nor the **Ahadith** - nor for that matter any of his followers, past present or future - can possibly give a logical and reasonable explanation for it.

In fact, to attribute to Allah – if Allah were God - such a need, is by itself an act of utter **Blasphemy.**

Al Nisa 4: 94 .... with Allah are profits and spoils abundant

*** Muhammad's Allah, rewards his followers with booty and spoils on earth and even greater ones in the afterlife, for massacring, murdering, despoiling, subjugating, raping, plundering and enslaving all those who do not believe in

"Allah and his messenger Muhammad"

Muhammad's **'Compassionate and Merciful'** Allah, deliberately **Pre-Destines** these wretched creatures to their undeserved fate; they had no choice or free will in the matter.

It is no great wonder then, that a great number of avaricious, ignorant and stupid men would follow and believe in such a 'generous' deity ***

Al Anfal{Booty} 8: 1 They ask thee concerning (things taken as) **spoils of war. Say: "(Such) spoils are at the disposal of Allah and the apostle...** *......41 And know that out of all the* **booty** *that ye may acquire (in war)* **a fifth share is assigned to Allah and to the apostle**

Sahih Muslim HadithHadith 4328   Narrated by Sa'd ibn AbuWaqqas

Mus'ab ibn Sa'd said: My father took a sword from **Khums** and brought it to the Prophet and said: Grant it to me. He refused. At this Allah revealed (the Qur'anic verse):

"They ask thee concerning the spoils of war. Say: **The spoils of war are for Allah and the Apostle"** *(viii.1).*

*** All the spoils of war are for Muhammad only to dispense with as he wished. He invariably used the booty and plunder to **bribe** and **intice** pagan Arabs to join his cult and to buy weapons to fight with.

As usual, a very convenient **MADE to ORDER** verse *'descends'* from Allah to justify it by divine order ***

Sahih Muslim HadithHadith 4346 Narrated byAbuHurayrah

The Messenger of Allah said....If a township disobeys Allah and His Messenger (and actually fights against the Muslims) **one-fifth of the booty seized there from is for Allah and His Apostle** and the rest is for you.

Sahih Al-Bukhari Hadith 5.637 Narrated by Buraida

The Prophet sent 'Ali to bring the **Khumus (of the booty)** and I hated Ali, and 'Ali had taken a bath **(after a sexual act with a slave-girl from the Khumus).**

When we reached the Prophet I mentioned that to him.

He said, "O Buraida! Do you hate Ali?"

I said, "Yes."

He said, "Do you hate him, for he deserves more than that from the Khumus."

*** **Ali** had no right to **RAPE** her without first getting permission from Muhammad***

Sunan of Abu-Dawood Hadith 2731   Narrated by Abdullah ibn Abbas

The Apostle of Allah said on the day of Badr: He who does such-and-such, will have such-and such. The young men came forward and the old men remained standing near the banners, and they did not move from there.

When Allah bestowed victory on them, the old men said: We were support for you. If you had been defeated, you would have returned to us.

Do not take this booty alone and we remain (deprived of it). The young men refused (to give), and said: The Apostle of Allah has given it to us.

Then Allah sent down: *"They ask thee concerning (things taken as) spoils of war, Say: (Such) spoils are at the disposal of Allah and the Apostle......*

Sunan of Abu-Dawood Hadith 2743 Narrated by Habib ibn Maslamah

The Apostle of Allah used to give a quarter of the booty as reward after the fifth had been kept off, and a third after the fifth had been kept off when he returned.

*** The so called rewards that Muhammad was giving were not actually his to start with, not as a product of honest sweat and toil but as the product of **Loot** and **Plunder** ***

Sunan of Abu-Dawood Hadith 2737 Narrated by Abdullah ibn Umar

The Apostle of Allah sent a detachment to Najd. I went out along with them, and got abundant riches. Our commander gave each of us a camel as a reward. We then came upon the Apostle of Allah (peace be upon him) and he divided the spoils of war among us. Each of us received twelve camels after taking a fifth of it. The Apostle of Allah (peace be upon him) did not take account of our companion (i.e. the commander of the army), nor did he blame him for what he had done. Thus each man of us had received thirteen camels with the reward he gave.

*** **Muhammadan Islam was, is and forever will be primarily, about booty, plunder, rape and enslavement** ***

#41. Muhammad the Sinful

Q: Based upon my own studies of the subject, the followers of Muhammad have turned him into a sinless human being in similitude to Jesus.
How accurate is their assertion?

A: It was the latter **Muhammadan** exegetes who created the **DOGMA** of **Isma/ Sinlessness** of **Muhammad** in emulation of the **Christian** one regarding **Jesus.**

This doctrine of **Muhammad's** alleged infallibility, impeccability and sinlessness emerged slowly over the centuries. This doctrine - **a total and undeniable perversion of reality and fact** - is based only on **dogma** and not on any truthful record since the **Quran** and **Ahadith** themselves repeatedly and **unequivocally** state and show that **Muhammad** was only a man, a mortal who suffered their strengths and weaknesses of fallibility and sinfulness.

Muhammadan scholars have only themselves to blame for their unsuccessful endeavours at perverting and tampering with the historical - and their own - theological records by attempting to make Muhammad seem incorruptible and infallible contrary to the evidence at hand.

These distortions of the reports of the **Ahadith** are contrary to the **Quranic** verses which repeatedly declare that **Muhammad** was only a human messenger subject to human frailties and temptations:

Ali Imran 3: ....144 Muhammad is no more than an Apostle: many were the Apostles that passed away before him.

Al Kahf 18: 110 Say: "I am but a man like yourselves (but) *the inspiration has come to me that **your Allah is one Allah***

*** This verse shows clearly that **Allah** was already known as a god of the **pagan Arabs** long before **Muhammad** and his **Quran**.

The only difference is **Muhammad's** insistence that **Allah** is **one** deity without any associates ***

Al Anbiya 21: 35 *Every soul shall have a taste of death: and* **We test you by evil and by good by way of trial: to Us must ye return.**

Al Ghafir 40:55 *Patiently then persevere: for the Promise of Allah is true:* **and ask forgiveness for thy fault** *and celebrate the Praises of thy Lord in the evening and in the morning.*

Al Ahqaf 46: 9 *Say: "I am no bringer of new-fangled doctrine among the apostles nor do I know what will be done with me or with you. I follow but that which is revealed to me by inspiration:* **I am but a Warner** *open and clear."*

Al Fath 48: 1 *Verily We have granted thee a manifest Victory:* **2 That Allah may forgive thee thy faults of the past and those to follow**

*** Some of the commentators take this to mean sins committed by **Muhammad** before his call and after it.

Others refer to the word to the liaison with the **Coptic** handmaiden **Mary,** and to his marriage with **Zainab,** the wife of his adopted son **Zaid.**

None of the commentators that have been researched, including **al-Baizawi, al-Jalalayin, al-Kamalan, and Husain,** give the last interpretation. They all say it refers to his sins before and after his call to the Apostleship***

The Hadiths are replete with sayings and stories that show Muhammad being as **sinful** as any other human being with similar weaknesses and strengths.

Sahih Al-Bukhari Hadith 1.46 Narrated by 'Ubada bin As-Samit

The Prophet said, "I came out to inform you about (the date of) the night of **Al-Qadr**, but as so and so and so **and so quarreled, its knowledge was taken away (I forgot it)** and maybe it was better for you. Now look for it in the 7th, the 9th and the 5th (of the last 10 nights of the month of Ramadan)."

*** Muhammad, allegedly the greatest of the prophets, **forgot** the date of the most momentous instance of his life; the night when the first verse of the Quran was allegedly revealed to him by the angel Gabriel***

Sahih Al-Bukhari Hadith 1.394 Narrated by Abdullah

The prophet turned his face to us and said, "If there had been anything changed in the prayer, surely I would have informed you **but I am a human being like you and liable to forget like you**. So if I forget remind me ...

Sahih Al-Bukhari Hadith 8.388 Narrated by Aisha

The Prophet used to say, 'O Allah! I seek refuge with You from the affliction of the Fire, the punishment of the Fire, the affliction of the grave, the punishment of the grave, and the evil of the affliction of poverty. ..**and cleanse my heart from all sins** ...

Sahih Muslim Hadith 328   Narrated by Abu Hurayrah

The Messenger of Allah, said: I found myself in Hijr and the Quraysh were asking me about my night journey. I was asked about things pertaining to Bayt al-Maqdis, **which I could not preserve (in my mind)**.

I was very much vexed, so vexed as I had never been before. Then Allah raised it (Bayt al-Maqdis) before my eyes. I looked towards it, and I gave them the information about whatever they questioned me.

*** Yet again, Muhammad - the alleged greatest of all the previous prophets - who had only hours earlier just returned from his mythical Night Journey, already **forgot** what the **Temple of Solomon** looked like although he had just declared that he had led all the other prophets in prayers there a few hours earlier .

Moreover, the listeners should be made aware that in the days of Muhammad there was no Temple of Solomon in existence since it had already **been destroyed by the Romans 550 years earlier**

Muhammad was blatantly deceiving & lying to his followers***

Sunan of Abu-Dawood Hadith 5036 Narrated by AbulAzhar al-Anmari

When the Apostle of Allah went to his bed at night, he would say... **O Allah! forgive me my sin**, drive away my devil, free me from my responsibility, and place me in the highest assembly.

Sunan of Abu-Dawood Hadith 5043 Narrated by Aisha, Ummul Mu'minin

When the Apostle of Allah awoke at night, he said: There is no god but thou, glory be to Thee, **O Allah, I ask Thy pardon for my sin and I ask Thee for Thy mercy.**

Tabari 6:75 "'Messenger, how did you first know with absolute certainty that you were a prophet?' He replied, 'Two angels came to me while I was somewhere in Mecca.... One angel said, "Open his breast and take out his heart."

He opened my chest and heart, **removing the pollution of Satan and a clot of blood, and threw them away.** ...

And last but not least are the **Satanic Verses** that he uttered as reported by:

Ibn Ishaq's *"Sirat Rassoul'Allah"*

as well as by

Al Wakidi (d 823/207H) in his *"Asbab al Nuzul"*;

Ibn Sa'ad (d 845/230H) in his *"Kitab al Tabaqat al Kabir"*;

Ibn Jarir al Tabari (d 923) in his monumental **Islamic** *"History of the world"*;

Bukhari Hadith 6:385 and others.

Originally the Quran followed

Al Najm 53: 19 "Have ye seen Lat and Uzza *20* And another the third (goddess) Manat?

"These are the exalted cranes (Gharaniq/intermediaries) whose intercession is to be hoped for".

These verses were later abrogated and edited out and replaced with *21* What! for you the male sex and for Him the female? *22*Behold such would be indeed a division most unfair!

*** There are hundreds more Ahadith that reflect very badly upon Muhammad's character that no one can actually challenge since they were written NOT by his enemies but by Muhammadan Muslims who had absolutely no reason whatsoever to deliberately make him look bad ***

#42. Quran & Mein Kampf

Q: I have recently read Hitler's Mein Kampf and was fascinated and struck by the similarities of thought, concepts, perverted ideas, racism, hatemongering and warmongering that fill its pages, with Muhammad's Quran.

Even in the Hadiths as well as in the Charter of Umar, the discriminatory and racist rules and regulations against Christians, Jews and Unbelievers are almost identical to the race laws of the Nazis.

Can you elaborate?

A: People who have not read the **Quran and Mein Kampf** will find it extremely difficult to accept what you have just said.

Unfortunately, the **facts** based upon the two books show remarkable similarities as I shall proceed to show with all the relevant references.

Only miles and years distinguished **Hitler** from his mentor, **Muhammad.**

Der fuhrer's methods for accomplishing his madness were identical to **der prophet's.**

Mein Kampf:676 "... men must threaten and dominate men by compulsion. Compulsion is only broken by compulsion and terror by terror."

The lever that coerces compulsion is terror. **Hitler** simply followed **Muhammad's** path.

Bukhari:4.220 "**Allah's Apostle** said, 'I have been made **victorious with terror.**'"

Mein Kampf:677 "Since our view of life will never share power with another, it cannot co-operate with the existing doctrines it condemns. It is obliged to fight by all available means until the entire world of hostile ideas collapses."

Throughout the entirety of the **Islamic** era we have heard a singular battle cry:

Bukhari:4.386 "Our Prophet, the Messenger of our Lord, ordered us to **fight you till you worship Allah Alone.**"

Both men envisioned an eternal battle and total submission.

Mein Kampf:677 "This corrosive fight...for the new program and new view of life, demands determined fighters...and a forceful fighting organization. The recipe for a favorable result requires the formulation of a **declaration of war against all existing order** and against all existing conceptions of life in general."

Just like **Islam,** it was the **Nazis** against the world. The *"House of Islam"* forever battles *"Dar al Harb/ the House of War."*

Tabari IX:69 "He who believes in Allah and His Messenger has protected his life and possessions from us. As for those who disbelieve, we will fight them forever in the Cause of Allah. Killing them is a small matter to us."

The **Nazis** usurped **Muhammad's** dogma. The recipe of **"submit and obey"** was perfect for empowering **[Hitler],** their tyrant.

Mein Kampf:679 "The strength of a party lies in the **disciplined obedience** of the members to follow their leadership. The decisive factors are leadership and discipline. When troops battle one another, the victorious one will be that which is **blindly obedient to the Superior Leader.**"

Ishaq:601 "The best men launch spears as if they were swords. **They devote their lives to their Prophet.** In hand-to-hand fighting and cavalry attacks they purify themselves with the blood of the infidels. They consider that, an act of piety."

It is hard to distinguish which doctrine was more fixated on violence.

Mein Kampf:680 "In order to lead a view of life to victory, we have to **transform it into a fighting movement."**

Ishaq:587 "Our onslaught will not be a weak faltering affair.

We shall fight as long as we live.

We will fight until you turn to Islam, humbly seeking refuge.

We will fight not caring whom we meet.

We will fight whether we destroy ancient holdings or newly gotten gains.

We have cut off every opponent's nose and ears with our swords. We have driven them violently before us at the command of Allah and Islam.

We will fight until our religion is established. And we will plunder them for they must suffer disgrace."

Like **Muhammad, Hitler** seduced men **before** he coerced them. **He made promises but never delivered.**

The following **Islamic** concepts made **Hitler's** list in *Mein Kampf* : "abrogation," "annulment of treaties," "confiscation of war booty," "distribution of spoils," the party's cut or **"fifth,"** "conquest," "expulsion of nonbelievers," "Jewish businesses to be looted and divided," "Jewish land to become communal," "Jews to be punished by death," "the establishment of the laws" **of der Fuhrer," the formation of** "an army," "restrictions on journalists," **and a** "recasting of Christianity."

Apart from time and place, **der fuhrer's** list was an awful lot like **der prophet's.**

Mein Kampf:698 "The **NAZIS** must not become a bailiff of public opinion, **but its ruler.** It must not be the masse's slave, **but their master!"**

Muhammad wasn't much of a listener either.

Qur'an 47.21 *"Were they **to obey**, showing their obedience in modest speech, after the matter of preparation for **Jihad** had been determined for them, it would have been better."*

If the definition of propaganda is artful deceit, Hitler and Muhammad were **grand masters.**

Mein Kampf:701 "On behalf of our view of life I will strike the weapon of reply from the enemy's hand personally."

And how might **Hitler** accomplish this?

***Mein Kampf:702* "Skillful propaganda**.... The best proof of this was furnished by the success of the propaganda.....I had before me a surging crowd filled with the most sacred indignation and utter wrath..... In this meeting I became familiar with the pathos and the gestures which mesmerizing a thousand people, demands."

Islam and **Nazism** share an unhealthy trait, the willingness to link **"sacred"** to **"wrath."**

Neither of them can be trusted as they are willing to abrogate treaties which they do not like.

Qur'an 9.3 *"And a declaration from Allah and His Messenger to all mankind: 'Allah is free from all treaty obligations with non-Muslims and **so is His Messenger."***

Confirming the role of seductive verbal expression in achieving victory, **der fuhrer** shared:

Mein Kampf:704 "The emphasis was put on the spoken word because only it, is in a position to bring about great changes for general psychological reasons. Enormous world revolutionary events have not been brought about by the written word, **but by the spoken word.**"

Bukhari:6.662 "Allah's Apostle said, 'Some **eloquent speech** is as effective as magic.'"

Bukhari:9.127 "The Prophet said, 'I have been given the keys of **eloquent speech** and given victory with terror, so the treasures of the earth were given to me.'"

The study of **Muhammadan Islam**, like **Nazism**, is an exposé on **gang mentality**. Uncorrupted by **Islam**, or left free to choose, few if any **Arabs** would have been capable of perpetrating such horrific deeds. Yet as part of **Muhammad's** gang of **ghouls**, they fed off each other's rage.

Then sounding like **Muhammad** in **Mecca, der fuhrer** preached these words in **Munich**,

Mein Kampf:715 "The man who is the first representative of a new doctrine is exposed to serious oppression and urgently needs the strengthening that lies in the conviction of being a fighter in an embracing body."

Muhammad found his soul mates in **Medina.**

Ishaq:596 "You came to us discredited, when your message was rejected and we believed you.

You were forsaken and deserted and we assisted you.

You were a fugitive and we took you in, sheltering you. You were poor and in need and we comforted you."

Mein Kampf:845 **"Nazism must claim the right to force its principles on the whole** and educate everyone about its ideas and thoughts without regard to previous boundaries."

This is an order to impose **Nazism** on the world and then to indoctrinate the victims.

Bukhari:4.196 "Allah's Apostle said, **'I have been ordered to fight all the people till they say,** *"None has the right to be worshipped but Allah."'*

This is Muhammadan Islam in a nutshell.

Islam and **Nazism** seduced a sufficient number of men to become popular enough to build a **coercive militant force.** Both usurped pagan traditions to condition adherents and then established absolute authority over them.

Writing words that would come to haunt the world **fifteen** and then later **seventy-seven** years after they were scribed by **Hitler's** hand, we discover:

Mein Kampf:787 "Terror which is derived from a religion can never be broken by a formal State power. It will only succumb to a new view of life that proceeds with equal ruthlessness and determination....."

By emancipating his **indoctrinated** followers from Muhammad's legacy, we free them & ourselves from its scourge.

The clues in ***Mein Kampf*** that the **Nazis** were intent on world conquest were not less clear than those found in the **Qur'an**.

Mein Kampf:953 "The German needs only to be given land by the sword."

Bukhari:4.288 "Expel disbelievers from the Arabian Peninsula.'"

Qur'an 2.191 "Slay them wherever you find and catch them, and drive them out from where they have turned you out; for persecution and oppression are worse than slaughter."

When will the world learn to read the words on the page?

When will we come to understand that tolerating evil leads to disaster?

Muhammadan Islam and **Nazism** are intolerant, dictatorial fighting machines.

I can recite you any of a thousand **Qur'an** and **Hadith** quotes to match these, but instead, I'd like our listeners to contemplate the overwhelming similarity of the message, the motivation, and the means **Hitler** and **Muhammad** used to attack mankind.

Then consider the **catastrophic** consequences of ignoring, or even tolerating, **Muhammadan Islam's Jihadi** message.

#43 Muhammad the Forgetful

Q: It is a fact that the majority of the followers of Muhammad, over One Billion of them, are illiterate in the Arabic language and hence must trust and depend on their Mullahs to explain the Quran to them.

Based upon your research of the subject as well as upon your personal contacts with different Muhammadan nationalities, what are your conclusions?

A: I must emphasize repeatedly that a **believer** will **not** be swayed by Logic or Facts which would **undermine** his or her beliefs. They must be able to **ignore** as well as **deny** both Reality and Facts.

My experiences even with many of the highly educated Muhammadan Muslims, any and all my **proofs** are IGNORED without challenge.

None the less, let us share a few examples with our listeners-

Sahih Al-Bukhari Hadith 1.777 narrated by Abu Salama

In the morning of the 20th of Ramadan the Prophet delivered a sermon saying, 'Whoever has performed Itikaf with me should continue it. I have been shown the **Night of "Qadr"**, but have **forgotten its date,** but it is in the odd nights of the last ten nights. ..

Sahih Muslim Hadith 2631 Narrated by Abdullah ibn Unays

Allah's Messenger said:

I was shown laylat al-Qadr; then I was made to forget it...

*** Muhammad, the self proclaimed *'greatest of all the other prophets'* could not **remember** the date of the most **momentous** event in his life, the night of *'revelation'* of the first verse of the Quran.

Since Muhammad could not even remember the date of a recent and extremely important event and was not able to predict any future event, by what standard of logic could he be called a **prophet?** ***

Sahih Muslim Hadith 328 Narrated by Abu Hurayrah

The Messenger of Allah, said: I found myself in Hijr and the Quraysh were asking me about my night journey.

I was asked about things pertaining to **Bayt al-Maqdis [Temple of Solomon]**, which I could not preserve (in my mind) **[forgot]**. I was very much vexed, so vexed as I had never been before.

*** Once more does Muhammad admit to **his fallible memory.**

Yet again, Muhammad could not **remember** another **momentous** event in his life.

Muhammad **forgot** what the Temple of Solomon looked like; the very same that he had only visited a few hours earlier - and led prayers at the head of all the previous Hebrew Prophets - on his alleged miraculous **Night Journey.**

The listeners should be aware that in the year 622AD there was no **Temple of Solomon** in existence since it had already been destroyed by the Romans 550 years earlier.

Muhammad was actually deliberately and mendaciously **deceiving** his gullible but believing followers ***

Sahih Al-Bukhari HadithHadith 1.394 Narrated by Abdullah

The Prophet turned his face to us and said,

"If there had been anything changed in the prayer, surely I would have informed you but I am a human being like you and liable to forget like you. So if I forget remind me

Sahih Al-Bukhari HadithHadith 3.244   Narrated byAbu Said Al Khudri

The Prophet said, "Whoever was in Itikaf with me should stay in Itikaf for the last ten days, for I was informed **(of the date) of the Night (of Qadr) but I have been caused to forget it.**

Sahih Al-Bukhari Hadith 6.550 Narrated by Abdullah

The Prophet said, "It is a bad thing that some of you say,

'I have forgotten such-and-such verse of the Qur'an,' for indeed, he has been caused (by Allah) to forget it.

So you must keep on reciting the Qur'an because it escapes from the hearts of men faster than camel do."

Sahih Al-Bukhari Hadith 6.558 Narrated by Aisha

Allah's Apostle heard a man reciting the Qur'an at night, and said, "May Allah bestow His Mercy on him, as he has reminded me of such-and-such Verses of such-and-such Suras, which **I was caused to forget.**"

Sahih Al-Bukhari Hadith 6.559 Narrated by Abdullah

The Prophet said, "Why does anyone of the people say, 'I have forgotten such-and-such Verses (of the Qur'an)?' He, in fact, **is caused (by Allah) to forget.**"

*** It was typical of Muhammad **never** to admit error or fault but **blame** everything on **outside** agents such as: Satan, Quraysh, Christians, Jews, Etc.

The followers of Muhammad at the present time walk perfectly in his footsteps by always **denying** any wrong doing and blaming everything on others ***

#44 Was Muhammad Illiterate ?

Q: One of the most ingrained dogmas among the followers of Muhammad is that he was illiterarte, ie he could not read and write.

They have created this dogma to prove to the world that Muhammad could not possibly have created the verses of the Quran and hence they had to have been revealed to him by Allah.

Are these assumptions factual?

A: The Quran and Muhammad's followers use his alleged illiteracy as a 'fact' and hence imply that the Quranic 'revelations are divine'.

This is of course utterly false and nonsensical since the greatest legacy of the pagan Arabs was their poetry. Their poets were able to recite excellent odes although they were illiterate. Their poetry did not depend on whether or not they could read and/or write.

According to the historical records, Muhammad actually plagiarized some very important verses from other poets and put them in his Quran. Such poets as Imrul Qays; Hasan bin Thabit; Zayd bin Nufayl, etc.

Most relevant of all are the following Hadiths/ stories written by his followers and NOT by his enemies that paint a completely different picture.

Sahih Al-Bukhari Hadith 7.573 Narrated by Ibn Abbas

When Allah's Apostle was on his death-bed and in the house there were some people among whom was **'Umar bin Al-Khattab,** the Prophet said,

"Come, let me write for you a statement after which you will not go astray."

'Umar said, "The Prophet is seriously ill and you have the Qur'an; so the Book of Allah is enough for us." The people present in the house differed and quarrelled. Some said, "Go near so that the Prophet may write for you a statement after which you will not go astray," while the others said as Umar said. When they caused a hue and cry before the Prophet, Allah's Apostle said, "Go away!" Narrated 'Ubaidullah: Ibn 'Abbas used to say, "It was very unfortunate that Allah's Apostle was prevented from writing that statement for them because of their disagreement and noise."

*** Muhammad demanded a pen and paper for himself to write a statement. The allegedly illiterate Muhammad was able to read and write after all.

His followers who were present, did not grasp the magnitude or the implications of such a request, since they truly believed that he was illiterate.

After all, he was 'the messenger of Allah' who could not possibly tell a lie. They thought that he was delirious and did not know what he was saying.

The fact is, that it is exactly when a person is delirious, that the truth comes out of him **because** one is not in full control of one's faculties which would otherwise have prohibited him from telling the **truth.**

Muhammad had been deceiving all his followers for almost 23 years and in this manner he made them believe that he was being 'inspired' by Allah.

He had mastered the perfect **scam** and succeeded and is still succeeding even as we are speaking today into having his followers believe all his lies and fabrications in his Quran.

In the Qarawiyoun Manuscript in Fez (MS fos 57b-59a), it tells that **Umar b al Khattab,** found his sister **reading a sheet of paper** on which was **Sura Ta Ha.** After reading it himself, he too converted to **Islam.**

All of a sudden, the illiterate Arabs became allegedly very literate even among the women, excepting of course, Muhammad, who was nonetheless, sent by his wife Khadijah on commercial endeavors that would have required writing, reading contracts as well as calculating ***

Sunan of Abu-Dawood Hadith 2993 Narrated by Yazid ibn Abdullah

We were at Mirbad. A man with disheveled hair and holding a piece of red skin in his hand came. We said: You appear to be a Bedouin. He said: Yes. We said: Give us this piece of skin in your hand. He then gave it to us and we read it.

It contained the text: "From Muhammad, Apostle of Allah to Banu Zuhayr ibn Uqaysh. If you bear witness that there is no god but Allah, and that Muhammad is the Apostle of Allah, offer prayer, pay zakat, pay the fifth from the booty, and the portion of the Prophet and his special portion (safi), you will be under the protection of Allah and His Apostle."

We then asked: **Who wrote this document for you? He replied: The Apostle of Allah.**

*** The writing on the piece of skin was done by Muhammad and no one else ***

Al-Tirmidhi Hadith 96 Narrated by Abdullah ibn Amr

Allah's Messenger went out and he had in his hand two books. He said: Do you know what these two books are?

We said: Allah's Messenger, we do not know but only that you inform us. Thereupon he said: This one which my right hand possesses is a Book from the Lord of the worlds. **It contains the names of the inmates of Paradise** and the name of their forefathers and those of their tribes. It is most exhaustive and nothing will be added to it nor anything eliminated from it up to eternity.

He then said: This one in my left hand is a Book from the Lord of the worlds.

It contains the names of the denizens of Hell and the names of their forefathers and their tribes. It is also exhaustive to the end and nothing will be added to it nor anything will be eliminated from it.

I.Q. Al Rassooli

The Companions said: Allah's Messenger,

(if this is the case)

then where lies the use of doing a deed if the affair is already decided?

*** Ladies and gentlemen, the most important item in this story is that it compromises the assertions by his followers, that he was illiterate, since the only way possible for Muhammad to have known the extensive contents of the two books so as to differentiate between them, was if he could **read,** especially since they were not *'revealed'* to him by either Gabriel or Allah. This was not a case of *'inspiration'* but of definite reading and evaluating the information within.

Just as important for the listeners to know is the comment made by his followers regarding the concept of **pre-destination** that fills many of the verses of the Quran.

Even they, who were among the most illiterate, the most unlearned and the most superstitious people in Arabia were **astute** enough to understand the **futility** of **life** under the concept or dogma of **pre-destination.**

If people are pre-destined, then they have no **free will** to make choices and hence there would be no need for religion, no need for prophethood and hence no need for Muhammad, for Satan or the Quran ***

And last but not least, the icing on the cake as they say:

Surat al Ankabut 29: 48 *"And thou wast not (able) to* **recite** *(tatloo) a Book before this (Book came) nor art thou (able)* **to** *transcribe it [takhuttuhoo] with thy right hand:* ...

*** This is an extremely illuminating verse which makes it clear that Muhammad, before his Quranic *'revelations'*, could neither **Recite** nor **Write** them down since he was ignorant of them.

Allah makes it clear that if Muhammad had known **previous** revelations, he would have **transcribed** them; that is **write** them down.

Was Allah **wrong ?*****

#45 A The Jews of Arabia

Q: According to my own observation of the subject, very few people in the world know that there were Judaized Arabs in the Arabian Peninsula, centuries before Muhammad.

These were native aboriginal pagan Arabs who had converted - without coercion I may add - to the religious beliefs of the Jews who had migrated to Arabia centuries earlier.

Can you elaborate?

A: Our readers should be made aware that contrary to what they have been taught that **Jews** are a **Religion** like **Christianity**, is totally wrong, since the word **Jew** denotes a **Nationality** (people born in the **Kingdom** of **Judea** or from parents who originated from there) whose religion was and still is **Mousawiyoon** (the followers of **Moses**).

In **Arabic** they are called **Al Taifa Al Mousawiya** meaning the followers of the **Mosaic Sect/Faith**.

Because of the uniqueness of their beliefs among all the pagan nations surrounding them, after their **Diaspora**, the **Nationality** of the **Jews** and their **Religion** became synonymous thus identifying them simply as **Jews**.

In all cases that the word Jew/Jews is read in this analysis, it means **MOUSAWI**, the religion of the Jews.

Hence the **'Jews'** of **Arabia**, like the **Christians** of **Arabia**, were mostly indigenous **native Arabs of the Peninsula** and **NOT foreigners;** they had willingly converted to these beliefs, centuries before **Muhammad** and his **Quran**.

Although **Arab** denotes a nationality (one who originated from the **Arabian Peninsula** or a descendant there of), it does not necessarily also mean one is a follower of **Muhammad/ 'Muslim'** because one can also be a **Christian Arab** or an **Arabized** – that is subjugated peoples - such as **Egyptians, Algerians, Iraqis etc** for example whose land, culture, religion, independence, traditions and language were almost completely taken over by those of the conquering **Arabs.**

In fact, no authentic history of the **Arabian Jews** exists in the world.

The reason there are no records of the historical existence of the **Jews** of **Arabia** in the **Penisula** of the **Arabs,** is simply because **Muhammad** and his followers completely subjugated or wiped out their villages, their books, their very existence in the years 622 to 635 CE.

They did exactly the same to the **Christians** and pagans of **Arabia**. Most of what we have are based entirely upon the one sided and **unsubstantiated** so called 'traditions' of the victorious **Arabs** that luckily contain within them **kernels** of exceptional **facts.**

According to **Arabian** records, the **Jews** of the **Hijaz** claimed that they had come to settle in **Arabia** during the **Kingdom of Solomon** who had trading relationships with the **Arabs**. It is a fact that in the **Bible,** it is only during the reign of **king Solomon** that the first mention ever of the **Arabs** is recorded; *KingsI 10:15*
.

He most certainly sent emissaries and traders - with military contingents for security- to the **Arabs** especially among the coastal areas for the trade routes to **Africa** and most probably, **India.** Since according to **Muhammadan** traditions, the **Queen of Sheba** was allegedly from the **Arabian Yaman**, then the above **Jewish** tradition is not baseless.

The second **Jewish** immigration, according to the **Jews,** took, place in **587 B.C.** when **Nebuchadnezzer,** the king of **Babylon,** destroyed **Jerusalem** and dispersed the **Jews** .

The **Arabian Jews** claimed that several of their tribes at that time had come to settle in **Wadi al-Qura, Taima,** and **Yathrib** as mentioned by *(Al-Baladhuri, Futuh al-Buldan).*

As a matter of fact, what is more concretely established is that when in A.D. 70 the **Romans** massacred tens of thousands of **JEWS** in **JUDEA**, and then in A.D. 132 forced many of them from that land, many of the **Jewish** tribes fled to find asylum in the **Hijaz**, a territory that is contiguous to the south of **Judea**.

There, being agriculturalists among other things, they settled wherever they found water springs and greenery, and occupied the fertile lands. **Ailah, Maqna, Tabuk, Taima, Wadi al Qura, Fadak** and **Khayber** came under their control in that very period, and the tribes of **Bani Quraiytha, Bani al-Nadir, Bani Bahdal,** and **Bani Qainuqa** also came in the same period and settled around **Yathrib**. They then built up their own communal village and called it **Madina**, meaning **'our country'** in **Hebrew** in memory of **Judea**.

Yahtrib became a suburb of **Madina** settled mostly by **pagan Arabs,** such as the **Aus** and **Khazraj**.

Among the tribes that settled in **Yathrib/Madina** the **Bani al Nadir** and the **Bani Quraiytha** were more prominent for they belonged to the **Cohen** or priestly class. They were looked upon as of noble descent and enjoyed religious leadership among their co-religionists. It is reported in the traditions, that the **Quraiytha** were allied to the **Khazraj** tribe while the other two tribes, the **Nadir** and **Qaynouqa** were allied to the **Aus**.

According to **Arabian** tradition, the first **Himyarite kingdom** (from the tribe of **Himyar**), in south-west **Arabia** - where modern **Yaman** is situated - was established in about 130 BCE and lasted till 525 CE. This kingdom stretched over the **Yaman** in the south to **Hadthramout** in the west and the town of **Najran** in the north.

Among the nine kings known to historians of this dynasty, **Abu Karib As'ad Kamil** (c.385-420) is reported to have conquered **Persia** and later **embraced the faith of the Jews** and propagated it among his subjects **(Ibn Ishaq p. 6-19).**

It is not commonly known that the last **Hymiarite king, Dhu Nuwas was** of the faith of the **Jews**. According to **Al Tabari**, he died in 525 in his wars with the **Abyssinians** who had conquered and subjugated south-western **Arabia**.

Arabic sources expressly state, that the religion of the **Jews** became widely spread among the **Bedouin** tribes of **Southern Arabia** and that converts to the faith of the **Jews** were also found among the **Hamdan**, a **North Yemenite** tribe especially among the upper strata of society. **Arab** historians also attest to the fact, that the **Judaized** tribes of **Arabia** always sided with the **pagan Arabs** against the **African Abyssinians.**

In A. D. 450 or 451, the great flood of **Yaman** occurred. As a result of this, different tribes of the people of **Saba** were compelled to leave **Yaman** and disperse in different parts of **Arabia and beyond.**

Thus, the Bani Ghassan went to settle in Syria, Bani Lakhm in Hirah (Iraq), Bani Khuzaah between Jeddah and Mecca and the Aus and the Khazraj went to settle in Yathrib.

By the time of the 5th century, the original **Israelites/Jews** had so totally assimilated into the **Arabian** environment that extremely few **Hebrew** names existed amongst them. Their tribal structure was **Arabian;** their alliances were with **pagan Arabian** tribes; they married and intermarried and were closely associated by blood ties with these tribes to such an extent that the **'Jews'** of one tribe fought the **'Jews'** of another tribe.

Of the **12 Jewish** tribes that had settled in **Hijaz**, none except the **Bani Zaura** retained its **Hebrew** name. In fact, there is nothing in the poetry of the **Jewish** poets of the **pre-Islamic** days to distinguish it from the poetry of the **Arab** poets in language, ideas and themes. Since the **Jews** and **Arabs** are **Semites,** they are also physically indistinguishable from each other.

By the time of **Muhammad**, the original **Jews** had given up their **Hebrew** culture and language, even their **Hebrew** names, and had become almost entirely **Arabized** by a long process of assimilation with the converted **Arabian** tribes by inter marrying with them.

Thus, by the beginning of the 7th century, the majority of **Arabian 'Jews'** were actually **Judaized Arabs** who had converted or married into the older but much diluted **Israelites** whom the **Quran** calls *" Allatheena Hadoo"* that is, those **Arabs** who had - **willingly and without coercion** - converted to the religion of the **Jews.** Their language, their dress and their poetry became indistinguishable from the other **Arabs.**

Al Jumahi (845 CE) devotes a section of his biographies *(Tabaqat al-Shu'ara)* to the Jewish poets of Al-Madina and its environs.

Abu'l Faraj al Isbahani in his *Al Aghani* cites a number of Jewish poets in Arabia.

In summation, the only difference between the Judaized Arabs and the pagan Arabs in the Peninsula, was their RELIGION.

Our listeners should clearly be aware, that the following are the Muhammadan, one- sided traditions of what allegedly transpired.

As usual in the Muhammadan *'traditions'*, there are no **primary** or even **secondary** independent and reliable eye witness reports to assert or contradict these alleged traditions.

Al Baqara 2: 62 those who believe and those who **are Jews** *[Allatheena Hadoo]*, and Christians, and Sabaeans ...

Al Nisa 4: 46 Some of those who **are Jews** *[Allatheena Hadoo]*...

Al Nisa 4: 160 Because of the wrongdoing of **the Jews** *[Allatheena Hadoo]*, We forbade them good things which were (before) made lawful unto them, ...

*** From the linguistic point of view, the Quran should have said *Al Yahood* = **the Jews** instead of *Allatheena [those who] Hadoo [became Jews]* if it meant **Jews** only and not **Converts** ***

The most astounding realization, based upon the Hadiths, is that their belief in the **One and Only God of Israel** never changed or wavered among these **Judaized Arabs** to such an extent, that even when the males of the **Quraiytha** tribe were being **butchered** (600-900 men and boys), by Muhammad and his companions, **only two of them** accepted that Muhammad was the messenger of Allah.

Their incredible tenacity to stick to their religious beliefs, and to deny Muhammad what they clearly knew were his utterly false claims to prophet-hood, is attested to by the fact, that among the thousands of Jews and Judaized Arabs, less then **ten** people were willing to convert to the cult of Muhammad even upon pain of death.

As a **testament** to their incredible display of loyalty to, and their refusal to betray their beliefs and traditions, in the following Hadith, Muhammad remarks ruefully upon this tenacity.

Sahih Al-Bukhari Hadith 5.277 Narrated by Abu Huraira

The Prophet said, "Had only **TEN JEWS** believed me, all the Jews would definitely have believed me."

*** From among the thousands of Jews in Arabia, **not even ten**, were willing to submit to Muhammad's false pretences and tyranny.

This **is**, the **ultimate measure of martyrdom** ***

Before **Muhammad** appeared on the scene, there was no religious or **'racial'** discrimination between the **'Jews'** and the **Arabs** especially since both are **Semites.** The concept of ethnic intolerance did not exist among the **pagan Arabs** until **Muhammad** created it in his **Quran** to justify the destruction of the **Judaized** and **Christianized Arabs** for having refused to accept him as a prophet.

#45B The Jews of Arabia

There is no historical proof to show that the **Jews** ever engaged in any proselytizing activities in the **Hijaz,** or that their rabbis invited the **Arabs** to embrace **Judaism** like the **Christian** priests and missionaries. None the less, this does not preclude the fact that ordinary **pagan Arabs,** or several of their leaders, for whatever reasons of their own, were willing to adopt the traditions of the **Jews.**

That is why **Judaism** did not spread as a religion and creed in the **Hijaz** but remained only as a mark of distinction of a few **Israelite** tribes, to start with. The **Jewish** rabbis, however, had a flourishing business in granting amulets, charms and fortune telling because of which they were held in great awe by the **pagan Arabs** for their **"knowledge"** and practical wisdom in: medicine, agriculture, metallurgy and literature unlike the nomadic **Arab** tribes and others semi sedentary **Arabs** who were generally illiterate, superstitious, ignorant of the surrounding civilizations, without art and with a very simple and uncomplicated religion.

Over the decades, the **Jews** and the **Judaized Arabs** became economically much stronger than the **pagan Arabs.** Since they had emigrated from the more civilized and culturally advanced countries of **Judea, Syria & Iraq,** they knew many such arts as were unknown to the **Arabs;** they also enjoyed trade relations with the outside world.

Due to their acumen and expertise, they captured the business of importing grain in **Yathrib** and the upper **Hijaz** and exporting dried dates to other countries. Poultry farming and fishing also were mostly under their control. They were good at cloth weaving too. They had also set up wine shops here and there, where they sold wine which they imported from **Syria.** The **Bani Qainuqa** generally practiced crafts such as that of the goldsmith, blacksmith and vessel making.

Those **'Jews'** - of **Israelite** descent or indigenous **Arab converts** - were integrated and accepted by the pagan natives. It is important to repeat yet again, that the **pagan Arabs** were almost entirely nomadic people who abhorred and looked with contempt at the concept of tilling the land.

In **(Ibn Ishaq's p:6/18)**, there are numerous passages that attest to the above facts. The stories about the **Tuba, Qurayza, Madina, Mecca** etc are very clear in showing the incredible intertwining between the **'Jews'** and the **Arab** tribes to such an extent, that they are indistinguishable from each other excepting for their religious beliefs.

According to the reports in Ibn Ishaq, it was **two Jewish rabbis who saved both the Madina and Mecca** from the wrath of **al Tubba (Ishaq 6-12)** ***

Philip Hitti in his monumental *"History of the Arabs"* asserts that it was the **Jews** who introduced the following fruit to the **Arabians:** Apples; apricots; watermelons; pomegranates; lemons; oranges, sugarcane; bananas and almonds among others.

The greatest and most important contribution by the Jews to Arabian agriculture and subsequently their heritage, was the introduction of the **palm tree,** which existed mostly in the fertile land of Iraq. It is called 'Tamr' in Arabic, whose root resides in the Hebrew 'Tamar' meaning 'dates'.

Furthermore, each of their tribes had to enter into alliances with one or another powerful **pagan Arab** tribe for the sake of its own protection so that no other powerful tribe should overawe it by its might. Because of this, they had not only to take part in the mutual wars of the **Arabs** but they often had to go to war in support of the **Arab** tribe to which their tribe was tied in alliance against another **'Judaized'** tribe which was allied to the enemy tribe.

In **Yathrib** the **Bani Quraiytha** and the **Bani an-Nadir** were the allies of the **Aus** while the **Bani Qainuqa** were allied to the **Khazraj.**

A few years before **Muhammad's** emigration to the **Madina,** these **'Judaized'** tribes had confronted each other in support of their respective allies in the war that took place between the **Aus** and the **Khazraj** at **Buath.**

The **Aus** and **Khazraj** were the ones who welcomed and protected **Muhammad** in the **Madina** and who were called the **Ansar** meaning supporters/helpers by **Muhammad.**

Because of their proximity and blood relations with their **Judaized Arab** brothers and sisters, they were the most prone to believe in the **One and Only God**. They were the same who later, after the death of **Muhammad,** had to contend with the religious and political discrimination fostered upon them by the **Qurayshites.**

The **'Jews/Judaized Arabs'** of **Madina** were almost totally **Arab;** they were after all, natives of **Arabia** and not foreign intruders or actual **'Jews'**, and even if they were originally from **Judea** - **by the way, there was no Palestine** - they became fully absorbed and assimilated by the time of **Muhammad.**

The **Judaized Arabs** at the beginning, welcomed him as a brother monotheist, who was attempting to convert his **pagan Arabian** tribes to the belief in the **One and Only God.**

Unfortunately, **Muhammad's** original perception of his mission as the **'Moses'** of the **pagan Arabs,** slowly transformed itself into a more militant and uncompromising self esteem as a prophet to all mankind and especially to the **Jews.**

Muhammad actually started to perceive himself and believe that **he was, the promised Messiah**.

The Judaized Arabs, for very good reasons, refused to accept Muhammad as a prophet - especially since he was not bringing about any new concepts or ideas which were either equal to, or superior to theirs.

Because of his grandiose claims to prophet-hood and his alleged revelations, they constantly questioned and ridiculed him, especially since his so called *'revelations'* **totally contradicted the original versions in their Hebrew Bible.**

These humiliating, but fully warranted disputations, became intolerable effrontery to him personally, and a threat to his inauthentic claims which were adding to his difficulty in 'converting' the pagans to his cultic beliefs.

In the end, he had no choice but to exterminate such witnesses to his lies and pretensions.

Muhammad's personal legacy of hate for the **Jews & Christians** who refused to believe in him, is inscribed in his **Quran.** The entirety of the **Quran after all,** is actually **Muhammad's** own

ALTER EGO

and thus, replete with innumerable verses attacking, insulting, denigrating and inciting **Muhammad's** followers against the **Judaized Arabs.**

Systematically and with afore thought, **Muhammad** broke all treaties with the **Pagan, Judaized & Christianized Arabian** tribes or found other excuses to **slaughter, convert, subjugate or enslave** them.

This subject is immense and cannot possibly be done in a few minutes and hence those who want to investigate it more should visit our website

www.inthenameofallah.org **or any other relevant site.**

Our readers **must** bare in mind that as usual with the Muhammadan *'traditions',* there are no **primary** or even **secondary** independent and reliable eye witness reports to assert or contradict these one sided and **uncorroborated** allegations made by the **victorious** Muhammadan Muslims against their **victims.**

#46. Altered Revelations

Q: The followers of Muhammad have been indoctrinated by their scholars about the alleged divine origins of the Quran, and the overwhelming majority do not know and have not been informed about the stories in the Hadiths and some verses in the Quran that actually point to the contrary.
Will you elaborate?

A: Your observations are correct and I shall recite the following more important and relevant examples-

Sahih Al-Bukhari Hadith 4.814 Narrated by Anas

There was a **Christian** who embraced **Islam** and read ***Surat-al-Baqara and Al-Imran,*** and he used to write (the revelations) for the Prophet. Later on he returned to **Christianity** again and he used to say:

"Muhammad knows nothing but what I have written for him."

*** This story relates to the fact that one of Muhammad's scribes used to modify his *'revelations'* so that they rhymed better with the full knowledge of Muhammad.

This made the scribe realize that they could not possibly have been **divinely revealed** if a mere mortal like him was allowed and able to alter them. So he left Muhammad and his Islam and reverted back to Christianity ***

The following is a shortened version of a Hadith regarding Muhammad's first alleged **violent** encounter with the angel Gabriel

Sahih Al-Bukhari HadithHadith 1.3 Narrated by Aisha

Thereupon he caught me for the third time and pressed me, and then released me and said,

I.Q. Al Rassooli

"Iqraa bismi rabbika allathee khalaqa, khalaqa^l Insan min Alaq"

'Read in the name of your Lord, who has created, has created man from a clot" (96.1, 96.2, 96.3)

Then Allah's Apostle returned with the Inspiration and with his heart beating severely.

Then he went to **Khadija bint Khuwailid** and said, "**Cover me! Cover me!**"

They covered him till his fear was over and after that he told her everything that had happened and said, "I fear that something may happen to me." Khadija replied, "Never! By Allah, Allah will never disgrace you......"

Khadija then accompanied him to her cousin **Waraqa bin Naufal bin Asad bin 'Abdul 'Uzza,** who, during the **Pre-Islamic Period** became a **Christian** and used to write with **Hebrew** letters. He would write from the **Gospel** in **Hebrew** as much as Allah wished him to write.

Another version of the same event goes like this-

Sahih Al-Bukhari Hadith 6.478 Narrated by Aisha

...... Khadija then took him to **Waraqa bin Naufil,** the son of Khadija's paternal uncle. Waraqa had been converted to **Christianity** in the **Pre-Islamic Period** and used to write **Arabic** and write of the **Gospel in Arabic** as much as **Allah** wished him to write.

*** Our readers should be made aware of the transition in the two Hadiths from **writing in Hebrew to writing in Arabic.**

This was part and parcel of the methods used by the later followers of Muhammad to deliberately distance Waraqa from the Jews as much as possible to make believe that the Quran was not influenced by anyone outside of Muhammad.

When one **studies** & I repeat **studies** the Quran, one will have no choice but to conclude that the Quran is based almost **entirely**

Lifting the Veil

on plagiarized, plundered, pirated and/or **perverted concepts, precepts, thoughts & ideas** from the **traditions, fetishes & scriptures** of the Pagan Arabs, Jews, Christians & Zoroasterians****

#47. Ancestry of the Arabs

Q: The Arabs claim that they are descendants of Ishmael and Abraham.
That Abraham and Ishmael actually built the foundations of the Ka'ba

Since there is no mention in the Bible of Abraham & Ishmael having ever set foot in Arabia and there is no mention in the Torah of Arabia, Arabs, Allah, Mecca or the Ka'ba.

On what foundations are their claims supported?

A: Like almost all the other claims made by the Arabs, they are all a **mirage** and their foundations are as solid as the shifting sands of the Arabian Desert.

Before Muhammad and his Quran, **the pagan Arabs had absolutely no knowledge** of Abraham, Ishmael or any other Biblical character.

To give himself and his followers an **Ancsetry** worthy of divine revelations, Muhammad **Plagiarized, Plundered, Pirated and or Perverted** all that his followers have from the Traditions, Scriptures and Fetishes of the Jews, Christians, Zoroasterians and Pagan Arabians.

Being consummate **pirates,** he and his followers did not only plunder wealth, peoples and assets but they upgraded to pirating even the religious beliefs of others to such an extent that they claim that **all** the previous Biblical Hebrew prophets are theirs. They did the same to the Churches, Synagogues and Temples of the conquered peoples by turning them into Mosques.

For three hundred years after the death of Muhammad, his followers were able to concoct all the traditions that allegedly connect the Arabs to Ishmael and Abraham.

Lifting the Veil

Let us look at the **facts**

1. When one investigates **all** the names of the Arabs at the time of Muhammad especially those mentioned in the Hadiths, **not** one of them carried a Biblical name

2. Moreover, it is inconceivable that **none** of them was called either Abraham or Ishmael, if they truly were their alleged ancestors, while Muhammad's name is used among at least 80% of his later male followers

3. The Tree lines concocted by Muhammad's later followers are historically and logically utterly improbable and incompatible with the original Biblical version

4. No where in all the poetry of Pagan Arabia were Abraham or Ishmael mentioned

The Muhammadan Arabs use the same Bible that they assert had been altered and/or perverted by the Jews and Christians to find their alleged ancestry from among the descendants of Ishmael.

Not only are these so called descendants not mentioned anywhere in Arabic folklore prior to Muhammad, there are of course no documents of any kind to back up their fanciful and imaginary ancestral tree. Moreover, the Ahadith themselves are at substantial variance with each other.

According to Arab 'historians' there are allegedly three types of Arabs:

1 Al Arab al Baida --- Those original Arabs who had been destroyed by Allah for their **unbelief** such as the Ad and Thammud.

2 Al Arab al Arabyia --- Who are the original Arabs of the Peninsula descended from the line of Shem- Arphaxad-Shelah-Eber- Joktan/ Qahtan -Jurhum

3 Al Arab al Musta'riba --- Who are the Arabized descendants of the Hebrew Ishmael and Ra'la d. of Mudad al Jurhumi, through Adnan and Ma'ad.

As can be seen, most of the names are plagiarized directly from the **Bible** and **Arabized** to make them sound original and authentic, which of course they are neither.

According to their alleged 'traditions', **Ishmael** ended up marrying an **Arabian** woman and was taught **Arabic** by the **Jurhum** tribe who adopted him.

They had to teach him **Arabic** because his native language was **Hebrew**. Hence **Muhammad** and his followers are descended from the **Hebrews** and are hence not pure **Arabs.**

It took Muhammad's followers almost 300 years of **plagiarism and fraudulence** to create **a worthy ancestry** for him and for themselves, not one of which is based on any solid fact either documentary or folkloric; only wishful and fanciful thinking.

#48. Characteristics of 'Muslim' Males

Dear readers or listeners, first and foremost, we would like to state clearly, that we are not **against** the followers of Muhammad - who are actually the **first & worst** victims of the **cult** of Muhammadan Islam - but we are without a shadow of a doubt, against the **teachings** of Muhammad's Quran.

Please bear in mind, that none of the followers of Muhammad are borne **evil,** but almost all of them are brainwashed by the Quran that turns them into Hatemongering, Warmongering, Racist & Unthinking individuals.

We have chosen the **male** followers of Muhammad only, because they are the **perfect** replicas – **clones** – of Muhammad. They have had no choice in the matter since they have been **programmed & indoctrinated** by their religious leaders to believe that Muhammad was the most **perfect male being** that has ever walked the surface of this Earth. Hence, all his Male followers must **emulate** his **sunna,** that is his deeds, behaviour, thoughts and sayings.

We have purposefully **ignored** the **female** followers of Muhammad since Muhammad and his **cloned** male followers, consider them as **inferior** beings not much higher in intellect than **domestic animals;** harbingers of EVIL thoughts; **seducers** of men, as well as constituting the largest number of the dwellers of Hell for being **disobedient** to their husbands.

We do not say these things to insult or out of malice to them, but because this was and is, **exactly** how Muhammad and his Male followers perceive them and the Hadiths are replete with stories that are **insulting, humiliating, outrageous** and **threatening** towards all the **females** of the human species.

The Male followers of Muhammad USE the Quran and Hadiths to **enslave, terrorize, subjugate** and **control** the **body, spirit and intellect** of their females.

We believe, without any reservations, that the **salvation** of Muhammadan Islam resides in the **enfranchisement** and **liberation** of their Female believers.

Since we support **wholeheartedly** the enlightenment and empowerment of all the female followers of Muhammad, we cannot include them as carrying the same characteristics as the males.

It is a fact that the Male followers of **Muhammad** have to live in a **warped & unreal twilight zone** of an intellectually & emotionally dysfunctional world of **denial! denial! denial!**

Because the moment they agree with **any** of our observations or statements, that would be the very beginning of the **disentegration** of their whole belief system.

Our audience should be aware of the following **characteristics** of the **male** followers of Muhammad – **irrespective** of **Nationality, Race, Colour or Culture**

1. They exhibit an **obscene** degree of **hypocrisy, mendacity & institutionalized racism**

2. These are compounded with a **pathological & depraved** indifference to **facts, reality, mercy, compassion, logic, morality, justice, knowledge, religion, verasity, loyalty & language**

3. Their **perverted** view of **unbelievers** (80% of **humanity** or 5.5 Billion human beings) is based entirely on the enormous number of verses in the Quran & Sunnah that are **hatemongering, warmongering, discriminatory , mendacious & vile** that permeate their chapters

4. Those **unbelievers** are, without exception : All **christians;** all **buddhists;** all **hindus;** all **sikhs;** all **jews;** all **animists** etc

5. Not a single one of these **male** Muhammadan Muslims, can **ever** counter **any** statement or observation made in this series about the Quran or Hadiths, using **logic**

or **knowledge** but only **ignoramous emotionional & outrageous outbursts** of **unrestrained anger** at being incapable of **disproving** any of our conclusions

6 They are the **only** followers – in the whole world - of a Cult Belief System that invariably show their **'resentment'** by holding their 'holy' Quran in one hand and weapons of death & destruction in the other, while screaming the **terror verse** of **"Allahu^Akbar"**

7 They are **masters** at the **art of denial** and the best in the world for **blaming** all others for their **own misfortunes, ignorance, shortcomings and stupidity**

8 Their hatred of the Jews especially is as **intense,** as **cowardly & lopsided** as that of the **nazis -** whom they make every effort to emulate - in spite of the **fact** that there are over **1.3 billion** followers of Muhammad against only a tiny **13 million** Jews worldwide

9 They are willing to commit suicide **only** because they actually **believe** – in their **warped, perverted & indoctrinated** mind – that they will end up having unlimited **sexual, sensual & carnal** pleasures with **72** virgins after **death;** the very **same** pleasures that they are **denied** in real **life** on Earth

10 No matter how many **facts** are shown to them based entirely on the Arabic language and their own books, they would **block** all this evidence and recede into the abyss of **mendacity,** of **denial** and the M**irage** of **alleged** past glories & fantasies. In short, they have mastered the art of **Intellectual, Theological and Political Masturbation.**

Let us now share with you a few **examples** about these characteristics some of which may overlap:

HYPOCRISY: They **demand** justice and equality under the law in the Western democracies but they deny any of them in their own Muhammadan Muslim states to all so called **unbelievers**

MENDACITY: They claim that the Quran was a divine revelation when in fact every Biblical reference therein **contradicts** the Hebrew Bible & the New Testament

INSTITUTIONALZED RACISM: It is a fact that they HATE and attack all those who do not believe as they do, 80% of humanity as well as they **blatantly** discriminate against their believing females

INDIFFERENCE TO FACTS & REALITY: No matter how much one can prove to them - based entirely on the Arabic language of the Quran, Hadiths and their books - the contradictions between the Quran and the Bible, they declare that the Jews and Christians had **perverted** these books while at the same time, they exhaustively quote from these same books and the Quran uses them as **witnesses** to its own veracity.

Moreover, although they watch daily on their TV regarding the depraved behaviour of other followers of Muhammad around the world – such as suicide bombings, butchering etc, they still deny all and everything

INDIFFERENCE to MERCY or COMPASSION: The world watches aghast and in terror the bestial acts committed in the name of Allah not only against **unbelievers** but also against other Muhammadan Muslims of a different sect or political affiliation

INDIFFERENCE TO MORALITY & JUSTICE: Their Shari'a laws discriminate against not only **Unbelievers** but also against all the Female followers of Muhammad as well as other sects of Muhammadan Islam

INDIFFERENCE TO KNOWLEDGE & RELIGION: They deliberately destroy the temples and objects of reverence that belong not only to Unbelievers but even to the shrines of other sects of Muhammadan Islam and teach their children that the Earth is **flat** and that Muhammadan Islam is the **only true** religion

INDIFFERENCE TO LANGUAGE: They deliberately **deceive** and **mislead** the unwary, and those who do not understand the Arabic language, that **Islam** means **peace** which is not **true** since it **only** means **submission;** that Allah is God when in fact Allah is **not** God but the **name** of the supreme pagan rock god of the Quraiysh tribe in Mecca long **before** Muhammad & his Quran.

INDIFFERENCE TO VERACITY & LOYALTY: No TRUE follower of Muhammad can **ever** be **loyal** to any state which is NOT a Muhammadan Muslim state.

The Quran, in perfectly clear and unambiguous Arabic, **forbids** the followers of Muhammad to **B**efriend Jews, Christians and all Unbelievers or be under their control.

The Male followers of Muhammad who have found security, freedom and financial success by **escaping** from their own God forsaken countries, now do their best to **undermine** the very states that have given them citizenship to pull them down into the **abyss** and **dark ages** of Muhammadan Islam.

To understand this **total illogic,** our listeners MUST remember the following :

"A belief, is not merely an idea that the mind possesses; it is in fact, an idea that totally **possesses** the mind."

We have had a **challenge** on our website as well as in our series to every follower of Muhammad to find fault or deliberate misrepresentation anywhere in our series. So far we have had no **takers.**

The **male** followers of Muhammad **'win'** their arguments **only** through **terror.** Muhammad did the same in his days when he had anyone criticizing him **murdered.**

We believe that it is better to die **once** a **free** human being than to **live** an eternity as a **slave.**

We would like our listeners to ponder the above issues and use them as means to counter the **lies** and **deceptions** perpetrated by the followers of Muhammad against all those who are **ignorant** of the **facts.**

We are grateful to all of you who listen to our series, to those who subscribe and to those who spread the word about it.

We need your support and comments so that those who are against us realize that it is **wake up time** about the **facts** regarding the **Cult Belief System** of **Muhammadan Islam** and that they cannot **any more** fool or terrorize **all** the people of the world.

#49. Isaac OR Ishmael ?

Q: The Muhammadan Arabs especially, tell the world that the Quran asserts that Abraham was attempting to sacrifice Ishmael and NOT - as the original story that appears only in the Bible tells us - that it was Isaac.

What are the Facts?

A: Isaac was **Sarah's only son** and hence the one who was to have been offered for sacrifice in the **Torah**

Genesis Chapter 22

*1. And it came to pass after these things, that God tested Abraham, and said to him, Abraham....****Take now your son, your only son Isaac, whom you love,*** *and go to the land of **Moriah; and offer him there for a burnt offering*** *upon one of the mountains which I will tell you.*

9. *And they came to the place which God had told him; and Abraham built an altar there, and laid the wood in order, and **bound Isaac his son,** and laid him on the altar upon the wood.*

10. *And Abraham stretched out his hand, and took the knife to slay his son.11. And the angel of the Lord called to him from heaven, and said, Abraham, Abraham...Lay not your hand upon the lad, nor do anything to him; for now I know that you fear God, seeing that you did not withhold your son, your only son from me.*

The version in the **Quran (S37:100/107)** is completely incompatible with and different from the **Biblical** narrative. More over, the **Quran** does not assert or allege that it was **Ishmael** who was being offered for a sacrifice, as the later **Muhammadan** scholars in desperation, concocted as an alternative story.

The Biblical verses above show repeatedly and with great precision that it is always **Isaac,** and **ONLY Isaac,** who is considered as **Abraham's foremost son,** as in the repeated description of

I.Q. Al Rassooli

"your son, your ONLY son, Isaac ".

Isaac's name appears in association with **Ishmael** in **four Suras (2:133&136&140; 3:84; 4:163; 14:39)**.

His name appears alone **(without Ishmael)** in association with **Abraham or Jacob** in **eight Surahs (6:84; 11:71; 12:6; 38; 19:49; 21:72; 29:27; 37:112 & 113; 38:45)**.

The Quran mentions **Isaac's** name on **Sixteen** occasions while that of **Ishmael** only **Eight** times.

*** It is a great insult to the human intellect, as well as a pitiable and pitiful endeavour that the followers of Muhammad attempt their best to **pervert, contort** and **twist,** Recorded History, Facts, Reality and Language in order to give themselves a **worthy ancestry,** at any cost ***

According to alleged, **unsubstantiated** and totally **fabricated Arab 'traditions'** and contrary to the original stories from the **Biblical** records, **Ishmael** is their **'father'** just as **Isaac** was the **'father'** of the **Israelites.**

From this very outset, let the listeners be aware that the above so called **'traditions'** did not exist in the mind of the **Pagan Arabians** prior to their **alleged 'revelations'** in **Muhammad's Quran and later Hadiths.**

In this chapter, I shall show the readers the **two versions of the story of Ishmael,** that of the **original** in the **Bible** and that of the **Quran** for them to compare and contrast.

According to the **Bible, Abraham** was of the **Hebrew (Ibri) tribe.**

*Gen 14:"13. And there came one who had escaped, and told **Abram the Hebrew;** for he lived in the plain of Mamre the Amorite, brother of Eshkol, and brother of Aner; and these were confederate with Abram"*

The **Hebrews** were one among hundreds of **Semitic** tribes that lived in the land of what is now called **Iraq.**

If historians are correct in surmising that the **Semitic tribes of Iraq & Syria** originated from **Arabia**, then the **Hebrews** were one of these tribes. If this were the case, then **Abraham** and **Ishmael** cannot **also** be the progenitors of the **Arabs** from whom they allegedly originated.

According to the **falsified** and **unsubstantiated** Arab 'traditions', Abraham journeyed with the **'BABY' Ishmael** and his mother **(Hagar)** to the valley of **Mecca** and together later on raised the **Foundations of the Ka'ba.**

*Al Baqara 2: 127 And remember **Abraham and Isma`il raised the foundations of the House** (with this prayer): "Our Lord! accept (this service) from us for thou art the All-Hearing the All-Knowing*

***128** "Our Lord! make of us Muslims bowing to Thy (Will) and of our progeny **a people Muslim** bowing to Thy (Will)*

*** The falsification of history, the contortion of facts and reality are the FORTE of most of the so called 'scholars of Islam'.

They know full well, that there exists no such 'Arab tradition' anywhere in either the pagan Arabian records nor in the Oral traditions of these Arabs to substantiate any of their allegations.

If the Muhammadan scholars are correct, then Allah must have spoken in **hebrew** to Abraham and the **first** language heard near the Ka'ba was also **hebrew** and **not** Arabic.

It is a measure of their intellectual desperation that the Muhammadan scholars even **contradict** the Quran which asserts in several verses that neither Muhammad nor the Pagan Arabs had any **knowledge** of **previous revelations.**

*Al Baqara 2: 78 And there are among them **illiterates** who know not the **Book [ummiyoona la ya'lamoona'l kitaba]***

The **Quranic** word **Ummi** is deliberately mis-interpreted as **"Illiterate"** by the Sunni (Orthodox) Muhammadans. Critical scholars **(Tabari in his *Tafsir*)** point out that this curious adjective is invariably used in the **Quran** in contradistinction and/or in apposition to the **People of the Book/ Ahl al Kitab** and should therefore be taken to mean one **ignorant** of **Holy Scriptures** and/or the earlier revealed religions; that is, un-scriptured.

The Almighty made it crystal clear to **Abraham** by emphasizing that his **'ONLY SON'**, **Isaac**, was the one from his first wife **Sarah** and not from his concubine **Hagar** thus eliminating **Ishmael** from both the attempted sacrifice as well as from the blessing of inheriting the **Promised Land.**

We are here confronted by an extremely serious and **monumental** dilemma; either the Bible is false or the Quran is. Both, cannot be correct when they are giving **contradictory** versions of the same events.

Since the Bible preceded the Quran by at least 2100 years, one has to believe that the angel Gabriel gave Muhammad a completely altered version of the Torah from what was given to **Moses 'FACE TO FACE'** by the **Almighty** and not passed down **second hand** and adulterated by any intermediary as is the case with the Quran.

One has to assume that Gabriel deliberately changed God's Bible which is also inconceivable.

Since it is impossible to believe, that **any** Omniscient, Merciful and Compassionate God would have ever revealed all the Discrepancies, Hatemongering, Warmongering, Discrimination, Grammatical Errors, as well as the Historical and Character dislocations, Mendacities, Abnormalities, Inconsistencies, Time and Space Displacements that permeate the Quranic versions of the Biblical events, then only **one** conclusion can be possible.

That every letter, every word, every verse and every chapter in the Quran are the product of Muhammad's personal thoughts and imaginings, the secretions of his mind based upon his distorted recollections of stories and tales he had heard from Jewish and Christian individuals.

They actually represent Muhammad's own **ALTER EGO,** but cleverly projected into the unsuspecting mouth of **Allah,** the supreme pagan rock god of Mecca embedded into the corner wall of the Ka'ba, called the Black Stone.

The authors of the Quran: Muhammad, Allah and Gabriel are one and the same.

They are **ALL** Muhammad himself, while Allah, Gabriel and Satan are mere props required to give his alleged revelations sanctity and divine authority.

#50. Battle of Yamama

Q: The battle of YAMAMA was a turning point in the history of the Quran.
Will you elaborate?

A: It was due to the aftermath of this battle that the followers of Muhammad were forced to put the Quran to writing

At the very beginning of **'Islam'**, the **Quran** was being **memorized** and not yet **compiled into a written form** especially since as long as Muhammad was alive and receiving **'revelations'** - over a very long period of 23 years - new **Suras** were **being added** while others were **being revised, deleted** and/or **abrogated.**

*** All verses in the Quran that speak of it as a Book are wrong and deceiving since the Quran was **NOT** in book form while Muhammad was alive ***

When **Muhammad** died, there existed **no singular codex** of the **Quranic** text, that is, there was not in existence any collection of **'revelations'** in a **Final Review** form.

Also, there was not a single memorizer who knew all the verses of the **Quran;** all these verses were scattered in the memories of hundreds of **Huffath, memorisers.**

Without a doubt, **Muhammad** failed utterly in his primary mission of giving his followers a **SINGLE Authorized Scripture** because in reality he died without authenticating a unified codex of the **Quran.** The fact that he left his followers with **SEVEN** modes/versions of the **Quran,** speaks volumes about his failure.

The consequences of this failure became paramount when his followers were reciting different versions of the alleged **'words of Allah'.** This failure has endured- **and continues** - for the last **1400 years.**

All attempts by his present followers to gloss over this fact are doomed to fail since the records of the **Muhammadan scholars** in the centuries after his death attest to **otherwise.**

After the death of Muhammad many Arab tribes broke into revolt against the **State of** Madina. Caliph Abu Bakr organized 11 corps to deals with these **Apostates.**

The **Battle of Yamama** was fought in December 632 AD in the plain of Aqraba in the region of Yamama between the forces of Caliph Abu Bakr and Musailima, a self-proclaimed prophet like Muhammad.

Musailima and most of his followers were massacred by the armies of **Abu Bakr** but at the same time, **hundreds** of those men who had memorized different sections of the **Quran** also perished and with them many verses of the **Quran.**

As the **memorizers (Huffath),** were becoming extinct through slaughter in battle or otherwise, Umar ibn al Khattab, recommended that the **Quran** should be committed to writing. Abu Bakr entrusted the task to **Zayd ibn Thabit** of al **Madina** who used to be Muhammad's secretary

Sahih Al-Bukhari Hadith 6.509 Narrated by Zaid bin Thabit

Abu Bakr As-Siddiq sent for me when the people of **Yamama had been killed** (i.e., a number of the Prophet's Companions who fought against Musailama). (I went to him) and found 'Umar bin Al-Khattab sitting with him. Abu Bakr then said (to me), "Umar has come to me and said:

'Casualties were heavy among the Qurra' of the Qur'an (i.e. those who knew the Quran by heart) on the day of the **Battle of Yamama,** and I am afraid that more heavy casualties may take place among the Qurra' on other battlefields, whereby a large part of the Qur'an may be lost. Therefore I suggest, you (Abu Bakr) order that the **Qur'an** be collected."

So I started looking for the Qur'an and collecting it from (what was written on) palmed stalks, thin white stones and also from the men who knew it by heart, till I found the last Verse of *Surat At-Tauba* (Repentance) with Abi Khuzaima Al-Ansari, and I did not find it with anybody other than him.

All were brought together and a text was constructed.

If it were true that there were many **'memorizers'** of the **Quran**, why then did they need to collect the **Quranic** verses from diverse and unrelated **'documents'** such as leafstalk, bone, parchments as well as the memories of men?

From the above quotes, it is clear that the **pagan Arabs** had not by then mastered the art of writing or the use of writing materials such as clay, papyrus, metal sheets or even skins of animals. The **Arabs** of the **Hijaz** - contrary to all the efforts of **Muhammadan** propaganda - were mostly illiterate, uneducated uncivilized nomadic and semi nomadic people.

Abu Bakr and Umar recognised that there were other masters of the text of the **Quran**, such as **Abdullah ibn Mas'ud, Ubayy ibn Ka'b, Mu'adh ibn Jabal, Ali bin Abi Talib** and others alongside **Zaid ibn Thabit,** who were authorities **of equal if not more** standing with him and who were qualified to produce authentic codices of the **Quran** in written form.

The manuscript compiled by Zaid, though highly prized as it was, nevertheless was not regarded with any greater authority than the others once these began to be put together and it was for this reason, therefore, that Zaid's codex was not publicly imposed on the whole community as the officially sanctioned text of the Quran.

Zaid's text was, in fact, virtually concealed after its compilation. Upon the death of Umar it passed into the private keeping of Hafsah, his daughter.

Far from being given official publicity, it was set aside and given no publicity at all.

By the time **Uthman** became caliph, although the other codices were gaining prominence in the various provinces, this codex had in fact receded into the private custody of **Hafsa, Muhammad's** widow who simply kept it indefinitely in her personal care.

It may have been compiled under official supervision, but it was never regarded as the actual official and solely authentic text of the Quran. It had become just one of many codices of equal authority that had been put together at roughly the same time.

It is **vital** to point out to our listeners that the compilations of the Quran were not under the supervision of **Muahammad** to give it authority and sanctity but done without his authority by his followers to mitigate against the very real chance that it would have otherwise been lost. In other words and contrary to what Muhammad's followers have us believe, there was no **divine guidance** in its collection.

Hence to **standardize** the Quran into a singular codex, the third Khalifa, Uthman bin Affan, instructed Zaid bin Thabit to compile a second **revised edition** of the Quran.

In 651AD, **Uthman bin Affan,** canonized the **Madina** codex and ordered all **SIX** other versions of the **Quran that were originally** collected by the most intimate companions of Muhammad to be destroyed.

Thus, based entirely upon the **Muhammadan** records themselves, any self respecting intelligent person must come to the conclusion that there were major discrepancies in the readings of the different **texts** that necessitated the **draconian** instruction to burn the alleged holy words of **Allah.**

The claims by the followers of **Muhammad** that the **Quran** that they have today is **exactly** the same as that revealed to **Muhammad** 1400 years ago, is a blatant lie as the **Muhammadan Muslim** records themselves clearly show.

The **Quran** that we have today is actually the product of almost **300 years** of editing and altering and all the **denials** by **Muhammad's** followers are **desperate** attempts to **deceive** the uninformed.

#51. Biblical Names in the Quran

Q: Are the Biblical names in the Quran based upon actual pagan Arabian Arabic sources?

A: I must answer this question on **three** levels **Historical, Ideological & Linguistic**

<u>Historically,</u> when one looks up the names of Muhammad's companions and the names of other **Pre Islamic Arabs,** one will not find a **single Biblical** name among the **Pagan Arabs.** Names such as **Ibrahim, Ismail, Ya'qoub, Moussa, Isa, Da^ood, Sulaiman** etc. are missing which should not be surprising since the Pagan Arabs had absolutely no inkling whatsoever that they were in any way associated with Abraham **until** Muhammad's alleged Quranic revelations.

If **Abraham & Ishmael** were truly the ancestral fathers of the **Arabs,** then it beggars belief and logic that they forgot them so completely especially when one takes into account fact that **Muhammad's** name is used by over **80%** of all the males of his followers even after **1400 years.**

Moreover, if **Abraham & Ishmael** were truly the ancestral fathers of the **Arabs,** it would make the **Arabs descendents** of the **Hebrews; Arabic** the **daughter** of the **Hebrew** language and **Mecca** and the **Ka'ba** holy shrines for the **Jews** also.

When the above subjects are looked at dispassionately and intelligently, the conclusions arrived at above, change the whole dynamic of Muhammadan claims to their language, their shrines and their **mythical** history.

Ideologically, the Quran **repeatedly** asserts that **both Muhammad** and the **Pagan Arabs** had no knowledge of previous revelations.

*Al A'raf 7: 157 "Those who follow the apostle the **unlettered prophet** "*

"Al Rassool al Nabi al Ummi"

Al Shura 42:52 And thus have We by Our command sent inspiration to thee: **thou knowest not (before) what was Revelation and what was Faith..**

"ma kunta tadri ma^l kitabu wa la^l iymanou"

*** Yet once more does the Quran **assert,** that the pagan Arabs and Muhammad were **ignorant of previous revelations prior to itself** ***

In *Al Jum'ah 62:2* "He who sent among the **unlettered** (people) a messenger from them"

"Houaa'llathi ba'atha fi'l Ummiyeena rasoolan minhum".

The claims by **Muhammad** and his later followers that the **Pagan Arabs** had any knowledge of **Abraham & Ishmael** as their ancestors are pure **fabrications** and blatant **lies** especially since they contradict the **Quran** itself.

Linguistically, our readers should be aware that the **Arabic** names of the **Biblical** characters are taken from the **Syriac Arabic** of the **Christians** who resided in the Byzantine Empire and the Arabian Peninsula.

At its broadest definition, *Syriac* is often used to refer to **all Eastern Aramaic languages** spoken by various **Christian** groups; at its most specific, it refers to the classical language of Edessa, which became the liturgical language of Syriac Christianity.

In summation, the **falsifications** of history and theology were needed by **both Muhammad** and his later followers to give themselves a worthy ancestry in line with the **Hebrew Prophets** and hence be able to claim the receiving of divine revelations also.

Being the best **pirates** of the desert, it was not enough for **Muhammad** and his followers to plunder the wealth of the **People of the Book** but they graduated to become also pirates and plunderers of their beliefs to such a depraved extent that they started claiming the **Hebrew Prophets** and kings as their own.

The followers of **Muhammad** continue unrestrained, to create for themselves a history, a lineage and a cult belief system that are based entirely on the **plundering, plagiarizing, pirating and/or perverting** of the histories, traditions, beliefs, fetishes & scriptures of other peoples.

#52. Christians of Arabia

Q: In our chapter about the Jews of Arabia, I mentioned that very few people in the world know that there were Judaized Arabs in the Arabian Peninsula centuries before Muhammad & his Quran.

The same is of course also true about the Christians of Arabia, who also preceded Muhammad by at least 300 years.

Why do you think this is the case? And who were these Christian Arabs?

A: In answer to the first part of your questions, it has been and still is, the deliberate policy of the Arabian followers of Muhammad **NOT** to inform a generally ignorant world, that there were **Christianized** as well as **Judaized Arabian** tribes in the Peninsula long before Muhammad & his Quran.

In this way, people would not **know** that he was influenced enormously by their Scriptures & Traditions without which there would have been no Quran. As almost all of our listeners realize now, Muhammad **plagiarized, plundered, pirated & or perverted** the Scriptures, Traditions & Fetishes of the Pagan Arabians, the Jews, the Christians, the Zoroasrerians and incorporated them in his Quran.

They want the world – including Muhammadan Muslims - to believe the self evident lies that **Muhammad discovered Monotheism, that Allah was god, and that he was a Prophet.**

Let us now **reveal** the **Facts** to those who are willing to listen and to learn.

Shortly after the conversion of the **Roman Empire** to Christianity in 325AD under the Emperor Constantine, Christianity started penetrating the **Arabian Peninsula** through hermits, traders and or emissaries sent by the Roman Emperors to discuss trade relations with the **Arabs** to get spices and other Eastern products.

I.Q. Al Rassooli

A long time before Muhammad, Christianity had already spread to Egypt, North Africa, Abyssinia, Syria and Iraq and was moving south to the Arabian Peninsula.

In A. D. 450 or 451, the great flood of **Yaman** occurred. As a result of this, different tribes of the people of **Saba** were compelled to leave **Yaman** and disperse in different parts of **Arabia and beyond.**

Thus, the Bani Ghassan went to settle in Syria, Bani Lakhm in Hirah (Iraq), Bani Khuzaah between Jeddah and Mecca and the Aus and the Khazraj went to settle in Yathrib.

Under the Byzantine Empire, the Bani Ghassan and other Arab tribes of the Syrian frontier followed **Monophysite Christianity** and controlled the northern end of the great road up through the Hijaz.

In the meantime, the Abyssinians, who invaded Southern Arabia, the Yemen, were also Monophysite. Hence, shortly before Muhammad's arrival on the scene, the Byzantine Empire had three major Christian sects in operation, not necessarily tolerant of each other and they were:

The state church, usually called Greek Orthodox or Malkite, the Jacobite and the Nestorians.

Most were actual Arabians who converted to Christianity and were in contact with the Pagan Arabs of the Peninsula through tribal affiliations and trading caravans. In fact, early Arabic poetry shows the Christian hermit as a familiar figure and the same is true in numerous verses of the Quran and Hadiths.

According to the historical records, Muhammad actually plagiarized some very important verses from other poets, both Pagan & Christian and put them in his Quran. Such poets as **Imrul Qays; Hasan bin Thabit; Zayd bin Nufayl,** etc.

There were Christian hermitages in **Wadi l-Qura,** well in the interior of the Peninsula, east of the Hijaz, whose monks attended the fairs during the holy forbidden months of the pagan Arabs where they traded, regaled listeners with stories and recited poetry. The Christians were able to spread the 'word' among the pagans and help increase conversion.

Arabic history relates that Christianity was introduced into South Arabia by a Syrian monk called **Faymiyoun (Phemion).**

The poetry of the Pagan Arabians show that they valued their nomadic way of life **infinitely more** than a settled one and looked with utter contempt upon agricultural people whom they could rob at will if and when circumstances arose.

We would like you to be aware, that almost all of the records that are available to the world regarding the history of the Arabian Christians, come from the **unsubstantiated** and one sided reports left to us by the Muhammadan Muslim victors who forced into conversion, slaughtered or exiled the original, native and indigenous population of Arabia's Christians and destroyed all their records and traces from the face of the Earth.

Since the Christians were associated with a civilized society, they too, like the **Jews** and **Judaized Arabs,** occupied the most fertile areas that they could find among the tens of thousands of square miles of otherwise scorching and sterile desert.

The chief centre of Christianity in Southern Arabia was the town of

Al Najran (Najjar, carpenter in honour of Jesus) situated in the one part that was fertile.

On the eve of Muhammadan Islam it had probably the wealthiest population in the area. It was famous for making textiles in which silk was employed. The **Yemeni** garments that figure so much in early pagan Arabic poetry were manufactured there. It was also famous for its leather and armaments industry.

Najran seems to have had a much more advanced political structure than other Arabian towns including Mecca or Madina. It was ruled by a triumvirate:

a *Sayyid,* an *A'qib & a Bishop*.

The *Sayyid* acted as **chief/ Sheikh** in the same tradition of Arab tribal leaders who dealt with all external affairs, exchanged treaties, controlled commerce, acted as host at the periodical fairs and led military expeditions.

Al A'qib seems to have dealt only with internal affairs such as administering the municipality and policing the city.

The Bishop was supreme in all ecclesiastical affairs and ruled over all the clergy & monks who formed a considerable section of the community.

It was through this town, which became the centre of Christianity in the Arabian Peninsula, that the Christian message was spreading.

Envied by the Pagan Arabs generally for their great wealth, the people of Najran were none the less held in great esteem for their nobility and the ancient poets seemed to have regarded them as the noblest of the Arabs.

This was of course at a date much earlier than the false pretensions of the **Quraiysh of Mecca,** whose repute for nobility became only recognized **after** the spread of Muhammadan Islam and based entirely for their kinship to him.

Like Mecca, the Arabian Peninsula had **SEVERAL** other holy places of pilgrimage called, also **Ka'ba,** one of which was in **Najran** even before the arrival of the Christian Arabs. The Byzantine Emperor spent a lot of money building a very imposing cathedral as a frontier bastion to impress the Pagan Arabs as well as a centre to spread Christianity.

This is described as a very splendid edifice adorned with marble and mosaic that had to be transported all the way from **Syria.**

Najran remained a Christian city into the **Muhammadan Muslim** era, until its inhabitants were expelled by **Umar Ibn al Khattab** the second Khalifa. Most of the exiles went to **Iraq** where they founded a town also called **Najran.**

The **Arabian Christians** endured much less than the fate of the **Judaized Arabs** who were mostly slaughtered or enslaved. Both communities suffered enormously and irreversibly at the hands of Muhammad and his followers under the pretext that Muhammad upon his death bed instructed his followers that *"Two religions cannot exist in the land of the Muhammadan Muslims"*

Al-Muwatta Hadith   Hadith 45.17

The Expulsion of the Jews from Madina

Yahya related to me from Malik from Ismail ibn Abi Hakim that he heard Umar ibn Abd al-Aziz say, "One of the last things that the Messenger of Allah, may Allah bless him and grant him peace, said was,

'May Allah fight the Jews and the Christians. They took the graves of their Prophets as places of prostration .

Two deens (religions) shall not co-exist in the land of the Arabs.' "

Al-Muwatta Hadith   Hadith 45.18

The Expulsion of the Jews from Madina

Yahya related to me from Malik from Ibn Shihab that the Messenger of Allah, may Allah bless him and grant him peace, said, **"Two deens shall not co-exist in the Arabian Peninsula."**

Malik said that Ibn Shihab said, "Umar ibn al-Khattab searched for information about that until he was absolutely convinced that the Messenger of Allah, may Allah bless him and grant him peace, had said, **'Two deens shall not co-exist in the Arabian Peninsula,'** and he therefore expelled the Jews from Khaybar."

In this, the 21st Century, Christians in almost **all** the Muhammadan Muslim States are being **persecuted** and reduced in numbers through emigration. The most **disgusting & disturbing** fact is **the deafening silence** about this subject emanating from the Media, the Politicians and the Churches in the **west**.

#53. Allah & his Apostle Know Best

Q: Another mantra that fills the Hadiths is "Allah & his apostle know best"
Will you explain?

A: The above expression is repeated in the Hadiths hundreds of times implying and equating Muhammad with Allah in knowledge especially.

In the Quran, during the **Meccan** period, this mantra did not exist because it was towards **Al Rahman or Allah** alone that his ideas were fixated. This changed after his arrival to **Madina** with his increasing political and military power where by the verses almost invariably associated

Allah with his messenger.

Muhammad's initial humility and humbleness were taken over by self assertion and extreme arrogance whereby he invariably **linked his name to that of Allah** creating a subliminal twinning and an inseparable association in the minds of his impressionable, ignorant and gullible followers as shown in only a **few** examples below:

This mantra is repeated in at least seventeen **Suras over 200 times.**

Other Suras-(4,5,7,8,9,24,26,33,40,48,49,57,58,59,61,63,64)

Sahih Muslim Hadith 6813 Narrated by AbuHurayra

We were in the company of Allah's Apostle and we heard a terrible sound. Thereupon Allah's Apostle said: Do you know what (sound) is this? We said: **Allah and His Apostle** know best.

Thereupon he said: That is a stone which was **thrown seventy years before in Hell** and it has been constantly slipping down and now it has reached its base.

Sahih Muslim Hadith 790 Narrated by Anas ibn Malik

The Holy Prophet said: Do you know what Kawthar is?

We said: **Allah and His Messenger** know best.

The Holy Prophet said: It (Kawthar) is a canal which my Lord, the Exalted and Glorious, has promised me, and there is an abundance of good in it....

Sahih Muslim Hadith 1768 Narrated by Ubayy ibn Ka'b

Allah's Messenger said: O AbulMundhir, do you know the verse from the Book of Allah which, according to you, is the greatest?

I said: **Allah and His Apostle** know best....

Al-Muwatta Hadith 13.4

"The Messenger of Allah, took the subh prayer with us at Hudaybiyya after it had rained in the night. When he had finished he went up to the people and

said, 'Do you know what your Lord has said?'

They said, **'Allah and His Messenger** know best.'

Sahih Al-Bukhari Hadith 7.850 Narrated by Muadh bin Jabal

While I was riding behind the Prophet ... he said, "o Mu'adh!" I replied, "Labbaik, o Allah's Apostle" he said, "Do you know what is Allah's right upon his slave?" I said, **"Allah and His Apostle** know best." ...

Then he said, "Do you know what is the right of the slaves upon Allah if they do that?" I replied, **"Allah and His Apostle** know best." ...

Sahih Al-Bukhari Hadith 6.326 Narrated by Abu Dharr

Once I was with the Prophet in the mosque at the time of sunset.

The Prophet said, "O Abu Dharr! **Do you know where the sun sets?"**

I replied, **"Allah and His Apostle** know best."

He said, **"It goes and prostrates underneath (Allah's) Throne**...

Sahih Al-Bukhari Hadith 9.520 Narrated by Abu Dharr

I entered the mosque while Allah's Apostle was sitting there. When the sun had set, the Prophet said, **"O Abu Dharr! Do you know where this (sun) goes?"**

I said, **"Allah and His Apostle** know best."

He said, **"It goes and asks permission to prostrate,** and it is allowed, and (one day) it, as if being ordered to return whence it came, then it will rise from the **WEST!"**

Al-Tirmidhi Hadith 259   Narrated bAnas ibn Malik

Allah's Messenger said: Do you know who is most generous?

They said: **Allah and His Messenger** know best.

Whereupon he said: Allah is the Most Generous, then I am most generous to mankind, and the most generous people after me would be those who will acquire knowledge and then disseminate it.....

*** Since neither Allah nor Gabriel ever addressed the followers of Muhammad, they, the **gullible, superstitious** and **ignorant** had no choice but to accept Muhammad's statements as **true,** which of course, they were not.

The proofs that Muhammad was **deceiving** and **betraying the trust** of his followers are obvious from the very fact that his statements are totally **selfserving** and bereft of any LOGIC, **facts or knowledge.**

Muhammad is equal to Allah since Muhammad knows what Allah knows ***

#54 Seven Versions of the Quran

Q: Why, if the Quran is the 'WORD' of an Omniscient god called Allah, was it revealed in SEVEN modes? Will you explain?

A: This is a question that every thinking and inquiring mind should ask whether they are **Believers** or **Unbelievers.**

After all, the Hebrew **Bible,** the New Testament, the scriptures of the great civilizations of India, China, Persia and others were all in **One** version, why did Allah, if he were the same as the **God of Israel & Jesus** need to reveal the Quran in not two, three or four modes but **Seven?**

Incredibly, the answer to this question, based upon the records of Muhammadan Islam, is **astoundingly simple.**

To start with, the **pagan Arabs** were mostly illiterate and very rarely had the facilities or the wherewithal to put down in writing the verses of the Quran. Most of the Quran had to be memorized by those who were attending Muhammad at any one time.

Since Muhammad had to inform some of his immediate followers of his alleged **'revelations' at different times, in different places to different companions - over the incredibly long period of twenty three years** - it was impossible for him to keep track of the verses, their contents and to which **Sura** they belonged. He was giving different versions of a verse to different companions at different times. This caused of course, dissent, consternation, infighting and bewilderment among his followers.

When these companions exchanged recitations, each believing that he had the correct and obviously the only **true** version, they started fighting and accusing each other of error or fraud.

They of course had no other recourse but to ask Muhammad for the true version. When Muhammad heard the **two** or more versions, he told them that **all** are **correct.**

Muhammad escaped this dilemma by informing his gullible and ignorant followers that the Quran was 'revealed' in SEVEN different ways, modes, versions or dialects.

Thus, at a stroke, the **sincere & truthful** apostle of Allah covered all his lies and deception with this convenient and very simple answer.

Why **seven** modes? because seven is a holy number in the Bible and hence Muhammad used it incessantly in the Quran and Hadiths

Allah, who gave the Torah to Moses in only one form and in a singular language, had to give the 'glorious and inimitable' Quran in **seven** different ways.

Our listeners should be reminded that many of the **memorizers** of the Quran perished in the earliest battles of Muhammadan Islam, **before** the Quran was finally collated and collected in book form.

Hence, even according to the Hadiths, innumerable verses were lost in that way as well as in other ways as detailed in our

'Compilation of the Quran' chapter 36.

Sahih Muslim Hadith 1787 Narrated by Ubayy ibn Ka'b

I was in the mosque when a man entered, and prayed and recited (the Qur'an) **in a style to which I objected.** Then another man entered (the mosque) and **recited in a style different from that of his companion.** When we had finished the prayer, we all went to Allah's Messenger and I said to him: This man recited in a style to which I objected, and the other entered and recited in a style different from that of his companion.

The Messenger of Allah asked them to recite, so they recited. He expressed approval of their efforts (their modes of recitation), **and there occurred in my mind a sort of denial which did not occur to me even during the Days of Ignorance.**

When the Messenger of Allah saw how I was affected (by a wrong idea), he struck my chest, whereupon I broke into a sweat and felt as though I were looking at Allah in fear.

He said to me: **Ubayy, a message was sent to me to recite the Qur'an in one dialect,** and I replied: Make (things easy for my people. It was conveyed to me for the second time that it should be recited in two dialects. I again replied to him: Make affairs easy for my people. It was again conveyed to me for the third time **to recite in seven**

modes ...

*** It is obvious then that Muhammad's Allah was **incapable** of knowing that the followers of Muhammad were such simpletons that they needed the Quran to be recited in **seven** different ways for them to comprehend it.

Muhammad's **all knowing** Allah, **did not know** their weaknesses.

No truly divine supreme being could **fail** to **know** the weaknesses of his own creation.

Sahih Al-Bukhari Hadith 3.601 Narrated by Umar bin Al Khattab

I heard Hisham bin Hakim bin Hizam reciting **Surat-al-Furqan** in a way different to that of mine. **Allah's Apostle had taught it to me (in a different way).** So, I was about to quarrel with him (during the prayer) but I waited till he finished, then I tied his garment round his neck and seized him by it and brought him to Allah's Apostle and said, "I have heard him reciting **Surat-al-Furqan** in a way different to the way you taught it to me." The Prophet ordered me to release him and asked **Hisham** to recite it. When he recited it, Allah's Apostle said, **"It was revealed in this way."** He then asked me to recite it. When I recited it, he said, **"It was revealed in this way.**

"The Qur'an has been revealed in seven different ways, so recite it in the way that is easier for you."

Sahih Al-Bukhari Hadith 4.442 Narrated by Ibn Abbas

Allah's Apostle said, "Gabriel read the Qur'an to me in one way and I continued asking him to read it in different ways till **he read it in seven different ways**."

I.Q. Al Rassooli

Al-Tirmidhi Hadith 2215 Narrated by Ubayy ibn Ka'b

Ubayy told of Allah's Messenger meeting Gabriel and saying,

"I have been sent, **Gabriel,** to a people who are **unlettered,** among whom are **old women** and **old men, boys** and **girls,** and **men who have never read a book."**

He replied, **"The Qur'an, Muhammad, has been sent down in seven modes."**

*** Ladies & gentlemen please remember that **the People of the Book,** the **Israelites,** when they left Egypt were also **unlettered** but the God of Israel did **not** need to recite the Torah to them in **seven** different ways ***

It was exactly because of these various versions of the Quran that Uthman bin Affan, the third Khalifa, allowed only **one** Quran to exist by **burning** the **six** other versions.

Since Muhammad accepted and allowed the seven variations of the Quran, as agreed upon with Allah through Gabriel, no **mortal** should have had the right to burn any of them as each one was supposedly divine.

This **unilateral** act of his, caused a rebellion and dissention among the Arabs that ended with his murder. This **sacriligious** act, nullifies the **unfounded** and totally **spurious** claims of the followers of Muhammad that the Quran was never changed or tampered with, in **defiance** of the reports in most of the books written by the earlier Muhammadan exegetes that show otherwise ***

All the above illogical, sacrilegious & unacceptable **anomalies** can be instantly resolved when our listeners realize that the Quran in its entirety is the product of Muhammad's imagination, his own **ALTER EGO,** but cleverly projected into the unsuspecting mouth of Allah, the **name** of the supreme rock god of the Quraysh thus giving his alleged *'revelations',* the authority of divine sanctity ***

#55. Muhammad & News Media

**Q: From my own studies of the subject, it seems that nothing whatsoever has changed in the relationship between Muhammadan Islam and the News Media over the last 1400 years.
Do you agree?**

A: Your observation is of course accurate since the followers of Muhammad are actually his **clones.** They have no choice, as believers, but to follow in his foot steps, his **Sunna** and **ape** and **imitate** all his actions, thoughts and deeds since he is supposed to be the **most perfect male** human being in all creation.

Our listeners should be made aware that the only **News Media** among the tribes of Arabia were their **poets.** It was they who memorized the lineage of the tribe, its history, its deeds and its myths. They were the ones who by their poetry and or oratory, disseminated the current affairs of their day.

The poets of the tribe were held in immense esteem and awe since an excellent poet of a small tribe could be more lethal than all the forces of a bigger tribe with a mediocre poet.

Poets invariably extolled the virtues of their tribe or those of certain individuals be they ordinary men or kings. At the annual fair of **Ukaz** held during the Forbidden Months, poets vied with each other in public contests that could bring great honour to them and their tribe when they won.

Among the ancient Arabian odes, seven were legendary and held first place and were called **'Mua'llaqat'** meaning **'Suspended'**.

They were magnificent poems composed by some of the most illustrious poets of Arabia long before Muhammad.

In the **Arab** world they are honoured as masterpieces of poetical composition.

The days before **'Islam'** are called in Arabic **Al Jahiliyya,** meaning the **'time of ignorance'** or barbarity. However, it was during this alleged time of **'ignorance'** that many of the best and most beautiful **Arabic** poetry were conceived - a fact recognized even by the **Muhammadan Muslims** themselves.

No poets during the whole period of **Pagan Arabia** were **murdered** for their poetry. This would have been unthinkable and almost sacrilegious. Unfortunately, Muhammad changed all these rules and prohibitions because they did not suit him or his agenda.

*** As will be shown in the following Ahadith, Muhammad sanctioned the **murder** and **assassination** of any and all those who **satrised** or **disagreed** with him and his ideas.

He instigated their butchery be they men or women, free or slave, young or old. He exhibits a **pathological & depraved** indifference to human suffering, human rights, justice and morality.

Those of his followers who were willing to commit these crimes at his prompting, did so with incredible **cowardice,** invariably against **unarmed civilians,** in the dead of **night.**

Muhammad was an **equal opportunity** destroyer of all those who did not accept his belief system.

Even today, in the 21st century, his followers exhibit **exactly** the same symptoms all over the world ***

Ishaq:597 "When the Apostle returned to Medina after his raid on Ta'if, **word spread that he had killed some of the men who had satirized and insulted him. The poets who were left spread in all directions.**"

" **Ka'b al Ashraf** began publishing poems about the wives of **Muslims.** He referred to the wives of **Muslims,** and damaging their honor. In other poems he would curse the **Prophet**, ridicule him, and say improper things about him. In a third type of poem, he would curse the **Prophet's** companions, and compare them to animals - dogs, sheep, and camels. This was a type of insult**.**

The Arabs of those times loved poetry, as the verse says: **'Poetry is the language of the Arabs.' For Arabs, poetry is sharper than the sword."**

Ishaq:368 "**Ka'b's** body was left prostrate [humbled in submission]. Sword in hand we cut him down. By **Muhammad's** order we were sent **secretly by night. Brother killing brother. We lured him to his death with guile** [cunning and deviousness]. Traveling by night, **bold as lions,** we went into his home. We made him taste death with our deadly swords. We sought victory for the religion of the Prophet."

"We carried **Ka'b's head** and brought it to **Muhammad** during the night. We saluted him as he stood praying and told him that we had **slain Allah's enemy.** When he came out to us we cast **Ashraf's** head before his feet. The **Prophet praised Allah** that the **poet had been assassinated** and complimented us on the good work we had done in **Allah's Cause....**

*** Again and again and again, the degree of cowardice and duplicity exhibited by Muhammad and his followers is unbelievable.

They **always murdered, assassinated** or **slaughtered,** their **defenseless** and unsuspecting victims, invariably **unarmed civilians** but at the same time boasted that they were *"bold as lions"*

Even today, **1400 years** later, nothing whatsoever has changed in the character of the Male Muhammadan Muslims; they still **butcher** their **manacled** and **defenseless** victims on TV while boasting about their own bravery***

ishaq: 676 Asma bint Marwan, the poetess, in protest over the cowardly assassination of Ka'ab al Ashraf, said to her people:

"'You obey a stranger who encourages you to murder for booty. You are greedy men. Is there no honor among you?'

Upon hearing those lines **Muhammad** said, **'Will no one rid me of this woman?'** Umayr, a zealous Muslim, decided to execute the Prophet's wishes.

That very night he crept into the writer's home while she lay sleeping surrounded by her young children. **There was one at her breast. Umayr** removed the suckling babe and then **plunged his sword into the poet.** The next morning in the mosque, **Muhammad,** who was aware of the assassination, said, 'You have helped Allah and His Apostle.' Umayr said. 'She had five sons; should I feel guilty?' 'No,' the Prophet answered. 'Killing her was as meaningless as two goats butting heads.'"

*** No prophet in recorded human history ever acted with such DEPRAVED PATHOLOGICAL INDIFFERENCE towards other human beings.

Muhammad is the only alleged *'divinely inspired'* messenger who acted in such manner.

Only after studying in depth, the subjects of the Quran, Ahadith, Arab and Islamic history could one come to the one & only logical conclusion that explains all the **hatemongering, warmongering, immorality, injustices, inconsistencies, absurdities, historical dislocation, theological contortions, grammatical errors, mendacities** and **stupidities,** that fill the Quran and Hadiths which is, that:

Every letter, every word, every verse/aya and every chapter/surah in the Quran could not have been 'revealed' by any **Omniscient, Compassionate and Merciful divinity,** because it is in reality the product of Muhammad's own ideas, hatreds, lusts, anger, jealousy, fears, cowardice and immorality, in other words, his own

ALTER EGO

but cleverly projected into the unsuspecting mouth of Allah, the Pagan Arabian supreme rock god of the Quraysh, embedded into the corner wall of the Ka'ba, called the **Black Stone.**

In a **nutshell,** Muhammad, Gabriel, Satan & Allah are **one** and the **same.**

They are all manifestations of Muhammad's own invented personal **Cult Belief System** ***

#56. Made to Order Revelations

Q: While reading Ibn Ishaq's "Sirat Rassool^ Allah" and the Hadiths, I came upon hundreds upon hundreds of instances of events or actions that were taken or ordered by Muhammad, for which only afterwards, a 'revelation' was 'descended', justifying or explaining it by an indisputable 'divine decree'.

Can you explain this?

A: Your observations and assessment are correct and any of our listeners who may have doubts need only go to our website to get many more examples and details.

There are literally hundreds of such examples and I can only recite a few of them that very clearly prove the depth of Muhammad's deception which he willfully and knowingly perpetrated against his believing but very gullible followers:

Sahih Al-Bukhari Hadith 6.318 Narrated by Aisha

Sauda (the wife of the Prophet) went out to answer the call of nature after it was made obligatory (for all the Muslims ladies) to observe the veil. She was a fat huge lady, and everybody who knew her before could recognize her.

So 'Umar bin Al-Khattab saw her and said, **"O Sauda! By Allah, you cannot hide yourself from us,** so think of a way by which you should not be recognized on going out."

Sauda returned while Allah's Apostle was in my house taking his supper and a bone covered with meat was in his hand.

She entered and said, "O Allah's Apostle! I went out to answer the call of nature and 'Umar said to me so-and-so."

Then Allah inspired him (the Prophet) and when the state of inspiration was over, the bone was still in his hand as he had not put in down, he said (to Sauda),

"You (women) have been allowed to go out for your needs."

*** Even to attend to the call of nature, the women needed dispensation and a *'divine'* revelation that was **instantly** attended to – while Muhammad was still having his supper - by the ever accommodating Allah, the alleged creator of the Universe ***

Sahih Al-Bukhari Hadith 6.175 Narrated by Ibn Abbas

When the Verse: *"If there are **twenty** steadfast amongst you, they will overcome **two hundred**."* (8.65) was revealed, then it became obligatory for the Muslims that **one (Muslim)** should not flee from **ten (non-Muslims).**

Then there was revealed: *"**But now Allah has lightened your (task)...**"* (8.66)

So it became obligatory that **one-hundred (Muslims)** should not flee before **two hundred (non-Muslims).**

*** It seems that Muhammad's Allah, the Omniscient, the all Knowing, did not realize that **ONE Believer** could not possibly fight against **TEN Unbelievers,** so Allah corrected this error and revealed another verse which over ruled the earlier one thus reducing the odds to the more realistic of **ONE Believer** being equal to only **TWO Unbelievers** ***

Sahih Al-Bukhari Hadith 6.311 Narrated by Aisha

I used to look down upon those ladies who had given themselves to Allah's Apostle and I used to say, "Can a lady give herself (to a man)?"

But when Allah revealed: *"You (O Muhammad) can postpone (the turn of) whom you will of them (your wives), and you may receive any of them whom you will; and there is no blame on you if you invite one whose turn you have set aside (temporarily),"* (33.51)

I said (to the Prophet), **"I feel that your Lord hastens in fulfilling all your wishes and desires."**

*** Even his **teenage** wife, Aisha was perplexed at the alacrity with which Allah very conveniently accommodated Muhammad's wishes and desires whenever he required

them ***

Sunan of Abu-Dawood Hadith 2304   Narrated by Jabir ibn Abdullah

Musaykah, a slave-girl of some Ansari, came and said: My master forces me to commit fornication.

Thereupon the following verse was revealed:

"But force not your maids to prostitution (when they desire chastity)."

Sunan of Abu-Dawood Hadith 3960   Narrated by Abdullah ibn Abbas

The verse *"And no Prophet could (ever) be false to his trust"* was revealed about a red velvet.

When it was found missing on the day of Badr, some people said; **Perhaps the Apostle of Allah has taken it.**

So Allah, the Exalted, sent down

"And no prophet could (ever) be false to his trust" **to the end of the verse.**

*** Even his followers suspected that he may have cheated them for which Muhammad shut them up with the conveniently *'revealed'* verse exonerating him ***

Ibn Ishaq P288: ... the Quraysh said

" Muhammad and his companions have **violated** the **sacred month,** shed blood therein , taken booty and captured men"

So Allah sent down to his apostle-

Al Baqara 2:217 "**They ask thee concerning fighting in the Prohibited Month.** *Say: "Fighting therein is a grave (offence);*

but graver is it in the sight of Allah to prevent access to the path of Allah to deny Him to prevent access to the Sacred Mosque and drive out its members. Tumult and oppression are worse than slaughter. ....

*** One does not have to be a scholar or a rocket scientist to realize, that there is something unusual and unsavoury about Muhammad's claims that all his 'revelations' were divinely inspired when in fact, based upon all the above stories alone, not one of them could have been.

Each one of these stories, and hundreds more in both the Quran and other Hadiths, prove beyond a reasonable doubt, that they were all

MADE TO ORDER

'revelations', authored by Muhammad, as and when he needed them and then very cleverly projected them into the unsuspecting mouth of Allah, the supreme rock god of the Quraysh to give them divine sanctification.

The most shocking and disturbing realization from all of the above, is the inescapable conclusion that the author of the Quran was Muhammad and that in reality, Allah, Gabriel and Satan are Muhammad's multiple personalities as clearly demonstrated in almost every verse of the Quran.

That is why that even among the most learned followers of Muhammad, it is **impossible** for any of them to admit these facts because such an admission would destroy and completely discredit Muhammad, his Quran and the whole of Muhammadan **'Islam'** ***

#57. Jizzya or Poll Tax

Q: The followers of Muhammad and their supporters in the News Media and among many Politicians, tell the world that Muhammadan Islam is egaliterian, tolerant, just & moral. That it does not discriminate against the People of the Book, the Christians & the Jews.

Since most of the people in the world are ignorant of the contents of the Quran, they tend to believe these what are in reality, outright lies & deceptions.

Will you enlighten us?

A: Your observations and remarks are correct and I would like our listeners to be made aware of the following very relevant points before I go into the details:

1. That according to the Hadiths, the earliest followers of Muhammad who were allegedly being persecuted by the Pagan Quraysh tribe to which Muhammad belonged, **escaped** to Abyssinia where the Christian king gave them shelter and safety.

2. That when Muhammad was a child of 12 on a trip to Syria, he met a Christian monk called Bahira who allegedly asserted that Muhammad was the Promised Prophet.

3. That the Christian uncle of Muhammad's first wife Khadijah, also allegedly asserted that he was the Promised Prophet.

4. When Muhammad and his followers escaped from Mecca to Madina from the wrath of the Pagan Quraysh, the Judaized Arab tribes of the Madina welcomed him as a brother **monotheist** leading the Arabs away from paganism.

5. It was while Muhammad was in the Madina among the Judaized Arabs that he instructed his followers to

> observe their Yom Kippur/ day of fasting called Ashura as it fell on the 10ᵗʰ day of Muharram.
>
> 6   It was also while he was in Madina that he instructed his followers to observe the Qibla of the Judaized Arabs; that is to pray towards the direction of Jerusalem.
>
> 7   It was also while he was among the Judaized Arabs in the Madina that many of the most important Legal, Moral, Temporal & Ritual rules of the Quran were allegedly revealed to him by Gabriel.
>
> 8   He filled his Quran with an impressive number of stories, events and traditions that were Plagiarized, Pirated, Plundered and or Perverted almost **verbatim** from the none canonical Hebrew & Christian scriptures as we have shown in several chapters of our series.

Muhammad's debt, both moral and religious, to the People of the Book is not only **immense** but is also **incontrovertible.**

Muhammad's **infatuation** with the **People of the Book** turned into **hatred** when they **rejected** his claims that he was the Prophet of Allah who was sent to **convert** not only the Pagans but them also. At this, they had to draw the line.

Since what Muhammad was offering in his Quran had absolutely **nothing** to compare with what the People of the Book already had, they **obviously** were not willing to accept his **dictates** and **presumptions.**

Muhammad was now like a **rejected suiter** who had no doubt whatsoever in his own self asserted grandiosity and claims to prophet hood and hence reacted with immense Hatred & Violence against the People of the Book.

He did so through his usual allegedly revealed verses by the angel Gabriel, hence giving his hatred and ill thoughts the **power** of **sanctity.**

His Sura 9, Al Tauba, in numerous verses, he **recites** his litany of Hatemongering & Warmongering thoughts against the Pagans as well as against the People of the Book.

*Al Tauba 9: 5 But when the forbidden months are past **then fight and slay the pagans wherever ye find them and seize them beleaguer them and lie in wait for them in every stratagem (of war)**; but if they repent and establish regular prayers and practice regular charity then open the way for them: for Allah is Oft-Forgiving Most Merciful.*

14   *****Fight them and Allah will punish them by your hands** and cover them with shame help you (to victory) over them heal the breasts of believers.*

24   *Say: If it be that your fathers your sons your brothers your mates or your kindred; the wealth that ye have gained; the commerce in which ye fear a decline; or the dwellings in which ye delight are dearer to you than **Allah or His apostle** or the striving in his cause; then wait until Allah brings about His decision: and Allah guides not the rebellious.*

*** Our readers, please notice the transition of Allah OR his Apostle**, which makes Muhammad EQUAL in importance to Allah *****

29   *Fight those who believe not in Allah nor the Last Day nor hold that forbidden which hath been forbidden by Allah and His apostle nor acknowledge the religion of truth (even if they are) of the **People of the Book** until they pay the **Jizya** with willing **SUBMISSION** and feel themselves **HUMILIATED**.*

#1281 The translator of the Quran explains this verse as follows:

Jizya: the root meaning is compensation. The derived

meaning, which became the technical meaning, was a poll-tax levied from those who did not accept Islam, but were willing to live under the protection of Islam, and were thus

tacitly willing to submit to its ideals being enforced in the Muslim State. There was no amount permanently fixed for it. It was in acknowledgment that those whose religion was tolerated would in their turn not interfere with the preaching and progress of Islam.

*** Ladies & Gentlemen, please be aware that the Jizya was an **onerous tax,** in many cases amounting to almost 50% of the income of the People of the Book, levied against them in their own **subjugated** lands to protect them. To protect them from Whom or from What? The explanation given by the translator, is bereft of Logic or Morality and adds **insult** to **injury** to the People of the Book.

Moreover, even as they pay this egregious tax, they are to be **humiliated** and reminded of their **inferior** status under the sword of Muhammadan Islam in their own conquered homelands.

It was to **escape** these debilitating taxes and humiliations, that hundreds of thousands of the subjugated peoples converted to Muhammadan Islam ***

*Al Tauba 9: 33 It is He who hath sent His apostle with guidance and religion of truth to proclaim it **over all religions** even though the pagans may detest (it).*

*** There is no **Ambiguity** regarding the **Suprimacist** meaning of *'over all religions'*. Believing that they are **Predestined** to conquer the world, the Arabs and Muhammadan Muslims went to war against all the surrounding civilizations, to mass murder, enslave, plunder, rape, destroy and dehumanize millions of peoples.

They did so on a colossal scale, on three continents covering almost TEN million square miles, slaughtering and enslaving hundreds of millions of people,

In The Name Of Allah

It should by now have become obvious to our readers that, Allah is **only** the **name** of a god [ilah] but is **not** and cannot be the same as the **god of Israel and Jesus** ***

*Al Imran 3:56 "As for those **disbelieving infidels [Jews, Christians & pagans]**, I will punish them with a terrible agony in this world and the next. They have no one to help or save them."*

61 *"If anyone disputes with you about **Jesus being divine**, flee them and pray that Allah will curse them."*

118 *"O you who believe! **Take not into your intimacy those outside your religion [pagans, Jews, and Christians].** They will not fail to corrupt you. They only desire your ruin. Rank hatred has already appeared from their mouths. What their hearts conceal is far worse.*

*** This verse is one among hundreds that **discriminate, incite hatred** and **villify** all humans who do not believe as the Muhammadans do, in

'Allah and Muhammad as his messenger' ***

Al Ma^ida 5: 51 O ye who believe! take not the Jews and the Christians for your friends and protectors:

*** Our readers should not need many more such **vile** verses to be convinced of Muhammad's Quran **racism, hatemongering** and **discriminatory** attributes ***

57 *"Believers, take not for friends those who take your religion for a mockery or sport, a joke, whether among those who received the Scripture before you or among those who reject Faith; but fear Allah."*

*** The People of the Book had very legitimate reasons for their mockery and sarcasm of the Quran because Muhammad was trying his best at making the Quran sound historical, spiritual, authoritative and divine through a continuous methodology of -

plagiarising, plundering, piratining and/or **perverting, concepts, precepts, thoughts** and **ideas** from their **scriptures**, their **fetishes,** their **traditions,** as well as those of the **zoroasterians** and the **pagan arabs;** all the time **pretending** that they were new **'revelations'**.

The People of the Book - as well as his own Quraysh tribe - knew better and in the end he resolved to destroy them since they were the **only** witnesses to his **mendacity** and **deception** ***

72 They do blaspheme who say: "Allah is Christ the son of **Mary [Miriam]**

*73 "They are surely **disbelievers [kafara]** who blaspheme and say: 'Allah is one of three in the Trinity for there is no **God [Ilah]** except **One God [Ilah]**. If they desist not from saying this (blasphemy), verily a grievous penalty will befall them-the disbelievers will suffer a painful doom."*

*** The Quran and the **believing** followers of Muhammad, consider **all** Christians who believe in the divinity of Jesus as **kafara/ unbelievers,** equal to the hated Pagans and hence subject to the choices of **conversion, subjugation** or **death.**

All those Christians who think that they can be friends with believing Muhammadans are **deceiving** themselves since the few verses of the Quran that we have so far quoted – without even referring to more of them in the Hadiths - prove otherwise

For those Believers & Unbelievers who would like to learn much more about the Status of the People of the book under Muhammadan Muslim rule, we recommend the very best on this subject: **Dhhimmis & Dhhimmitude by the author Bat Ye'or*****

#58A. Quran Unravelled

Ladies & Gentlemen, Believers & Unbelievers, the debate and arguments about the authenticity and the alleged divine origin of the Quran goes on and will continue to do so **interminably.**

Although our series does its best to show in Part after Part, based entirely upon the Arabic language of the Quran & Hadiths, their own books, recorded History & Theology, that the Muhammadan **circular logic** in **defence** of their position is **untenable,** none the less, they persist in their arguments of Denial! Denial! Denial! While in the meantime Attacking our Veracity, by using Abusive language and by Threatening us.

So we have decided, that we should **all,** with our God given or Nature given thinking abilities, scrutinize a **short list** of the internal & external self evident **contradictions** in the Quran & Hadiths, and **once &** for **all,** put to rest the usual Muhammadan Muslim arguments that are repeated by the Ignorant News-media, the Ignoble Politicians and the Academia, which assert:

1. That Islam means **peace** when in fact in Arabic language of the Quran, Islam means SUBMISSION

2. That Islam belongs to the followers of Muhammad **only** when in **fact** this is one of the greatest linguistic and religious deceptions that has ever been perpetrated upon humanity, since according to the Quran itself, any human being who believes in the One and Only God is automatically a **muslim** and has absolutely nothing to do with either Muhammad or his Quran

3. That Muhammadan Islam is tolerant when any reasonable person reading the Quran and observing current events **should** conclude otherwise

4. That Allah revealed the Torah to Moses, **directly** 'Kalimu^Allah' and yet they claim, without a single proof, that the Torah that we have today had been perverted by the Jews

5   That Allah revealed the Gospels to Jesus, when we know, based upon the historical records, that this is **not** the case since the Gospels were written decades ***after*** the death of Jesus.

6   That the Gospels that we have today had **also** been perverted by the Christians this time, when no follower of Muhammad can ever prove these allegations

7   That the Quran that we have today is **exactly** the same, **unaltered,** as the one that Muhammad transmitted to his followers, when the Muhammadan records themselves, as we have shown, and will continue to show, **prove** beyond a shadow of a doubt that this is a **fallacy**

8   That the same god revealed the Bible **and** the Quran when in fact this is an **impossibility** since the Quran **contradicts** the Bible in every verse or **aya**

9   That Mankind was created from either a **clot** or a **leech** when the Bible tells us that it is descended from Adam who was created from **dust**

10   That Allah said 'BE' to Adam and he was, where as the Bible asserts that the Almighty **breathed** into the nostrils of Adam and gave him life

11   That Adam & Eve ate from the Tree of Life when in the Bible it is crystal clear that they ate from the Tree of Knowledge

12   That it was Satan who deceived Adam & Eve whereas the Torah has no concept of Satan and mentions the Serpent instead

13   That Adam & Eve were thrown **down** from the Garden of Eden in Heaven to Earth, while in the Biblical **original** they were thrown **out** of it, on Earth

14   That the number of days of creation are **eight** while the Biblical version states that they are only **six**

15   That there were **seven** heavens created when only **one** is mentioned in the Bible

16   That the Sun – which is one Million times bigger than the Earth - sets in a puddle of murky water, when humanity has known this is to be **untrue**

17   That Haman was the Prime Minister of Pharaoh the Egyptian at the time of Moses, when we recognize him as the Prime Minister of Xerxes the Persian, at the time of Esther **1000 years** earlier

18   That Pharaoh commanded Haman to build the Tower of Babel in Egypt when according to the Bible it was built in Babylon in modern day Iraq

19   That the Quran asserts that it was Allah himself who 'CHOSE' the Israelites above all other people, and yet the Muhammadans condemn the Jews for calling themselves the 'Chosen People' and label them **racists**

20   That actually it was Allah in the Quran who promised the **land** to the Israelites **but** the Arabs nonetheless claim it to be theirs

21   That the Quran states that Muhammad was **predicted** in the Torah when we have shown that this is a **lie**

22   That the Quran states that Muhammad was predicted in the New Testament also, when we have proven that this is a deliberate **perversion** of language

23   That Muhammad in his alleged **Night Journey** landed in **Jerusalem** when in **fact** the name of Jerusalem is **never** mentioned in the Quran while it appears <u>667</u> **times** in the Bible

24   That Muhammad saw Moses – who died at least 2100 years earlier - praying in his grave, when **resurrection** of the dead has not yet occurred

25   That Allah is Merciful & Compassionate when in fact he is **neither** since he **pre destines** humanity to be either

Lifting the Veil

believers and go to Paradise or to be **disbelievers** and end up in **hell.**

26 By depriving humanity of any **free will**, thereby having no **choice** in the matter, they are actually **innocent** of their **pre ordained** actions, showing Allah to be **immoral & unjust,** clearly **not** merciful or compassionate.

27 That Muhammad was a prophet when they cannot point to a single prophecy anywhere in the Quran

28 That the Hadiths enumerate a great number of **unsubstantiated & impossible** miracles that were performed by Muhammad thus contradicting the Quran which asserts **otherwise**

29 That Muhammad had knowledge of all subjects from astronomy to mathematics when all the relevant verses of the Quran & Hadiths show his incredible **ignorance & naivity**

30 That Muhammad was the **last** of the prophets when we have demonstrated this to be a deliberate misrepresentation and perversion of the meaning of the word **khatim,** thus **disproving** the allegation

31 That Muhammad was **sinless** when the Arabic of both the Quran and Hadiths assert otherwise

32 That Adam, Abraham, Moses, Jesus etc knew Allah when in fact the name Allah does not appear anywhere in the Hebrew Bible or the New testament since it was the Arabic name of the god of the Pagan Arabs

33 That it was Ishmael who was being sacrificed by Abraham while the original story in the Bible asserts repeatedly & **unambiguously** that it was in fact, Isaac

34 That Abraham & Ishmael built the foundations of the Ka'ba in Arabia when in reality the names Allah, Arab, Arabia, Mecca & Ka'ba are NEVER mentioned in the

Torah and neither Abraham nor Ishmael had ever set foot in Arabia

35. That the angel Gabriel was the same who appeared to Abraham, Moses & Jesus when anyone who has read the Bible would know this is **untrue**

#58 B. The Quran Unravelled

36 That the mother of Jesus, Mary, is the SAME as Mariam the sister of Moses and Aaron from **1400 years earlier**

37 That Mary gave birth to Jesus **under** a palm tree while the Gospels are totally ignorant of such an event

38 That Jesus did **not** die on the cross, thus denying his resurrection and thereby with a **single** sentence, completely destroying the very foundation of Christianity

39 That Abraham, Jacob, Ishmael, Isaac, Moses, the Israelites, Jesus, Mary & the Apostles – all of whom incidentally are Hebrews, Israelites or Jews - were **all muslims**, meaning believers in the ONE & **only god,** Yet the followers of Muhammad have **falsely** arrogated this title **only** to themselves so that they **can discriminate, humiliate & subjugate** the People of the Book

40 That the Quran states that the Jews - who have been and are, the most ardent **monotheists** - allegedly believe that the **uzair** is the son of god, thus making them **kafara &** Unbelievers, when it is impossible for **anyone** to substantiate such an **obscene lie.**

41 That the Quran was a book revealed to Muhammad when all the records of Muhammadan Islam prove this to be a **falsehood** since the Quran was compiled into book form only **after** Muhammad was dead

42 That Muhammadan Islam is a **religion** when in fact it is the **Cult** of Muhammad since his followers **must** emulate his **Sunna**

43 That Muhammadan Muslims have various beliefs and traditions when in reality they are **entirely** based upon

perverted, contorted & twisted historical and religious events as shown in our series.

44. That **jihad** is a **spiritual** struggle, when all the verses of the Quran & Hadiths clearly depict it otherwise. The **ultimate** goal of all **male** followers of Muhammad is to die fighting all **unbelievers**

"fi Sabilil Allah', that is 'for the sake of Allah'. It is considered the 6th Pillar of Muhammadan Islam.

And in the ultimate of circular logic of Muhammadan Islam, it is Allah in his infinite Wisdom & Compassion who has predestined certain Believers to righteously massacre and slaughter all Unbelievers, whom Allah also predestined as such in the first place.

Ladies & Gentlemen, it is common knowledge that the Almighty, by whatever name we may give him, must be **all knowing,** that is **omniscient** as well as **infallible,** Merciful & Compassionate.

Blasphemously, the Quran **proves** that Allah – if Allah were God - is otherwise: **uncertain, vacillating, fallible, merciless, immoral & unjust**

There are hundreds more of such differences & inconsistencies between the Quran and the Bible

As far as we know, based upon all the above information, we have very limited choices in trying to understand how this is possible; how the divine who allegedly revealed the Quran can be so wrong and so full of **hate!**

You our listeners, have the **freedom** to make up your own mind and conclusions.

We, none the less, would like to share our own conclusions with you.

We believe that the answer is very simple:

Since it is Illogical to accept that **any** Omniscient, Merciful and Compassionate God would have revealed all the Discrepancies, Hatemongering, Warmongering, Discrimination, Racism, Hypocrisy,

Grammatical Errors, as well as the Historical and Character dislocations, Mendacities, Abnormalities, Inconsistencies, Time and Space Displacements, that permeate the verses and chapters of the Quran, then only **one** conclusion can be possible.

That every letter, every word, every verse/aya and every chapter/sura in the Quran, are the product of Muhammad's personal thoughts and imaginings, his own hatreds, anger, lust, jealousy, fears, envy & incomprehension.

They are totally the secretions of his mind based upon his distorted recollections of stories and tales he had heard in earlier times from Jewish and Christian individuals.

In summation, they actually represent his own **ALTER EGO,** cleverly projected into the unsuspecting mouth of Allah the **name** of the supreme pagan rock god of Mecca embedded into the corner wall of the Ka'ba, called the **Black Stone.**

The major players in the Quran: Muhammad, Allah, Gabriel & Satan are actually one and the same. They are **all Muhammad himself,** while Allah, Gabriel and Satan are mere props required to give his alleged revelations sanctity and divine authority.

After 13 years of preaching to his own tribe and relatives among his pagan Arab audience, consisting mostly of illiterate, superstitious, unlearned and gullible people, even so, less than one hundred of them swallowed Muhammad's claims and posturing for prophet-hood.

Muhammad was not able to convince even most of his own kith and kin of his claims as the messenger of Allah let alone the more educated Judaized and Christianized Arabians, who knew that every Ethical, Judicial & Moral Precept, Concept, Thought or Idea in the Quran, had been Plagiarized, Plundered, Pirated and/or Perverted from their Bible and Scriptures.

In the end, he had to use Terror, Bribery and Slaughter to bring them **all** under his control and **force** them to **submit** to him.

There is, in the final analysis, absolutely nothing **divine** about the Quran and any follower of Muhammad, anywhere on this planet, who would attempt to challenge these statements and conclusions based entirely on the Muhammadan records themselves, will have the same probability of success, as finding a snowflake in **Muhammad's Inferno.**

#59. Muhammad the Coward

Q: The picture that the world receives from the followers of Muhammad paints him as a valiant, honourable, just & fearless warrior.

What is the reality and what are the facts?

A: Even though we may **repeat** ourselves when introducing a new chapter of our series, we do so to enlighten new listeners who may not access the others and hence miss these very important introductions.

That the greatest threat to the exposure of the falsehood of the Quran **are knowledge** of the Quran, Hadiths, the Hebrew Bible, the New Testament and related scriptures & history.

As we have repeatedly shown – and will continue to do so – in our series, that without a doubt, it is by **Divine Justice** that the very **hadiths** that explain the Quran to the followers of Muhammad, are the very ones which **completely & utterly** destroy its alleged divine origin and its **veracity** as we shall prove yet again in this chapter.

Sahih al-Bukhari hadith 4.54 narrated by abu Huraira The Prophet said, "By Him in Whose Hands my life is**... I would certainly never remain behind** any army-unit setting out in Allah's cause.

By Him in Whose Hands my life is**! I would love to be martyred in Allah's cause and then get resurrected, and then get martyred, and then get resurrected again, and then get martyred and then get resurrected again, and then get martyred.**

*** Muhammad, in his own words, admits that he did not fight in most of the raids that he either initiated or conducted.

He preferred death in **jihad** than life, as long as it was the Death & Jihad fought by his followers and not himself.

What a **spineless** coward.

He sent his simpleton and gullible followers to their demise with promises of booty and rape if they survived and unlimited sensual and sexual pleasures in his perverted version of Paradise if they got slaughtered.

With such promises, they could not go wrong, whether dead or alive.

Then, the brave Muhammad, who did not fight, boasts of how he would have preferred to die, in the way of Allah in **jihad, again & again & again** ***

Ibn Ishaq 373

The apostle **wore two coats of mail on the day of Uhud,** and he took up a sword and brandished it saying

"Who will take this sword with its right?" and he gave it to Abu Dujana Simak bin Kharasha, adding " That you should smite the enemy with it until it bends"

*** Muhammad did not get in the pitch of battle but retired to the top of the hill surrounded by his body guards. That is why he gave his own sword to someone else to fight with

It is obvious that Muhammad was no Alexander the Great nor a Julius Caesar but a pure coward who had to wear **two** coats of mail even though he had no intention of exposing himself to danger but relying on others to die for him, his ideas and his fraudulent promises ***

Sahih Al-Bukhari Hadith 4.276 Narrated by Al Bara bin Azib

The Prophet appointed 'Abdullah bin Jubair as the commander of the archers who were fifty on the day (of the battle) of Uhud. He instructed them, "Stick to your place, …. you should not leave your place till I send for you."

Then the infidels were defeated. By Allah, **I saw the women fleeing lifting up their clothes revealing their leg-bangles and their legs.** So, the companions of 'Abdullah bin Jubair said, *"The booty! O people,* **the booty !** *Your companions have become victorious, what are you waiting for now?"* '

Abdullah bin Jubair said, "Have you forgotten what Allah's Apostle said to you?" They replied, *"By Allah! We will go to the enemy and collect our share from the **war booty**."*

But when they went to them, they were forced to turn back defeated. At that time Allah's Apostle in their rear was calling them back. Only twelve men remained with the Prophet and the infidels martyred seventy men from us.

Then Abu Sufyan (the leader of the unbelievers) asked thrice,

"Is Muhammad present amongst these dead people?"

The Prophet ordered his companions not to answer him. ....

Abu Sufyan ... started reciting cheerfully, "O Hubal, be high! On that the Prophet said (to his companions), "Why don't you answer him back?"

They said, "O Allah's Apostle! What shall we say?"

He said, "Say, Allah is Higher and more Sublime."

(Then) Abu Sufyan said, "We have the (idol) Al Uzza, and you have no Uzza."

The Prophet said (to his companions),

"Why don't you answer him back?"

They asked, "O Allah's Apostle! What shall we say?"

He said, "Say: Allah is our Helper and you have no helper."

*** The Hadiths and their history amply prove, that those who converted to be followers of Muhammad did **not** do so for sublime **spiritual** reasons, but, for **booty, plunder, rape & enslavement** of the wealth, hard work and the fruitful produce of other peoples.

Why did Muhammad cower and ask his companions to answer Abu Sufyan? ***

Sahih Muslim Hadith4413 Narrated by Anas ibn Malik

It has been reported on the authority of Anas ibn Malik that (when the enemy got the upper hand) on the day of the Battle of Uhud, the Messenger of Allah was left with only seven men from the Ansar and two men from the Quraysh. When the enemy advanced towards him and overwhelmed him, he said:

Whoever turns them away from us will attain Paradise or will be my companion in Paradise.

A man from the Ansar came forward and fought (the enemy) until he was killed. The enemy advanced and overwhelmed him again and he repeated the words: Whoever turns them away from us will attain Paradise or will be my companion in Paradise.

Another man from the Ansar came forward and fought until he was killed.

This state of affair continued until the seven Ansar were killed (one after the other). Now the Messenger of Allah said to his two companions: We have not done justice to our companions.

***I would like our listeners to remember what I assert again, that it is by **divine justice** that the Hadiths **invariably & repeatedly** expose Muhammad's **true** characteristics for all to study.

The **gutless** but self declared **jihadi** Muhammad, **pretended** to be among the **muslim** dead and would not answer Abu Sufyan's plain and clear challenges. As usual with Muhammad, he expected others to expose themselves to danger.

Any fair-minded and inquisitive person would ask the following questions:

- a) Why was not Muhammad at the forefront of the battle instead of being at the **rear?**

- b) Why did he give his own sword to someone else to do the killing with?

- c) Why did he wear two coats of mail especially since he had no intention of fighting?

- d) Why did he not fight to defend his position but begged others to die for him?

e) Why did he pretend to be dead if he believed he was the messenger of Allah and that Allah was on his side?

f) Why, at the very end, did he not answer the challenges of the leader of the Quraiysh but expected others to do so?

Can any follower of Muhammad answer these simple questions?

ibn ishaq 380

....When the enemy hemmed Muhammad in, he said:

Who will sell his life for us?

five of the Ansar arose. They fought in defense of the apostle, man after man, all being killed....

*** Even though Ibn Hisham had edited Ibn Ishaq's version of events by taking out items that were not complimentary to Muhammad, even so, the story as depicted, shows an extremely **craven** and **unpricipled** man, who would send any number of his gullible and unsuspecting believing followers to certain death, without lifting a finger to defend himself ***

Ibn Ishaq 381

Abu Dijana made his body a shield for the apostle. Arrows were falling on his back as he leaned over him, until there were many stuck in it.

Ibn Ishaq 381

The first man to recognize the apostle after the rout when men were saying

"The apostle has been killed" was Ka'b b Malik, according to what al Zuhri told me.

Ka'b said **I recognized his eyes gleaming from beneath his helmet,** and I called on top of my voice

"Take heart, you Muslims, this is the apostle of Allah"

but the apostle signed to me to be silent.

*** Muhammad – who was pretending to be dead - signaled to him to be silent because he did not want his victorious enemies to know that he was still alive and may attack him again.

It was Muhammad who ordered the **murder** of Ka'b al Ashraf and Asma bint Marwan, both of them poets, the former 120 years old man and the latter a woman with a suckling child, who criticized Muhammad's slaughter of the Quraiysh leaders at the ambush of al Badr.

It was Muhammad who always had others among his followers to do his dirty work just like the modern heads of **MAFIA Crime Syndicates.**

Ladies & gentlemen, when the Ahadith are studied carefully, they single handily help obliterate & destroy all the myths of chivalry, bravery, compassion, intelligence, knowledge, veracity, miracles, etc, that were later concocted by the thousands on behalf of, and heaped upon the **undeserving** persona of Muhammad.

60. Anything New in Quran?

Q: The followers of Muhammad tell the world that Islam is a religion and that the Quran is Allah's final revelations to humanity.

As you know, I have read and studied the Quran exhaustively and have not found a single new practical, spiritual & intellectual precept, concept, thought or idea beyond the hatemongering, warmongering, terroristic & hellish verses that fill the chapters of the Quran.

Will you please tell us the facts?

A: Although we sometimes repeat the same themes, sentences and conclusions in our series, this is absolutely necessary to counter the innumerable cases of identical and or similar verses or statements that are replicated in the Quran and by the followers of Muhammad. Repetition, after all, creates **memory** retention.

First and foremost, Muhammadan Islam is a **cult** and **not** a Religion. It is the Cult of Muhammad since his **male** followers have to emulate him perfectly according to his **Sunna.**

Secondly, the concept of the belief in the One & Only God preceded Muhammad and his Quran by at least 2500 years by the examples of the Hebrew Abraham and his Israelite descendants. The concept of Islam, **submission** to the will of one God was not Muhammad's idea or invention, he simply **stole** it like he did with everything else in his lifetime.

Thirdly, you are perfectly correct about the contents of the Quran since **all** the traditions, fetishes and rules contained there in were **plagiarized, plundered, pirtaed & or perverted** from the Traditions, Fetishes & Scriptures of the Pagan Arabs, the Christians, the Jews, the Sabeans and the Zoroasterians.

Now let us share the following with our audience:

    1   All the Muhammadan Muslim traditions such as Salat/

I.Q. Al Rassooli

Prayer, Hajj/Pilgrimage, Sawm/Fasting, Zakat/Charity, Shahada/Witness,

Pre existed among the Pagan Arabs as well as among the Judaized & Christian Arabs centuries before Muhammad & his Quran.

2 During the Hajj to Mecca, circumambulating the Ka'ba, wearing the white seamless tunic, the shaving of the hair, the kissing of the Black Stone, the running between the two mountains of **safa & marwa,** the throwing of the stones at **al jamra/satan,** the sacrificing of animals, etc etc were **pagan** rituals that Muhammad very conveniently **subsumed** and wrapped up them with the new mantle of his version of Islam.

3 The prohibitions in the Quran regarding marriage, divorce and inheritance pre existed Muhammad & his Quran among the Pagan Arabs and the Judaized & Christian Arabs.

4 The concepts of Janna/Paradise, the Garden of Eden, Mallaa^ika/Angels, Shaytan/Satan, Jahannam/Hell, etc, were Plagiarized from the Bible of the Jews and Christians since these did not exist in the simple religion of the Pagan Arabians either as concepts or in their language.

5 Every single Biblical name in the Quran was not known to the Pagan Arabs but were stolen from the Syriac language of the Arabian Christian Bible.

6 The ideas about the Houris/Celestial Virgins and the opulence of Paradise were plundered from the Persian Zoroasterians.

7 Almost every story in the Quran regarding Biblical characters such as Adam, Abraham, Moses, Pharaoh, Ishmael, Isaac, Jacob, Jesus, Mary etc are actually from non Canonical stories in the Midrash of the Jews and Apocrypha of the Christians that Muhammad heard and incorporated with **errors** in his Quran.

8   Other stories were copied from the Greek, Latin or Persian ones

9   The words Masjid/ Mosque, Ka'ba, Allah, Jinn, etc were Pagan Arabian long before Muhammad & his Quran.

10   Almost **all** of the most important religious terms in the Quran – numbering about 118 – without which, the Quran cannot exist, were Plagiarized, Plundered, Pirated and or Perverted from Aramaic, Greek, Hebrew, Ethiopic, Indian, Syriac & Persian languages as agreed upon by the Muhammadan Exegetes themselves especially **al Suyuti**. Words such as:

Ahhbar / Jewish Doctors at Law; Istabraq/ Persian Silk Brocade; Umma/ People from Hebrew Aam; Injil/ Gospel from Greek Angelos meaning messenger; Aya/ Sign from Aramaic;   Barzakh/ Barrier from Pahlavi Persian; Burhan/ Proof from Amhari Ethiopic are only a few samples.

11   Muhammad's most spectacular contributions to his followers and humanity are his Hatemongering, Warmongering, Racist & Hellish verses that fill most of the chapters of his Quran.

12   Muhammad's Quran does not contain a **single spiritual** verse since he was totally engrossed in the **physical** concept of the Afterlife. In his versions of Hell & Heaven, the dead exist in a **physical** and **not** a **spiritual** state; that is why his Martyrs are able to enjoy having **sex** with **72** virgins besides the unlimited food, drink and other pleasures.

13   Muhammad's Quran is bereft of any precept of **salvation or redemption.** He promises his followers eternal Sensual, Carnal & Sexual pleasures after death, the same that he **prohibits** them from having in real life on Earth. It is no wonder then that his Believing **male** followers would commit all these barbaric and heinous suicide bombings to attain these goals.

14 The Quran is the **only** alleged holy book on Earth that turns usually **decent** human beings into **depraved** and **unthinking robotic** mass murderers.

15 No follower of Muhammad, or any other human being on Earth for that matter, can show a **single** new Practical, Spiritual, Moral & Intellectual verse in the whole of the Quran that is in any way shape or form Equal to or Superior to what exists in the Bible.

16 Based upon all the research that we have conducted in the last **23 years** about these subjects, we come again and again to the **only** logical and Possible conclusion which we shall repeat as many times as we deem necessary:

Every letter, every word, every verse/aya and every chapter/ surah in the Quran are the product of Muhammad's imagination, his own **ALTER EGO** but cleverly projected into the unsuspecting mouth of Allah, the pagan rock god of the Quraiysh tribe of Mecca to give his Quran divine sanctions and foundation.

If any of our readers who may have a better conclusion, we would like to hear it.

#61 Fight/Kill/Slay in the Quran

Q: I have researched the Hebrew Bible, the New Testament, Hinduism and Zoroasterian religions and could not find as many verses that incite their followers to fight and kill as those that fill the Quran and Hadiths.

Will you elaborate?

A: In the English language, Fight can mean to : Combat, Struggle, Resist, Strife, War, do battle.

In the Arabic language, one word **Qatl** with its **derivatives** can mean all of the following:

Fight: Qital, Kifah, 'Airak, Harb, etc

Kill: Qatl, Thabh, Jazr

Murder: Qatl

Slaughter: Thabh, Jazr

Slay: Qatl

kill, murder, fight, combat, slay, put to death, slaughter, etc.

Invariably, the interpreters of the Quran use the more 'sanitized' terms to convey a more moderate connotation so as to deceive the readers. This word Qital, Qatl, Qatala, Yaqtulu, Youqatilou, is usually used against all those who do not believe in Allah and Muhammad as his messenger.

This word and its derivatives are repeated in the Quran and Ahadith at least **35,213 times.**

So much for Muhammad's version of 'Peaceful Islam'.

Muhammad allegedly 'received' the first among many verses allowing and sanctioning him to fight against all non believers (those who do not believe in Allah & his apostle, almost **80%** of humanity) in the following:-

Al Tauba 9: 5 *But when the forbidden months are past then fight and* **slay [f'aqtulou]** *the pagans wherever ye find them and seize them beleaguer them and lie in wait for them in every stratagem (of war)...*

Al Baqara2: 191 *And* **slay them [wa^ qtulouhum]** *wherever ye catch them and turn them out from where they have turned you out; for tumult and oppression are worse than* **slaughter [al qatl]**; *but* **fight them not [taqtulouhum]** *at the Sacred Mosque unless they (first)* **fight you [youqtilukum]** *there; but if they fight you* **[qatalukum] slay them [fa'qtulouhum]** *Such is the reward of those who suppress faith."*

Al Ma'idah 5: 28 *"If thou dost stretch thy hand against me to* **slay me [litaqtulani]** *it is not for me to stretch my hand against thee to* **slay thee [liaqtulaka]:** *for I do fear Allah the Cherisher of the worlds.*

30   *The (selfish) soul of the other led him to the* **murder [qatla]** *of his brother: he* **murdered him [qatalahu]** *and became (himself) one of the lost ones.*

32   *On that account: We ordained for the Children of Israel that if anyone* **slew [qatala]** *a person unless it be for murder or for spreading mischief in the land it would be as if he slew [qatala] the whole people: and if anyone saved a life it would be as if he saved the life of the whole people.*

33   *The punishment of those who wage war against Allah and His Apostle and strive with might and main for mischief through the land is:* **execution [youqattalou]** *or crucifixion [youslabou] of the cutting off of hands and feet from opposite sides or exile from the land.*

*** 'Muhammadan Islam' the 'religion of peace' uses the word 'fight' and its derivatives **fifteen** times in only these three verses, as an example of **Thousands** more in both the Quran and Hadiths.

The Quran is full of **warmongering, hatemongering, satanic** and **racist** verses that could not have possibly emanated from any Omniscient, Compassionate and Merciful Divinity.

This 1400 years old **unilateral** declaration of **total** war against all those who do not believe in ***"allah & in muhammad as his messenger"***, to force into conversion, to subjugate or to annihilate them, continues unabated, by the followers of Muhammad, up to the present moment and the foreseeable future.

All the denials by the followers of Muhammad that Muhammadan Islam is a religion of peace run against **logic, facts, veracity** and **morality** since we see on TV their heinous actions of mass murder, of slaughter, of hijackings, of kidnapping, of butchering, of wanton destruction of holy places all over the world, invariably against defenseless civilians both against Unbelievers as well as other Believers of a different sect or thought.

Humanity is slowly **waking** up to these realities and the **facts** about the **true** nature of Muhammadan Islam as sanctioned by his Quran***

#62. Allah's Chosen People

Q: It is astounding how the followers of Muhammad, even in this 21st century continue to be in DENIAL of ALL facts shown to them that contradict their Quran.

Even more disturbing are the instances where the Quran asserts certain issues, events or concepts and yet the Muhammadans contort, twist and deform these items and try to Deceive the public both the unbelievers as well as the believers.

Will you show us some of these important instances?

A: Our audience has come to realize by now the near **impossibility** of getting through intellectually and or academically to the followers of Muhammad concerning the subjects of Muhammad, his Quran & Hadiths.

We do understand the Three fundamental items that **prohibits** them from thinking **rationally** which are:

a) Their total and very long term **indoctrination**

b) Their incredible **ignorance** of the Bible and other scriptures since the Quran **forbids** them from investigating or studying other than the Quran

c) And the very real threat of being **butchered** if they contradict their elders, question their scripture or apostatize.

Although we do understand their dilemma &

predicament if they are living in Muhammadan Muslim states, nonetheless, those who live and are brought up in the freedom of Western democracies, have absolutely no excuse to claim **ignorance** or **fear** and remain silent.

Let us look now at the Two of the most prominent issues that are reflected into the political and religious arena of today which are the issues of the Jews and their Promised Land.

Whenever useful, I shall **recite** in Arabic the translated verses for those of the followers of Muhammad who will **still** claim to have doubts about the veracity of what we **prove** in our series.

Al Israa 17:104 *And We said thereafter to the Children of Israel "Dwell securely in the land (of promise)":*

"wa qulna min b'adihi li bani Israiil, uskunoo^l arththa"

A' A'araf 7:137 *And We made a people considered weak (and of no account) inheritors of lands in both east and west lands whereon We sent down our blessings. The fair promise of the Lord was fulfilled for the children of Israel because they had patience and constancy and We levelled to the ground the great works and fine buildings which Pharaoh and his people erected (with such pride).*

138 We took the Children of Israel (with safety) across the sea...

*** The expression 'inheritors of East & West lands' reflects the Divine distribution of the land among the tribes of Israel on **both** sides of the river Jordan ***

Yunus 10:93 *We settled the Children of Israel in* **a beautiful dwelling-place,** *and provided for them sustenance of the best...*

Al Ma'ida 5: 20   *Remember Moses said to his people: "O my people! call in remembrance the favor of Allah unto you when He produced prophets among you made you kings and gave you what He had not given to any other among the peoples.*

21*"O my people! enter the* **holy land** *which Allah hath assigned unto you ....*

[Ya qawmi, udkhuloo^l arththa^l muqqadassata

al lati kataba^l allahu lakum...]

I.Q. Al Rassooli

*** Now, I would like our listeners to pay very keen attention to the following remarkable verses from two suras and their explanations at the hands of the Muhammadan translator of the Quran ***

Al Israa 17:1 *Glory to (Allah) Who did take His Servant for Journey by night from the Sacred Mosque to the Farthest Mosque whose precincts We did Bless in order that We might show him some of Our Signs: for He is the one Who heareth and seeth (all things).*

[Subhana^l lathee ASRA bi abdihi laylan mina^l masjid al haram ila^l masjid Al aqsa állathee barakna hhawalhoo linurihee min ayatina innahoo^l samee'u^l basseeroo]

2168 The translator explains that The Farthest Mosque must refer to the site of the Temple of Solomon in Jerusalem on the hill of Moriah, at or near where stands the Dome of the Rock,

Al Rum 30: 2 *The Roman Empire has been defeated*

3 In a land close by...

[Ghulibati^l Room fi ADNA^l arthth]

*** The translator of the Quran explains to the readers these verses as follows:

3505 The remarkable defeats of the Roman Empire under Heraclius and the straits to which it was reduced were not merely isolated defeats; the Roman Empire lost most of its Asiatic territory and was hemmed in on all sides at its capital, Constantinople. The defeat,

"in a land close by" must refer to **Syria and Palestine,** Jerusalem was lost in 614-15 A.D., shortly before this Sura was revealed.

*** Ladies and Gentlemen, please reflect upon what has been written and spoken in the Arabic of the Quran:

That Muhammad went on a Night Journey to the Furthest Mosque which is not identified in any manner and yet, the world is deceived into believing that it had to be the Temple of Solomon on the Temple Mount in Jerusalem. As you all should know by now, the name of Jerusalem is **NEVER** mentioned in the Quran.

Hence what we have here are pure **Myths.**

Let us for an instance assume that the Furthest Mosque is in the far off land of **Judea/Palestina.**

But, lo and behold, the translator of the next verse tells us that the **'land nearby'** mentioned in the Quran must be **Syria/Palestine.**

Which case is the **true** one? Either Jerusalem is very far or it is very near. As far as we know, it cannot be **BOTH.**

Now, the newest followers of Muhammad of the 21st century, have moved the goal post completely by denying the very existence of the Temple of Solomnon.

They are trying their worst to deny the followers of Moses, the Jews, and the followers of Jesus, the Christians, any religious or political associations with the land of Israel.

If this is the case, then they have done us ALL a great favour by actually agreeing with us that **both** the Quran & Hadiths are **lies** and **falsehoods.**

As we mentioned before, the followers of Muhammad, **never miss a chance to miss shooting themselves in the mouth** because to cover one set of lies, they need to create another set and so on and so forth. In the end, when one unravels any part of the chain, the whole edifice of falsehoods and deception breaks down and falls in the gutter where it belonged in the first place.

Hence, from both points of view, Muhammad could not have visited Jerusalem

Now we shall address the issue of the 'Chosen People':

Al Baqara 2:47 *O Children of Israel! call to mind the (special) favor which I [Allah] bestowed upon You and **that I preferred you to all others***

[wa anni faththaltukum a'la^' a'lameena]

Al Baqara 2:122 *O Children of Israel! call to mind the special favor which I bestowed upon you and **that I preferred you to all others***

[wa anni faththaltukum a'la^' a'lameena]

*** According to the Quran, it was Allah who 'preferred' the **Children of Israel** above all other peoples; it was **not** the Israelites, after all, who declared that they were the **'Chosen People'** ***

Al A'araf 7: 140 *He said: "Shall I seek for you a god other than the (true) Allah when it is Allah who hath endowed you with gifts above the nations*

[wa huwa fatthalakum a'la^l a'lameen]?"

Al Sajdah 32:23 *And certainly We gave the Book to Moses, so be not in doubt concerning the receiving of it, and We made it a guide for the Children of Israel ... 24 And We made of them Guiding Lights and leaders to guide by Our command as they were patient, and they were certain of Our communications.*

*** In very clear verses, Allah is declaring that the Torah that he revealed to Moses was a Guiding Light to the Israelites ***

Al Dukhan 44: 30 *We did deliver aforetime the Children of Israel from humiliating Punishment*

*32 And We have **chosen them** (the Children of Israel) **above** the 'Alamîn **[mankind,** and jinns] and our choice was based on a deep knowledge.*

[Wa Laqad akhtarnahum a'la 'ilmin a'la^l alameenaa]

Al Jathiyah 45: 16 *We did aforetime grant to the Children of Israel the Book the Power of Command and Prophethood; We gave them for Sustenance things good and pure; and We favored them above the nations*

[wa faththalnahum a'la^l a'lameenaa].

*** Repeatedly, in numerous verses as shown, the Quran asserts that it was Allah who did the choosing ***

It was **not** the Israelites or the Jews who declared that they are the "Chosen People" but it was Allah after all who **favoured** the Children of Israel and asserted that he "***favored them above the nations***" ***

As usual in our series, we have pointed out the relevant, very clear verses of their Quran to **disprove** and put to rest the **lies** and **deceptions** perpetrated by the followers of Muhammad as they **contradict** their own holy Quran.

#63. No Compulsion in Religion

Q: Most of the followers of Muhammad who have read the Quran, invariably quote a particular verse to PROVE that Muhammadan Islam is both tolerant & peaceful.

Can you enlighten us?

A: As we repeatedly declare, out of necessity, that the Muhammadan Muslim agenda by those who wield authority and power is invariably **three** fold:

1. To deceive the people who are ignorant of the Quran into believing that it is a Divine revelation and hence must be Peace loving, Merciful & Compassionate, which of course it is not.

2. To **Mislead** those who have doubts about their own faith and might want to convert to **Muhammadan Islam**

3. To **indoctrinate** its own members into believing in the above so that they do not look for answers somewhere else.

They have succeeded in this subterfuge for the last **1400 years** and continue to do so for the time being.

Al Baqara 2: 256 Let there be no compulsion in religion. Truth stands out clear from error; whoever rejects evil and believes in Allah hath grasped the most trustworthy hand-hold that never breaks. And Allah heareth and knoweth all things

This is a beautiful and highly moral verse

"Let there be no compulsion in religion".

The greatest tragedy is that among the hundreds of millions of humanity both among both the Believers and the Unbelievers they

Lifting the Veil

do not know the **facts** or many, especially among the followers of Muhammad, are not even willing to **face** Reality.

Unfortunately, the Facts & Reality are actually so **ungodly** and **obscene** that it is our duty as well as the duty of all those who **know** to enlighten the world and make them aware of the current **deadly** situation.

Let us now explore the issues, point by point based entirely, as usual, on all the Arabic references that are available to all those who want to research the subjects at hand.

1 Almost all the conciliatory verses that emanated from **Muhammad's** mouth during the **Meccan** period were **Abrogated/ Unsikhoo** during his **Madinan** period and among them is the verse above. For those who may not know, **abrogation** means this verse was over ruled and made null and void by the later allegedly revealed verses.

*al Tauba 9:5 But when the forbidden months are past then **fight** **and slay the pagans** wherever ye find them and seize them beleaguer them and lie in wait for them in every stratagem (of war);*

29 Fight those who believe not in Allah nor the Last Day nor hold that forbidden which hath been forbidden by Allah and His apostle nor acknowledge the religion of truth [Islam] (even if they are) of the People of the Book [Jews & Christians] until they pay the Jizya [Poll Tax] with willing submission and feel themselves humiliated.

Al Imran 3:19 The Religion before Allah is Islam *(submission to His will):*

> *3: 75 And believe no one unless he follows **your religion***
>
> *3: 85 If anyone desires a **religion other than Islam** (submission to Allah) never will it be accepted of him*
>
> **** Can anyone listening to these verses **doubt** their meaning?*
>
> Where in these verses can one find **tolerance** and no **compulsion?**

Except of course, the believing followers of Muhammad ***

2 Muhammadan Islam is such a peace loving, tolerant and wise Belief System that it **sanctions** the slaughtering of any and all those who change their mind and try to opt out of it.

You don't believe me? You think I am exaggerating?

al nahl 16: 106 *Anyone who after accepting faith in Allah utters unbelief - except under compulsion his heart remaining firm in faith - but such as open their breast to unbelief on them is Wrath from Allah and theirs will be a dreadful Penalty.*

*** According to the Muhammadan exegetes, this verse clearly sanctions the killing or slaughtering of any who willingly and freely **apostatizes** ***

Sahih Al-Bukhari 9.17 Narrated by Abdullah

Allah's Apostle said, "The blood of a Muslim who confesses that none has the right to be worshipped but Allah and that I am His Apostle, cannot be shed except in three cases: In Qisas for murder, a married person who commits illegal sexual intercourse and the **one who reverts from Islam (apostate) and leaves the Muslims.**"

Sahih Al-Bukhari Hadith 9.57 Narrated by Ikrima & 9.58

Some **Zanadiqa (atheists)** were brought to 'Ali and he **burnt them.** The news of this event, reached Ibn 'Abbas who said, "If I had been in his place, I would not have burnt them, as Allah's Apostle forbade it, saying, 'Do not punish anybody with Allah's punishment (fire).' I would have killed them according to the statement of Allah's Apostle, **'Whoever changed his Islamic religion, then kill him.**

Changing one's mind after entering 'Muhammadan Islam' is punishable by decapitation and death. **It is the only Belief System ever that ordains the murder of a follower who wants to change his/her mind!**

Just like in the **MAFIA Crime Syndicates,** one can join,**but** one cannot leave and still breathe!

We rest our case.

64. Islam: Cult or Religion ?

Q: I am outraged and distressed that the Media & Academia call Muhammadan Islam a Religion when in fact it is a Cult.

The level of Political Correctness that permeates both of the Media & Academia is stifling and destroying people's ability to Question, to Debate and to Disagree about the subjects of Religion, Ethnicity, Race, Colour , etc.

Will you elaborate?

A: Political correctness has sunk the level of intellect, of enquiry, and of debate, to the abyss of utter stupidity and cowardice. Our series does its best, to correct this abject surrender, imbalance & abdication of logic & morality.

In the Oxford dictionary a **cult** is described as: A system of veneration and devotion, **directed towards a particular figure or object,** such as the cult of Stalin, Mao Tse Tung and others.

Religion, on the other hand, is the ideas, rituals and institutions, that bind a certain community or even a group of communities creating a distinctive tradition and belief system in worshipping a superhuman controlling power especially a **personal God** or gods.

Let us now look at just a few **references** as they are recorded in the Quran and Hadiths:

Al Baqara 2: 119   *Verily We have sent thee in truth as a bearer of glad tidings and a **warner [natheera].***

Al Imran 3: 132   *And obey Allah and the Apostle; that ye may obtain mercy.*

*** In numerous verses of the Quran, they instruct the followers of Muhammad to obey **Allah & his apostle.** That is, they must follow the Quran and Muhammad's **SUNNA.**

Moreover, all of the above verses assert that Muhammad is only a **warner** and bringer of Glad Tidings. The word **messenger/ rasool** does not appear in any of them ***

Al A'araf 7: 188 Say: *"I have no power over any good or harm to myself except as Allah willeth.* ***If I had knowledge of the unseen****, I should have multiplied all good and no evil should have touched me, I am but a **warner [natheera]** and a bringer of glad tidings to those who have faith."*

*** Muhammad asserts in the verse above that he is not even a **prophet** since he cannot **predict** the **future:** as he had no **knowledge** of the **unseen** ***

Sad 38: 65 Say: *"Truly am I a **warner [natheera]**: no god is there but the One Allah Supreme and Irresistible*

Al Ahqaf 46: 9 Say: *"I am no bringer of new-fangled doctrine among the apostles, nor do I know what will be done with me or with you. I follow but that, which is revealed to me by inspiration: I am but **a warner**, open and clear."*

*** This verse, is among one of the most important in the Quran since Muhammad is asserting that he is **not** bringing a **new religion** *"I am no bringer of new-fangled doctrine"* **nor** was he a **prophet** foretelling the future *"nor do I know what will be done with me or with you"* ***

Al Thariyaat 51: 51 And make not another an object of worship with Allah: I am from Him a **warner [natheera]** to you clear and open!

*** I would like our listeners to be aware that almost every verse above was allegedly revealed to Muhammad during his **Meccan conciliatory period** even if some of the verses appear mixed among the Madina ones as repeatedly and erroneously happened during the **compilation** of the Quran.

Most of these verses were subsequently **abrogated,** that is overturned or over ruled by several of the later ones from the Madina period ***

AlAhhZab 33:21 "You have indeed a noble paradigm in the Apostle of Allah." [A second translation reads:] "You have in (Muhammad) the Messenger of Allah a beautiful pattern of conduct for anyone to follow." [A third reads:] "Verily in the Messenger of Allah you have a good example for him who looks unto Allah and the Last Day." [A fourth reads:] "Certainly you have in the Messenger of Allah an excellent prototype." [A fifth says:] "You have indeed a noble paradigm [archetype, exemplar, standard, model, or pattern] to follow in Allah's Apostle."

33:36 "No Muslim has any choice after Allah and His Apostle have decided a matter."

*** It was during Muhammad's Madina period that he started associating himself **equally** with Allah with an unending number of **"Allah and His Apostle"** mantra

Sahih Al-Bukhari Hadith 8.689 Narrated by Said bin Ubada Al Ansari

that he consulted the Prophet about a vow that had been made by his mother who died without fulfilling it. The Prophet gave his verdict that he should fulfill it on her behalf. **The verdict became Sunna** (i.e. the Prophet's tradition).

Muwatta, 46/3

Muhammad said in his last sermon:

I leave with you the **Quran and** my **Sunn**a**h**

Sahih Al-Bukhari Hadith 9.381 Narrated by Hudhaifa

Allah's Apostle said to us: ... the Qur'an was revealed and the people read the Qur'an, (and learnt it from it) and also learnt it from the **Sunna."**

Both Qur'an and Sunna/ Prophet's Traditions, strengthened the faithful believers' honesty."

Ishaq:391 "O people, this is Allah's Apostle among you. Allah has honored and exalted you by him. So help him and strengthen him. Listen to his commands and obey them."

Ishaq:467 "Allah addressed the believers and said, 'In Allah's Apostle you have a fine example for anyone who hopes to be in the place where Allah is.'"

Tabari VIII:182 "The people assembled in Mecca to swear allegiance to the Messenger in submission. He received from them the oath of allegiance to himself, to heed and obey."

*** Hitler too, received the oath of allegiance to himself ONLY ***

Like all 'living' institutions, religion cannot stand still but has to adapt, evolve and change in order to survive.

Since the Quran and the Ahadith instruct his **male** followers to emulate Muhammad's deeds, behaviour and thought, as the ultimate manifestation of the **perfect man,** Muhammadan 'Islam' is not a **religion** but definitely the **Cult** of Muhammad

As a Cult, it remains and will continue to remain, stuck in the **TIME WARP** of the 7th Century ***

#65. Ka'ba or Solomon's Temple?

Q: According to the records of Muhammadan Islam, Muhammad, at the very beginning of his perceived mission, had greater veneration and regard to Jerusalem and the Temple of Solomon because he considered them holier than Mecca and its Ka'ba.

Will you explain?

A: Our readers should share with us the most astounding **facts** that in the Quran, the names of Mecca Madina & Jerusalem/Al Quds are **never** mentioned although they were supposed to have been the most important cities for the Pagans as well as for the Muhammadan Muslims.

On the other hand, the Bible mentions the name of **jerusalem** at least 667 times.

During his first **thirteen** years in Mecca, neither Allah nor Muhammad saw fit to tell their followers about any Qibla – that is the direction of prayers – towards Mecca.

When in c. 622AD Muhammad migrated to Madina, among the Judaized Arabs, he was very impressed with **two** of their most important traditions:

1. Fasting on Yom Kippur of the Jews, which was evidently observed then on tenth day (Ashurah) of Muharram

2. And their praying facing the direction [**qibla**] of Jerusalem. He instructed his followers to do the same. This lasted for about 16-17 months.

Leviticus 16:29 *" And this shall be a statute forever to you, that in the 7th month (Tishri), on the 10th day of the month, you shall afflict your souls, and do not work at all, whether it be one of your own country, or a stranger who sojourns among you"*

This day happens to also be the one during which the Shi'a commemorate the martyrdom of Husayn bin Ali and his followers at the hands of the Ummayad Caliph Yazid bin Mu'awiya.

Sahih Al-Bukhari Hadith 3.222 Narrated by Ibn Abbas

The Prophet came to Medina and saw the Jews fasting on the day of Ashura.

He asked them about that.

They replied, "This is a good day, the day on which Allah rescued Bani Israel from their enemy. So, Moses fasted this day."

The Prophet said, "We have more claim over Moses than you."

So, the Prophet fasted on that day and ordered (the Muslims) to fast (on that day).

***Since Moses was not an Arab, nor was he a descendant from the line of Ishmael, then by what stretch of the imagination could Muhammad and his Arabian followers claim more rights to him than the Jews?

This is one more example - if any more could possibly be needed - of Muhammad's Plundering, Plagiarizing, Pirating and/or Perverting all his ideas, concepts, precepts and thoughts from the Bible and the traditions of the Jews – as well as others - and put them in his Quran to suit his agenda of pretending to be the messenger of Allah following in the footsteps of the Hebrew Prophets ***

Sahih Al-Bukhari Hadith 3.223 Narrated by Abu Musa

The day of 'Ashura' was considered as 'Id/ Feast day by the Jews.

So the Prophet ordered,

"I recommend you (Muslims) to fast on this day."

All the Hadiths above assert that Muhammad only found out about the significance of **Ashura/ Yom Kippur after** he had arrived in Madina among the Judaized Arabs.

When Muhammad first arrived in Madina, he wanted very much to have the Judaized Arabs accept him as a prophet similar to the Hebrew ones of old.

The Hadiths above are crystal clear in confirming this statement.

The Judaized Arabs did not accept him as a prophet because he was not offering them a single new practical, spiritual, moral and or intellectual precept, concept, thought or idea that was in any way shape or form either equal to or superior to what they already had.

They knew that he was a **false pretender** to prophet-hood

And out of their **thousands,** only **two** of them **submitted** to Muhammad even when they knew they were going to be slaughtered.

This is the mark of true **martyrdom.** Not Muhammad's **ungodly** and **cowardly** version.

After 16-17 months of having failed miserably to 'convert' the Judaized Arabs of the Madina to his new Cult Belief System, he turned into their bitterest and most implacable enemy and made a 180* about turn thus instituting Ramadhan as the month of fasting and changed the direction of the Qibla from Jerusalem to Mecca.

Let us together with our readers ponder the following points:

The fact that Muhammad had the first Qibla towards Jerusalem, shows the immense reverence that he had for its holiness - more at that time – than he had for the Ka'ba which was associated in his Monotheistic mind purely with Paganism.

The word Qiblah appears first in *Al Baqara 2:142/5.* The Quran never mentions **Jerusalem** by name or even **Al Quds.** Since pre Islamic pagan Arabs had absolutely no affiliations or regard for Jerusalem and had no idea as to what it was or even where it was, they could not have faced Jerusalem in prayer prior to Muhammad.

The Quran does not ordain that at prayers, the Muhammadan Muslims should face Jerusalem; this is found only in the Ahadith. These acts of **convenient afterthought reversals** became the pattern in Muhammad's life as reflected both in his Quran and the Hadith verses.

If the Ka'ba was the original 'House of Allah' as the Quran asserts, then there is absolutely no logical or theological reason as to why Muhammad directed the **first** Qibla towards Jerusalem unless he knew and believed that it was holier than the Ka'ba, especially since neither Allah nor Gabriel had **instructed** him to do so in the first place.

Muhammad after all, chose the first Qibla towards Jerusalem, all by himself, **without** any prodding or hint from Allah or Gabriel.

To explain away his convenient politico/theological reversal and change of mind, he gave the untenable and lame excuses in the following verses-

Al Baqara 2:142 *The fools among the people will say: "What hath turned them from the Qiblah to which they were used?" Say: To Allah belong both East and West; He guideth whom He will to a Way that is straight.*

> **143** ...and We appointed the Qiblah to which thou were used only to test those who followed the Apostle from those who would turn on their heels (from the faith).
>
> **144** We see the turning of thy face (for guidance) to the heavens; now shall We turn thee to a Qiblah that shall please thee. Turn then thy face in the direction of the Sacred Mosque; wherever ye are turn your faces in that direction.

So presumably, it was all a 'test' for his followers. This is a stupid and meaningless excuse since there is no 'test' or challenge either intellectual or physical in changing one's direction of prayer. The Ahadith make it very clear that the change in the direction of the Qibla was acted upon immediately and without hesitation or questioning by his gullible and unthinking robot-like followers.

Sahih Al-Bukhari Hadith 1.392 & 9.358 Narrated by Bara bin Azib

Allah's Apostle prayed facing **Baitul-Maqdis** [Temple of Solomon in Jerusalem] for sixteen or seventeen months but he loved to face the Ka'ba (at Mecca) so Allah revealed:

"Verily, We have seen the turning of your face to the heaven!" (2.144) So the Prophet faced the Ka'ba ...

*** If Muhammad truly **'loved' to face the Ka'ba** in the first place, why then did he not do so? After all, no one had put a sword to his neck to force him to face 'Jerusalem'.

Neither the Quran nor Gabriel had instructed him or directed him to face the 'Sham' to begin with. There was no *'revelation'* pertaining to such a Qibla.

It was Muhammad who **unilaterally** decided to face the direction of the **Temple of Jerusalem** because in the Meccan period and the very early Madinan period, he truly believed in the **primacy** of Jerusalem and Solomon's Temple over the Ka'ba, **which was still harbouring the pagan rock gods of Arabia.**

Muhammad only changed his mind about the Ka'ba when he realized that the Judaized Arabs were not going to change their religion and believe in his version of Islam nor in him as the prophet of Allah.

He therefore conveniently & instantly told his followers that a Made to Order 'revelation' from Allah has changed the Qibla towards the Ka'ba, his **secondary** choice, so as to placate his Quraiysh tribe also***

#66. Gabriel or Jibril

Q: According to my research, the Arabic name Jibril [angel Gabriel] was plagiarized by Muhammad from the Syriac language of the Christian Bible since it was not known to the pagan Arabs.

Will you tell us why & how the angel Gabriel became Islamized by Muhammad?

A: Muhammad's knowledge of the Hebrew Bible and the New Testament was based **entirely** upon **apocryphal** stories that he had heard from Priests, Rabbis or story tellers. Being **ignorant** of the facts, he got most of them mixed up in his Quran as we have shown repeatedly in our series.

Of the 1.4 Billion followers of Muhammad that exist today, not more than a few hundred people can tell us where and when the angel Gabriel first appeared in the Bible and what his actual **Hebrew** name is and what it means.

Muhammad too, was obviously totally ignorant of all of the above. The most important item that stuck in his mind, was that the angel Jibril was the messenger of God who **revealed** to Mary the arrival of Jesus as the **redeemer** of humanity.

Being the consummate desert **pirate** that he was, he not only plundered the wealth, produce and lives of others but **graduated to plundering, plagiarizing, pirating & perverting** the **thoughts, precepts, concepts** and **ideas** of other people and **claimed** them to be his own.

Our readers should bare in mind a most important and relevant piece of information that the followers of Muhammad do not mention for obvious reasons:

That the first men & women from the tribes of the Aus & Khazraj from the Madina who swore allegiance to Muhammad, although they were pagan to start with, they were none the less, very intimately related by blood and intermarriage to the **Judaized Arabian tribes in Madina.**

They were hence very receptive to the concept of a **Messiah** who would appear in the religions of **both** the Jews & Christians. Muhammad was not working out his **Cult Belief System** in a vacuum.

Since these men and women were mostly Illiterate, Superstitious and very Ignorant of the contents of the Bible, Muhammad was clever enough to **deceive** them into believing that he too was a prophet following in the footsteps of the earlier Hebrew ones.

Sunan of Abu-DawoodHadith 2159 Narrated byAbdullah Ibn Abbas

Ibn Umar misunderstood (the Qur'anic verse, "So come to your tilth however you will")--may Allah forgive him. The fact is that this clan of the Ansar, who were idolaters, lived in the company of the Jews who were the people of the Book. They (the Ansar) accepted their superiority over themselves in respect of knowledge, and they followed most of their actions. The people of the Book (i.e. the Jews) used to have intercourse with their women on one side alone (i.e. lying on their backs). This was the most concealing position for (the vagina of) the women. This clan of the Ansar adopted this practice from them.

By associating himself with the Ishmaelite branch of Abraham and by alleging that the Arabs were descended from that branch, he became in their mind, **the Arabian version of the promised Hebrew Messiah.** Muhammad has been getting away with his **deception** to this day.

I would like to share some very simple **logic** with our listeners by pointing out the following:

1. Let us assume for arguments sake, that Allah of the Quran is actually God

2. That Allah is the same god as that of Moses & Jesus

3. The Quran asserts **repeatedly** that it was Allah who revealed the **Taurat/ Torah** – Face to Face – to Moses **kalimu^allah** and the **injil/gospels** to Jesus

4   That they are all **preserved** incorruptible with him in heaven

5   The Quran also states that it was the angel Gabriel who revealed even earlier revelations to the other prophets of the Quran such as Noah, Abraham, Job, King Solomon etc

Let us now **examine** these Quranic statements, one by one:

1   In which language did Allah reveal the Taura to Moses and later the Gospels to Jesus?

2   Since, as every one who has studied Christianity knows, that the Gospels were written **after** the death of Jesus, then how can the Quran assert that they were revealed to him in his lifetime?

3   Since **both** the Taurat & the Gospels are **true** revelations from Allah, then how can **anyone** explain all the contradictions, discrepancies, historical & theological dislocations and contortions that fill the Quran when comparing its stories with the same events in their **Original** form in the Bible, the very **first** revelation?

4   Why would the angel Jibril/Gabriel, who predicted the arrival of the Messiah Jesus, change his message and claim that Muhammad was the one?

5   How is it logical to accept and believe, that the same angel Gabriel would **deny** the **death** of Jesus on the cross?

6   No where does the Bible mention any other **books** that were revealed to any of the Hebrew prophets besides Moses

7   Can any follower of Muhammad give us the names of the other **revelations** in **book** form to the other prophets of the Quran and where they are?

I can go on reciting at least 60-70 other differences but I believe that the above are enough since finding an answer to them would also be an answer to all of the others.

It is **inconceivable** to believe, accept, agree or even **imagine,** that the Quran could have been revealed to Muhammad by the **same** Gabriel as that of the Bible or that the god who instructed him to reveal its contents is the same as the God of Moses & Jesus.

It is **not** up to us, the so called **unbelievers** to **prove** our **veracity** because the **burden** of proof actually resides with the followers of Muhammad to provide the answers to these questions and anomalies, based entirely on **facts,** if that is at all humanly possible.

We await with great anticipation, any and all comments that may emanate from the followers of Muhammad.

#67 Dilemma of Muhammadan Muslims

Q: We have so far explored a lot of facets of Muhammadan Islam. More will be forthcoming. What I find difficult to understand is the almost total inability of the followers of Muhammad to face facts, truth & reality

Can you explain?

A: As I mentioned on several previous occasions when we were accused of being anti Muslims, that our exploration of the Quran and Hadiths is **not** an attack on believing Muhammadan Muslims but at the **mendacities, hatemongering, warmongering & racism** that fill the verses of the Quran which is supposed to be a divine revelation. Well, it is **not** a divine revelation! and no amount of **denial** by the followers of Muhammad can change a jot of the **facts** that it is **not**.

I would like those followers of Muhammad who listen to this series to know that we are not **against** them as individual human beings. We cannot be since they are its **worst victims** to start with.

We are, nonetheless, totally against their Cult Belief System that instructs them to **hate** us; to **war** against us; not to have us as their **friends;** to **discriminate** against us; to **betray** us, to **humiliate** us; to **subjugate** or to **slaughter** us.

It is a **fact** that it was Muhammad who **unilaterally** declared this war against us 1400 years ago as well as against ALL human beings who do not believe as he does.

Since those Muhammadans who are listening to our series **must** or **should** know these **facts** based entirely on the Arabic language of the Quran and Hadiths, why would they think that these instructions are morally and intellectually acceptable?

How could they believe that they could have possibly emanated from any Merciful & Compassionate god who created us in the first place?

What would they do, think and feel, if it was our Beliefs that ordained the indiscriminate Slaughter of the men, women and children of the followers of Muhammad just because they do not believe in Christianity or Buddhism or Hinduism and are not willing to convert to them?

I have no doubt that all our of listeners understand the immense difficulty of trying to **disbelieve** decades of **indoctrination.** The followers of Muhammad are the worst **victims** of the most **diabolical** intellectual, moral & spiritual deception that has ever been perpetrated upon the human consciousness by the Quran & Hadiths.

They have been brought up to believe in the utter **supremacy** of Muhammadan Islam. They are not **allowed** to study other Religions.

They are not **allowed** to Question their own Belief System

Throughout the history of Muhammadan Islam, all those who questioned the Quran were slaughtered, burnt or exiled from their own lands.

We do not even need books to read about these facts since we see their **depraved** acts daily on our **TV** and read about them in the news.

We fully understand and empathize with those followers of Muhammad who are confused and do not know whom to believe and what course of action to take.

We also appreciate their loyalty to their families and culture that would inhibit them from taking any action contrary to their traditions and sense of honour.

While we do sympathize and take all of the above into account, none the less, **every** human being has been given the **intellect** to comprehend, compare, contrast, analyze and then make an independent evaluation of one's situation at any time in their life.

The followers of Muhammad, Contrary to the teachings of the Quran, have the **free will to chose**. No god or divinity has Pre **destined** their lives, because Pre-Destination makes religion **null & void**.

The first humans, according to the Bible & the Quran were Adam & Eve. They were **forbidden** by the Almighty from eating of the fruit of the **tree of knowledge**. They were given a **choice**: to **eat** or **not** to **eat**. To **break** God's commandment or to **obey** it.

There was no Pre **destination,** because Predestination **excludes** Free Will. Without Free Will, there is no Choice.

The serpent or Satan did **not** threaten their lives or force them into breaking God's instruction.

Eve Chose to eat. Adam chose to follow Eve. Maybe they chose **wrong;** none the less, they made an intellectual & moral choice.

The same choices are available to those who are borne into Muhammadan Islam, or any other belief system. They have **all** the information available to them at the click of a 'Mouse'. They can choose another belief or they can choose none. If one believes in a god or not will not ever detract from one's humanity. **One can be a believer but a mass murderer and another can be an atheist but a saint.**

The greatest **fear** that those among the followers of Muhammad who want to change, is the fear of being **slaughtered** by their own brothers or sisters for apostatizing.

I would have thought that this **fact** alone shows the **depravity, inhumanity, injustice & Immorality** of a Belief System that FORBIDS one from **choice.**

Why, if Muhammadan Islam is such an allegedly great Belief System, resort to **violence & terror** to keep its followers in line?

I repeat, that as much as we do understand the **unenviable** situation and predicament of those borne into Muhammadan Islam, none the less, those Muhammadans who are citizens of democracies **do** have a **choice** and cannot hide behind any excuse except that they do not have the **will to choose** and hence remain till the end of their lives **hostages** to an **evil** and **ungodly** Cult Belief System.

#68. Hagar & Ishmael

Q: According to the original and only story in the Bible pertaining to Ishmael's ancestry, Hagar was the mother of Ishmael and the servant of Sarah.

Her name - as the mother of the most illustrious forefather of the Arabs, Ismail - is conspicuously and surprisingly absent from the Quran.

What are the facts?

A: You are of course correct in saying that the name of Hagar is **never** mentioned in the Quran **but** this should not be a surprise to anyone who has studied it or listened to our series.

After all, the following extremely important names are also absent from the All Knowing Quran: Mecca, Madina, Jerusalem, Sarah – the wife of Abraham & Eve, the mother of humanity.

As we have amply and repeatedly shown, the Quran is a **tossed salad of plagiarized, plundered, pirated & perverted , precepts, thoughts, concepts** and **ideas** from the Bible, New Testament, Pagan Arabian religion & Zoroasterian Persian religion, their fetishes, their traditions and their scriptures.

Muhammad in his Quran, conveniently & mendaciously, **islamized** all of them pretending they are **novel** and Newly Created Concepts & Revelations.

We **all** know, based entirely on the evidence at hand, that these are pure **fabrications & lies.**

In the whole Biography of Muhammad, *'Sirat Rassool^l Allah' by Ibn Ishaq*, the name of Hajar, the mother of Ishmael is not mentioned at all also.

In fact, the name Hagar/Hajar appears only once in the interpretations section of the ***Quran by Abdullah Yusuf Ali*** to explain ***al Baqara 2:158, note 160.*** According to imaginary & falsified Arab 'traditions', Hagar & Ishmael - in this case as a baby and accompanied in their exile by Abraham - had their thirst quenched at the well of Zamzam, near Mecca, almost 1000 desert miles away from Beer Sheba in Canaan.

According to the Torah - which is after all the **original** and **only** source of the story – Hagar & Ishmael found water near Beersheba and not in the desolation of Arabia near Mecca.

The alleged Arab traditions – which are of course totally unfounded, unsubstantiated and contrary to the historical and archaeological records - Canaan and Mt Sinai too are in Arabia.

Let us now visit the **original** and **only** source in the Bible:

***Genesis 16. 1.** Now **Sarai Abram's wife** bore him no children; and she had a maid servant, an Egyptian, whose name was Hagar.2. And Sarai said to Abram, Behold now, the Lord has prevented me from bearing; I beg you, go in to my maid; it may be that I may obtain children by her. And Abram listened to the voice of Sarai.3. And Sarai Abram's wife took **Hagar her maid** the Egyptian, after Abram had lived ten years in the land of Canaan, and gave her to her husband Abram to be his wife.4. And he went in to Hagar, and she conceived; and when she saw that she had conceived, her mistress was despised in her eyes.5. ....*

Abram said to Sarai, Behold, your maid is in your hand; do to her as it pleases you. And when Sarai dealt harshly with her, she [Hajar] fled from her face.7. And the angel of the Lord found her by a fountain of water in the wilderness, by the fountain in the way to Shur.8. And he said, Hagar, Sarai's maid, where did you come from? and where will you go? And she said, I flee from the face of my mistress Sarai.9. And the angel of the Lord said to her, Return to your mistress, and submit yourself under her hands.....

11. And the angel of the Lord said to her, Behold, you are with child, and shall bear a son, and shall call his name **Ishmael**; because the Lord has heard your affliction.12. And he will be a wild man; his hand will be against every man, and every man's hand against him; and he shall live in the presence of all his brothers.

....15. And Hagar bore Abram a son; and Abram called his son's name, whom Hagar bore, Ishmael.16. And Abram was eighty six years old, when Hagar bore Ishmael to Abram.

Genesis 21. 1. And the Lord visited Sarah as he had said, and the Lord did to Sarah as he had spoken.2. For Sarah conceived, and bore Abraham a son in his old age, at the set time of which God had spoken to him.

3. And Abraham called the name of his son who was born to him, whom **Sarah bore to him, Isaac**.4. And Abraham circumcised his son Isaac being eight days old, as God had commanded him.5. And Abraham was a hundred years old, when his son Isaac was born to him

...8. And the child grew, and was weaned; and Abraham made a great feast the same day that Isaac was weaned.9. And Sarah saw the son of Hagar the Egyptian, whom she had born to Abraham, mocking.

10. And she said to Abraham, Cast out this slave and her son; for the son of this slave shall not be heir with my son, with Isaac.11. And the thing was very grievous in Abraham's sight because of his son.

12. And God said to Abraham, Let it not be grievous in your sight because of the lad, and because of your slave; in all that Sarah has said to you, listen to her voice; **for in Isaac shall your seed be called.**13. And also of the son of the slave will I make a nation, because he is your seed.14. And Abraham rose up early in the morning, and took bread, and a bottle of water, and gave it to Hagar, putting it on her shoulder, and the child, and sent her away; and she departed, and **wandered in the wilderness of Beersheba.**

15. And the water was spent in the bottle, and she cast the child under one of the shrubs....17. And God heard the voice of the lad; and the angel of God called to Hagar from heaven, and said to her, What ails you, Hagar? fear not; for God has heard the voice of the lad where he is.18. Arise, lift up the lad, and hold him in your hand; for I will make him a great nation.19. And God opened her eyes, **and she saw a well of water; and she went, and filled**

the bottle with water, and gave the lad to drink.**20*. *And God was with the lad; and he grew, and lived in the wilderness, and became an archer.21. And he lived in the **wilderness of Paran; and his mother took for him a wife from the land of Egypt.

*** Believers & Unbelievers, should take note of the following important items when comparing the Quranic version of the same events with the Biblical originals above:

1. Ishmael was born in Canaan near Beersheba to a Hebrew father and an Egyptian mother.

2. God repeatedly asserts that **only** Isaac is deemed the Divinely elect son and **not** Ishmael.

3. **Only** the seed of Isaac was to inherit the Blessing of the Promised Land.

4. Ishmael was a teenager of over 14 years of age when he and his mother were sent away from Abraham's tribe and **not** the **baby** that the Quran asserts he was.

5. Ishmael and his mother Hagar, resided there after in the 'wilderness of Paran', in southern Canaan, and **never** in the Arabian Peninsula near the Ka'ba or Mecca.

6. Neither the Ka'ba nor Mecca or Allah are ever mentioned in the Bible. It stands to reason that, if the god of the pagan Arabs, Allah, was the same as the God of Israel, He would have at the very least mentioned their name somewhere in His Torah.

7. Abraham **never** visited the Ka'ba nor Mecca in the Biblical narrative.

8. Abraham, Ishmael and Isaac had no knowledge of a god called Allah.

9. Abraham, Hagar and the 'baby' Ishmael **never** went to the Ka'ba or to Mecca according to the **original** and **only** Biblical story.

10 Since the Torah, as asserted by the Quran itself, was revealed **directly** to Moses "Kalimu^l Allah" by Allah, and is considered **divine**, it beggars logic and intellect to believe that Allah - if he were the **God of Israel** - would have revealed **two contradictory versions of the same events.**

11 If Ishmael were the elect of Allah instead of Isaac, why are **all** the prophets of the Bible from the seed of Isaac and none from Ishmael's seed?

In conclusion, it is self evident as usual, that the Quranic stories are unfounded, untrue, inauthentic and total lies and no follower of Muhammad in the world can, based on **all** the knowledge that is available to every one, disprove our accusations or statements ***

Hom

#69. Ilm or Knowledge

Q: We are reminded repeatedly by the followers of Muhammad, of the immense contributions that the Muhammadan Muslims had given to humanity. That this was because Muhammad in his Quran instructed them to do so.

What are the facts?

A: **Islamists** and **Muhammadan Muslims,** invariably quote the following and similar verses in the **Quran** to perpetuate the myth that **'Islam'** encourages **all** branches of **knowledge: of Sciences, Philosophy, Medicine, Art, etc.**

They deliberately and very understandably ignore the fact, that **Muhammad,** his tribe and the **Arabs** of the **Hijaz** especially, were among the most uncivilized, generally illiterate and ignorant people in that part of the world **although surrounded** by many of the **oldest and greatest civilizations.**

Al Zummar 39: "9 .... Say: "Are those equal those who know [ya'alamoona] and those who do not know [la ya'alamoona]? It is those who are endued with understanding that receive admonition."

The **knowledge *[ilm]*** that is alluded to in the verse above, as well as in those in the **Ahadith,** refers to **religious knowledge only**, and not the branches of knowledge of **Sciences, Philosophy, Medicine, Art, etc., since all of the latter contradict the traditions**, especially pertaining to the creation and other natural items mentioned in the **Quran.**

Muhammadan orthodoxy does not encourage unrestricted intellectual inquiry, since it is deemed dangerous to the faith of the believer. The best **knowledge** that is accepted by the **tradition,** is the one that is helpful for the **practice of religion,** and ONLY **religion**

Lifting the Veil

Ibn Khaldun, the historian & philosopher - a true **Muhammadan Muslim;** born in Tunisia 1332 AD - reminds us, that **Arabs** did not play a great part in the development of **'Islamic Science'**:

" It is strange, that **most of the learned among the Muslims who have excelled in the religious or intellectual sciences, are not Arabs,** even those with rare exceptions; and even those savants who claimed Arabian descent, spoke a foreign language, grew up in a foreign land and studied under foreign masters"

Al-Tirmidhi Hadith 257 Narrated by Abdullah ibn Amr

Allah's Messenger happened to pass by two groups (of Muslims) in the mosque and he said: Both of them are good, but one is superior to the other. One group is supplicating Allah and praying Him. If He so wills He will confer upon them and if He so wills He will withhold. So far as those who are **acquiring the understanding of religion** and its **knowledge *[ilm]*** and are busy in teaching the ignorant, they are superior. Verily I have been sent as a teacher (of religion).

Al-Tirmidhi Hadith 259   Narrated by Anas ibn Malik

Allah's Messenger said: Do you know who is most generous?

They said: **Allah and his Messenger know best.**

Whereupon he said: Allah is the Most Generous, then **I am most generous** to mankind, and the most generous people after me would be those who will acquire **knowledge *[ilm]*** (of religion) and then disseminate it.

*** Muhammad makes it crystal clear that the **knowledge** he is alluding to is **Knowledge** of **religion only** ***

Al-Tirmidhi Hadith 279 Narrated by Abdullah ibn Mas'ud

Allah's Messenger said to me: Acquire the **knowledge *[ilm]*** and impart it to the people. Acquire the **knowledge *[ilm]* of Fara'id (laws of inheritance)** and teach it to the people, **learn the Qur'an and teach it to the people...**

Al-Tirmidhi Hadith6111 Narrated by Anas ibn Malik

The Prophet said, "The most compassionate member of my people towards my people is AbuBakr, ... the one who knows best how to recite the **Qur'an** is Ubayy ibn Ka'b, and the one who has most **knowledge [ilm] about what is lawful and what is prohibited** is Mu'adh ibn Jabal. ..

*** **Knowledge** in this instance as in all of the above - has nothing to do with science or literature but only with information regarding religious beliefs since all these men were **memorizers** of the Quran ***

Sunan of Abu-Dawood Hadith 2879 Narrated by Abdullah ibn Amr ibn al-'As

The Prophet said: **knowledge [ilm]** has three categories; anything else is extra; a precise verse, or an established **sunnah** (practice), or a firm obligatory duty.

*** All the above **Knowledge/Ilm** pertain **only** to **religious knowledge** ***

Sahih Al-Bukhari Hadith1.75 Narrated by Ibn Abbas

Once the Prophet embraced me and said, "O Allah! Bestow on him the **knowledge [ilm]** of the **Book (Qur'an)."**

Sahih Al-Bukhari Hadith 1.98   Narrated by Abu Huraira

'Umar bin 'Abdul 'Aziz wrote to Abu Bakr bin Hazm, "Look for the knowledge of Hadith and get it written, as I am afraid that **religious knowledge [duroos^l Ilm]** will vanish and the **religious learned men [Ulamaa]** will pass away (die). Do not accept anything save the **Hadiths of the Prophet.** Circulate **knowledge [Ilm]** and teach the ignorant, for **knowledge [Ilm]** does not vanish except when it is kept secretly (to oneself)."

*** There are hundreds more of the same that confirm the fact that **ilm / knowledge** in the Quran refers invariably to the sciences of the Quran and Hadiths; that is, to **religious knowledge** only.

It is very important to point out to our listeners that almost **all** those who **excelled** in the none religious sciences under the umbrella of Muhammadan Islam were **free** thinking & Secular men who broke away from the intellectual chains that bind the absolute majority of the Muhammadans to the **Dark Ages of Muhammad's 7th century Arabia.** Many of them were murdered, burnt, imprisoned or exiled.

Neither the Muhammadans – for obvious reasons - nor the Politically Correct in Academia and the Media make the world aware of these **facts.**

Nothing of value can ever grow under the **oppressive** and **grave** shadow of **Fundamentalist Muhammadan Islam.**

That is why, in the last **700 years** of human history, not even a handful of the hundreds of millions of the followers of Muhammad have contributed anything of value to the advancement of human civilization in any worthy field.

That is why also, that in the **21st century,** the most backward, least intellectually productive people in any and all branches of human knowledge, are among the **1.4 Billion** followers of Muhammad.

Ladies & Gentlemen, please be aware that the very best example of the most perfect **Fundamentalist Muhammadan Muslim** state was that of the **Taliban** in Afghanistan.

A state of **perpetual terror, ignorance, fear, stupidity, irrationality, injustice, immorality & most assuredly, ungodly**.

Reality and facts are the best at demonstrating the veracity of what we recite***

#70. Read or Recite

Q: Most people, when reading the Arabic of the Quran, are confused regarding Muhammad's alleged first encounter with the angel Gabriel.

Did Gabriel instruct Muhammad to Read or to Recite and what are the differences if any between the two words?

A: The **Oxford Dictionary** makes a very important **distinction** between **Reading & Reciting-**

Read: **Look at and comprehend the meaning of (written or printed matter)** by mentally interpreting the characters or symbols of which it is composed.

Recite: **Repeat aloud** or declaim (a poem or a passage) from **memory** before an audience.

In the **Arabic** language also, there are **TWO** distinct words describing the two actions of **Reading & Reciting-**

IQRA means to **Read**. That is to read from a **document** or from **writings.**

Yatloo on the other hand, means to **Recite**. That is to declaim words from memory.

Iqra is actually the first word of the first verse/aya of the first chapter/sura of the **Quran** but for **ungodly** reasons during the compilation of the **Quran,** it was relegated to the **96th Sura** instead.

Surat Al A'laq 96:1 "Proclaim! (or Read!) in the name of thy Lord and Cherisher Who created *2 Created man* out of a (mere) *clot of congealed blood (Leech):*

In Arabic: Iqraa bismi rabbika^l Lathee khalaqa

khalaqa ^l insana min alaq

*** As usual in hundreds upon hundreds of important verses in his Quran, Muhammad, once more, plagiarized and used the story of a vision in the Bible - ***Isaiah 29:11 & 40: 6*** - that was taught to him by either a learned Jew or a Christian - to dramatic effect as the first of his Quranic 'revelations' in his alleged confrontation with the angel Gabriel as depicted in the altered version of events in...

Bukhari Hadith 1.3:"......suddenly the Truth descended upon him **[Muhammad]** while he was in the cave of **Hira**. The angel came to him and asked him to **read [Iqra]**. The Prophet replied,

"I do not know how to read."

The Prophet added, "The angel caught me (forcefully) and pressed me so hard that I could not bear it any more. He then released me **and again asked me to read** and I replied,

'**I do not know how to read.**'

Thereupon he caught me again and pressed me a second time till I could not bear it any more. He then released me and **again asked me to read** but again I replied,

'**I do not know how to read** (or what shall I read)?'

Thereupon he caught me for the third time and pressed me, and then released me and said,

'**Read [Iqra]** *in the name of your Lord, who has created man from a clot.*

This version of the alleged story of *'revelation'* produces **TWO** extremely contentious and important question marks that have to be pointed out that require some logical answers:

a) It is **inconceivable** to accept, based on theological grounds alone, that the angel Gabriel, the supreme messenger of Allah, **did not already know** that Muhammad could not **read.**

b) It goes even beyond **credibility or logic,** that the angel Gabriel could have 'revealed' to Muhammad a completely **different** version of the creation of man to that found in its original in the **Bible.**

It is a measure of the complete lack of **veracity** and **accuracy** of the **Quran** that its first verse ever, displays a remarkable ignorance of the **Biblical** story of the **creation** of **Mankind;** after all, he was created from **dust** and **not** a **clot.**

The same **Torah,** that the **Quran** itself repeatedly asserts to have been the word of **Allah, is perverted and given a completely different version.**

Why would **Allah** give **TWO completely and utterly incompatible versions** of His own creation story to two different messengers of His

(**Moses** and presumably **Muhammad**)?

It is utter **blasphemy** to imply that **Allah - if Allah is the God of Israel & Jesus -** could be so inconsistent about the method of His own creation.

According to the Ahadith (stories about the sayings and way of life of Muhammad), **he was unable to read and write.** This is totally contradicted by the report mentioned in

Ibn Ishaq's *"Sirat Rasullullah"* the first biographer of his life (c 130AH), about **120 years** after his death.

In this very first and **original** version of the alleged encounter between **Muhammad** and the angel **Gabriel,** the angel actually produced

"a coverlet of brocade whereon was some **writing**".

(A. Guillaum's *'The Life of Muhammad'* p106).

Hence, verse **96:1** can **only** make sense if **Muhammad** could **read** what was **written** on the coverlet. This would obviously change the whole state of affairs - as deliberately **altered & falsified** by the later Muhammadans - dramatically and fundamentally.

Our readers should be aware that, since **Ibn Ishaq** was both an **Arab** and a **Muhammadan Muslim and was historically the nearest to the sources of information,** his report should have obviously **greater reliability** than the ones that were **mass produced** much later.

He cannot be accused of **fabrication** as a **foreigner** or as an **enemy of Muhammadan Islam.**

When **Gabriel** ordered him to **Read/Iqra, Muhammad** asked him correctly and sensibly, *" What shall I read"?*.

Since the coverlet had **writings on it,** as **Muhammad** himself asserts, then it is obvious and totally rational to assume that **Gabriel** wanted him to read the writing on the coverlet. Why else would **Muhammad,** on three consecutive occasions reply by asking **Gabriel** *"What shall I read?"*.

The astoundingly **simple** conclusion, based upon Muhammad's answer alone by asking Gabriel with *"What shall I read?"* instead of the altered versions of *"I cannot read", asserts* the fact that he **could read**.

In the altered version of the story, the answer *"I cannot read"* is totally meaningless implying the **utter stupidity and ignorance** of **Gabriel** regarding **Muhammad's** ability to read or not.

Our readers should be aware that for doctrinal and theological reasons, the later followers of Muhammad had done their best to **obfuscate** and **confuse** their followers and others as to the real meaning of the words depicting to **read** and to **recite.**

This is **confirmed** in the altered and corrupted texts of Bukhari Hadith 1:3 & 9:111,

Hence, in our analysis and investigation to discover the **facts** we must address the meanings of both words individually and thoroughly even if we have to repeat certain ideas more than once.

A.1) Let us assume to start with, that **Bukhari's** version of events is the **factual one** and that **Iqra** does mean **READ; that is to read from the words from a document or writings.** Hence the logical question to be asked yet again is:

how is it possible or logical that the angel of **Allah** did not know that **Muhammad** was unable to read? That he was illiterate?

Moreover, according to the above version of the event, the **Hadith** does **not** mention any **item or document** that was displayed by **Gabriel** for **Muhammad** to **READ from.**

A.2) Now we take **Bukhari's** version and assume that **Iqra** means **RECITE, that is to repeat from memory.**

In this manner also, **Muhammad's** answer *"I cannot read"*, or in this instance, *"I cannot recite"* **makes absolutely no sense** since **Gabriel** had not **yet** informed him of the **Quranic** verses to recite and **Muhammad** was obviously at a loss as to what he was supposed to recite and hence Muhammad should have replied

" What should I recite"?

Once more, we have to come to the unavoidable conclusion that, **Gabriel, Allah's** messenger was yet again, being depicted as **ignorant** and **clueless.**

B.1) Now, let us investigate, in the same manner, **Ibn Ishaq's original** version of the events and that **Iqra** means to **READ**, to start with.

When **Gabriel** ordered him to **Read/Iqra - implying the writing on the coverlet - Muhammad** asked him correctly and sensibly, *" What shall I read"* ? because maybe he was not sure. In this case **Gabriel** obviously and correctly, knew that **Muhammad could read.**

B.2) But, if **Iqra** in this instance meant **RECITE**, **Gabriel's** command and **Muhammad's** answer *" What shall I recite"* ? becomes once again meaningless and irreconcilable since **Gabriel** had, we reiterate again, not told **Muhammad** the **Quranic** verses that he wanted him to **RECITE**, rendering **Gabriel**, once again, as **ignorant** and **clueless.**

We have now covered all the possible versions of the event resulting in only **one** version that can possibly make any sense whatsoever, which is

B.1,

Ibn Ishaq's original, wherein **IQRA** means to **READ** the writings from the coverlet.

Lifting the Veil

What is most important in all of the above analysis and investigation, is the fact, that the original story as given by **Ibn Ishaq** - who was after all the **first and nearest writer** to the events that transpired during the life of **Muhammad** - had been materially, linguistically and grammatically, **deliberately** altered and tampered with to suit the subsequent theological arguments to fit the **dogma** of the **'divine'** source of the **Quran.**

Hence **Gabriel's** request **WAS** correct since actually, **Muhammad** was able to **READ.**

#71. Good or Bad Muslims

Q: So called moderate Muhammadan Muslims, many academicians as well as the media, tell a generally ignorant world that those who are committing suicide bombings, mass murder, slaughter, decapitations etc are not true Muslims. They are the extremists; the radicals.

From my own understanding of the Quran & Hadiths, this is an absolute fallacy. Can you elaborate?

A: Your assessments are perfectly correct. The world is being deliberately deceived by the so called Moderate Muhammadan Muslims while the Media & Academicians are betraying us through their will full **ignorance** bordering on criminal negligence & stupidity.

Let me tell you the **facts** in a Nutshell:

1. The very best Muhammadan Muslims are JIHADI Warmongering, Hatemongering & Intolerant Racist ones such as Osama bin Laden, al Zawahiri, The mullas of Iran etc.

2. The very best type of a Fundamentalist Muhammadan form of government is that of the Taliban of Afghanistan and the Mullas of Iran. Muhammadan Islam is totally & irreconcilably **anti democratic, racist, intolerant, ignorant** & full of **hate.**

3. The very **worst** type of Muhammadan Muslims are ones who believe in a **"Live & Let Live"** state of affairs; ones who can have as friends Christians, Hindus, Buddhists, Jews, Sikhs & Animists. Ones who although they believe in Allah as the one and only god, do not subscribe to the depraved and inhumane, immoral & unjust Shari'a rules and doctrines.

Now let us **together** explore in detail the **reasons** for the above statements, based entirely on the Quran or Hadiths:

Warmongering **Jihadi** Muhammadan Muslims have to follow and abide by the following **few** samples of Quranic verses:

Al Nisaa 4:89 – *"They wish that you would reject Faith, as they have, and thus be on the same footing: Do not be friends with them until they leave their homes in Allah's Cause (Jihad). But if they **turn back from Islam**, becoming renegades, **seize them and kill them** wherever you find them."*

Al Tauba 9:38 – *"Believers, what is the matter with you, that when you are asked to march forth in the Cause of Allah (Jihad) you cling to the earth?* ***Do you prefer the life of this world to the Hereafter?"**.......*

44 – *"Those who believe in Allah and the Last Day do not ask for an **exemption from fighting (in Jihad)** with your goods and persons. And Allah knows well those who do their duty."*

88 – *"The Messenger and those who believe him, strive hard and **fight jihad** with their wealth and lives (in Allah's Cause)."*

Muhammad 47:20 – *"Those who believe say, 'How is it that no surah was sent down (for us)?' But when a categorical (decisive or uncompromising) surah is revealed, and **fighting and war (Jihad, holy fighting in Allah's Cause)** are ordained, you will see those with diseased hearts looking for you (Muhammad) fainting unto death. Therefore woe unto them!".*

Tabari IX: 13 – *"Muhammad turned to see Umm, a pregnant woman, who said, "O Messenger!* ***Kill those (Muslims) who flee from you as you kill those who fight you***, *for they deserve death. Here is my dagger. If any come near me I will rip them up and slit open their belly with it!".*

We would like our readers to be aware of the **subtle** but actually **vital** differences between what Muhammad in his Quran calls all those Arabs who were **not** willing to fight in his cause as **hypocrites** or **unbelievers** while the Judaized and Christainized Arabs are called **disbelievers** and/or **hypocrites**.

Al Nisaa 4:97 – *"Verily, when angels take the souls of those who die wronging themselves (by staying at home) they say: 'In what*

(Jihad) were you?' They reply: 'Weak on the earth.' Such men will find their abode in Hell, and evil resort!".

Al Tauba 9:68 – *"Allah has promised the **Hypocrites,** both men and women, and the **disbelievers** the **Fire of Hell** for their abode: Therein shall they dwell. It will suffice them. On them is the curse of Allah, and an enduring punishment, a lasting torment."*

75 – *"Some of you made a deal with Allah, saying, 'If you give us **booty** we shall pay You the tax.' But when He gave them booty, they became greedy and refused to pay..."*

120 – *"It is not fitting for the people of Medina and the Bedouin Arabs to refuse to follow Allah's Messenger (Muhammad when fighting in Allah's Cause **(nor to prefer their own lives to his life).....***

Ishaq:603 – *"Some Bedouins came to apologize for not going into battle, but Allah would not accept their excuses".*

Muhammadan Islam is all about **terror, fighting, plundering, booty & slavery.** There are no **redeeming** of **saving graces** anywhere in over 6000 verses of the Quran.

The best teachers about Muhammadan Islam are the horrible **deeds, actions** and **public pronouncements** that the world watches and reads in all forms of the Media, by the followers of Muhammad.

The followers of Muhammad **never** miss a chance **not** to shoot themselves in the mouth. They are the very best advertisers of the REAL qualities and **actual** aspirations of Muhammadan Islam to **rule** the world by the use of indiscriminate **terror & force.**

It was Muhammad who pitted sons against fathers, brothers against sisters, clans against clans and Arabian tribes against Arabian tribes finally ending with the current state of affairs whereby Muhammadan Muslims are against 80% of humanity.

Ibn Ishaq in his Sirat Rassool Allah P204, reports:

When the people came together to plight their faith to the apostle, al Abbas al Ansari pointed out –

"O men of Khazraj, do you realize to what you are committing yourselves in pledging your support to this man?

<u>It is to WAR against all and sundry</u>"

*** The above Hadith is remarkable because it shows that even 1400 years ago, among the most ignorant and uneducated people, there were some who realized the enormity of the future consequences of following Muhammad's dictates***

Tabari VIII:130 – The Messenger said, "**Two religions cannot coexist in the Arabian Peninsula**". Umar investigated the matter, then sent to the Jews, saying: 'Allah has given permission for you to be expelled'.

Pursuant these instructions, the Arabian followers of Muhammad unto this day, consider the Arabian Peninsula a sacred land not to be polluted by any and all other religions which are not allowed to practice their faith under any circumstances unless they do it in **private** and in specially enclosed areas.

So much for the alleged **tolerant** and **peaceful** characteristics of Muhammadan Islam that they repeatedly ram down our throat in spite of all obvious proofs to the **contrary.**

Muhammadan Islam is **Intolerant, Ractist. Discriminatory, Immoral & Unjust** and no one can dispute these assertions based entirely upon their books, facts & reality.

#72. Promised Land in the Quran

Q: The Promised Land for the Israelites is of course mentioned only in the Bible.

The Quran too, echoing the Bible, asserts that it was Allah who Promised the land to the Israelites in very clear and precise Arabic verses.

So, on what grounds do the Arabs claim the land of Israel as well as the whole of Arabia as their own?

A: The land of Israel was promised by God in very clear Biblical verses to the descendants of **Isaac ONLY**.

The expressions **Promised Land** or **Land of Promise** (al Arth al Mow'ouda or Arth al Mi'ad) do not appear in such manner in the Quran, but in the Arabic translation of the Bible.

In the Quran, the Promised Land or Land of Promise is mentioned in:

Al Ma^idah 5:21 '*O my people! enter the **holy land [Al Artha al Muqadassa]** which Allah hath unto you assigned **[Allah had written/kataba Allah lakum]** and turn not back ignominiously for then will ye be overthrown to your own ruin.*

*** Muqadassa/ Holy is from the Hebrew (Qodesh) and is not Arabic in origin since the Arabs used the term Muharrama/Forbidden regarding their holy places.

This verse is extremely important since it verifies and confirms the claim of the Jews to the land of Israel***

22 "They said: "O Moses! in this (land) are a people of exceeding strength: never shall we enter it until they leave it: if (once) they leave then shall we enter..... He said: "O my Lord! I have power only over myself and my bother so separate us from this rebellious people!" 26 Allah said: "Therefore will (the land) be out of their reach for forty years; in distraction will they wander through the land: but sorrow thou not over these rebellious people."

*** All the Quranic verses of this *Sura* are obviously not found in the same manner in the Bible. They are all **composed, altered & recited** from Muhammad's own fertile **imagination** ***

Al A'araf 7:137 And We made a people considered weak (and of no account) **inheritors of lands [al arth] in both east and west** lands whereon We sent down our blessings. **The fair promise of the Lord was fulfilled for the children of Israel** because they had patience and constancy and We levelled to the ground the great works and fine buildings which Pharaoh and his people erected (with such pride).

*** By *"both east and west lands"* the Quran affirms the Biblical narrative that assigned the Promised Land among the Twelve tribes of Israel on **both** sides of the river Jordan ***

Yunus 10:93 We settled the **Children of Israel in a beautiful dwelling-place** and provided for them sustenance of the best: it was after knowledge had been granted to them that they fell into schisms. ..

*** This is Muhammad's re phrasing of the Biblical description of the Promised Land as a "Land of Milk & Honey" ***

Al Israa 17: 104 "And We said thereafter to **the Children of Israel "Dwell securely in the land : [uskunoo^l Ardtha]** but when the promise of the Final Days come to pass We shall gather you together in a motley crowd.

Al Noor 24: 55 "Allah has promised to those among you who believe and work righteous deeds that He will of a surety grant them in the land inheritance

[la-yastakhlifannahum fi^l ardthi] (of power) as He granted it to those before them; that He will establish in authority their religion the one which He has chosen for them...

Al Roum 30:6 (It is) the promise of Allah. **Never does Allah depart from His promise:** but most men understand not.

*** Since Allah - *"Never does Allah depart from His promise"* - then the claim by the Arabs and the followers of Muhammad to the land of Israel is obviously **null & void** ***

Genesis 17: 7 *And I will establish my covenant between me and you and your seed after you in their generations for an everlasting covenant, to be a God to you, and to your seed after you.8. And I will give to you, and to your seed after you, the land where you are a stranger*, **all the land of Canaan, for an everlasting possession;** *and I will be their God*

9. *And God said to Abraham...This is my covenant, which you shall keep, between me and you and your seed after you; Every male child among you shall be circumcised...*

12. *And he who is eight days old shall be circumcised among you, every male child in your generations, he who is born in the house, or bought with money from any stranger, who is not of your seed......*

20. *And as for Ishmael, I have heard you; Behold, I have blessed him, and will make him fruitful, and will multiply him exceedingly; twelve princes shall he father, and I will make him a great nation.*

21. But my covenant will I establish with Isaac, *whom* **Sarah** *shall bear to you at this set time in the next year"*

*** Since the alleged Arab *'traditions'* are derived entirely from the Bible - the pagan Arabs having had no knowledge of the Biblical events before Muhammad's Quran - then they should accept the crystal clear fact, that the Land of Promise was for the Israelites only, just as the Quran itself also asserts***

Furthermore, it is alleged that Muhammad instructed that

"Two religions cannot exist in the country of Arabia"

from Hidaya B9 c 8

and subsequently, almost all the **Judaized and Christianized Arabs** were expelled from their own native lands by the followers of Muhammad

So the Arabs claim **BOTH Arabia & the Holy Land** as theirs contrary to the historical records and the religious ones.

All the Arab & Muhammadan *'theological'*, historical and political contortions cannot, should not and must not be allowed to succeed ***

#73. Apostacy Wars

Q: We are assured by the followers of Muhammad, that the Pagan Arabs accepted Muhammad's Islam because of its sublime, moral, spiritual & judicial messages.

How true are these claims?

A: In Arabic, the word for Apostasy is **RIDDA** which means the renunciation or abandonment of a religious or political belief or principle.

Apostasy in Muhammadanism (**irtidad or ridda)** is commonly defined as the rejection of Muhammad's version of Islam in word or deed by a person who has been a Muhammadan Muslim.

When Muhammad died, Abu Bakr was chosen by a very small clique of Muhammad's companions to take over the leadership of the Muhammadan Muslim community called Al Khalifa. However, many Bedouin tribes that had converted to Muhammad's version of Islam through **terror, bribery** or **greed,** refused to recognize Abu Bakr's leadership.

They regarded their allegiance to the Muhammadan Muslim community as having been a personal allegiance to Muhammad himself – hence, when Muhammad died, so did their allegiance. In **fact,** this was the reality.

Abu Bakr refused to accept this and launched the Wars of the **Ridda, or wars of Apostasy,** in order to combat and defeat the many apostates who existed throughout the Arabian Peninsula. Eventually, through slaughter and mass murder, Abu Bark was able to re-impose the authority of **Muhammadan Islam** once again, upon the **unwilling** Arabs of the Peninsula under the leadership of Mecca.

All major schools of Islamic jurisprudence agree that a **sane male apostate must be killed.** A female apostate may be put to death, according to some schools, or imprisoned, according to others.

It is clear from the verses of the Quran that "the apostate is threatened with punishment in the next world only" however "in traditions, there is little echo of these punishments in the next world ... and instead, we have in many traditions a new element, the death penalty, by decapitation, in this world"

Al Baqara 2: 217 *.. And if any of you turn back from their **faith** [yartad] and die in **unbelief [kafiroo]** their works will bear no fruit in this life and in the Hereafter; they will be Companions of the Fire and will abide therein*

*** The jurist Al-Shafi'i, interpreted this verse as providing the main evidence for apostasy being a capital crime in Islam ***

Al Baqara 2:256. *"Let there be no compulsion in religion: Surely the Right Path is clearly distinct from the crooked path."*

*** This particular verse is used by the modern followers of Muhammad to **deceive** those **ignorant** of the **facts** about Muhammadan Islam.

The unwary are of course unaware that this particular verse, among another **120 conciliatory verses,** were **abrogated/overturned** by the subsequent more devastating **fighting & aggressive** verses of the Madina Period. In this manner, people would be lulled into believing that Muhammadan Islam is a truly peaceful Belief System ***

Al Imran 3:90 *"But those who reject **Faith [kafaroo]** after they accepted it, and then go on adding to their defiance of Faith,- never will their repentance be accepted; for they are those who have gone astray. As to those who **reject Faith [kafaroo]**, and die **rejecting [kuffaroo]** ,- never would be accepted from any such as much gold as the earth contains, though they should offer it for ransom"*

Al Nisaa 4: 89 *[the Hypocrites] but wish that ye should **reject faith [kafaroo]** as they do and thus be on the same footing: but take not friends from their ranks until they flee in the way of Allah. But **if they turn renegades seize them and slay them [wa-qtuloohum] wherever ye find them;** and (in any case) take no friends or helpers from their ranks.*

137 *"Those who believe, then reject faith [kafaroo], then believe (again) and (again) reject faith [kafaroo], and go on increasing in unbelief,- Allah will not forgive them nor guide them on the way."*

Al Tauba 9:5 *But when the forbidden months are past then* ***fight and slay the pagans wherever ye find them*** *and seize them beleaguer them and lie in wait for them in every stratagem of war...*

Al Nahhl 16:106-109 *"Any one who, after accepting faith in Allah, utters* **Unbelief [kafara],-** *except under compulsion, his heart remaining firm in Faith - but such as open their breast to Unbelief, on them is Wrath from Allah, and theirs will be a* **dreadful Penalty.** *This because they love the life of this world better than the Hereafter... Without doubt, in the Hereafter they will perish."*

*** **Al Nisaa 4: 89** is the clearest instruction to kill those who turn away since they are considered treators.

The Sharia' follows in fact the SUNNA of Muhammad ***

Article 18 of the Universal Declaration of Human Rights.

"Everyone has the right to freedom of thought, conscience and religion; this right includes freedom to change his religion or belief, and freedom, either alone or in community with others and in public or private, to manifest his religion or belief in teaching, practice, worship and observance."

Article 306 of the Mauritanian Constitution-

"**If a Muslim is found guilty of the crime of apostasy, either** through words or through actions, he will be asked to repent during a three day period. If he has not repented within this time limit, **he will be sentenced to death as an apostate** and his property will be seized by the Revenue office.

Every Muslim who refuses to pray will be asked to comply with the obligation to pray within the prescribed time limit. If he persists in his refusal, **he will be punished by death.**"

*** Muhammadan Islam is the **only ' belief system' in the world** that mandates the murder of anyone who joins it but later changes one's mind and decides to leave it.

If it were such a great and *'peaceful religion'*, why act with such depraved indifference and brutality towards the conscience of the individual? ***

Sunan of Abu-DawoodHadith 4487 Narrated byUthman ibn Affan

AbuUmamah ibn Sahl said: We were with Uthman when he was besieged in the house. ..He came out to us, looking pale.

He said: They are threatening to kill me now.

We said: Allah will be sufficient for you against them, Commander of the Faithful!

He asked: Why kill me? I heard the Apostle of Allah say:

It is not lawful to kill a man who is a Muslim except for one of the three reasons:

Kufr (disbelief) after accepting Islam, fornication after marriage, or wrongfully killing someone, for which he may be killed. I swear by Allah, I have not committed fornication before or after the coming of Islam, nor did I ever want another religion for me instead of my religion since Allah gave guidance to me, nor have I killed anyone. So for what reason do you want to kill me?

*** Uthman bin Affan, the third Khalifa was subsequently murdered by other so called Muslims ***

Ladies & gentlemen, the **facts** as recorded by the Muhammadans themselves prove that most of the Bedouin Arabs who had rallied out of fear to the banner of 'Islam' under Muhammad, changed their mind after his death.

It took almost two years of bloody fighting under the first Khalifa, Abu Bakr and under the generalship of Khalid Ibn al Walid, the mass murderer called **(The Sword of Allah),** to subdue, subjugate and force those secessionists and apostates to return them - once more

- to the fold of **peaceful** 'Islam'; but of course, not through dialogue & conviction, but at the point and edge of **swords.**

Contrary to all the platitudes, disinformation, misinformation, lies and falsifications of the historical records conducted by the followers of Muhammad, his version of 'Islam' was born by the shedding of a **SEA** of blood in the Arabian Peninsula, followed by the shedding of an **OCEAN** of blood of millions of subjugated, humiliated and plundered peoples on three continents.

Muhammadan Muslim bloodshed by bombs, guns and swords continues to this day, not only against so called 'Unbelievers' but also against other **believers** as we see daily in the news media, all over the world***

#74. Muhammad's Psychological Profile

Q: We have shown in our series so far the full extent of the falsehoods, the mendacities, the hatemongering & warmongering that fill the chapters of Muhammad's Quran.

To understand the reasons for all the above characteristics, we must understand Muhammad's background which would explain his psychological profile

A: You are correct since to fully understand **Muhammad**, his sayings and his deeds, one must study his formative life and his experiences as he grew up. Everything he did in his life depended entirely upon his upbringing and the influences of the people who took care of him as he matured.

Muhammadans tell us all kinds of myths and fairy tales about the childhood of their religious founder **Muhammad.** The reality is that these are no better than make believe stories and fables old women tell their grandchildren.

Unfortunately these stories have been adopted into the mainstream of **'Muhammadan Islam'** as **irrefutable fact.**

'Abd al-Muttalib was Muhammad's grandfather, from the Quraiysh tribe in Mecca. He traded with **Syria** and the **Yemen** and had obtained certain profitable privileges at the pagan shrine of **Mecca.** It was he who supplied the pilgrims with food and water. He had a number of wives from different tribes who gave him ten sons, **Muhammad's** father and uncles, as well as six daughters.

One of these children was **'Abdallah.** His father, no doubt seeking an alliance with the clan of the Banu Zuhra, asked for the young **Amina bint Wahb** as a bride for his son. **Muhammad** was the first and only child of this marriage.

Muhammad's father **Abdallah** died, either during his wife's pregnancy or shortly after her delivery. He left his wife very little, only one slave, five camels and a few sheep. **Amina** gave her son to a suckling woman called **Halima**. **Amina** died later when **Muhammad** was only six years old.

'Islamic' Myths about Muhammad-

Nothing is known for certain about **Muhammad's** childhood.

The void was gradually filled with legends that grew ever more beautiful and edifying with the passage of time. Even the earliest and most moderate accounts, must be treated with great caution and suspicion.

When **Muhammadan Islam** became the religion of a powerful Empire, precepts were needed to regulate social life. Divergent opinions and interests naturally existed. Political parties also grew up, centered round **Muhammad's** family and **Companions.**

In addition, a great many people - impelled by curiosity, piety or even historical interest - demanded information about **Muhammad's** life. Men began to appear who were professional repositories of traditions; **actually, inventors of stories;** they would spread a tale to satisfy this curiosity or that piety, or to provide a ruling as occasion demanded; for **Muhammad's** deeds and sayings had an exemplary value.

Like the modern historians, the keepers of tradition were expected to quote their sources; **but these were oral ones.** Such a story came from such a one who in turn heard it from another, and so on all the way back to one of **Muhammad's** contemporaries who had seen him do it or heard him say it.

It was of course a very simple matter to make up **false traditions** (the **Arabic** word **Hadith,** meaning `narratives') to support one's own party or opinion.

The **Muhammadan** records show that the great **Arab** historians and jurists **knew this perfectly well.** They tried to do away with the false traditions - those, for example, where the chain of authorities cited was manifestly impossible - **but they made no**

claims to any degree of certainty. Instead, they were content to repeat contradictory traditions on the same subject, one after the other, quoting their sources for each. It was up to the reader to decide which one he liked to believe. **'But Allah knows best'**, they would often add.

The oldest collections of historical traditions available to us date from about **125 years** after **Muhammad's** death.

Much imagination had gone to work in the meantime. And yet, many facts can be established, as the parties who differ most widely are agreed on the main events of the **Muhammad's** life.

Unfortunately there are many points on which we are very far from certain; in particular, it is clear that extremely little was known about the early years of **Muhammad's** life, and that much has been made up about it.

According to the **Qurayshites'** custom, the young **Muhammad** had a nurse from a nomadic clan. In this way, it was thought, the children of **Quraysh** would be filled with the pure air of the desert and grow strong.

Muhammad's nurse was a woman called **Halima,** of the clan of the **Banu Sald,** a branch of the great tribe of **Hawazin.**

Muhammad's mother died when he was six years old. His grandfather, the venerable **'Abd al-Muttalib,** who was then eighty years old, took him to live with him. But he died two years later.

Muhammad was then taken in by one of his uncles, **Abu Talib.** He was a merchant in comfortable circumstances, and is said to have been the person who took over the leadership of the **Hashim** clan.

Muhammad seems to have remained a bachelor for longer than was usual among his people. The reason for this was probably poverty. He asked, it is said, **Abu Talib** for the hand of his cousin **Umm Hani.** Marriages between cousins were approved of in **Bedouin** society; but the suitor was rejected, probably in favour of a more illustrious rival.

This is virtually all we know about the childhood and young manhood of **Muhammad**, at least from the earliest sources, before the proliferation of legends & myths of all kinds grew out of all reasonable control.

No matter what the **'facts'** of his upbringing are, what we have on hand is more than enough to build a realistic picture of **Muhmmad's** childhood and upbringing.

From the very beginning, he did not have an auspicious start to life. **Muhammad** was totally deprived of any parental love and affection as well as the security and warmth of belonging.

Neither his soul nor his body were properly nourished. He was not necessarily attended to when he cried.

He did not get picked up, hugged, cuddled and sweet loving words whispered in his ears.

He did not have a father figure to love him, guide him, play with him and make him feel protected and secure.

He did not have the love and warmth of his mother's body and sense of belonging that every child needs.

It is impossible for a surrogate mother, a grand father or an uncle to show as much love, affection, understanding and comprehension of a child as a father and mother.

Any child growing up under these **desolate spiritual and physical depravations cannot and will not mature into a humane and normal human being.** **Muhammad** ended up as a spiritually empty vessel with no understanding of **love, compassion** or **mercy.** His condition in modern medical terms is that of:

Pathological Narcissism.

In verse after verse in the **Quran,** it is always towards **Muhammad** that they point. **Allah** is only used as the **'divine threatening whip'** to put his followers in line. The verses of the **Quran** instruct **Muhammad's** followers:

That they should obey him blindly and unquestioningly;

that they should follow whatever example he may set **(his Sunna);**

that they should believe that he is the messenger of **Allah;**

that they should know that he **Muhammad,** is superior to any and all other **Arabs** - if not humanity;

that he **Muhammad,** has intercessory powers with **Allah;**

that revelations come to him whenever and wherever he needs them;

that **Allah** hates the enemies of **Muhammad** in even greater measure than **Muhammad;**

that everything **Muhammad Covets, Wants, Needs** or **Lusts** for is made **Halal** to him by the will of **Allah** through the usual convenient and **MADE To ORDER 'revelations';**

that all those who do not believe in him or insult him will end up **Dead - usually Murdered -** and their bodies will suffer the eternal and numerous tortures of **Allah's Hell;**

that he is the beloved of **Allah;**

that the enemies of **Muhammad** are automatically the enemies of **Allah** (there is no difference in the association)

that even the gossip of his wives is monitored by **Allah;**

that he is in touch with the angel **Gabriel** a lot of the time especially when a necessary **'revelation'** is required;

that those who die fighting at the behest of **Muhammad** will go to a **Paradise** full of **sensual** and **carnal** pleasures with **males OR females** infinitely more rewarding than anything on **Earthly Life.**

*** When the verses of the Quran are studied carefully, anyone who knows the different characteristics of **Pathological Narcissism** will be able to - without any difficulty whatsoever - to fit one or more of them, perfectly, with verses from the Quran.

It is inconceivable that any **Omniscient, Compassionate & Merciful** God would have revealed all the **Anomalies, Inconcistencies, Incongruities, Contradictions,**

Misinformation, Grammatical Errors, Disinformation, Absurdeties and **Mendacities** that fill the verses of the Quran.

All these facts can be **Fully** and **Easily** explained, the moment the listener comes to the **only** logical conclusion possible:

That every letter, every word, every verse/Aya and every chapter/Surah in the Quran are the product of **Muhammad's** own imagination, his

ALTER EGO,

but cleverly projected into the **UNSUSPECTING** mouth of **Allah, the Supreme Rock god of Pagan Mecca,** embedded in the corner wall of the **Ka'ba,** called the **BLACK STONE.**

Hence, Allah, the Rock god of Pagan Arabia and the Quran, is **not** and cannot be the God of Israel, of Christianity, of Zoroaster or of anybody else.

Neither could a rock **'reveal'** anything to anyone.

The **Conundrum** is now immediately and very logically **resolved:** The **Quran** is **Not** divine

Muhammad, Allah, Gabriel & Satan are **ALL** one and the same: **Muhammad himself** ***

#75. Plagues or Commandments ?

Q: Will you please explain how Muhammad, the greatest of all the prophets, with his usual keen intellect, was able to mix up the Ten plagues of Egypt with the Ten Commandments at Mt Sinai?

A: Like **eveything** else in his **Quran**, **Muhammad's** comprehension of the **Biblical** stories was minimal to say the least. He invariably got them mixed up both in **time & space.**

The stories of the **Ten Plagues and the Ten Commandments** are very clearly portrayed in the **Bible.** They are totally **incomprehensible** and in **error** in **Muhammad's Quran** as we shall presently show.

What shall transpire even worse than these errors are the attempts by the **Muhammadan** scholars of the **Quran** to **brazenly** explain the unexplainable with **lies, deception** and contortion of both **Facts** and **Religion.**

We would like to point out to our listeners, especially those who are followers of **Muhammad,** that there is not a single **Quranic** verse in the following examples that represents anything actual from the **original Biblical** story. All of the following dialogue and story lines were created by **Muhammad** himself.

*Al Isra 17: 101 To Moses We did give **NINE** Clear Signs: ask the Children of Israel*

*** Well, we asked the **Children of Israel,** just as Muhammad requested, and they told us that to start with, the clear signs/ Miracles were **TEN** in number and not **NINE** ***

*Al Naml 27: 9 "O **Moses!** verily I am Allah the Exalted in Might the Wise!...*

10 "Now throw down thy rod

12 *"Now put thy hand into thy bosom and it will come forth white without stain (these are) among the **nine Signs** (thou wilt take) to **Pharaoh** and his people.*

Al A'araf 7: 130 *We punished the people of **Pharaoh** with years (of drought) and shortness of crops; that they might receive admonition.*

*** I would like to remind our readers that the stories of the Seven good and Seven bad crop years were in the days of Joseph and not Moses, a lapsed period of almost 400 years. Muhammad was wrong as usual, yet again***

Al A'araf 133 *So We sent (plagues) on them **wholesale death (1); Locusts (2); Lice (3); Frogs (4); and Blood (5):** signs openly Self-explained*

> **134** *Every time the penalty fell on them they said: "O **Moses!** ... if thou wilt remove the penalty from us we shall truly believe in thee and we shall send away the **children of Israel** with thee."*
>
> **135** *But every time We removed the penalty*
>
> *from them ... they broke their word!*
>
> **136** *So We exacted retribution from them: We drowned them in the sea because they rejected Our signs and failed to take warning from them.*
>
> **137** *And We made a **people [the Israelites]** considered weak (and of no account) inheritors of lands in **both east and west lands** whereon We sent down our blessings. The fair promise of the Lord was fulfilled for the **children of Israel** because they had patience and constancy*
>
> **138** *We took the **children of Israel** (with safety) across the sea.*

1091 The translator of the Quran, Abdullah Yusuf Ali, who is extremely knowledgeable in the Bible, none the less, enumerates with deliberate falsehood the following signs/miracles that allegedly befell Egypt:

The NINE Clear Signs are: (1) the Rod (vii. 107), (2) the Radiant Hand (vii. 108), (3) the years of drought or shortage of water (vii, 130), (4) short crops (vii. 130), and the five mentioned in this verse, viz., (5) epidemics among men and beasts, (6) locusts, (7) lice, (8) frogs, and (9) the water turning to blood.

*** Ladies & Gentlemen, anyone who has read the **original** Biblical version would immediately realize that the so called miracles of the Rod, the Radiant hand, the years of draught and shortage of water are **not** in the story of the Exodus.

The Bible recites the following Plagues:

Water turning to Blood; Frogs; Lice; Swarm of wild beasts; Epidemic; Boils; Hail; Locusts; Darkness & finally the Death of the First Born; making **TEN** plagues and not **NINE** ***

Muhammad's acquaintance and knowledge of many of the important precepts and concepts of the **Bible and Apocrypha** is impressive in its broadness but extremely deficient in its understanding; none the less he made use of them in his **Quran** as the basis of his legislation.

From the very beginning, the foundation stones of **Muhammadan Islam** reside in the two commandments of the **Hebrew Decalogue, the Ten Commandments of the Torah:**

Genesis 20:3 "There is no God but God ; There is no image or likeness to God"

This should bring to the attention of the listeners the incredible similarity also between **Muhammad's Shahada/Testimony,**

"there is no God but Allah" (Surah 3:18 & 13:30)

and the **Hebrews' Shema'**

"Hear O Israel, the Lord God is only one Lord" (Deut.6:4).

I.Q. Al Rassooli

The **Quran** states that **Allah** gave **Moses** certain monitions on tablets (of stone), and also that he gave him **nine clear signs.** (Surah vii. 145, and Surah xvii. 103.) These two statements have perplexed the **Muhammadan** commentators very much, and every effort is made by them to reconcile the **nine signs** with the **Ten Commandments,** although it is evident from the **Quran** itself, that the **nine clear signs** actually refer **ONLY** to the miracles of **Moses. [Plagues Of Egypt]**

According to the **Muhammadan** traditions, **Muhammad** was very confused in the matter and was **himself** responsible for the mistakes of the commentators on his book, for it is related in **Mishkat al-Masabih** (book i. c. ii. pt. 2) which is the improved version of <u>Masabih al-Sunnah</u> **by** <u>Al-Tabrizi</u> **that:**

"A **Jew** came to **Muhammad** and asked him about the *nine (sic)* wonders which appeared by the hands of **Moses.**

Muhammad answered him: "Do not associate anything with **Allah** (1) do not steal (2) do not commit adultery (3) do not kill (4) do not take an innocent before the king to be killed (5) do not practice magic (6) do not take interest (7) do not accuse an innocent woman of adultery (8) do not run away in battle (9) and especially for you, **O Jews**, not to work on the **Sabbath** (10)"

*** Muhammad was of course his **usual & understandable** ignorant self, in **error** on **five** of the items he mentioned as well as having given the **wrong** answer to the question which related to the **ten** plagues and **not** the **Ten Commandments** ***

Al Muhaddith `Abdu 'l-Haqq al Dehlawi remarks on this tradition that the **Jew** asked **Muhammad** about the **nine** *(sic)* miracles (or plagues) of Egypt **BUT Muhammad** answered him in **error** with the **Ten Commandments.**

A comparison of the **Ten Commandments** given by the great **Hebrew** law-giver **Moses** with those recorded in the above tradition, and in the *6th Surah* of the **Qur'an,** *verse 152,* will show how imperfectly **Muhammad** was acquainted with the **Biblical** scriptures.

Lifting the Veil

The commentator **Husain**, who wrote four hundred years ago, says that the following verses in the ***Suratu 'l-An`am (vi.)*** are those **Ten Commandments** which in every dispensation are incumbent on mankind, and cannot be abrogated (meaning undoubtedly the **Ten Commandments** from **Moses**).

Al An'am 6: 151 "SAY: Come, I will rehearse what your Lord hath made binding on you –

(1) that ye assign not aught to Him as a partner:

(2) that ye be good to your parents:

(3) that ye slay not your children

(4) and that ye come not near to pollutions, outward or inward:

(5) that ye slay not anyone whom Allah hath forbidden you, unless for a just cause.

(6) Come not nigh to the substance of the orphan but to improve it, until he came of age:

(7) Use a full measure, and a just balance

(8) And when ye give judgment, observe justice, even though if be the affair a kinsman,

(9) Fulfill the covenant of Allah.

(10) Follow not other paths lest ye be scattered from His path. This hath He enjoined so that we may fear Him"

Compare the above with the Biblical Ten Commandments:
1. ***Exod. 20:3*** You shall have no other gods beside Me

2. ***Exod. 20:4*** You shall make no graven images....

3. ***Exod. 20:7*** You shall not utter the name of God in vain.

4. *Exod. 20:8* Remember the Sabbath day....

5. *Exod. 20:12* Honour your father and mother...

6. *Exod. 20:13* You shall not murder...

7. *Exod. 20:13* You shall not commit adultery...

8. *Exod. 20:13* You shall not steal...

9. *Exod. 20:13* You shall not bear false witness...

10. *Exod. 20:14* You shall not covet your neighbour's wife...

In conclusion, Ladies & Gentlemen-

There is no human being on Earth who can show a single verse in Muhammad's Quran that represents a new intellectual, moral, spiritual and original Concept, Precept, Thought or Idea, which in any way shape or form, is **equal** to or **superior** to these that **Muhammad Plagiarized, Plundered, Pirated and/or Perverted from the Hebrew Bible.**

#76. Debating Muhammadans

Q: According to the huge amount of mail that we receive from our audience, they encounter exactly the same extremely frustrating, ignorant and totally unrealistic replies and comments from the followers of Muhammad in defense of their Quran and beliefs.

A: We have been asked to explain this phenomenon, hence I would like to recite two very **APT** examples that are relevant to this chapter:

In Bukhari Hadith *Volume 2. 667:* Narrated 'Abis bin Rabia: 'Umar ibn al Khattab came near the **Black** 'Umar ibn al Khattab came near the **Black** Stone and kissed it and said: **"No doubt, I know that you are a stone and can neither benefit anyone nor harm anyone. Had I not seen Allah's Apostle kissing you I would not have kissed you."**

It is very revealing that although Umar knew that the gesture was empty and false he nonetheless copied Muhammad in kissing the stone! Just like Umar, most Muhammadans follow **blindly & unthinkingly** their leader in their shameful practice of venerating what was and continues to be a pagan ritual as well as all the other practices, thoughts & deeds of Muhammad.

Further more, to explain away the incompatibilities of the stories as depicted in the Quran vis a vis their originals in the Bible, the earlier Muhammadan scholars in general, alleged that the People of the Book, the Jews and Christians had altered/corrupted the meaning and or interpretations of their Holy Books.

Unfortunately, his later followers, because of their enormous frustration in trying to reconcile these irreconcilable differences, started the process of character assassinating the Holy Books of the Jews and Christians by alleging that their **texts** were actually perverted, altered and doctored at least one thousand years before - or even after- just to deny Muhammad and his Quran their rightful position as a prophet and scripture of Allah!

Besides being a preposterous and disgusting allegation, neither the Quran nor any of its followers can substantiate any of their uncorroborated, hatemongering, asinine, baseless, desperate and infantile allegations.

Theirs, are acts of intellectual, literary, historical and theological perversions and fraudulence resulting from their desperate need to explain away the unexplainable.

None the less, these allegations have become part and parcel of their dogma justifying them to slaughter, dispossess, plunder, subjugate or force into conversion the People of the Book.

Like all criminals, the Muhammadan exegetes **project upon their victims** –the Jews and Christians in this particular case- the very characteristics, deeds and perversions that they themselves actually possess, exhibit and do. It is, after all, easier to claim that one's opponent is a fraud without having to prove that they are.

The word used by Muhammadan writers for this supposed corruption/alteration of the sacred Scriptures of the Jews and Christians is *Tahrif [Corruption]*.

What is actually astounding, and contrary to these allegations, is that it is a documented fact that most of the early Muhammadan exegetes, understood Tahrif to mean altering the Meaning but not the Text of some of the Biblical verses

It was **Ibn Hazm** (994/1064 born in Cordoba, Spain), in his *Al-Fisal fi al-Milal wal-Ahwa wal-Nihal,* who carefully built a case for the verbal corruption of the biblical text because he could not accept that the Quran could possibly be wrong.

In psychology, this is called **Projective Identification** where by the criminal accuses his victim of his own intended criminal action. To explain away the unacceptable, Ibn Hazm alleges that the Bible is not a message from Allah which contains some erroneous passages and words, but is of the status of an anti-Scripture, "an accursed book," the product of satanic inspiration.

His conclusions marked a departure from the prevailing opinion before his time and was followed by subsequent writers only with careful qualifications. Although the majority of later polemicists rejected Ibn Hazm's conclusions as extreme, by the strength of his argumentation he influenced all subsequent polemical literature.

I gave these two examples as an illustration of the incredible power of **belief** in denying **facts, reality, logic & intellect.**

Our listeners must appreciate that if many of the most educated scholars of Muhammad Islam could subscribe to such **imbecile** logic, how can we blame the mostly **unlearned** and generally **unthinking** ordinary men & women followers of Muhammad in believing otherwise?

Their only escape from **reality** is **denial! denial! denial!** Even when you quote to them Chapter & Verse of their own scripture, because admitting to any of our revelations is tantamount to **religious suicide!**

That is why when our audience or ourselves have a discussion with a follower of Muhammad **it has to go through the following sequence:**

We are first accused that we do not read/ write Arabic and hence cannot possibly know what we are discussing

When we point out that our mother tongue is Arabic and that we do read & write it, they go to the next line of defense

It is not good enough to read the Quran because you must study it. We inform that we have.

Have you studied at the hands of a Muslim scholar who would explain to you the hidden and elaborate meanings of the verses?

We do not need anyone else to explain the meaning of the verses of the Quran since we are reading it in our own mother tongue.

OK where are your references upon which you are basing your allegations?

But we have been quoting to you Chapter & Verse from the Quran and Hadiths. These **are** the references.

I.Q. Al Rassooli

You are lying. You are deliberately perverting the noble message of the Quran by taking everything out of context. You must quote from reliable sources.

What other more reliable sources are there than the Quran & Hadiths that you believe in?

You are anti Muslim, a Christian Kafir or a Zionist Imperialist dirty Jew bastard!

End of communication **NEXT!**

This may sound like a comedy script but frighteningly, it is a **fact** that no follower of Muhammad could ever **admit** to any of our statements and conclusions without **apostatizing!**

As we have pointed out on several occasions, that the **male** followers of Muhammad **never** miss a chance from shooting themselves in the mouth is their **total** inability to use their brain or intellect **independently** from their elders or leaders.

> In the script above we are told that if we do not know the Arabic language we cannot possibly understand the Quran. We agree with this statement fully.
>
> How then can the same followers of Muhammad BRAG that it is the fastest growing belief on Earth when in reality & in fact over **one** Billion of the 1.3 billion followers of Muhammad do not **understand** Arabic and especially the Arabic of the Quran!
>
> Under what category are they? **kafirs?** Ignorant Muhammadans? Imperialist Agents? Tools of Zionists? Can they in fact be considered even **muslims?** Hence their first, foremost **& only** line of defense is **obliterated** leaving them nothing more than circular and hence endless **illogic** to try and defend the indefensible.

As we have mentioned before that: "A belief, is not merely an idea that the mind possesses; it is in fact, an idea that totally possesses the mind."

Hence it is **almost** impossible to get through to people who are too **scared** to **listen** lest they have to **discard** all their views on Muhammadan Islam!

In conclusion; talking to the followers of Muhammad is exactly the same as Umar ibn al Khattab intoned: **Like talking to the Black Stone**

#77 Miriam or Mary ?

Q: During my study of the Quran I was astounded to find out that Muhammad had even less knowledge and understanding of the New Testament than he had of the Hebrew Bible, particularly in the case of Mary the mother of Jesus.

Can you elaborate?

A: The Quran, as we have shown and continue to show, is replete with historical, theological, character and events errors that are so immense in magnitude and so numerous, that they can boggle the mind of any learned and unbiased person.

In this particular case, the Quran has mixed up the Biblical character of **Miriam - the sister of Moses and Aaron** and the daughter of **Amram** their father *(1450 BCE)* - with the New Testament **Mary the mother of Jesus** *(1 BCE)*, a time difference of **1450 years.**

Because of these irreconcilable & astounding historical and theological errors, the exegetes of Muhammadan Islam unashamedly continued - and still continue - to perpetuate many blatant lies and deceptions upon humanity for the last 1400 years.

In fact, in the Quran, the name **Mary** does not exist but only the Arabic **Mariam,** forcing the translators and interpreters to use the name Mary so as to deliberately mislead the readers or listeners who either do not know Arabic or are ignorant of the New Testament, or both.

Even the translation of the Quran by Pickthall, a Christian convert to Muhammadan Islam, continued this deception.

The verses that appear in the Quran were copied and altered by Muhammad almost verbatim from the ***Gospel of Luke Chapter 1*** and interspersed them among his *Suras* as and when he saw fit.

As usual with Muhammad, he did not fully understand the context of the original stories, from the points of view of both the theological and the historical, and hence got all of them jumbled up.

***Al Imran 3: 35** Behold! a **woman of Imran** said: "O my Lord! I do dedicate unto thee what is in my womb for Thy special service so accept this of me for Thou hearest and knowest all things."*

***36** And when she was delivered she said: My Lord! Lo! I am delivered of a female... have named her **[Mariam]**, and Lo! I crave Thy protection for her and for her offspring from Satan the outcast.*

*** It is a fact that not a single word in the verses above was uttered by any New Testament character as alleged in the Quran, and since [Mariam] was a Jewess, she could not possibly have known the name Allah as it does not exist in the Hebrew Bible.

It is imperative that our listeners are made aware of a most fundamental issue regarding the Quran and Muhammadan Islam:

Allah is NOT God but the NAME of the supreme pagan rock god of the Quraysh, embedded in the corner wall of the Ka'ba called the **Black Stone** almost 1000 desert miles away from Judea.

Mariam could have only addressed herself to the God of Israel & Jesus as **Hashem [Elohim]** - since the God of Israel has no name - and was never **Allah** ***

***Al Imran 3: 42** Behold! the angels said: "O **[Mariam]**! Allah hath chosen thee and purified thee; chosen thee above the women of all nations.*

***3: 45** Behold! the angels said "O **[Mariam]**! Allah giveth thee glad tidings of a Word from Him: his name will be **Christ Jesus the son of Mariam** held in honor in this world and the Hereafter and of (the company of) those nearest to Allah.*

*** The Quran is obviously wrong again here also since Christ was **not** part of the name of Jesus **but** a **title** meaning **messiah** given to him **after** his death and **not** before his **birth*****

Mariam 19: 28 "O sister of Aaron! thy father was not a man of evil nor thy mother a woman unchaste!"

*** The above verse asserts in no uncertain terms, that the [Mariam] repeatedly mentioned in the Quran as the mother of Jesus, is the same as the sister of Aaron in the Bible also called [Mariam] which obviously makes her the daughter of **Imran [Amram]**.

The confusion is completely on the side of Muhammad and his Quran and no where else. All the convoluted explanations by **Abdullah Yusuf Ali** - and all other Muhammadan Muslims like him - are as **untruthful** as Muhamnmad's Quranic verses above ***

Al Tahreem 66: 12 And [Mariam] the daughter of 'Imran [Amram] who guarded her chastity; and We breathed into her (body) of Our spirit; ...

*** As usual in the Quran, this is erroneous since according to the **Gospel of Luke 3:24**, Mary's father's name was **Heli** and **not Imran**. It is impossible that the angel Gabriel who predicted the arrival of Jesus, could have told Muhammad such blatant lies.

The angel who informed Muhammad could not have been Gabriel nor could he have been a messenger from the God of Israel & Jesus.

Either way, it adds to the lack of veracity of the Quranic verses which are totally at odds with the historical and theological records that had pre existed both Muhammad and his Quran by SIX hundred years ***

Sahih Al-Bukhari Hadith 4.570 Narrated by Ibn Abbas

The Prophet entered the **Ka'ba and found in it the pictures of (Prophet) Abraham and Mary.** On that he said' "What is the matter with them (i.e. Quraish)? They have already heard that angels do not enter a house in which there are pictures; yet this is the picture of Abraham. And why is he depicted as practicing divination by arrows?"

*** Bukhari should have known better than to incorporate this blatantly false **isnad** in his Sahih Hadith.

Muhammad after all, was visiting the Ka'ba **most** of his life without once mentioning these alleged pictures in it ***

Sahih Al-Bukhari Hadith 4.623 Narrated by Abu Musa

Allah's Apostle said, "Many amongst men reached (the level of) perfection but none amongst the women reached this level except Asia, Pharaoh's wife, and Mariam, the daughter of 'Imran.

*** Those of us who know the Bible, also know that the name of Pharaoh's wife is **not** mentioned anywhere. This is another one of Muhammad's concoctions

Moreover Muhammad asserts that Mariam is the daughter of Imran/Amram***

Sahih Al-Bukhari Hadith 4.642 Narrated by Ali

I heard the Prophet saying, **"Mariam, the daughter of 'Imran, was the best among the women** (of the world of her time) and Khadija is the best amongst the women. (of this nation)."

Sahih Muslim Hadith 5326 Narrated by Mughirah ibn Shu'bah

When I came to Najran, they (the Christians of Najran) asked me: You read

"O sister of Harun" (i.e. Maryam) in the Qur'an, whereas Moses was born much before Jesus.

When I came back to Allah's Messenger I asked him about that, whereupon he said:

The (people of the old age) used to give names after the names of Apostles and pious persons who had gone before them.

*** This is a most remarkable hadith since it challenges the veracity of both Muhammad and his Quran by one of his followers and not by an enemy of Muhammad.

Muhammad's answer is as **false** as the Quranic assertions regarding Mariam. Being the *'apostle of Allah'* he forbade any of his followers to pursue the question lest they end up in Hell.

The unwillingness of the followers of Muhammad to question anything in the Quran continues unabated to this day.

His followers of **today** are as **ignorant** of **previous revelations** as the pagan Arabs were 1400 years ago.

The name of Mariam is repeated 34 times in 12 Suras in the Quran.

There are **hundreds** of other instances in the Quran, similar to the ones above in their total lack of veracity, historicity and accuracy when they are compared to their originals in the Bible.

No intelligent, decent, just, moral and fair human being, would accept that the Almighty would give **two** completely **different** and **contradictory** Divine Revelations and assert that **both** are **true.**

Such an act cannot possibly be divine and hence the Quran is the **singular** product of Muhammad's fertile imagination***

#78 Missing Verses in the Quran

Q: Muhammadan Islam is the only Belief System on Earth that forbids any questioning, investigating, comparing & contrasting its holy book the Quran.

Will you provide details of this interesting phenomenon?

A: I repeat once again, that the greatest threat to the exposure of the falsehood of the Quran are knowledge of the Quran, Hadiths, the Hebrew Bible, the New Testament and related scriptures & history.

As we have repeatedly shown – and will continue to do so – in our series, that it is by **divine justice** that the very **hadiths** that explain the Quran to the followers of Muhammad are the ones which **completely & utterly** destroy its alleged divine origin as we shall prove yet again in this chapter.

We have a report from `Umar ibn al Khattab that he said, 'The Messenger of Allah stoned, Abu Bakr stoned and I have stoned. I am not prepared to add to the Book of Allah [Quran] otherwise I would write it into the mushaf, for I fear that there will come some people who, not finding it, will not accept it.'

[That is, NOT finding the Stoning Verse in the Quran]

(Ahmad b. al Husain al Baihaqi, "al Sunan al Kubra", 10 vols., Haiderabad, 1925-38/1344-57, vol. 8, p. 213)

[`Umar summoned] a group of the Muhajirs and the Ansar and inscribe[d] their testimony on the margin of the mushaf: 'The testimony of `Umar that the Messenger of Allah stoned adulterers.'

(K. al Mabani", in A. Jeffery, "Two Muqaddimahs", Cairo, 1954, p. 78)

Muhammad bin Abu Bakr Shams ul-Imam Sarakhsi reports,

`Umar said from the pulpit, '**... and part of what was revealed in Qur'an read,** *"the shaikh and the shaikha, when they fornicate, stone them outright"*. Some will repudiate this, and that men would say, "`Umar has added to the Book of Allah," I will write it on the margin of the mushaf.'

(p. 78-79, al Sarakhsi, "Mabsut", 30 vols., Cairo, 1324, vol. 9, p. 36)

*** If Umar knew about such a verse or Sura, then why is it not in the Quran?***

Where did it use to be in the Quran?***

Ubayy asked Zirr b. Hubais, 'How many verses do you recite in surat al Ahzab, 33?'

Zirr replied, 'Seventy-three verses.'

Ubayy asked if that was all. 'I have seen it,' he said, 'when it was the same length as Baqara [of 286 verses]. It contained the words "The shaikh and the shaikha, when they fornicate, stone them outright, as an exemplary punishment from Allah. Allah is might, wise."'

(p. 78-79, Ahmad b. al Husain al Baihaqi, "al Sunan al Kubra", 10 vols., Haiderabad, 1925-38/1344-57, vol. 8, pp. 210-11)

Ubayy said, '**It used to equal the length of surat al Baqara and we used to recite in Ahzab/33 the stoning verse.**'

(p. 80, Jalal al Din al Suyuti, "al Itqan fi `ulum al Qur'an", Halabi, Cairo, 1935/1354, pt 2, p. 25)

*** Ladies & Gentlemen, this Sura must have been similar in length to that of **al Baqara of 286 but ended being one of 73 only.**

Where are Allah's missing verses?

How could any one in his/her right mind accept such degradations in the Quran and still contend that it is divine ?

That its prototype is in heaven and that it has not been altered since it was revealed to Muhammad?

Is the prototype also truncated, perverted and tampered with?

What answers can the followers of Muhammad conjure up to explain away these catastrophic facts?***

Al Ahzab/33 was identified as the sura originally containing the stoning verse, and, in addition to Ubayy and Abu Musa,

`Aisha reports that **Ahzab used to be recited, in the lifetime of the Prophet, as having 200 verses,** but when `Uthman wrote out the mushafs, all they could find was its present length.

(Jalal al Din ` al Suyuti, "al Itqan fi `ulum al Qur'an", Halabi, Cairo, 1935/1354, pt 2, p. 25)

Aisha explains how the wording came to be omitted from the mushaf:

The stoning verse and another verse were revealed and recorded on a sheet (sahifa) which was placed for safe-keeping under her bedding.

When the Prophet fell ill and the household were preoccupied with nursing him, **a domestic animal got in from the yard and gobbled up the sheet.**

(p. 86, Burhan al Din al Baji, "Jawab", MS Dar al Kutub, Taimur "majami`", no. 207, f. 15)

Jalal Al Din reports, 'The Messenger of Allah said "Allah has commanded me to instruct you in the reciting of the Qur'an."

He then recited: "Did not those who rejected the Prophet among the people of the Book and the associators…" *The verse continued, "Did ibn Adam possess a wadi of property", or, "Were ibn Adam to ask for a wadi of property and he received it, it would asked for a second, and if he received that, he would demand a third wadi. Only dust will fill the maw of ibn Adam, but Allah relents to him who repents. The very faith in Allah's eyes is the Hanifiya, not Judaism nor Christianity. Whoso does good, it will never be denied him."*

(p. 82-83, Jalal al Din al Suyuti, "al Itqan fi `ulum al Qur'an", Halabi, Cairo, 1935/1354, pt 2, p. 25)

Ibn `Abbas said, '*Had ibn Adam possess two wadis of pelf, he would have desired a third. Only dust will fill the mouth of ibn Adam, but Allah relents to him who repents.*' `Umar asked, 'What is this?' ibn `Abbas replied that Ubayy had instructed him to recite this. `Umar took ibn `Abbas to confront Ubayy. `Umar said, 'We don't say that.' Ubayy insisted that the Prophet instructed him. `Umar asked him, 'Shall I write it into the mushaf, in that case?'

*** This too is not written in the Quran***

Buraid claims to have heard the Prophet recite *ibn Adam* at prayer. The aya was in surat Yusuf/12.

(p. 83, Burhan al Din al Baji, "Jawab", MS Dar al Kutub, Taimur "majami`", no. 207, f. 18)

Ubayy said, 'Yes.' This was before the copying of the `Uthman mushafs on the basis of which the practice now rests.

(p. 83, Burhan Baji, "Jawab", MS Dar al Kutub, Taimur "majami`", no. 207, f. 17)

Zuhri reports, 'We have heard that many Qur'an passages were revealed but that those who had memorized them fell in the battle of Yamama fighting. Those passages had not been written down, and following the deaths of those who knew them, were no longer known; nor had Abu Bakr, nor `Umar nor `Uthman as yet collected the texts of the Qur'an.

Those lost passages were not to be found with anyone after the deaths of those who had memorized them.

This was one of the considerations which impelled the Muhammadans to pursue the Qur'an during the reign of Abu Bakr, committing it to sheets for fear that there should perish in further theatres of war men who bore much of the Qur'an which they would take to the grave with them on their fall, and which, with their passing, would not be found with any other.

Anas is reported in the two Sahih's as declaring:

'There was revealed concerning those slain at Bi'r Ma`una a Qur'an verse which **we recited until it was withdrawn:**

"Inform our tribe on our behalf that we have met with our Lord. He has been well pleased with us and has satisfied our desires.'"

(pp. 48-49, Jalal al Din al Suyuti, "al Itqan fi `ulum al Qur'an", Halabi, Cairo, 1935/1354, pt 2, p. 26)

*** No doubt this verse was removed from the Quran because it alleged that those who died met with Allah which is contrary to the Muhammadan doctrine that **no human** can meet face to face with Allah***

The extreme Sh`ia, the Rafidis, alleged that the impious rulers of Muhammadan Islam had expunged from the mushaf some 500 verses including those which most unambiguously marked out `Ali as the appointed successor to the Prophet.... The rebels against `Uthman, justifying their revolt, enumerated amongst their grievances their resentment at his 'having expunged the mushafs.'

(Abu Bakr `Abdullah b. abi Da'ud, "K. al Masahif", ed. A. Jeffery, Cairo, 1936/1355, p. 36)

All the above are only a small sample of a ripple in a **Tsunami** of such abrogations, missing verses, missing Suras, added verses and interloped Suras that can never be attributed to any Omniscient Divinity.

Contrary to all the allegations and dogma of the followers of Muhammad, the Quran that we have today is NOT the same that was allegedly 'revealed' to Muhammad but has been repeatedly and deliberately tampered with to fulfill sectarian agendas.

What is extremely relevant to point out is, that the Ahadith and 'Traditions', were written by Muhammad's contemporaries and companions, in Arabic, and are the ones that are making these assertions and not some outsiders or enemies to the faith of Muhammadan Islam

As I mentioned before, that it is **indisputably** by **Divine Justice**, that the very Hadiths that explain the Quran to its followers, without the need for outside help or interference, single handily, **destroy** the alleged divine origin & veracity of the Quran.

#79. Fall of Adam

Q: When reading the stories about Adam in the Quran, I was shocked to realize that Muhammad believed that Adam was thrown down from a heavenly paradise to Earth instead of the original version in the Bible wherein he was thrown out of paradise on Earth.

How was it possible that Gabriel – if he were the angel of God - could have misled Muhammad so disastrously and falsely?

Is there an explanation?

A: As usual with Muhammad Quran's version of the stories that he plagiarized from the Bible, the one about that of the creation leading to Adam's 'Fall' is devoid of any background in Time or Space and is utterly insipid unlike the vivid and captivating original in the Bible.

Genesis 2: "7 Then the LORD God formed man of the dust of the ground, and breathed into his nostrils the breath of life; and man became a living soul.

8 And the LORD God planted a garden eastward, in Eden; and there He put the man whom He had formed.

9 And out of the ground made the LORD God to grow every tree that is pleasant to the sight, and good for food; the tree of life also in the midst of the garden, and the tree of knowledge of good and evil.

15 And the LORD God took the man, and put him into the garden of Eden to dress it and to keep it.

16 And the LORD God commanded the man, saying: 'Of every tree of the garden you may freely eat;

*17 but of the **tree of knowledge** of good and evil, thou shalt not eat of it; for in the day that you eat thereof you shall surely die.'*

Genesis 3 "*1 Now the serpent was more subtle than any beast of the field which the LORD God had made. And he said unto the woman: 'Yea, hath God said: Ye shall not eat of any tree of the garden?'*

6 And when the woman saw that the tree was good for food, and that it was a delight to the eyes, and that the tree was to be desired to make one wise, she took of the fruit thereof, and did eat; and she gave also unto her husband with her, and he did eat.

17 And unto Adam God said: 'Because thou hast hearkened unto the voice of thy wife, and hast eaten of the tree, of which I commanded thee, saying: Thou shalt not eat of it; cursed is the ground for thy sake; in toil shalt thou eat of it all the days of thy life.

19 In the sweat of thy face shalt thou eat bread, till thou return unto the ground; for out of it wast thou taken; for dust thou art, and unto dust shalt thou return.'

23 Therefore the LORD God sent him forth from the garden of Eden, to till the ground from whence he was taken.

24 So He drove out the man; *and He placed at the east of the garden of Eden the cherubim, and the flaming sword which turned every way, to keep the way to the tree of life.*

*** It is obvious that God **evicted** Adam and his wife **out** of the **Garden of Eden on EARTH** to toil, suffer and sweat to earn their livelihood ***

Amongst Muhammadan writers, the **fall** is called Dthallatu Adam, or the slip of Adam. The term **Dthallah,** meaning "a slip" or "error", being applied to prophets, but not **Thamb,** which is " sin", since Muhammadan Islam has the **dogma** that prophets **do not** commit sin, hence instantly exonerating all of Muhammad's Evil deeds.

The following is the account of Adam's "slip", as given in the Quran-

Al Baqara 2:35 *"And we said, 'O Adam! Dwell thee and thy wife in the Garden [Janna] , and eat ye plentifully there from* *wherever ye list; but to this tree come not nigh, lest ye become of the transgressors.'*

36 "*But Satan made them slip [fa aTHallahuma] from it, and caused their banishment from the place in which they were. And we said,* **'Get ye down [ahbittou]**

Al A'raf 7:19 '*And, O Adam! Dwell thou and thy wife in Paradise [Janna] and eat ye whence ye will, but to this tree approach not, lest ye become of the unjust doers."*

22 "*So SATAN beguiled them by deceits and when they had tasted of the tree, their nakedness appeared to them, and they began to sew together upon themselves the leaves of the garden. And their Lord called to them 'Did I not forbid you this tree, and did I not say to you, "Verily, Satan is your declared enemy?"*

24 *He said,* **'Get ye down [ahbittou]**, *the one of you an enemy to the other; and on earth shall be your dwelling, and your provision for a season."*

25"*He said, 'On it shall ye live, and on it shall ye die, and from it shall ye be taken forth.'"*

*** Our readers should be aware of the following Quranic **falsehoods** when compared to the **original** Biblical version:

1. **satan is never** mentioned in Genesis nor in the whole of the Torah

2. It was the **serpent** and **not** Satan that **tempted** Eve

3. The serpent beguiled **only eve** and **not both-** Adam & Eve

4. God, in the Bible ordered them **out** of the Garden of Eden – on Earth – and **not** told them to **jump** down from Paradise to earth

5. God of the Bible did not warn either Adam or Eve of the Serpent's enmity beforehand

Ta Ha 20:115 "*And of old We made a covenant with Adam; but he forgot it; and we found no firmness of purpose in him.*

120 "*But Satan whispered to him: said he, 'O Adam! Shall I show thee* **the tree of Eternity [Shajarati^l Khuldi]** *, and the Kingdom that faileth not?*"

*** For those who do not know, the serpent tempted Eve with the fruit of the **Tree of Knowledge** and **not Adam** of the **Tree of Life/Eternity** ***

121. "*And they both ate thereof, and their nakedness appeared to them, and they began to sew of the leaves of the Garden [Janna] to cover them, and Adam disobeyed his Lord and went astray.*" .

123 He said: "*Get ye down [ahbita] both of you all together (from the Garden) with enmity one to another...*

*** As usual, the Quranic version of the Biblical story is totally at variance with the original. Further **errors** & **falsehoods** are repeated, and so we repeat our objections accordingly:

- 1   The serpent **tempted** EVE **not** Adam

- 2   The serpent tempted Eve about the tree of **knowledge** and **not** the tree of **life** or Tree of Eternity

- 3   God **evicted** them from the Garden of Eden on Earth and did not **drop** them from it to Earth

We would like to share with our readers the following lines of reasoning:

Since the Bible is described in the Quran as the Word of Allah, that was revealed to Moses **directly,** without any intermediaries, then how is it possible that the Quran's version, which is also allegedly revealed by Allah, is utterly different and contradictory to it if Muhammad's Allah is the same as the God of Israel?

The Muhammadan commentators are much perplexed as to the scene of the fall of Adam. In the Bible, Adam and Eve were '**cast out**' from the Garden of Eden [on Earth]; they were **not thrown down** from anywhere [Heaven to Earth].

After all, two of the four rivers that encompassed the Garden of Eden are earthly rivers such as the Euphrates and Tigris.

From the text of the Quran it is very clear that the Paradise spoken of and envisioned is in heaven and not on earth. To substantiate this, there is a Muhammadan Muslim tradition, that when Adam was cast down, he fell on the island of Ceylon, would support this view.

Ali ibn Babwayh Al-Qummi was a Shi'a scholar who records the opinion that Eden was not on earth but in heaven. After having disobeyed Allah, Allah sends Adam and Eve to earth, arriving first at two holy **pagan** mountain peaks outside Mecca; Adam on Safa, and Eve on Marwa.

Other Muhammadan traditions hold that Adam was moved to Sri Lanka, Ceylon, as the next best thing to Eden, and, viewing Adam as having been a giant, human size having shrunk drastically before the great flood, Adam's Peak in Sri Lanka is said to contain his giant footprint.

Al-Baizawi maintains that the Garden of Eden was in the heavens, and that the fall occurred before Adam and Eve inhabited this earth of ours.

At the very beginning of our series, we mentioned that we are putting Muhammad & his Quran on trial and that you will be the Jury.

So, Ladies and gentlemen of the **jury** even though we do put our own conclusions forth for each chapter for all to hear, as required by Trial rules, nonetheless, in the final analysis, it is up to you to make your own minds up.

Once again, we leave it to you, our listeners, to make your own intelligent conclusions, based upon all the **facts** that we have provided to you from the Biblical and Muhammadan sources, if it is at all logical and moral that any **omniscient** divinity, would have provided **two** or more contradictory versions of Adam's story.

#80 Muhammad's Sunnah

Q: According to my studies, I found out that in several important instances Muhammad's Sunnah superseded the Quran and that without knowledge of the Sunnah the Quran cannot possibly be a guide to the believers.

Will you elaborate?

A: The Sunna is the practice and example of Muhammad, and is the second authority for Muhammadan Muslims besides the Quran.

A Hadith is supposed to be a reliably transmitted report of what Muhammad allegedly said, did, or approved. Belief in the divine inspiration of the sunna is as important in the Muhammadan Muslim faith as belief in the Quran.

Sahih Al-Bukhari 7.822 Narrated by Alqama

'Abdullah cursed those women who practiced tattooing and those who removed hair from their faces and those who created spaces between their teeth artificially to look beautiful, such ladies as changed what Allah has created.

Um Ya'qub said, "What is that?"

'Abdullah said, **"Why should I not curse those who were cursed by Allah's Apostle** and are referred to in Allah's Book?"

She said to him "By Allah, I have read the whole Qur'an but I have not found such a thing.

'Abdullah said, "By Allah, if you had read it (carefully) you would have found it. *(Allah says:) 'And what the Apostle gives you take it and what he forbids you abstain (from it).' - (59.7)*

*** Um Ya'qub was absolutely correct to say that such a verse does not exist in the Quran.

Abdullah was also correct by insisting that Muhammad's **sunna** is **equal** to the Quran ***

Sahih Al-Bukhari 8.689 Narrated by Said bin Ubada Al Ansari

that he consulted the Prophet about a vow that had been made by his mother who died without fulfilling it. The Prophet gave his verdict that he should fulfill it on her behalf. The verdict became Sunna (i.e. the Prophet's tradition).

*** This means that this **verdict** became part of Sharia law, just like the rules of the Quran, which cannot ever be changed***

Sahih Al-Bukhari Hadith 8.816 Narrated by Ibn Abbas

'Umar said, "I am afraid that after a long time has passed, people may say, 'We do not find the Verses of the Rajam (stoning to death) in the Holy Book,' and consequently they may go astray by leaving an obligation that Allah has revealed. Lo! I confirm that the penalty of Rajam be inflicted on him who commits illegal sexual intercourse, if he is already married and the crime is proved by witnesses or pregnancy or confession." Sufyan added, "I have memorized this narration in this way." 'Umar added, "**Surely Allah's Apostle carried out the penalty of Rajam, and so did we after him.**"

*Al Nur 24:2 The woman and the man guilty of adultery or fornication **flog each of them with a hundred stripes**: let not compassion move you in their case in a matter prescribed by Allah if ye believe in Allah and the Last Day: and let a party of the Believers witness their punishment.*

Dear readers, while the Quran mandates inflicting **only** 100 stripes for **fornication,** Muhammad's Sunna on the other hand punishes with **death** by **stoning.**

Hence Muhammad's Sunna, supersedes the Quran

Sahih Al-Bukhari 9.387 Narrated by Abu Musa

The Prophet said, "My example and the example of what I have been sent with is that of a man who came to some people and said, 'O people! I have seen the enemy's army with my own eyes, and I am the naked warner; so protect yourselves!' Then a group of his people obeyed him and fled at night proceeding stealthily till they were safe, while another group of them disbelieved him and stayed at their places till morning when the army came upon them, and killed and ruined them completely So this is the example of that person who obeys me and follows what I have brought (the Qur'an and the Sunna), and the example of the one who disobeys me and disbelieves the truth I have brought."

*** It is abundantly clear from the above that Muhammad made his deeds, sayings and rules **equal** to Allah's Quran ***

*Al Israa 17:78   Establish regular prayers at the sun's decline till the darkness of the night **(Asr prayer)** and the morning prayer **(Fajr prayer)** and reading: for the prayer and reading in the morning carry their testimony.*

*Al Baqara 2: 238   Guard strictly your (habit of) prayers especially the middle prayer**(Thuhr prayer)** and stand before Allah in a devout (frame of mind).*

Sahih Al-Bukhari Hadith 9.88   Narrated by Talha bin Ubaidullah

A bedouin with unkempt hair came to Allah's Apostle and said, "O Allah's Apostle! Tell me what Allah has enjoined on me as regards prayers." The Prophet said, "You have to offer perfectly the **five (compulsory) prayers** in a day and a night (24 hrs.)...

*** While the Quran in the above two verses stipulates **three** prayer sessions a day, Muhammad's Sunna and practice follow **five** prayer sessions.

Once more does the Sunna over-rule the Quran ***

Sahih Al-Bukhari Hadith9.381 Narrated by Hudhaifa

Allah's Apostle said to us, "Honesty descended from the Heavens and settled in the roots of the hearts of men (faithful believers), and then the Qur'an was revealed and the people read the Qur'an, (and learnt it from it) and also learnt it from the Sunna." **Both Qur'an and Sunna** strengthened their (the faithful believers)' honesty."

*** Our readers should be aware that **no one** in Arabia **ever** read the Quran while Muhammad was alive since it was only compiled in **book** form long after he was dead. This Hadith, like tens of thousands of others is, to put it **charitably**, in **gross error** ***

Sahih Al-Bukhari 9.382 Narrated by Abdullah

The best talk (speech) is Allah's Book (Qur'an), and the best way is the way of Muhammad, (his **SUNNA)**

Sahih Al-Bukhari Hadith 9.415 Narrated by Humaid

I heard Muawiya bin Abi Sufyan delivering a sermon.

He said, "I heard the Prophet saying, "If Allah wants to do a favor to somebody, He bestows on him, the gift of understanding the **Qur'an and my Sunna…**"

*** The Sunna of Muhammad is deemed, in the tradition of his followers, divinely inspired and hence equal to the Quran.

That is why, the Fundamentalist **male** followers of Muhammad have remained and will continue to remain, **stuck** in the **primitive TIME WARP** of Muhammad's 7th **Century.**

The historical records **prove** beyond a reasonable doubt that nothing of value **intellectual, spiritual, artistic, scientific, joyful, philosophical**, **moral** or **judicial** can **ever** bloom under **Fundamentalist Muhammadan Islam.**

Anyone who doubts the above statements, all he/she needs to know is that the most **perfect** Muhammadan Muslim State was that of the Taliban in Afghanistan.

>A state of Depraved indifference to Justice, Morality and Intellect.

>A state **devoid** of any Joy and Happiness.

>A state of **abject** Tyranny and **fear**.

>A state of Mind-boggling stupidity and Ignorance.

A state of the living dead.

That the most **Perfect** representative of a **Fundamentalist Male Muhammadan Muslim** is **Osama** bin Laden who, **contrary** to what the Media & others describe him, is **not** a **terrorist**. He is a **believer** who is only following the Quran & Muhammad's Sunna.

That Muhammadan Muslims of 1.3 billions, almost **20%** of the human population, produce the least number of Intellectual, Philosophical, Scientific, Artistic or Spiritual Books or Papers in the world is only **one testimony** to the assertions that we make

That among about 55 countries that are either totally Muhammadan Muslim or have a majority of them, are **undemocratic, racist, hatemongering, warmongering, & unjust.**

They treat their women – who represent more than **50%** of their population - with contempt, with terror, with subjugation, with humiliation and with degradation because of the ordinances of the Muhammad's Quran and his Sunna.

As we have shown repeatedly that, all the above anomalies, absurdities, inconsistencies and abnormalities can **only** make sense when the listeners realize that, **both** the Quran and the **sunna** are the product of Muhammad's own **ALTER EGO,** and have absolutely nothing to do with Allah or Gabriel, who are used only as props by Muhammad, to give his alleged revelations and speech, divine sanction.

#81 Poitier: Saviour Battle

Q: We were requested by one of our listeners to describe the Battle of Poitier - also called battle of Tours - between some Christian armies and the armies of Muhammadan Islam.

We believe that it is a very relevant and important subject to discuss regarding the real intentions of the followers of Muhammad towards Europe & Christianity in current times.

Will you explain.

A: Let me first start with a **resume** of the background of this battle and then the details.

The **Battle of Tours** (October 10, 732) is also known as the Battle of Poitiers. The battle was fought near the city of Tours in France, close to the border between the Frankish realm and independent Aquitaine. The battle pitted Frankish and Burgundian forces under Charles Pepin, later titled MARTEL, against an army of the Arabian Umayyad Caliphate led by 'Abdul Rahman Al Ghafiqi, Governor-general of al-Andalus.

The Arabian Umayyad Caliphate, at the time of the Battle of Tours, was perhaps the world's foremost military power. Great expansion of the Caliphate occurred under the reign of the Umayyads. Muhammadan Muslim armies pushed across North Africa and Persia through the late 600s.

Forces led by Tariq ibn-Ziyad crossed Gibraltar and established Muhammadan power in the Iberian/ Spanish peninsula which subsequently crossed into southern France with the intention of expanding as far into Europe as their victories permitted. The Muhammadan Muslim empire under the Umayyad Arabs was now a vast domain that ruled, colonized and subjugated a diverse array of tens of millions of peoples on three continents: Christians, Zoroasterians, Jews, Hindus and others.

It had destroyed what were the two formerly super military powers: the Sassanid Persian Empire, which it absorbed completely, and the Byzantine Christian Empire, most of which it had absorbed, including Armenia, Syria, Judea/ Palestina, Egypt and North Africa.

The Frankish realm under Charles Pepin was the foremost military power in Western Europe. It consisted of what is today most of France, most of Western Germany and the low-countries. The Frankish realm had begun to progress towards forming the first real imperial power in Western Europe since the fall of Rome.

On his march through the southern districts of France in the land of the Franks, Abd-er-Rahman utterly destroyed many towns and villages, killed and enslaved a great number of the people, and seized all the booty & property that he could carry off.

He plundered the city of Bordeaux and, it is said, that he obtained so many valuable things that every soldier "was loaded with golden vases and cups and emeralds and other precious stones."

'Abd-al-Rahmân trusted the tactical superiority of his cavalry, and had them charge the Franks repeatedly. This time, the faith the Umayyads had in their cavalry, armed with their long lances and swords, which had brought them so many victories in previous battles, was not justified.

In one of the rare instances where medieval infantry stood up against cavalry charges, the disciplined Frankish soldiers withstood the assaults, though according to some Arab sources, the Arab cavalry was able to break several times into the interior of the Frankish square.

"The Muhammadan horsemen dashed fearlessly and frequently against the battalions of the Franks, who resisted heroically, and many fell dead on both sides." Despite these determined assaults, the Frankish wall did not give in. It appears that the years of year-round training that Charles had instilled in his men, paid off brilliantly.

In fact, his hard-trained soldiery accomplished what was not thought possible at that time: that infantry could withstand the determined onslaught of cavalry. For the first time, this was exactly what happened as the Frankish **infantry** withstood the repeated assaults of the Umayyad heavy **cavalry.**

Charles had created an army of professional infantrymen which was both highly disciplined and well motivated, "having campaigned with him all over Europe". They were buttressed by levies that Charles basically used to raid and disrupt his enemy lines, and gather food for his infantry.

The ***Mozarabic Chronicle of 754*** says: "And in the shock of the battle the men of the North seemed like a sea that cannot be moved. Firmly they stood, one close to another, forming as it were a bulwark of ice; and with great blows of their swords, they hewed down the Arabs. Drawn up in a band around their chief, the people of the Franks carried all before them. Their tireless hands drove their swords down to the breasts of the foe".

Those Umayyad troops who had broken into the square had tried to kill Charles, but his bodyguards who surrounded him would not be broken. The battle was still in flux when Frankish histories claim, that a rumor went through the Umayyad army that Frankish scouts threatened the booty that the Muhammadans had plundered from Bordeaux.

Some of the Umayyad horsemen, without permission from their officers, at once broke off the battle and returned to camp to secure their loot. According to Muhammadan accounts of the battle, in the midst of the fighting , scouts from the Franks sent by Charles began to raid the camp and supply train (including slaves and other plunder).

Charles presumably had sent scouts to infiltrate and cause chaos in the Umayyad base camp, and free as many of the slaves as possible, hoping to draw off part of his foe. This tactic, succeeded way beyond his wildest expectations, as many of the Umayyad cavalry, unilaterally broke ranks and returned to their camp. To the rest of the Muhammadan army, this appeared to be like a retreat, but soon it became an undisciplined route.

Both Western and Muhammadan records agree, that while trying to stop the debacle, 'Abd-al-Rahmân became surrounded and was cut down and the Arabian troops then withdrew altogether to their camp. ***"All the host fled before the enemy"***, candidly wrote one Arabic source, ***"and many died in the flight"***.

The Franks resumed their phalanx, and rested in place throughout the night, believing the battle would resume at dawn the following morning.

When the Arab forces did not renew the battle the next day, the Franks feared an ambush. Charles at first believed that the Muhammadan forces were trying to lure him down the hill and into the open. This tactic he knew, he had to resist at all costs. He had in fact disciplined his troops for years, that under no circumstances whatsoever, would they break formation and come out in the open.

Only after extensive reconnaissance of the Umayyad camp by Frankish soldiers was it discovered that the Muhammadans had escaped by stealth during the night.

Both historical accounts assert, that the Muhammadan Muslims had so hastily abandoned their camp, that even the tents were abandoned, as the Umayyad forces headed back to Iberia/Spain with whatever loot remained that they could carry.

The Franks were victorious, 'Abdul Rahman Al Ghafiqi was killed, and Charles subsequently extended his authority in the south.

Ninth-century chroniclers, who interpreted the outcome of the battle as divine judgment in his favour, gave Charles the nickname ***Martellus*** **("The Hammer"),** recalling the title heaped upon Judas Maccabeus ("The Hammerer") of the Jewish Maccabean revolt against the Seleucid Greek Empire.

Exact details of the battle, including its exact location and the number of combatants, cannot be determined from the accounts that have survived. Only one thing remains certain:**the Frankish troops won the battle without cavalry.**

History is peppered with **singular** battles, the outcome of which did actually change the course of human history such as those of: Marathon & Arbela.

Without a shadow of a doubt, the battle that was won by Charles Martell at Tours was **seminal** since it **saved** the whole of Christian Europe from becoming **Islamized** and thus actually preserving **Christianity.**

Muhammadan Islam at this moment of history and in the foreseeable future, is in the process of re-conquering Christian Europe without **war**. They are slowly but most assuredly, **conquering her demographically from within:**

Through immigration and a much higher birth rate.

#82 Was Muhammad Predicted?

Q: Muhammad's Quran asserts that he, Muhammad was predicted in both the Torah & the New Testament.

Will you enlighten us about the veracity or lack there of such claims?

A: The greatest tragedy that has faced humanity for the last **1400 years** is the fact that most of the followers of **Muhammad** are **prohibited** by their religious leaders from **EVER** questioning the **Quran** or from studying the previous revelations, those of the **Torah** and the **New Testament**.

An even greater, more sinister and frightening reality is the fact, that because of their continuous and relentless **indoctrination** from a very early age, not even the most learned among the followers of **Muhammad** are willing or able to accept **facts** or **reality** but continue to wallow in a culture of **total denial.**

Up to a certain psychological point, this can be understood because the moment these learned people admit that there is something seriously wrong with the stories of the **Quran**, they have to lose faith and that is an incredibly difficult intellectual, spiritual and moral hurdle to overcome.

It is much easier to remain in **denial,** forever.

*Al A'raf 7:157 "Those who follow the apostle the unlettered prophet whom **they find mentioned in their own (Scriptures);** in the **law and the Gospel;** for he commands them what is just and forbids them what is evil.....*

The translator of the **Quran** in this case, was an extremely learned gentleman by the name of **Abdullah Yusuf Ali.** His knowledge of the **Hebrew Bible & the New Testament** was superb.

He even quotes repeatedly, chapter and verse from these books to explain the **Quranic** verses. None the les, this learned man would stoop to any abysmal level of **deception, contortion** of history

& religion as well as the **perversion** of Language so that he can attempt to explain the unexplainable.

Let me share with you his explanations of this verse and those that follow as he asserts: " In this verse is a prefiguring, to **Moses,** of the Arabian Messenger, the last and greatest of the messengers of Allah. Prophecies about him will be found in the **Taurat** and the **Injil/Gospels**.

In the **reflex** of the **Taurat** as now accepted by the **Jews, Moses** says

*"The Lord thy God will raise up unto thee **a Prophet** from the midst of thee, of thy brethren, **like unto me**" (Deut. xviii. 15)*

The only Prophet who brought a **Shari'at** like that of Moses was **Muhammad Al- Mustafa,** and he came of the house of **Ismail** the brother of **Isaac** the father of **Israel**.

In the **reflex** of the **Gospel** as now accepted by the **Christians, Christ** promised another **Comforter (John xiv. 16):** the **Greek** word **Paraclete** which the Christians interpret as referring to the Holy Spirit is by our Doctors taken to be **Periclyte,** which would be the Greek form of **Ahmad**.

*** First I would like our readers who are followers of Moses or Jesus to understand the term **reflex** used by **Yusuf Ali.**

According to Muhammadan Muslim scholars, the books that we have today, the Hebrew Bible and the

New Testament are **not** the originals **but** are ones that have been Altered & Perverted and hence are **inauthentic.**

Only in the **wishfull** thinking and self inflicted deception of the followers of Muhammad could they **prove** that Muhammad was ever mentioned or predicted anywhere in the Torah especially since he is not of the descendants/seed of Issac.

The Biblical verse mentioned above pertained **only** to the descendants of Jacob - of whom Moses was one - and to no other branch of the family of Abraham; Muhammad after all, is allegedly descended from Ishmael and hence cannot be the one among those predicted.

Neither is Muhammad mentioned anywhere in the New Testament no matter how his followers, in **desperation,** try their best to contort the Greek language, deform history and twist logic.

Besides, I would like our listeners to know that from the death of Moses to the advent of Muhammad there were numerous **other** Hebrew prophets, every-one of them was a descendant from the line of Isaac **but** not **one** of them from the seed of Ishmael.

In fact, the Torah instructs the Israelites -

Deut. 13:2-4 *"... if there arises amongst you **a prophet or a dreamer** ...urging you to follow other gods...pay no attention to the words of that prophet or dreamer.."*

Sahih Al-Bukhari Hadith 5.277 Narrated by Abu Huraira

The Prophet said, *"Had only **ten Jews believed me,** all the Jews would definitely have believed me."*

*** Muhammad fitted this description so completely that among the **tens** of **thousands** of Judaized Arabs in the Arabian Peninsula, not even **ten** individuals were willing to follow Muhammad even upon **pain** of **death** ***

*Al Saff 61:6 "And Jesus, the son of Mariam, said: 'Children of Israel, I am the Messenger of Allah (sent) to you, confirming that (which was revealed) before me in the **Torah,** and giving Glad Tidings of a **Messenger to come after me, whose name shall be Ahmad, the Praised One....!'"*

*** It is not for the followers of Moses or Jesus to prove the veracity of their books because it is incumbent upon the followers of Muhammad to show a single verse in the New Testament mentioning the name Allah or predicting the arrival of one called Ahmad, especially one such as Muhammad who turned out to be a blood thirsty theological, sexual and economic **predator** and not a 'comforter' in the mold of the saintly Jesus ***

Al-Tirmidhi Hadith 5772 Narrated by Abdullah ibn Salam

The description of Muhammad is written in the Torah and also that Jesus, son of Mariam, will be buried along with him. **AbuMawdud** said that a place for a grave had remained in the house.

*** There is not one single Muhammadan on the face of planet Earth - or anyone else in the universe - who can point out such a **prediction** anywhere in either the Hebrew Bible or the New Testament.

As usual with the Quranic stories, the moment they are properly investigated and put to the test, they fail miserably and very clearly due to their lack of veracity and or historical foundations.

As we have shown in chapter after chapter in this series that the Quran and Hadiths are built upon foundations of **quicksand** made up of **mendacities, deceptions & lies** cemented with **perversion of facts history & real**

#83. Messengers & Prophets

Q: Many people who read of Muhammad are confused about the titles Rassool meaning Messenger & Nabi meaning Prophet.
Will you please explain the differences?

A: In **Arabic, Messenger** is **Rassoul,** the conveyor of the messages of **Allah;** an **Angel.**

Angel is fundamentally a **Christian** term, applied to a man who is sent by **God.** It is based upon the **Hebrew Bible** which had several stories regarding **God's messengers** - in the form of human beings - manifesting themselves to Abraham for example.

At least **four** of the most important verses of the **Quran** reiterate that **Muhammad** was **ONLY** a **messenger of Allah.**

That he was not creating a new religion but was passing on the **Abrahamic** religious **practices (Rituals)** which existed before Muhammad and his Quran.

That **Muhammad's** sole role was to deliver the **Quran,** the message of the **One and Only Allah** which the **Pagan Arabs** had allegedly forgotten.

*Al Imran 3:81 Behold! Allah took the **covenant** of the **Prophets** [Nabiyeen] saying: "I give you a Book and Wisdom; then comes to you an **Messenger** [Rassoul] confirming what is with you...*

*** It is very clear from the verse above that according to the Quran, a **Prophet is given Scripture and Wisdom** while a **Messenger** would come only to **Confirm** existing Scripture & Wisdom ***

*Al Ma'idah 5:99 " The **messenger** [al rassoul] has no function **except** delivering the message....";*

*Al R'ad 13:40 " ....your **ONLY** mission (O Muhammad) is **to deliver** (Quran), while it is **we** who will call them to account"*

Al Nahl 16:123 " Then **we inspired you** (O Muhammad) to follow the **religion of Abraham, monotheism;** never was he an idol worshipper"

Al Hajj 22:52 Never did We send an **messenger [rassooli]** or a **prophet [nabi]** before thee but when he framed a desire Satan threw some (vanity) into his desire

Al Shura 42:48 "....you (O Muhammad) **have no duty EXCEPT delivering the message** (Quran)"

*** The above verses make it crystal clear that there is a definite **distinction** between a Prophet and a Messenger ***

The pagan Arabs and the idolaters of Quraysh used to observe prayers [salat] as shown in-

Al Anfal 8:34-35 "...Their **prayer [salatuhum]** at the House (Ka'aba) were nothing more than **deceit and repulsion...**".

A few weeks after this revelation, the following was commanded in the Quran-

Al Muddaththir 73:20 " ....and observe regular **prayers [salawat]** and give regular **charity [zakat]**,

*** These verses can only make sense if the listeners, the Arabs (pagan or 'Muslim'), were already practicing these deeds or understood their functions.

A Messenger (Rassoul) is commissioned by Allah to confirm **exsting** Scripture while a Prophet (Nabi) is a messenger of God who delivers **new** Scripture.

All Prophets are Messengers but not all Messengers are Prophets.

Muhammad does not create a **new religion** in his Quran. He only **confirms** previous revelations.

Muhammad did **not prophesy** anything.

Muhammad **was not** a **prophet** ***

The **Arabic** term for Prophet is **(Nabi)** and is a loan word plagiarized from the **Hebrew (Nabi); Admonisher/Prophet especially since the pagan Arabs had no such concept.**

Among most other peoples, their great men came forth as reformers, philosophers or legislators; not so among the **Semitic** peoples whose great men invariably came as **self proclaimed spokesmen for God, as prophets.**

The characteristics of the prophets as portrayed in the Bible are:

1. Impassioned poetical utterances

2. Intense preoccupation with **God,** morality and above all, **justice**

3. **An inordinate and fearless compulsion urging him to declare the will of the Almighty.**

Prophethood should be seen as a sort of spiritual and mental compulsion - **in the order of genius** - peculiar to extraordinary and visionary individuals who in the depth of their soul and mind conceive the idea of an **Absolute Deity Who is inspiring them.**

The title of a **NABI/ Prophet** - **like so many others copied from the Bible** - did not exist in the **Arabic** language since the **concept** itself was alien to them.

Just as the whole history of **Israel** centered upon the prophets, so has - **in emulation** - **Muhammad** created his own image in his **Quran.**

Invariably, **the divinely appointed prophets of Israel** acted as if they were **God's Vice Regents on Earth.**

Muhammad acted and arrogated to himself, in the final analysis, exactly this position as made very clear when comparing the **Quranic** verses of **Mecca** when it is only

'**Allah Who was to be obeyed**' while in the **Madinan** verses it is invariably '**Allah & his messenger**'.

Muhammad's preaching in **Mecca** was a copy-cat of concepts and ideas plundered and pirated from **Jewish** and **Christian** traditions and beliefs such as:

1. **Judgement Day**

2. The **resurrection** of all humans, the just and the unjust

3. The accounting for their sins when the **books** are opened

4. The rewards of **Heaven/Pardise/ Garden and** the punishment of **Hell**

5. The doctrines of angels and evil spirits personified in **Gabriel** and **Satan**

6. The **creation** of Heaven and Earth, of Man and of Nature

7. **The belief in the One and Only God**

8. The retributions that **Allah** would inflict on all those who break his rules

9. The idea of the **Chosen People** which he stole from the **Jews** and arrogated to himself and his followers.

While the concept of **'chosen'** actually meant that the **Jews** - as descendants of the **Israelites** - were **chosen** to be a *'Light unto the Nations'*, as an example to be emulated, **Muhammad** turned it into a different and totally aggressive and unmerciful dogma that required him and his followers to **impose** their beliefs by **force upon all of humanity.**

*Al Imran 3:81 Behold! Allah took the **covenant** of the **Prophets** [Nabiyeen] saying: "I give you a **Book and Wisdom**; then comes to you an **Messenger [Rassoul]** confirming what is with you;*

*** It is very clear from the verse above that according to the Quran, a **Prophet is given Scripture and Wisdom** while a **Messenger** would come only to **Confirm existing Scriptures*****

Most important of all is that a **prophet** by definition is **one who can predict future events. Moses** was able to do that in his confrontations with **Pharaoh** while Muhammad **never** predicted anything.

According to the following hadith, **Aisha** confirms that Muhammad was not able to predict the future, **hence he could not have been a prophet.**

Sahih Al-Bukhari Hadith 6.378 Narrated by Masruq

I said to 'Aisha, "O Mother! Did Prophet Muhammad see his Lord?" 'Aisha said, "What you have said makes my hair stand on end ! Know that if somebody tells you one of the following three things, he is a liar: Whoever tells you that Muhammad saw his Lord, is a liar." Then Aisha recited the Verse:

"No vision can grasp Him, but His grasp is over all vision. He is the Most Courteous Well-Acquainted with all things." (6.103)

"It is not fitting for a human being that Allah should speak to him except by inspiration or from behind a veil." (42.51)

'Aisha further said,

"And whoever tells you that the Prophet knows what is going to happen tomorrow, is a liar." She then recited:

"No soul can know what it will earn tomorrow." (31.34)

Tabari 1:181 " The Prophet said **'I was sent immediately before the coming of the Day of Doom.** I preceded it like this one preceding that one' -referring to his index and middle finger"

> **182** "he said 'Allah will not make this nation [of Islam] incapable of lasting half a day -a day being a thousand years- ...Consequently, based upon the Prophet's authority, what remained of time was half a day that had elapsed to the Prophet's statement ...

*** Ladies & gentlemen, based upon Muhammad's prophecy, **Dooms Day** should have occurred 500 years after his alleged 'revelation' which occurred about 610 AD.

I.Q. Al Rassooli

Well, as we all know, **the year 1110** had passed and we are in the year 2008 AD without the prophecy of the infallible 'Prophet' having come true***

Muhammad's alleged prophesies could be counted on one hand none of which ever came true.

Our listeners should remember the following **facts:**
1. Almost **all** of the Quranic verses refer to Muhammad as **rassool**/ Messenger and **not nabi**/Prophet

2. Muhammad had his **signet** ring inscribed with "Muhammad Rassool^Allah" **not** Nabi^Allah

3. The Hadiths address Muhammad with the **mantra** " Allah & His Messenger/Rassool" and **never** "Allah & his **nabi**/Prophet

4. The title Prophet was conferred upon Muhammad posthumously, after his Death ***

#84. Islam Before Muhammad

Q: I find it amazing how the followers of Muhammad who read his Quran assiduously in clear Arabic are still totally oblivious or unwilling to understand the actual meaning and or implications of what they are reading.

You & I have discussed this matter recently and I would like you to share this subject with our listeners

A: It is a great tragedy that part and parcel of the **burden** of being a follower of Muhammad is to be in a state of total **denial** all of one's life.

I do not say this jokingly but as a very **frightning** manifestation of the incredible depth of their **programming & indoctrination.**

Let us look for example at the earliest and most relevant Quranic verses on this subject starting with

Surat Al Baqara 2: 127   *And remember Abraham and Isma`il raised the foundations of the House (with this prayer): "Our Lord! accept (this service) from us for thou art the All-Hearing the All-Knowing.*

128 *"Our Lord! make of us*

Muslims bowing to Thy (Will) [Rabbina wa^ja'lna Muslimeeni laka]

and of our progeny a people Muslim bowing to Thy (Will) [wa min thurriyatina ummata Muslimata laka]

132 *And this was the legacy that*

Abraham left to his sons and so did Jacob;

"O my sons! Allah hath chosen the faith for you; then die not except in the faith of Islam."

[fala tamootoona illa wa antum Muslimoona]

133 *Were ye witnesses when death appeared before*

I.Q. Al Rassooli

Jacob? Behold he said to his sons: "What will ye worship after me?"

They said: "We shall worship thy Allah and the Allah of thy fathers of Abraham Isma`il and Isaac the one (true) **Allah to Him we bow (in Islam)."[wa nahhnoo lahoo Muslimoona]**

136 *Say ye: "We believe in Allah and*

the revelation given to us and to Abraham Isma`il Isaac Jacob and the Tribes and that given to Moses and Jesus and that given to (all) Prophets from their Lord we make no difference between one and another of them **and we bow to Allah (in Islam)."[wa nahhnoo lahoo Muslimoona]**

I have recited the relevant parts in the Arabic language so that the listeners, whether they are English or Arabic speakers hear the words **muslimoona** as it actually appears in the Quran and we cannot be accused of any falsification.

These verses very clearly refer to Abraham, Ishmael, Isaac, Jacob and their descendants, the Tribes of Israel.

Let us now point out the **obvious** that invariably escapes the intellect of the followers of Muhammad:

1. All of the above named Biblical characters were Hebrews and **not** Arabs

2. Every one of them lived at least 2500 years **before** Muhammad & his Quran

3. Since the Quran itself **asserts** that they were all **muslims,** because they believed in the one & only Allah, then Islam as a **concept preceded** Muhammad and his Quran by at least 2500 years.

4. By what standard of logic or morality then, do Muhammad and his followers appropriate this concept as if it were their own invention and hence belongs to them alone?

5. For **1400 years** and unto this day they pride themselves at being the **only** true Muslims and hence **superior** to all other beliefs when in **fact & reality** they had Plagiarized, Plundered, Pirated & Perverted this concept from the **Jews.**

Let us now examine more relevant verses:

Al Imran 3: 52 When Jesus found unbelief on their part he said: "Who will be my helpers to Allah?" Said the Disciples: "We are Allah's helpers we believe in Allah and do thou bear witness that **we are Muslims**

[wa^shhad bi anna Muslimoona].

64 Say: "O people of the Book! come to

common terms as between us and you: that we worship none but Allah; that we associate no partners with Him; that we erect not from among ourselves Lords and patrons other than Allah." If then they turn back say: "Bear witness that **we (at least) are Muslims** (bowing to Allah's will)

[wa ashhadoo bi-anna Muslimoona]."

Al Ma^idah 5: 111 "And behold! I inspired the Disciples to have faith in Me and Mine Apostle: they said `We have faith and do thou bear witness that

we bow to Allah as Muslims'. [wa ashhad bi-anna Muslimoona]"

Al Hajj 22: 78 And strive in His cause ... He has chosen you and has imposed no difficulties on you in religion; **it is the cult of your father Abraham.** It is He Who has named you **Muslims [al Muslimeena] both before** and in this (Revelation);

*** This verse makes it **crystal clear** that it was Allah who named the Hebrews & the Israelites **[before]** and the Muhammadan Arabs **[after]** as Muslimeena***

Al Qusas 28: 53 And when it is recited to them they say: "We believe therein for it is the Truth from our Lord: indeed **we have been Muslims** (bowing to Allah's Will) **[Muslimeena]** from before this."

*** It is important that our listeners should grasp the following **FACTS,** based upon the verses above, as well as others in the Quran, that Adam, Noah, Abraham, Ishmael, Isaac, Jacob, the Tribes, Moses, Jesus, Mary and the Apostles, existed thousands of years **BEFORE** Muhammad and his Quran.

They all believed in the One and Only God of Israel and hence were, by definition of the word and its implication in the Quranic verses, **MUSLIMS.**

In fact, any creature, from anywhere **in the** universe, who submits to the will of, or believes in the One and Only God, is automatically, a MUSLIM and has absolutely nothing to do with either Muhammad or his Quran.

It is an affront to logic and to human intelligence in general, that the followers of Muhammad have **ARROGATED** the term **ISLAM** only to themselves, for the last 1400 years, while it is neither the truth nor the reality.

What is even more relevant is another **fact** and that is, there were people in Arabia, long before Muhammad & his Quran who believed **only** in the God of Abraham and who were neither followers of the faith of the Jews nor of Christianity who were called Hanifs.

Khadijah, Muhammad's first and most important wife in his life was one of them, a **hanifiyah.**

The **Muhammadan Muslim** exegetes do not dwell at all upon her **incaculable** influence upon **Muhammad's** religious beliefs, his psychology and the course of his life.

Her belief in the **One & Only God of Abraham,** was the cause that turned **Muhammad** away from his **Paganism** and made such an impact upon his mind, to such an extent, that he took it upon himself to bring **all** of the **Pagan Arabians** to **monotheism.**

In conclusion, Islam as a concept preceded Muhammad & his Quran by at least 25 centuries.

Islam as a way of life preceded Muhammad & his Quran by at least 2100 years.

There is absolutely nothing new of value in the Quran.

#85 Muhammad's Surgeries

Q: Although the Quran asserts Muhammad's fallibilities, sins and errors as an ordinary human being, all be it as a messenger of Allah, his followers have created the myth of his sinlessness called Isma' in similitude to that of Jesus.

What are the facts and the fictions?

A: It is with great regret that I have to remind our listeners repeatedly every single time that they or you ask a question, that what they have read in the **Quran** & **Hadiths** or heard from the followers of **Muhammad are lies, deceptions, mendacities and illusions.** I have no choice but to do so since they truly are what I label them to be.

Here also, what the followers of Muhammad have concocted regarding his character are **pure myths** that have been repeated by them for so many centuries that they now actually believe them to be true. The perpetrators of the **deception** have become its foremost **victims.**

(I)

In **Alfred Guillaum's** translation of *Sirat Rassul'llah* by **Ibn Ishaq- (P71-72)**, there is a tradition that when **Muhammad** was a little child **(two to three years old)**, **Halima** his foster mother, was informed by **Muhammad** that ....

"Two men in white raiment came to me with a gold basin full of snow, who opened up my belly, extracted my heart and split it; then they extracted a leech/clot (Alaqa) from it and threw it away; then they washed my heart and belly with that snow until they had thoroughly cleaned them"

*** It is beyond belief to assume that a child of that age was alone tending flocks of animals, who knew about snow in the unforgiving heat of the Arabian desert, as well as about leeches in waterless Arabia.

What the story actually relates is that the surgery removed Muhammad's SINS at the age of 2/3 years.

I would like to point out to our listeners is the fact that Muhammad used the term **'alaq'**, once again later on,

as the **source** of **human creation,** in the first allegedly revealed verse of the Quran as in :

Al Alaq 96: 1 Proclaim! (or Read!) in the name of thy Lord and Cherisher Who created

2 Created man out of a (mere) **clot of congealed blood** *[alaq]*

In Arabic   *Iqraa bismi Rabbika^ allathi khalaqa*

Khalaqa^l Insana min Alaq

This is obviously contrary to the Biblical Story of the Creation ***

(II)

Sahih Al-Bukhari Hadith 4.770 Narrated by Sharik bin Abdullah bin Abi Namr

I heard Anas bin Malik telling us about the night when the Prophet was made to travel from the Ka'ba mosque. Three persons came to the Prophet before he was divinely inspired as an Aspostle, while he was sleeping in Al Masjid-ul-Haram. The first said, "Which of them is he?" The second said, "He is the best of them." That was all that happened then, and he did not see them till they came at another night and he perceived their presence with his heart, for the eyes of the Prophet were closed when he was asleep, but his heart was not asleep. This is characteristic of all the prophets: Their eyes sleep but their hearts do not sleep. Then Gabriel took charge of the Prophet and ascended along with him to the Heaven.

*** In the Muhammadan traditions, it is the **heart** which contains the human consciousness and **not** the **brain** ***

(III)

Sahih Al-Bukhari Hadith 4.429 Narrated by Malik bin Sasaa

The Prophet said, "While I was at the House in a state midway between sleep and wakefulness, (an angel recognized me) **as the man lying between two men.**

A golden tray full of wisdom and belief was brought to me and **my body was cut open** from the throat to the lower part of the abdomen and then my abdomen was **washed** with **Zam-zam water** and **(my heart was) filled with wisdom and belief.**

*** According to Muhammad, **wisdom & belief** are **physical** and **not intellectual & spiritual**

Once again at the age of about 50 years, Muhammad needed another **physical/ spiritual** and **intellectual cleansing** to remove his **sins** and **unbelief.**

The inquisitive listener should wonder at the expression: "*as the man lying between two men*". Why was Muhammad, who already had several wives, be sleeping in the mosque and not his own house, lying between **Two** men?

The answer to this question, took me a very long time to figure out. Muhammad never missed a chance at **emulating** any Biblical story regarding a **prophet,** this time from the New Testament about Jesus, who was crucified **between two men.**

Once more, Muhammad needed **surgery** to remove his **sins** from his **body** and **not** from his **brain*****

(IV)

Sahih Al-Bukhari Hadith 5.227 Narrated by Abbas bin Malik

Malik bin Sasaa said that Allah's Apostle described to them his **Night Journey** saying, "While I was lying in **Al-Hatim or Al-Hijr,** suddenly someone came to me and cut my body open from here to here." I asked Al-Jarud who was by my side, "What does he mean?" He said, "It means from his throat to his pubic area," or said, "From the top of the chest." The Prophet further said,

"**He then took out my heart.** Then a gold tray of Belief was brought to me and my heart was washed **and was filled (with Belief)** and then returned to its original place"

Then a white animal which was smaller than a mule and bigger than a donkey was brought to me." The Prophet said, "The animal's step (was so wide that it) reached the farthest point within the reach of the animal's sight. I was carried on it, and Gabriel set out with me till we reached the nearest heaven.

*** The traditions that Muhammad needed two or three surgeries to have his body operated upon and filled with belief, is astounding in its implications.

Why should the most 'perfect' of men need to have himself 'scourged' from unbelief several times in his lifetime is beyond comprehension. On the contrary, this shows that Muhammad was **sinful** and repeatedly failing in **belief.**

In conclusion, the Hadiths above which contradict each other, completely and utterly **destroy, demolish** and **contradict,** all of Muhammad's followers' assertions that he was **sinless,** in their **dogma of 'isma'.**

The listeners furthermore, should appreciate the enormous implications of these stories since they were made by Muhammad's own **followers** and **not** by his **enemies** **

#86. Mu'allaqat or Pre Islamic Poetry

Q: The followers of Muhammad assert that the Quran is so beautifully written in the best Arabic language, an allegedly illiterate person like Muhammad could not have possibly been able to compose it & hence it could only have been divinely revealed.

Can you shed light on these assertions?

A: Like everything else in our series, we shall use the records of the Arabs and Muhammadan Islam to **disprove** & **dismantel** their LIES one by one.

In Arabic, Mu'allaqat means **suspended.**

These were magnificent poems composed by some of the most illustrious poets of Arabia long before Muhammad and his Quran.

Even in the **Arab** world of today they are honoured as masterpieces of poetical composition.

The days before *'Islam'* are called in **Arabic Al Jahiliyya**, meaning the *'time of ignorance'* or barbarity. However, it was during this alleged time of *'ignorance'* and barbarity, that many of the best and most beautiful and **romantic Arabic** poetry were conceived - a fact recognized even by the Muhammadan Muslims themselves.

In those days, the Arabian Peninsula was divided among many small tribal territories and sheikhdoms; and in each tribe there was a poet, **Sha'ir**, who was second in importance only to the **Sheikh**, the head of the tribe.

The poet was responsible for keeping the history and the genealogy of the tribe, and in his poems he glorified the tribe and mocked its enemies. In reality, these poets were the **News Repoters** par excellence of **pagan Arabia.**

The names of some of these poets are: **Labid; Tarafah ibn al Abd; al Harith ibn Hillizah; Amr ibn Kalthum; Antara ibn**

Shaddad al Absi;Imru al Qays. (In some other traditions, three other names are also added).

The lives of these poets were spread over a period of more than a **hundred years**. The earliest of the seven was the **Arabian Christian Imru' al-Qais,** regarded by many as the most illustrious of **Arabian Mu'allaqa** poets.

His exact date cannot be determined; but probably the best part of his career fell within the midst of the 6th century.

It is a phenomenon which deserves the fullest recognition, that the needy inhabitants of a barren land should thus have produced an artistic poetry distinguished by such a high degree of uniformity.

Even the extraordinary strict metrical system, was observed by poets, who had no inkling of theory and no knowledge of an alphabet, excites enormous surprise. In the most ancient poems, the metrical form is as scrupulously regarded as in later compositions.

The **Muallaqat** are seven **Pre-Islamic Arabic** poems from around the 6th Century AD that are considered the best of their kind. They are called the **'suspended'** due to **the myth which developed about them during the 'Islamic' period** - that, being the best poems of their time, they were written on parchments using golden ink, and hung on the walls of the **Ka'ba** for all to see.

However, that name first appeared only a **long time after** the poems had been composed, since the title **Mu'allaqat is not mentioned at all, in the sources from that period.** It is therefore a **false myth**, which comes from romancing the Pre-Islamic period by the later Muhammadan scholars.

Since the Arabic culture of that time was mainly oral, these poems were at first not written down, but recited and later memorized by individuals, usually the poets' apprentices.

The first Muallaqat compilations were written in the beginning of the Islamic period ,7th - 8th Centuries AD (about 200 to 300 years **after they were composed).**

The number of poems that were included varied, but seven of these poems are considered a canon to this day, and at the head of those seven is the one written by the **Christian Arabian** poet **Imru al Qays**.

Al Muallaqat belong to a poetic genre called al **Qasida**. Nowadays, almost every long poem can be called a **Qasida**, but in the ancient times the definition was more distinct: a **Qasida** was a long poem with very strict form.

The **stanzas** of the **Qasida** are divided into **two parts** with identical **metre**; the metres of **Arabic poetry**, like those of **Grecian poetry**, are based on **short and long syllables**, and the ones used for the **Qasidas** were usually the long metres, which helped create the typical long descriptive segments.

The **rhyme** is consistent throughout all the stanzas, and the two parts of the first stanza often rhyme as well. The classical **Qasidas** are constructed of three main themes, written according to certain fixed conventions (though not every poet used all three together).

1. In the first part of the **Qasida**, which is called **Nasib** in **Arabic**, the poet describes his arrival to the campgrounds of his love's tribe, expecting a romantic rendezvous, and his discovery that the tribe had left the place to look for other pastures. The poet halts the friends that have ridden with him, and sits down to cry, remembering the love that has been and is now gone.

2. After reflecting on his lost romance, the return to reality hurts the poet so much that he cannot stay near the campgrounds anymore, and he mounts his riding animal and goes out to the desert. This part, called **Rihla (journey)**, is usually longer than the **Nasib** and has a faster pace, and it contains many descriptions of the dangers of the desert and of the poet's riding animal, whose loyalty is portrayed as a contrast to the disloyalty of womankind.

3. In the third part of the **Qasida** the poet **praises the traits of the ideal man** by glorifying himself or his tribe, or by tongue-lashing other tribes.

It is very hard to translate classical **Arabic** poetry into **English as** the language of the ancient poets in particular, **is amazingly rich,** where complex notions can be expressed with very few words.

Perhaps the oldest passage where it is stated that the poems were hung up, occurs in the *'Iqd al-Farid* **(The Precious Necklace)** by the Spaniard **Ibn Abd Rabbih**. We read there:

"The Arabs had such an interest in poetry, and valued it so highly, that they took seven long pieces selected from the ancient poetry, wrote them in gold on pieces of Coptic linen folded up, and hung them up on the curtains which covered the Ka'ba.

Against this, we have the testimony of **al-Nahhas**, who says in his commentary on the **Mu'allaqat:**

"As for the assertion that they were hung up in the Ka'ba, it is not known to any of those who have handed down ancient poems." This cautious scholar is unquestionably right in rejecting a story so utterly unauthenticated.

Even more pertinent is the fact, that most of the **pagan Arabs** were **illiterate** and hence, hanging these poems to be read, would have been a useless exercise especially since the **Arabic** writing of those days, did not yet have vowels and there were several different **Arabic** dialects.

The customs of the Arabs before Muhammad are pretty accurately known to us; we have also a mass of information about the affairs of **Mecca** at the time when **Muhammad** arose; **but there is no trace** of this or anything like it to be found in really good and ancient authorities.

To account for the disappearance of the **Mu'allaqat** from the **Ka'ba** we are told, in a passage of late origin "**that they were taken down** at the capture of Mecca by Muhammad".

But in that case, we should have expected some hint of this event being mentioned in one or more of Muhammad's biographies, and in the works on the history of **Mecca; in all the extant records of the period concerned, we find no such thing.**

Up to a time when the art of writing had become far more general than it was before the spread of Muhammadan Islam, **poems were never or very rarely written, with the exception, perhaps, of epistles in poetic form.**

Based upon all the information available, the diffusion of poetry was exclusively committed to oral tradition.

In **fact,** even the Quran was memorized and transmitted **orally,** to start with, before it was committed to writing after Muhammad's death.

In short, this legend, so often retailed by Arabs, and still more frequently by ignorant Europeans, must be entirely rejected.

The most important conclusion derived from all the above has nothing whatsoever to do about the actual existence of the Mu'allaqat or not but upon the **fact** that Pre Muhammadan **illiterate** poets were able to compose **divine** odes **without** divine intercession.

Since Muhammad was not born in a vacuum, but was surrounded by both pagan and other religious influences, Muhmmad's Quran too, is also in the format of a Qasida with a similar repetitive theme based upon the following:

1. A people are in error

2. A prophet declares himself calling them to believe in the One and Only Allah

3. Most of his tribe ridicule and oppress him and continue in unbelief

4. Allah visits them with catastrophes destroying most of them

5. The prophet and a few of his followers are vindicated

6. Muhammad also, praised himself just as the Jahiliyah poets did.

Muhammad's Quran, did not have to originate from a divine being, since the Odes of the seven Muallaqat are even more beautiful, both in meaning and in structure, than the Quranic verses.

The poets who recited these odes were just as illiterate as allegedly Muhammad was, but no one ever considered their poems the result of *'divine revelations'*.

So why Muhammad's Quran?

We have after all, only Muhammad's unsubstantiated assertions that they were revealed to him by Allah.

#87 Jesus in the Quran

Q: The Quran asserts that Jesus was a Muslim and hence is one of their prophets. The Quran also asserts that Jesus did not die on the cross.

Moreover, excluding Muhammad, every important prophet mentioned in the Quran is either an Israelite or a Jew.

Could you please explain these strange anomalies?

A: Most of the followers of Muhammad as well as most other human beings, are totally ignorant of what you have just mentioned.

In our Chapter 4, 'Who is a Muslim?', we explained that any creature from anywhere in the universe who believes in the concept of the One & Only God, is automatically a Muslim: That is one who submits to the will of **One Divine Entity**. This has nothing whatsoever to do with either Muhammad or his Quran.

All the Israelites and their descendants the Jews were and are **Muslims;** so were Jesus and all the Hebrew prophets.

Al Baqra 2: 136 Say ye: "We believe in Allah and the revelation given to us and to Abraham Isma'il Isaac Jacob and the Tribes and that given to Moses and Jesus and that given to (all) Prophets from their Lord we make no difference between one and another of them and we bow to **Allah (in Islam) [wa nahhnoo lahoo Muslimoon]."**

Al Imran 3: 45 Behold! the angels said "O Mariam! Allah giveth thee glad tidings of a Word from Him: his name will be Christ Jesus the son of Mariam held in honor in this world and the Hereafter and of (the company of) those nearest to Allah.

3: 55 Behold! Allah said: "O Jesus! **I shall take thee and raise thee** *to Myself and clear thee (of the falsehoods) of those who blaspheme....*

*** There is a deliberate miss-translation of the verse above to cover up the inconsistencies of the Quran.

" *I shall take thee...*" should have actually been translated to " ***I shall cause thee to die and then raise thee...***"

[inny **mutawaffika** *(I shall let you die) wa rafi'uka ilayya (and will raise you to me)]*

which completely changes the meaning and hence the implications of the verse because it contradicts the earlier assertion in the *Quran (4:157)* that Jesus did not die.

Moreover, based upon the general theme of the Gospel accounts, the Jews would have rightly rejected Jesus for the following theological reason:

If he had declared himself the son of God, this would have been against their strict monotheism just as it would have been totally unacceptable to Muhammad and his followers who would have executed him also.

Al Imran 3: 59 *This similitude of Jesus before Allah is as that of Adam: He created him from dust then said to him: "Be" and he was.*

*** As usual, the Quran is again in **error** since only **adam** was created from a **mould** and **not** by the **word** of God***

Al Nisaa 4: 157 *That they said (in boast) "We killed Christ Jesus(Massih Isa) the son of Mariam the Apostle of Allah";* **but they killed him not nor crucified him** *but so it was made to appear to them and those who differ therein are full of doubts with no (certain) knowledge but only conjecture to follow for of a surety they killed him not.*

*** The unlearned Muhammad who arrived on the scene of history at least 620 years after the events of Jesus, presumes to know more than the Gospels and the Christians. Muhammad had even the name of the mother of Jesus, Mary, mixed up with the name of the sister of Moses & Aaron, Mariam of 1400 years earlier.

Moreover, this verse **contradicts** *Al Imran 3:55.*

Most important of all, this verse completely **destroys** the Christian **religion** since **without** the **death** of Jesus, there is no **resurrection** and hence, without **death & resurrection,** there is neither meaning nor purpose for **Christianity** ***

Al Ma'ida 5: 46 *And in their footsteps We sent Jesus the son of Mariam confirming the law that had come before him: We sent him the Gospel: therein was guidance and light and confirmation of the law that had come before him: a guidance and an admonition to those who fear Allah.*

Al Hadid 57: 27 *Then in their wake We followed them up with (others of) Our apostles: We sent after them Jesus the son of Mariam and* **bestowed on him the Gospel...**

*** Yet once more is the Quran in **error (twice** in this case) since neither the God of Israel or Jesus nor Allah ever sent him the Gospels.

The Gospels, after all, were **written** down **decades after** the death of Jesus ***

Al Saff 61: 6 *And remember Jesus the son of Mariam said: "O Children of Israel! I am the apostle of Allah (sent) to you confirming the Law (which came) before me and giving glad Tidings of an Apostle to come after* **me whose name shall be Ahmad."** *But when he came to them with Clear Signs they said "This is evident sorcery!"*

*** No follower of Muhammad – or anybody else in the universe - could point out such a statement **anywhere** in the whole of Christian Scripture ***

Sahih al-Bukhari Hadith 3.656 & 3.425 narrated by abu Huraira

Allah's Apostle said, "The Hour will not be established until the son of Mariam (i.e. Jesus) descends amongst you as a just ruler, he will break the cross, kill the pigs, and abolish the Jizya tax. Money will be in abundance so that nobody will accept it

Sahih al-Bukhari Hadith 4.658 narrated by abu Huraira

Allah's Apostle said "How will you be when the son of Mariam (i.e. Jesus) descends amongst you and he will judge people by the Law of the Qur'an and not by the law of Gospel

Sahih al-Bukhari Hadith 7.209 narrated by Nafi

Whenever Ibn 'Umar was asked about marrying a Christian lady or a Jewess, he would say: "Allah has made it unlawful for the believers to marry ladies who ascribe partners in worship to Allah, and I do not know of a greater sin, as regards to ascribing partners in worship, etc. to Allah, than that a lady should say that Jesus is her Lord although he is just one of Allah's slaves."

Sunan of Abu-Dawood Hadith 4310 Narrated by Abu Hurayrah

The Prophet said: There is no prophet between me and him, that is, Jesus. He will descent (to the earth). When you see him, recognize him: a man of medium height, reddish fair, wearing two light yellow garments, looking as if drops were falling down from his head though it will not be wet. He will fight the people for the cause of Islam. He will break the cross, kill swine, and abolish jizyah.

Allah will perish all religions except Islam. He will destroy the Antichrist and will live on the earth for forty years and then he will die. The Muslims will pray over him.

*** The Quran asserts that **all** the prophets of Israel, including Jesus, Mary and the Apostles **were Muslims:** Believers in the One and Only God; which of course they were.

But **not** in Allah, that neither the Israelites & Jews nor the Christians had any knowledge of nor is his name mentioned anywhere in the Bible or the New Testament.

This chapter confirms yet again, all our previous assertions, that Muhammad **Plagiarized, Plundered, Pirated and/or Perverted Precepts, Concepts, Thoughts & Ideas from the Hebrew Bible & the New Testament** and inserted them in his Quran to give it an aura of authenticity and divinity.

#88. Days of Creation

Q: If Allah is the same god that revealed the Torah to Moses, as the Quran asserts, then why is the story of the creation in the Quran very different from, and incompatible with that of the original in the Bible? Will you please explain these strange contradictions?

A: As you well know, and as our audience is also becoming aware of, that the Quranic versions of the Biblical events are totally out of **synchronous** in **Time & Space** with their **originals** in the Bible.

Muhammad had actually no idea where and when these events occurred and invariably got them all mixed and jumbled up as he did with the Biblical Characters also.

His knowledge and understanding of the Biblical **creation** story suffered just as badly as all the others as shown repeatedly in his Quran.

In the Bible, God clearly indicates that the Universe and all living things were created in **six** days; as in Genesis 1:1-31.

The Bible describes the creation step by step, day by day in beautiful detail. **nothing** like this is explained in the Quran. As usual, the Quran has no details, no rhyme, no rhythm and no beauty.

The Quran – which is allegedly the 'Word of the all knowing Allah', is remarkably **uncertain about the number of days of the creation:**

*Al Sajdah 32: 4 It is Allah Who has created the heavens and the earth and all between them in **six Days** and is firmly established on the Throne*

*Al Fussilat 41:9 Say: Is it that ye Deny Him Who **created the earth in two Days?**....10 He set on the (earth) Mountains standing firm high above it and bestowed blessings on the earth and measured* *therein all things to give them nourishment in due proportion **in four Days** in accordance with (the needs of) those who seek (sustenance).12 So He completed them as seven firmaments in **two Days** and He assigned to each heaven its duty and command*

*** If we add all the days of creation above, we come to **eight** days. Moreover, the Bible mentions **only one** firmament and not **seven.**

How is it possible to imply that the angel Gabriel, the messenger of Allah lied and deceived Muhammad regarding these primal subjects?

In fact, it is easier and infinitely more logical to come to the conclusion that **it was Muhammad who actually 'revealed' all the verses of the Quran** but cleverly projected them into the mouth of the unsuspecting Allah to make them sanctified, than to accept that both Allah & Gabriel were misinforming and misleading Muhammad***

Al Qaf 50:38 *We created the heavens and the earth and all between them in Six Days nor did any sense of weariness touch Us*

*** It was beyond Muhammad's intellect and comprehension to understand the Hebrew concept of a

"Day of Rest, the Sabbath". He misunderstood it to mean that God rested out of weariness or tiredness.

He did not comprehend that the God of Israel finished all His creation in **six** days and had nothing further to **create** on the seventh; that is, he ceased the process of creating.

It was the God of Israel and **not** Allah, who mandated upon his followers, the Israelites, that on the Seventh day, the Sabbath, they must all stop their usual daily labour and sweat to earn their living during the first six days of the week.

Instead, God made the Sabbath a holy day, a day of rest, a day of cessation of all labour so that humanity could enjoy each others' company, especially their families & friends and admire the wonders of his creation.

Moreover, this Day of Rest was **not** and is **not** exclusive to the Israelites **only** but was & is also a day of rest, that is no labour being done, for their servants, the strangers amongst them, all their animals and all their lands (no tilling).

This very simple, incredibly Merciful, Compassionate and **historically, culturally and theologically unique and revolutionary concept,** was truly beyond Muhammad's Intellectual and Moral grasp and comprehension.

Because of Muhammad's utter failure to understand this sublime concept, there is no provision for a day of rest for his Muhammadan Muslim followers.

Friday, the Jumua' is **not** a day of **rest** for the followers of Muhammad but a day when they all are instructed to attend noon prayers ***

According to some other Muhammadan Traditions **(Mishkat, xxiv. c. I pt 3),** Allah created the **earth on Saturday,** the **hills on Sunday,** the **trees on Monday,** and **unpleasant things on Tuesday,** the **light on Wednesday,** the **beast on Thursday** and **Adam,** who was the last of Creation, was created after the time of afternoon prayers **on Friday.**

*** Our readers should be made aware that these alleged 'Traditions', were invented **like TENS of thousands of others,** over a period of almost **300 years** after the death of Muhammad and have absolutely nothing to do with facts or reality especially, since neither Muhammad, nor his pagan Arab tribe, the Quraysh, had any knowledge of previous revelations, such as the Bible.

Moreover, if these 'traditions' were true, then on which day were the Sun, Moon, stars and the remainder of the cosmos created? They are missing in the above list.

Also, how could Adam have been created on Friday, after the time of afternoon prayers, when in reality, **there could have been no people to pray and no mosque to pray in?** After all, Adam and

Eve only started copulating after the 7th day of creation and after their expulsion from the Garden of Eden.

Throughout their history, and unto today, the first day of the Muhammadan Muslim week is called **Ahhad** which is from the Hebrew root **ehad** meaning **first** or **one**!

So how could have Allah started his creation on **Saturday,** the **Sabbath** which was the **last** day and **not** the first, the day that He ordained as a day of cessation of creation, even according to the Quran itself?

As usual with Muhammadan Islam, their own words, from their own mouth, whether from the Quran, Hadiths or their alleged traditions, expose their **mendacity, irreverence, stupidity, ignorance, irrelevance & total lack of authenticity.**

Once again, our listeners, so called Believers & Unbelievers have a lot to digest, think about and evaluate regarding the veracity or lack there of, the alleged divine origin of the Quran***

#89 Muhammad & Astronomy

Q: The world is repeatedly reminded by the follower of Muhammad that the Quran is not only a spiritual revelation but actually contains almost all knowledge that humans need to conduct their lives with.

How accurate are these declarations?

A: Muhammadan scholars assert in no uncertain terms, that **Muhammad had full knowledge of almost everything under the sun.** They have hundreds if not thousands of books printed, desperately trying to prove the unprovable.

The following is only a small sample of traditions; let our listeners make their own minds up:

Al Baqara 2:189 *"They ask you about the New Moons. Say: They are but signs to mark fixed seasons in (the affairs of) men, and for Hajj Pilgrimage."* *** Allah created the Moon so that the Hajj can be performed on time by the followers of Muhammad***

Al Kahf 18:83 *"They ask you about Dhu'l-Qarnain [Alexander the Great]. Say, 'I will cite something of his story. We gave him authority in the land and means of accomplishing his goals. So he followed a path until he reached the setting place of the sun.* ***He saw that it set in black, muddy, hot water. Near it he found a people."***

*** As our readers know, we receive a lot of e mail and videos attempting to prove the mathematical and astronomical miracles of the Quran, from the speed of light and nuclear energy to outer space explorations.

The verse above, in **unambiguous** Arabic, is asserting that Allah – the all knowing – is informing Muhammad that the Sun sets in a puddle of murky water on Earth.

For those followers of Muhammad who are listening and like to play with numbers, please be aware that the Sun is over 1,000,000 times bigger than the Earth and yet, according to Muhammad's Quran, it sets every evening in a puddle of muddy waters.

Of course we are willingly ignoring its gravitation and

temperature to suit this verse ***

Al Anbiyaa 21:26 *"Don't the unbelievers see that the* **heavens and earth were joined together in one piece** *before we clove them asunder? ...Will they not believe?*

And We have set on the earth mountains as stabilizers, lest the earth should convulse without them. ...

*** The verse is not only **illogical** but also contrary to the Bible which is the only source of the creation process that Muhammad is alluding to.

It is illogical because no where in human history was there a report regarding the heavens and earth being joined and then separated, and once more we are willingly ignoring the impossibility of such a scenario.

Moreover, Muhammad's Quran, in its **infinite wisdom** has concluded that Allah created the **mountains** to act as **Stabilizers** and to hold the Earth together.

These stories and ideas, are as usual, the product and conclusions that emanated entirely from Muhammad's own vivid but entirely illogical and **uncomprehending** imagination***

Al Mulk 67:3 *"We created seven heavens, one above the other. Muhammad, can you see any fault in Ar-Rahman's creation? ...We have adorned the lowest skies with lamps, and We have made them missiles to drive away the devils and against the stone Satans*

*** Maybe I have missed something in my study of the Bible, because as far as I know, there is no mention of Even Two heavens let alone **seven**

Did Allah forget to mention this to Moses in his Torah?

What are these missiles that are scaring and warding off Devils?

Lifting the Veil

What and who are the **stone satans?**

The **enigma** deepens with every **aya** ***

Bukhari: 4.421 "I walked hand in hand with the Prophet when the sun was about to set. We did not stop looking at it. The Prophet asked,

'Do you know where the sun goes at sunset?'

I replied, 'Allah and His Apostle know better.' He said,

'It travels until it falls down and prostrates itself underneath the Throne. ... Allah will order the sun to return whence it has come and so the sun will rise in the west. And that is the interpretation of the statement of Allah in the Qur'an.'"

*** Even the oldest civilization upon earth knew that the sun rises in the **east** and sets in the West. But of course they must have all been wrong ***

Tabari I:204 "I asked the Prophet, **'Where was Allah before His creation?'** Muhammad replied: 'He was in a cloud with no air underneath or above it.'"

*** And all of us thought we need air to have clouds. Silly ignorant fools that we are ***

Tabari I:219 "When Allah wanted to create the creation, He brought forth smoke from the water. The smoke hovered loftily over it. He called it 'heaven.' Then He dried out the water and made it earth. He split it and made it seven earths on Sunday. He created the earth upon a big fish, that being the fish mentioned in the Qur'an. By the Pen, the fish was in the water. The water was upon the back of a small rock. The rock was on the back of an angel. The angel was on a big rock. The big rock was in the wind. The fish became agitated. As a result, the earth quaked, so Allah anchored the mountains and made it stable. This is why the Qur'an says, 'Allah made for the earth firmly anchored mountains, lest it shake you up.'"

*** It should be apparent to even the most simpleton of minds, that **before** the **creation,** there could not have been either water, smoke or anything else for that matter.

There really is not much that we can possibly add upon the remainder of this 'creation story' as explained by Muhammad, the ***'greatest and most knowledgeable of all the prophets'*** ***

Tabari I:232 "Gabriel brings to the sun a garment of luminosity from the light of Allah's Throne according to the measure of the hours of the day. The garment is longer in the summer and shorter in the winter, and of intermediate length in autumn and spring. The sun puts on that garment as one of you here puts on his clothes."

Tabari I:233 "When the Messenger was asked about that, he replied, 'When Allah was done with His creation He created two suns from the light of His Throne. His foreknowledge told Him that He would efface one and change it to a moon; so the moon is smaller in size."

*** As usual, Muhammad's thought processes and logic, leave a lot to be desired.

In this instance, ***'When Allah was done with His creation'***, should mean that he **Finished** the process of creation; hence why did he **continue** with the creation of the Sun and the Moon, if he had already finished?

More over and even more important, since Muhammad is only plagiarizing from the Bible regarding the story of **creation,** then yet again, he is wrong and misleading his ignorant listeners because in the Bible, the Sun and the Moon were **actually created** on the **fourth day,** and definitely **not after** the **creation.**

Genesis 1: 14 God said, " let there be luminaries in the firmament of the heaven to separate between the day and the night; **15** *and they shall serve as luminaries in the firmament of the heaven to shine upon earth" And it was so*

16 *And God made the two great luminaries, the greater luminary to dominate the day and the lesser to dominate the night...*

19 *and there was evening and there was morning, a fourth day"*

Muhammad's Allah cannot possibly be the same as the God of Israel***

Lifting the Veil

Tabari I:234 "Allah thus sent Gabriel to drag his wing three times over the face of the moon, which at the time was a sun. He effaced its luminosity and left the light in it.

Tabari I:235 "Allah's Apostle said, 'Allah created an ocean three farsakhs (918 kilometers) removed from heaven. Waves contained, it stands in the air by the command of Allah. No drop of it is spilled....

Tabari I:236 "Allah created two cities out in space, each with ten thousand gates, each 6 kilometers distant from the other. By Allah, were those people not so many and so noisy, all the inhabitants of this world would hear the loud crash made by the sun falling when it rises and when it sets. Gabriel took me to them during my Night Journey from the Sacred Mosque [the Ka'aba] to the Farthest Mosque [the none existant Jewish Temple in Jerusalem]. I told the people of these cities to worship Allah but they refused to listen to me

Tabari I:332 "The sun and the moon were in eclipse for seven days and nights."

*** It must have been Only in Arabia that they suffered total darkness for **seven** days and nights.

With such lucid depth of knowledge, one cannot possibly add any further comments to Muhammad's cosmic explanations and his **current** followers' undeniable belief in his genius, even with all of the

21st century's actual knowledge.

What is most frightening and disturbing of all, is the fact that those of Muhammad's followers who are reading or listening, would rather get angry with our statements than actually give them food for thought & reflection about the veracity of the Quran and Hadiths and Muhammad's supreme knowledge of everything***

#90 Errors in the Quran

Q: Studying the Quran has been an incredible eye opener. What I found most disturbing - considering that it is supposed to have been a divine revelation – are the astounding number of grammatical, historical, linguistic, theological and Biblical errors that fill its pages.

How can any thinking human being accept so many inconsistencies, disrepencies and outright falsehoods as having been revealed to Muhammad by the angel Gabriel?

A: The **Quran & Hadiths** have been studied in minute details, both by the followers of **Muhammad** and by Orientalists over the centuries. In the latter two hundred years, many very eminent Europeans, studied the Arabic language, the Quran and Ahadith and mastered both to an incredible degree. It is on record that the Muhammadan exegetes as well as the European Arabists have come to the following conclusions:

    a) That the Quran contains a great number of grammatical and lexical errors.

    b) It contains a significant number of words - in fact the most important ones in the Quran, about 108 of them - which are entirely foreign to the Arabic language. Most are based on and or borrowed from the Syriac, Hebrew, Aramaic, Ethiopic, Persian and others.

    c) It contains a number of names of Biblical characters not congruent with those in the Bible.

    d) It contains an enormous number of historical and theological errors.

    e) It also contains a significant number of differences & contradictions as compared with the same stories as originally written in the Hebrew Bible or the New

Lifting the Veil

Testament.

f) It has copied almost the entire Pagan Arabian traditions and fetishes but cloaked them with the wrappings of 'Islam' with only a minute number of changes.

g) It contains major historical displacements that are completely at odds with the written records and knowledge.

Based upon all the above contradictions, inconsistencies and displacements in Time and Space, Allah cannot be the God of the Bible, the God of Israel or the God of Jesus.

God by definition, is Omiscient, as the Quran asserts to be *"ALL KNOWING"* and would not have given two or more different versions of the same events dislocated in Time, in Space and in Names of characters. This attribute is, by itself, an enormous **blasphemy.**

The following are only a **fraction** of these manifest errors and contradictions from among **hundreds** upon hundreds of others:

After Cain killed his brother Abel, The Quran says

Surat Al Ma'idah 5: *" 31 Allah sent a raven who scratched the ground to show him how to hide the shame of his brother."*

The Quran in **Sura HHud 11:42 & 43** says that one of the sons of Noah refused to go into the Ark and was drowned in the flood,

the Bible says that all three sons of Noah went into the Ark with him and were saved from the flood **(Genesis 7:7).**

In **Al HHud 11:44** the Quran says that the Ark came to rest on top of mount Judi, the Bible says that it was Mount Ararat **(Genesis 8:4).**

Abraham's father, according to the Quran, is Azar *(Surat Al **An'am** 6:74),* while the Bible says that his name is **Terah (Genesis 11:26).**

The Quran says Abraham had two sons,

the Bible says they were eight (**Genesis 25:2**)

The Quran says some of Abraham's descendants lived in the valley of Mecca *(Surat Ibrahim 14:37)*,

while the Bible says they lived in Hebron *(Genesis 13:18)*.

The Quran says that Abraham had two wives, in the Bible he had three.

The Quran says that he built the Ka'ba *(Surat Al Baqara 2:125-127)*.

The Bible has no such record.

The Hadiths assert that it was Ishmael who was being sacrificed while the Bible tells us it was Isaac

The Quran states that the one who adopted Moses was Pharaoh's wife *(SuratAl Qasas 28:9)*,

While the Bible says it was Pharaoh's daughter *(Exodus 2:5)*

The Quran states that Haman lived in Egypt during Moses' time c. 1450 BCE *(28:6)*,

while the Bible says that Haman lived in Persia during King Ahasuerus time c. 400 BCE *(Esther 3:1)*.

The Quran states that Mary's brother was Aaron *(Surat Maryam 19:28)*,

while the Bible says that Aaron lived 1450 years before Mary *(Numbers 26:59)*.

The Quran asserts that she gave birth to Jesus under a palm tree *(19:23)*,

while the Gospel says it was in a stable *(Luke 2:7)*.

The Quran also mentions that Jesus spoke and made miracles at the time when he was a baby *(19:24-26)*.

The New Testament has no record of this.

Lifting the Veil

The Quran asserts that Jesus did NOT die on the cross *(Surah Al Nisaa 4:157)*

But the Gospels DISAGREE.

Surat Al Khaf 18:86 "Until, when he reached the setting of the sun, he found it set in a spring of murky water: Near it he found a People: We said: "O Zul-qarnain! (thou hast authority,) either to punish them, or to treat them with kindness."

*** According to the Quran, the **sun** sets in a murky puddle of water; but the **sun** is over **one million** times bigger than the Earth ***

Surat Al Qasas 28:38 Pharaoh built the tower of Babel in Egypt

According to the historical record, the Tower of Babel was built in what is now **Iraq** and **not** in Egypt.

Surat Al Kahaf 18:83-88 *"They ask thee concerning Zul-qarnain (Alexander the Great) Say, " I will rehearse to you something of his story"*

Verily We established his power on earth, and We gave him the ways and the means to all ends..

*** Alexander was a **pagan** and had absolutely nothing to do with prophet-hood except in the Quranic version***

The Quran states that Zacharias could not speak for three nights *(Surat Maryam 19:10),*

while the New Testament says he could not speak until the child was born (or for about 9 months) *Luke 1:20.*

*** So far, ladies & gentlemen, not a single verse above has any resemblance to any original one in the Hebrew Bible and the New Testament hence cannot possibly have been a revelation from either the angel Gabriel or the God of Israel & Jesus.

But, it could have easily been from **Satan** pretending to be the angel Gabriel. After all, he, Satan, was able to deceive Muhammad with the notorious but astounding **Satanic Verses** when Muhammad was more than willing to compromise his newly found Monotheism by reverting to Paganism

The followers of Muhammad who believe the Quranic version of the Biblical events, have not read, let alone studied either the Bible or the New Testament to compare and contrast these events since they are actually **prohibited** from doing so by their political & religious leaders.

Even when and if some of them do attain such knowledge, they are then told that both the Hebrew Bible & the New Testament have been perverted over the centuries by the followers of Moses & Jesus and hence are not the original versions that would have otherwise agreed with the Quran.

There is obviously not a single follower of Muhammad on Earth who can produce the **original** versions of these books upon which they rest their case.

Hence it would take a monumental intellectual & spiritual effort for any follower of Muhammad to use his or her own logic to overcome decades of **indoctrination** and accept the reality that it is the Quran and **only** the Quran that is in **total** and **manifest** error and falsehood***

#91. Slew the Whole World

Q: There is a verse in the Quran that is used invariably by Muhammadan apologists which declares that:
*"if anyone slew a person unless it be for murder or for spreading mischief in the land it would be as **if he slew the whole people: and if anyone saved a life it would be as if he saved the life of the whole people**"*

Are they being truthful?
A: It gives me absolutely no pleasure whatsoever, to tell our audience again & again & again that like everything else that we have been showing regarding Muhammadan Islam & its followers; the above verse is misquoted with deliberate falsification to pretend to the mostly **ignorant** and trusting world that Muhammadan Islam is a **peaceful & peaceloving** Belief System.

We heard this very verse recited by Iqbal Sakrani of the Muslim Council of Great Britain in public, in Trafalgar Square, in front of **millions** of viewers **after** the London suicide bombings on the

7th July 2005.

This was in response to the fact, that the suicide bombers were Muhammadan Muslims, raised, educated and taken care of by the tax paying people of Britain and in return, with typical **loving islam**, they mass slaughtered innocent civilians in the Name of Allah.

All of a sudden, the Muslim Council was galvanized into action to distance itself from such barbaric acts and blame the so called **radical muslims** for these misdeeds.

The very same Muslim Council, which **never** demonstrated against any and all outrages committed in the name of Allah, Muhammad or Islam, anywhere and everywhere in the world during the past decades, was then doing its utmost to pretend that it cared for the welfare of the people of this nation.

With their usual **deceitfulness,** Iqbal Sakrani, Muhammad abd al Bari, Enayat Banglawala – all of whom are of none Arabic background - & Tariq Ramadhan, as well as many other luminary Muhammadans, pretended to be outraged at these **insane** acts.

They then shed **floods of crocodile tears** in public, with the assistance and compliance of the **stupid** & criminally negligent British media.

I needed to give our listeners this background especially for those who are **not** British.

Now, I shall address the Quranic verse above from Surat al Ma'idah which tells a perverted version of the Biblical story of Cain & Able **after** Cain had murdered his brother.

I would like our audience to **listen** very carefully to the beginning of the verse which is actually the **crux** of this chapter:

Al Ma'idah 5: 32 On that account: We ordained for the Children of Israel, that if anyone slew a person unless it be for murder or for spreading mischief in the land, it would be as if he slew the whole people: and if anyone saved a life, it would be as if he saved the life of the whole people. ...

This verse, like **hundreds** of others in the Quran, is **plundered & perverted** from the Bible and or from Jewish Rabbinic traditions.

This particular one is from Pirque Avot (Sayings of the Fathers) in the Mishna.

Ladies & gentlemen, when the above verse is **recited** in full, one would understand that it was Allah addressing the People of Israel and **only** the People of Israel **but** neither Muhammad nor his Arab followers.

By deliberately, willfully and with aforethought cutting out *"We ordained for the Children of Israel ---* Iqbal Sakrani and all the others who quoted – and still quote – this **truncated** verse, changed the perception of the **unwary** listeners and made them believe that it is part of **peaceful** Muhammadan Islamic teachings.

That was and still is, their whole purpose and intent and they have been and still are succeeding in their **deception** and **fraudulence!**

If any of you need further **proof,** you can look at **hundreds** upon hundreds of Muhammadan preachers on U tube who quote the **truncated, edited or perverted** version ONLY of this verse!

If this action is **not dishonourable,** what is?

Why would such educated & learned men, stoop to these abysmal levels of **hypocrisy & mendacity** if their Muhammadan Islam is so superior to **all** other beliefs?

Why would they need to **distort** the Quranic verse if the Quran is as holy as they pretend it to be?

Is this **not** a deliberate alteration of Allah's words?

Does this not constitute **blasphemy?**

How can any of them **justify** such **dishonesty** both religious & intellectual?

How could they treat their listeners, so called Believers or Unbelievers with such **contempt?**

Since Muhammadan Muslims can do this shameless and systematic editing in the 21st century, in front of millions of people, then how dare they tell us that the Quran that we have today has never been altered in the last 1400 years?

They have been getting away with these **intellectual, MOral & religious** perversions because most human beings do not know the subjects at hand and hence are easily **duped** by well dressed & well spoken people whom they think are paragons of virtue and knowledge!

Well Ladies & gentlemen, they **are not!** as we have been demonstrating repeatedly in our series, using the very Muhammadan Arabic sources to PROVE the opposite?

The very internet that is used by the followers of Muhammad to propagate their messages of Hate, of War, of Superiority, of Racism & of Intellectual Fraud, is also **enlightening** a mostly **ignorant** world about the real characteristics of Muhammadan Islam.

In fact, the internet shows all their **depraved** behaviour of Mass Murder, Kidnappings, Beheadings, Stoning to death, Genital Mutilation, Desecration of all kinds of Holy places etc etc perpetrated upon **both** Unbelievers as well as other Believing sects of Muhammadan Islam.

Can any follower of Muhammad **prove** what we are revealing here as **erroneous** or **mendacious?**

We await their usual attacks based upon **denial! denial! denial!** Of Facts & Reality.

#92. Suckling a Grown Man/Rath'at al Kabir

Q: It seems that your repeated assertion that it is by Divine Justice that the Hadiths destroy Muhammadan Islam has recently been vindicated by the Fatwa (Muhammadan religious ruling) regarding the Breast feeding of a grown man by a grown woman among the Believers.

Will you please explain?

A: Although the statements that we make are **always** based upon **Muhammadan Muslim** authorities, many of our listeners still remain in doubt because of the incredible depravity, immorality or stupidity of many of the subjects that we are investigating.

It is hence extremely gratifying when some of the statements that we make, are **inadvertently** further authenticated by some of the highest scholars of **Muhammadan Islam.**

Recently, the head of the Al-Azhar Hadith Department, put out a religious opinion called a **fatwa** asserting that in Muhammadan Islam, **breastfeeding allows a woman to be with a man in private.**

I shall now read to our listeners the official sequence of events:

Dr. Izzat Atiyya explained his fatwa in an interview with *Al-Watani Al-Yawm,* the weekly of Egypt's ruling National Democratic Front party. He said: "The religious ruling that appears in the Prophet's conduct [Sunna] confirms that breastfeeding allows a man and a woman to be together in private, even if they are not family and if the woman did not nurse the man in his infancy, before he was weaned - providing that their being together serves some purpose, religious or secular...

"Being together in private means being in a room with the door closed, so that nobody can see them... A man and a woman who are not family members are not permitted [to do this], because it raises suspicions and doubts.

A man and a woman who are alone together are not [necessarily] having sex, but this possibility exists, and breastfeeding provides a solution to this problem... I also insist that the breastfeeding relationship be officially documented in writing... The contract will state that this woman has suckled this man... After this, the woman may remove her **hijab** and expose her hair in the man's [presence]...

Dr. Atiyya further explained that the breastfeeding does not necessarily have to be done by the woman herself. "The important point," he said, "is that the man and the woman must be related through breastfeeding.

[This can also be achieved] by means of the man's mother or sister suckling the woman, or by means of the woman's mother or sister suckling the man, since [all of these solutions legally] turn them into brother and sister...

"The logic behind [the concept] of breastfeeding an adult is to transform the bestial relationship between [two people] into a religious relationship based on [religious] duties... Since [this] breastfeeding takes place between [two] adults, the man is still permitted to marry the woman [who breastfed him], whereas [a woman] who nursed [a man] in his infancy is not permitted to marry him...

"The adult must suckle directly from the [woman's] breast... [This according to a *hadith* attributed to Aisha, wife of the Prophet Muhammad], which tells of Salem [the adopted son of Abu Hudheifa] who was breastfed by Abu-Hudheifa's wife when he was already a grown man with a beard, by the Prophet's order

I shall now **confirm** the scholar's statements based upon the following accepted Hadiths:

Al-Tirmidhi Hadith 3173 Narrated by Umm Salamah Allah's Messenger said, "The only suckling which makes marriage unlawful is that which is taken from the breast and enters the bowels, and is taken before the time of weaning."

Sahih Al-Bukhari Hadith 1.88   Narrated by Abdullah bin Abi Mulaika

'Uqba bin Al-Harith said that he had married the daughter of Abi Ihab bin 'Aziz. Later on a woman came to him and said, "I have suckled (nursed) you Uqba and the woman whom you married (his wife) at my breast." 'Uqba said to her, "Neither I knew that you have suckled (nursed) me nor did you tell me." Then he rode over to see Allah's Apostle at Medina, and asked him about it. Allah's Apostle said, "How can you keep her as a wife when it has been said (that she is your foster-sister)?" Then Uqba divorced her, and she married another man.

Sahih Muslim, Suckling a Young boy, Tradition #3428.

Zainab daughter of Abu Salama reported: I heard Umm Salama, the wife of Allah's Apostle saying to Aisha: By Allah, I do not like to be seen by a young boy who has passed the period of fosterage, whereupon Aisha asked: Why is it so?

Umm Salama answered: because Sahla daughter of Suhail came to Allah's messenger and said: Allah's messenger, I swear by Allah that I see in the face of Abu Hudhaifa – her husband - (the signs of disgust) on account of the entering of Salim (in the house), whereupon Allah's messenger said: Suckle him.

Sahlah said (in astonishment): **(But) He has a beard!.**   But Muhammad said again: **Suckle him,** and it would remove what is there (expression of disgust) on the face of Abu Hudhaifa.

She said: **(I suckled him)** and , by Allah, I did not see (any sign of disgust) on the face of Abu Hudhaifa.

Sahih Muslim, Suckling a Young boy, Tradition #3426.

Ibn Abu Mulaika reported that al-Qasim b.Abu Bakr had narrated to him that 'A'isha reported that Sahla bint Suhail b. 'Amr came to Allah's Apostle and said: Messenger of Allah, Salim (the freed slave of Abu Hudhaifa) is living with us in our house, and he has attained (puberty) as men attain it and has acquired knowledge (of the sex problems) as men acquire, whereupon he said: **suckle him** so that he may become unlawful (in regard to having **sex** with you)

Ibn Abu Mulaika conitnued: I **refrained from** (narrating this hadith) **for a year or so on account of fear**. I then met al-Qasim and said to him: You narrated to me a hadith which I did not narrate (to anyone) afterwards.

He said: What is that? I informed him, whereupon he said: Narrate it on my authority that 'A'isha had narrated that to me.

Ladies & Gentlemen, Believers & Unbelievers, here was a man who was afraid to narrate what he had heard and decided to keep this story to himself for more than a year! The man viewed this Hadith with obvious trepidation regarding the innocence of this story and knew that there was something morally wrong with this unbelievable event.

Even 1400 years ago, this type of story, of a grown and married woman who would breast feed any grown man, not her husband, so that she can be at home so to speak while he is around, was so immoral that it boggled the mind of its listener.

That is why he kept his mouth shut for almost a year thereafter. But as a believing Muhammadan Muslim, he had to accept it as a divinely sanctioned order.

The Azhar council decided to dismiss the Doctor **not** because he was telling a **lie** but because he was telling the **truth** thus exposing Muhammadan Islam to ridicule. They even go so far as to accuse those who support his deductions as **perverts.**

In light of the foregoing, then all the preceding Muhammadan scholars must have been perverts since they too read the same hadiths and walked away with the same understanding that I do. They saw that the logical implication one derives from them is that Sahla, against her natural instincts, breast-fed a young man at the express orders of Muhammad.

There are of course more Hadiths regarding the above, but I am sure these will suffice.

Believers & Unbelievers, I shall repeat yet again, as I shall do so at every opportunity, that the worst NIGHTMARE of Muhammadan

Islam is KNOWLEDGE of the Quran, of the Hadiths & all their related subjects.

Muhammadan Islam can only survive through **subjugation, intimidation, terror, indoctrination & the ignorance** of its followers. They are after all, its **worst & foremost** innocent **victims.**

We have repeatedly made it **crystal** clear that the objective of this series is **not** to insult, humiliate or degrade the followers of Muhammad, the so called **believers,** but to **enlighten** them as well as all those so called **unbelievers** around the world.

believers, all we have ever asked you to do, is to use your God given faculties to **think indpenendently** for yourselves. To read and investigate the very Bible that the Quran asserts was revealed **directly** to Moses and the Gospels to Jesus.

Why depend on or accept the Mulla's or anybody else's versions that are passed on to you with deliberate falsifications?

You should ask yourselves **why you are forbidden** from studying the scriptures of other peoples IF the Quran is allegedly so superior to them?

If the Quran is so superior, then you should not be afraid or hesitate from reading them. What could you possibly loose?

After all, we are repeatedly told by the scholars of Muhammadan Islam that the Quran **loves knowledge.**

So **learn!** & hence **unchain** your **minds & liberate** your **souls!**

#93. Muhammad the pagan

Q: The followers of Muhammad assert that he was never an idol worshipper. That Allah guided him from childhood away from the pagan beliefs of his parents and tribe.

Are these statements borne by the records of Muhammadan Islam?

A: As usual with the followers of Muhammad, they **invent & concoct** mythical stories about Muhammad thus shooting themselves in the mouth because they contradict the very exegetical **Muhammadan** sources, in the **Arabic** language, that **prove** otherwise.

It is an absolute fact that Muhammad was born of pagan parents. His father, Abdullah and his mother, Amina were both pagans and they used to worship many idols. His entire childhood till the age of 25 years at least, was spent in paganism.

Today, many Muhammadans will find it extremely hard to digest this fact. However, Muhammad's pagan origin is disclosed by **Hisham ibn al-Kalbi.**

On page 17 of his very important work, ***Kitab al-Asnam***

(The Book of Idols) he writes :

'We have been told that the Apostle of Allah once mentioned al-Uzza saying, **"I have offered a white sheep to al-'Uzza, while I was a follower of the religion of my people."**

In the statement above Muhammad clearly admits his past adherence to the paganism of his tribe - the then religion of the Quraysh.

When Muhammad married Khadijah his first wife, who was a **Hanifiyah,** that is one who believed **ONLY** in the God of Abraham being neither a follower of the Laws of Moses nor of Jesus, she introduced him to her uncle, Waraqa bin Nawfal, who had converted from Paganism to Christianity. There is absolutely no doubt that Khadija's and Waraqa's religious influences were singularly instrumental in making Muhammad think deeply about his Pagan religious beliefs.

As he attended the annual assembly of poets at Ukaz he was deeply impressed and moved by the thoughts, eloquence, sentiment, freethinking and humanism expounded by many of those poets. He started questioning the idol-worshipping of his tribe and began, at the age of 40 years - 15 years after marrying Khadija - to start preaching the concept of the one God, the creator - similar to the concept of the Jews & Judaized Arabs of his days.

Nonetheless, as the Quranic verses amply demonstrate, he was confused as to which god ought to be his one and only God. Allah, at that time, was the supreme rock god of the pagan Quraysh. From Muhammad's perspective, their only fault was that besides Allah, the Quraysh used to worship as intercessors with Allah, other smaller gods/goddesses like: **Hubal, Al-Lat, Al-Uzza, Manat…etc.**

So, at the start of his new concept of an almighty creator, Allah was out of the question. Besides, at that time, even the magicians, the soothsayers, the sorcerers and the Satan worshippers used to vow by Allah. Thus, Muhammad, at the very beginning, found it utterly unacceptable to make Allah his one & only God (ilah).

During those pagan days, the people of Yemen used to worship another deity whose name was Ar-Rahman who was coincidentally, also the Jewish word Rahmana which was a name for God in the Talmudic period.

(Noldeke: The Koran, The Origins of the Koran, p.53).

They were still influenced by the legacy of the Judaized Hymiarite kingdom of the Yemen.

Muhammad, for a while, adopted the name Ar-Rahman for **God (ILAH)** in place of Allah. Muhammad believed, that by using the name **Ar-Rahman** he ought to be able to get the support of the Judaized Arabs to his new belief system.

*** Please note that no where in the Quran does Allah say that he has 99 additional names including Ar-Rahman.

In fact these alleged 'names' are actually **attributes/ sifat** and **not names** that were heaped later on, on Allah by the followers of Muhammad***

So, when he declared himself to be the messenger of Ar-Rahman, the Meccans, too, were at a loss and confused. The Meccans did not know of any Ar Rahman, other than the Ar-Rahman of al Yemen.

When we read, with an unbiased mind, the first *50 Suras*

(in chronological order) of the Quran, we note Muhammad's confusion regarding Lord/Rabb, Allah and Ar-Rahman. He was quite unsure of whom he should consider as his only God (Ilah).

Here is a summary of the first *50 Suras* regarding Muhammad's idea of his only God:

Lord/Rabb — 68, 92, 89, 94, 100, 108, 105, 114, 97, 106, 75

(11 Suras) in which the name of Allah is not mentioned

Ar-Rahman & Lord/Rabb— 36, 55

(2 Suras) in which the name of Allah is not mentioned

Ar-Rahman, Allah, Lord— (1 Sura) 20

Allah, Lord/Rabb— 96, 73, 74, 81, 87, 53, 85, 50, 38, 7, 72, 25, 35, 56, 26, 27, 28, 17 (18 Suras)

This demonstrates Muhammad's initial vacillation, confusion and ignorance of the affairs of his only God (Ilah).

The Quran also confirms that when he started to preach his brand of faith Muhammad was lost, confused and did not know much of religion. Here is what the Quran writes:

Yusuf 12.3 *We do relate unto thee the most beautiful of stories, in that We reveal to thee this Qur'an: before this, thou too was among those who knew it not*

Al Shu'araa 42.52 And thus have We, by Our Command, sent inspiration to thee: thou knewest not (before) what was Revelation, and what was Faith

Al Thduha 93.7 And He found thee wandering, and He gave thee guidance.

*** In all three verses, they **assert** that previously, Muhammad, as a **pagan,** had no knowledge of earlier revelations: the **Bible** ***

Maryam 19: 58   ... We carried with Noah and of the posterity of Abraham and Israel of those whom We guided and chose; whenever the Signs of al Rahman were rehearsed to them they would fall down in prostrate adoration and in tears.

61 Gardens of Eternity those which al Rahman promised to His servants

Al Anbiyaa 21: 112   Say: "O my Lord/ Rabbi judge Thou in truth!" "Our Lord/ Rabbina Al Rahman is the One Whose assistance should be sought....!"

Initially, Muhammad even eulogized the important gods (or idols) of the pagans by agreeing with the Quraysh- at some point that these gods were the intercessors of Allah (The Satanic Verses). On the same page

Hisham ibn al-Kalbi writes:

The Quraysh were wont to circumambulate the Ka'ba and chant:

Al Najm 53.19   By Allat and al-'Uzza,

.20 And Manah, the third idol besides.

21 Verily they are the most exalted females [al Gharaniq al U'laa]

22 Whose intercession is to be sought.

Al Lat, al Uzza & al Manat were **"the Daughters of Allah"** who supposed to intercede before Allah, the supreme pagan god of the Quraysh.

Muhammad, in a moment of desperation and weakness, to try and bring his Quraysh tribe to his way of thinking, compromised his monotheism by allowing himself to state that he received the **above** 'revelation' from Allah.

The above represent the **Satanic Verses** controversy, whereby Satan allegedly was able to easily mislead Muhammad into allowing his followers to have partners with Allah, as they had under paganism; that is to allow the three daughters of Allah to share his divine throne by being intercessors between humanity and Allah.

When Muhammad realized the enormity of his error, that he had compromised his Monotheism, he later very conveniently, **abrogated** verses 21 & 22 and replaced them with the following:

Al Najm 53.19 Have ye seen Lat and 'Uzza,

.20 And another, the third, Manat?

.21 What! for you the male sex, and for Him, the female?

.22 Behold, such would be indeed a division most unfair

*** To cover up the fact that he had compromised his monotheism, Muhammad found that the best **scape goat** is to very conveniently blame the unsuspecting and totally innocent: **Satan**

Being the self proclaimed *'prophet of Allah'*, Muhammad always **blamed others** for **all** his **own** errors, troubles and failures.

I would like our listeners, both Believers & Unbelievers, to ponder the following **irrefutable** fact:

That the alleged Monotheist Muhammad **venerated**, Circumambulated, kissed & hugged the Black Stone **even** when the Ka'ba still contained all 360 **idols** of the Quraysh and was still a Pagan Temple all his adult life.

He only destroyed the idols of the Ka'ba - except the Black Stone - after he conquered Mecca a year before he died.

Whom would you listeners believe, the records of Muhammadan Islam or the Apologists and perverters of facts & reality who serve their agenda of deceiving humanity about the very essence of Muhammad?***

#94. Stoning Verse or Ayat al Rajm

Q: We are told repeatedly by the followers of Muhammad that the Quran that we have at hand is exactly the same as that allegedly revealed to Muhammad 1400 years ago.

How accurate are these statements and are they borne by the records of Muhammadan Islam?

A: It is very unfortunate but essential that we repeat the same statement again & again & again that invariably, **Muhammadan Muslims,** invent & concoct unsubstantiated stories about **Muhammad** and his **Quran** thus requiring them to create more lies to cover the earlier ones especially since their falsehoods contradict the very exegetical **Muhammadan** sources, in the **Arabic** language, that **prove** otherwise.

In our series we may touch upon **many** similar subjects under different headings because they overlap and it gives our listeners different facets of our research.

The Stoning Verse is called in Arabic, Ayat al Rajm

Hadith Muslim maintains that key passages were missing from Zaid bin Thabit's collection of the Quran. The most famous is the **verse of stoning.**

All the major traditions speak of this missing verse. According to **Ibn Ishaq's version (p. 684)** we read:

"Allah sent Muhammad, and sent down the scripture to him. Part of what he sent down was the passage on stoning.

Umar ibn al Khattab asserts, 'We read it, we were taught it, and we heeded it. **The apostle [Muhammad] stoned, and we stoned after him.** I fear that in the time to come men will say that they find no mention of stoning in Allah's book, and thereby go astray in neglecting an ordinance which Allah has sent down.

Verily, stoning in the book of Allah is a penalty laid on married men and women who commit adultery."

Therefore, according to Umar [ibn al Khattab], the stoning verse was part of the original Quran, the revelation which Allah allegedly sent down. But now it is missing from the Quran. In many of the traditions we find numerous reports of adulterous men and women who were stoned by Muhammad and his companions.

Yet we read in today's Quran:

Al Nur 24:2 *The woman and the man guilty of **adultery** or fornication flog each of them with **a hundred lashes**: let not compassion move you in their case in a matter prescribed by Allah if ye believe in Allah and the Last Day: and let a party of the Believers witness their punishment*

*** Umar said, adultery was not only a capital offence, but one which demanded stoning.

This verse is now missing from the Quran, and that is why Umar raised this issue.

Believers need to ask themselves whether indeed their Quran can be claimed to be the same as that passed down by Muhammad to his companions?

With evidence such as this here addressed - as well as of hundreds of other discrepancies - the Quran in our possession today becomes all the more suspect ***

Sahih Muslim Hadith 4191 Narrated by Ubadah ibn as-Samit

Allah's Messenger said: When an unmarried male commits adultery with an unmarried female (they should receive) one hundred lashes and banishment for one year. And in case of married male committing adultery with a married female, **they shall receive one hundred lashes and be stoned to death.**

Sahih Muslim Hadith 4214 Narrated by Al-Bara' ibn Azib

There happened to pass by Allah's Apostle a Jew blackened and lashed. Allah's Apostle called them (the Jews) and said: Is this the punishment that you find in your Book (Torah) as a prescribed punishment for adultery? They said: Yes. He called one of the scholars amongst them and said: I ask you in the name of Allah Who sent down the Torah to Moses if that is the prescribed punishment for adultery, which you find in your Book.

He said: Had you not asked me in the name of Allah, I should not have given you this information. We find stoning to death (as the punishment prescribed in the Torah). However, this (crime) became quite common … so we decided to blacken the face with coal and flog as a substitute punishment for stoning. Thereupon Allah's Messenger said: O Allah, I am the first to revive Thy command when they had cancelled it. He then gave the order and he (the offender) was stoned to death.

Al-Muwatta Hadith 41.1 Stoning

Malik related to me from Nafi that Abdullah ibn Umar said, "The Jews came to the Messenger of Allah and mentioned to him that a man and woman from among them had committed adultery. … So the Messenger of Allah gave the order and they were stoned . "

Abdullah ibn Umar added, "I saw the man leaning over the woman to protect her from the stones."

Sunan of Abu-Dawood Hadith 4443 Narrated by An-Nu'man ibn Bashir

Habib ibn Salim said: A man called AbdurRahman ibn Hunayn had intercourse with his wife's slave-girl. The matter was brought to an-Nu'man ibn Bashir who was the Governor of Kufah. He said: I shall decide between you in accordance with the decision of the Apostle of Allah If she made her lawful for you, I shall flog you one hundred lashes. If she did not make her lawful for you, I shall stone you to death. So they found that she had made her lawful for him. He, therefore, flogged him **one hundred lashes.**

Sahih Al-Bukhari Hadith 5.188 Narrated by Amr bin Maimun

During the pre-Islamic period of ignorance I saw a **she-monkey** surrounded by a number of monkeys. They were all stoning it, **because it had committed illegal sexual intercourse.**

I too, stoned it along with them.

*** Believers & Unbelievers, this Hadith is a real gem, and I cannot understand how Bukhari actually included it among the **sahih** traditions:

Even the **monkies** had knowledge of the Stoning Verse **before** Muhammad's Quran and applied it amongst themselves.

They must have obviously learned about it from a Divine revelation similar to the ones that were descending upon Muhammad ***

Sahih al-Bukhari hadith8.804 narrated by al Shaibani

I asked 'Abdullah bin Abi Aufa, -Did Allah's Apostle carry out the Rajam penalty (i.e., stoning to death)?" He said, "Yes." I said, "Before the revelation of Surat-ar-Nur or after it?" He replied, "I don't know."

Sahih Al-Bukhari Hadith 8.806 Narrated by Abu Huraira

A man came to Allah's Apostle while he was in the mosque, and he called him, saying, "O Allah's Apostle! I have committed illegal sexual intercourse." The Prophet turned his face to the other side, but that man repeated his statement four times, and after he bore witness against himself four times, the Prophet called him, saying, "Are you mad?" The man said, "No."

The Prophet said, "Are you married?" The man said, "Yes." Then the Prophet said, "Take him away and stone him to death." Jabir bin 'Abdullah said: I was among the ones who participated in stoning him and we stoned him at the Musalla. When the stones troubled him, he fled, but we over took him at Al-Harra and **stoned him to death.**

*** All the above reports and many many more, indicate that there was the verse of **rajm** as part of the Quran but is **not** in the Uthmanic and current Qurans.

The most extraordinary fact is that it is Umar ibn al Khattab, one of the most intimate of Muhammad's companions and also the Second Khalifa of 'Islam' who is asserting that the Stoning Verse existed and does **not** exist in Uthman's Quran.

Any intelligent and independently inquiring mind would raise the following points:

Why is the **Stoning Verse** missing from Uthman's Quran?

Umar is not the **only** one asserting the previous existence of this verse.

We have also shown that **numerous** other verses are **missing** from Uthman's **edited** version of the Quran!

Ladies & Gentlemen, as we have **repeatedly** demonstrated, based entirely upon the Muhammadan records themselves, that many others attest to Umar's assertion that Muhammad **stoned** those who committed adultery without any basis in the Quran.

Further more **how many** other verses are missing because the **huffath/ memorizers** who heard them from Muhammad died in the 'Muslim' slaughters after his death?

How can even a **single revelation** from Allah be missing from the Quran? If Allah is the same as the God of Israel & Jesus?

Why does the Sunna over-rule the Quran?

Can **any** follower of Muhammad explain these incredibly disturbing **facts,** in a **rational manner?**

Personally, I have absolutely no doubt that no one can***

#95. Muhammad & Deception

Q: The followers of Muhammad tell the world that he was the most perfect male human being ever. That he was decent, valiant, brave, compassionate, honourable etc etc.

My own studies of Muhammad's character based upon the very records of the Muhammadans indicate otherwise.

What is your input?

A: As we progress with our series, every single characteristic of Muhammad will be scrutinized and we shall enlighten our audience about them based, as usual, entirely upon the Muhammadan records themselves that **invariably** prove the opposite of what the Muhammadan scholars do their best to deceive both the **Believers & the Unbelievers.**

So far we have touched on several of his characteristics in our chapters 33,38,41, 43, 59,89 & 93.

Muhammad was actually the most consummate artist on deception, fraud and lying. The Arabs of the so called 'Jahiliya'/ Days of Ignorance had more honour, veracity and decency than they ever had or could ever have after Muhammad and his Quran have done to pervert them.

He encouraged treachery, lying, betrayal, deception, and all other similarly nefarious characteristics for as long as they were useful to his agenda to convert the whole of mankind to his **twisted** vision of 'Islam'.

These accusations are not based on anger or hate but are based **entirely** upon the Muhammadan Muslim records themselves, in the Quran, in the Hadiths and in their history as we shall show.

Al Baqara **2:6** *"As for the disbelievers, it is the same whether you warn them or not; they will not believe.* ***Allah has set a seal***

upon their hearts, upon their hearing, *and a covering over their eyes. There is a great torment for them."*

*** The 'disbelievers' will not believe because Allah had already pre-destined them to **BE** so

" Allah has set a seal upon their hearts, upon their hearing…".

They are not at fault since they have **no choice** in the matter; yet, the merciful and compassionate Allah, none the less, sends them to eternal damnation in his Hell.

In fact, Allah's **Predestination** is the ultimate form of **deception** ***

2:9 *"They deceive Allah and those who believe, but they only* ***deceive [yukhadioona]*** *themselves, …*

*** How is it possible, from both the intellectual and theological points of view, to claim that mere human beings can **deceive** Allah if Allah is the **God of Israel**?

This statement is unadulterated **blasphemy** ***

Al Nisaa 4:142 *"Surely the* ***hypocrites strive to deceive [yukhadioona]*** *Allah. He shall retaliate by* ***deceiving them khadi'uhum]*** *."*

*** This verse reduces Allah to a petulant child perpetrating schemes and deception upon his own creation. This depiction is also, pure **blasphemy** ***

Al A'raf 7:186 *"Whomever Allah wants to deceive [youthlili] you cannot help. Allah does not want them to know the truth because he intends to disgrace them and then torture them."*

*** It is a pathetic belief system if its god, Allah, conspires and deceives his own creation, and then without mercy or justice have them tortured in his Hell.

If a human beig is deceived by Satan, he/she have recourse to **repent** to God. But there is no possibility of salvation when it is Allah who is deceiving one.

In fact, the above verse is pure idolatry to give human attributes of deception, scheming and plotting to any divine entity ***

Al Maida 101 *"Believers! Do not ask questions about things which if made plain and declared to you, may vex you, causing you trouble."*

102 *"Some people before you did ask such questions, and on that account they lost their faith and became disbelievers."*

*** Muhammad could not tolerate being asked questions that he could not answer. Hence, to mitigate against this happening, so that he can continually deceive his followers, he conveniently revealed the above verses hence, as always, sanctifying his prohibition ***

Al Anfal 8:30 *"Remember how the unbelievers plotted against you (Muhammad). They **plotted [yamkuroona]**, and **Allah** too had arranged a **plot**; but **Allah** is the **best schemer [khayru^l Makireen]**"*

Ishaq:323 *"**I am (Allah) the best of plotters.** I deceived them with My guile so that I delivered you from them."*

*** What kind of a god would extol the failings of mortals such as deception, scheming, plotting and counter plotting?

What kind of a god is so immoral & unjust as to consign innocents to the tortures of his Hell and gloat over the prospect?

Are these verses not blasphemous when applied to any supreme creator? ***

Al Anfal 8:71 *"If they try to deceive you, remember **they have deceived Allah before.**"*

*** How could mere mortals deceive the allegedly All Knowing Allah?

Only if Allah is not God, can this be possible***

Al Ra'ad 13:27 *"Say, 'Allah **leads** whosoever He wills **astray.**'"*

*** Does the reader need any more unambiguous statements asserting the pre-destination of mankind?

If mankind is pre-destined, what for is then the need for religion?

And, if there is no need for religion, then there is obviously no need for prophets or for Satan.

Hence, there is no purpose for Muhammad or his Quran***

Al Ahzab 33:11 *...The Hypocrites and those in whose hearts is a disease said:* **'Allah and His Messenger promised us nothing but delusion; they have promised only to deceive us."**

Al Ghafir 40:32 *"... Any whom Allah causes to err, there is no guide. That is how Allah leads the skeptic astray."*

*** Muhammad's Quran, being a reflection of his own character, is full of **deception & betrayal** ***

Bukhari:4.268 "Allah's Apostle said, **'War is deceit.'"**

Bukhari:5.369 "Allah's Apostle said, 'Who is willing to kill Ka'b bin Ashraf who has hurt Allah and His Apostle?'

Thereupon Muhammad bin Maslamah got up saying, 'O Allah's Apostle! Would you like me to kill him?' The Prophet said, 'Yes,'

Maslamah said, 'Then allow me to say false things in **order to deceive him.'**

The Prophet said, 'You may say such things.'"

*** It is crystal clear from the above hadith, that Muhammad allowed and sanctioned murder, deception and lies to achieve his ends. Since Ka'b bin Ashraf was an Arabian of the faith of the Jews, **he could not have been the enemy of Allah, if Allah is the same as the God of Israel.**

Hence Muhammad's accusation, that he was an enemy of Allah is a deception and a blatant lie, used only to justify his murder because he opposed Muhammad's slaughter of the Quraysh leaders at Badr ***

Bukhari:7.427 "The Prophet said, 'If I take an oath and later find something else better than that, then I do what is better and expiate my oath.'"

*** Does any **reader** need more confirmation of the depraved indifference shown by Muhammad regarding any **truth?** ***

Ishaq:365/Tabari 7:94 "Muhammad bin Maslamah said, 'O Messenger, we shall have to tell lies.'

'Say what you like,' Muhammad replied. **'You are absolved,** free to say whatever you must.'"

*** Only in Muhammad's twisted morality could a so called prophet allow **deceptions,** betrayals and murder **assassinations.**

What is most revealing in the verses of this section is the fact that his newly converted followers were actually apprehensive to tell lies or to betray trust in their earlier state of **ignorance.**

In reality, they were much more decent and nobler when they were Pagans and **before** becoming 'Muhammadan Muslims' ***

Ishaq:383 "One of the young men's fathers confronted Muhammad and said,

'You have robbed my son of his life by your deception and brought great sorrow to me.'"

*** Even the illiterate pagan Arabs, his own people and tribe, knew how false Muhammad was ***

Ishaq:519 "Hajjaj said to the Apostle, 'I have money scattered among the Meccan merchants, so give me permission to go and get it.' Having got Muhammad's permission, he said,

'I must tell lies.' The Apostle said, **'Tell them.'**"

*** Again and again and again, the Hadiths paint a disgusting and unholy but **truthful & factual** portrayal of Muhammad

Deception, Betrayal and Lying were and are the **hallmark** of Muhammad and his followers; unto this day ***

tabari 8:23 "...Nu'aym came to the Prophet. 'I 've become a Muslim, but my tribe does not know of my Islam; so command me whatever you will.' Muhammad said, 'Make them abandon each other if you can so that they will leave us; for war is deception.'"

Even in the 21st Century, **1400 years later,** nothing has changed.

The modern followers of Muhammad, politicians, educators, leaders and their media, do their best to **deceive** the Unbelievers as well as the Believers by doing their best to pretend at distancing themselves from those whom they call 'Radical Muslims'.

In **fact** and in **reality,** they actually agree, condone & support suicide bombings, assassinations, terror and the **undermining** of our **Democracies** with the sole aim of **islamizing** the whole of humanity ***

#96. Let There be Light

Ladies & gentlemen, U Tube have **terminated** our series without any justification.

They did so without a single prior warning given to us as to which, if any, rules were broken.

They did so totally **arbitrarily** and without giving us the opportunity to explain our side of the story.

This is a **draconian** act against all known judicious laws whether Judeo-Christian or not, excepting of course Shari'a law.

We have not broken a **single** one of their terms and conditions but this did not stop them from **knuckling** under to the followers of Muhammad who **flag** any and all sites that EXPOSE the **truth & facts** about Muhammad and his Quran.

Paraphrasing (Edmund Burke), I say

"All that is necessary for evil to triumph, is that good men & women do nothing."

A lot of the history of the struggle, between good and evil, can be explained by Edmund Burke's observation.

Time and again, those who profess to be good, clearly outnumber those who are evil, yet, those who are evil, prevail far too often.

It is almost **never**, that numbers determine the outcome of a struggle, **but** whether those who claim to be good men & women, are willing to stand up and fight for what they know, to be right.

There is an enormous number of examples of this sad and awful scenario being played out over and over again in scriptures and in history.

FREEDOM is never handed **FREELY!** People must and have to **struggle** and go to war to secure their freedom. It is humanity's most precious treasure.

Without it, we are nothing more than **domesticated** animals being herded and controlled by **tyrants.**

To keep this most precious treasure safe & sound, we must **all** be vigilant as well as ready to **defend** and to preserve it at All costs.

We are free **because** our fathers, mothers, brothers, sisters & or grandparents, fought and **died** to keep us free! **We** have not **earned** this freedom. It was bequeathed to us through the sacrifices of others in its **defense!**

As the guardians & custodians of the **liberty** of our own children, our grandchildren and all our future generations, we have no other choice but to continue the process of preserving it.

We have absolutely no right to squander it and let our descendants live as **slaves** to any political or religious organization.

When good men & women do nothing, they get nothing good done.

When good men & women do nothing, evil triumphs by default!

The fundamentalist followers of Muhammad have had and continue to have a **single** and very publicly declared objective in mind:

To 'Islamize' the whole of Humanity, to Subjugate it or to Slaughter it!

You must all remember, that it was Muhammad in his Quran that **unilaterally** declared **total & eternal** war against us – the so called Unbelievers - and not the other way round!

We, who are **free** human beings, **outnumber** the followers of Muhammad 5 to 1 and yet, it is not inconceivable that they could win because of our self interests, **divided** agendas and differences.

In **reality,** we have the collective ability, Technologically, Intellectually, Numerically & Militarily, if the **will** were there, to completely overcome and re educate the followers of Muhammad in a short period of time!

We have been **terminated** because of the **facts** that we have been **revealing** in every single chapter of ours, that addressed different facets of either Muhammad or his Quran, based entirely upon their own records in the Arabic language, our own mother tongue.

I would like to repeat yet again, to those who have not listened to our series and even to those who have, that our issue is not with the majority of the followers of Muhammad who are the **first & worst** victims of the Cult of Muhammadan Islam, but with the message of Muhammad's Quran especially and the Fundamentalists who believe and act upon its verses.

We, as any believers in the One & Only God are **muslims,** a **fact** that has been deliberately and willfully **ignored& falsified** by the followers of Muhammad for the last 1400 years.

I would like to re iterate once again, that it is entirely by **DIVINE JUSTICE,** that the very **hadiths** that explain the Quran and traditions to the followers of Muhammad, are the same that utterly **discredit the veracity** & alleged **divine** origin of the Quran as we have been able to demonstrate in 101 chapters before we were **silenced!**

The Fundamentalist followers of Muhammad demonstrate their **depravity, hatemongering, racism, warmongering, tyranny, disloyalty, hypocrisy, cowardice, stupidity & ignorance,** in almost every corner of the globe, perpetrated not only against so called defenseless **Unbelievers** but also against other sects of so called **Believers.**

All of you who want to actually see them in action, should go to www.memri.com **memri** which is the **middle east media research institute** which has a library of thousands of videos from all over the Islamic world in their own Arabic language with translations, from their own media.

You will, I guarantee you, find the most mind **boggling** videos ever about Muhammadan Islam not scripted by 'Christian pigs, or apelike Jews, or Western Imperialists or Hindu kuffar' but by the followers of Muhammad themselves!

You will be able to see and listen, for example, to a Muhammadan scholar, in this 21st century, refuting the spherical shape of the earth because the Quran states that it is **flat.** He asserts that all the satellite pictures that we have are **false** since they contradict the Quran!

Of mullahs screaming at their congregations assuring them that Muhammadan Islam is **superior** to all other belief systems and without so called Islamic science, the west would still be living in caves!

As I mentioned previously, any **belief**, is not a negotiable item no matter how contrary to **facts & reality** it may be. That is exactly why the followers of Muhammad who made comments to our chapters could not and would not agree to any of our statements without having to abandon their Muhammadan Islamic beliefs; that is, without **apostatizing!** They thus must remain in **denial** for the rest of their lives.

The worst to suffer among the Muhmmadans are their women folk, who are considered by Muhammad and his male followers – as we have amply demonstrated - as just one rung up the evolutionary ladder than Domestic Animals.

They are **enslaved, terrorized, subjugated**, kept in most cases as **ignorants, humiliated** & subjected to **genital mutilation** by their males so as to control their Mind, their Body & their Soule!

The ability of the followers of Muhammad to coerce our spineless and mindless political, religious, media & academic elites is based upon two items: Fear of violence & petro dollars!

It is left to all of US, the neglected & marginalized people, the absolute majority in all of our countries, to achieve what our ignoble leaders are not willing to do.

We, in the Western democracies especially wield infinitely more power **together** than we as individuals can ever imagine.

We are the ones who **elect** and pay the taxes that keep most of these **imbeciles** in power.

We are the ones who surf and keep the internet, Google & U tube alive and going!

We together can move not only mountains but governments out of power when we act together and in concert regarding very legitimate issues that concern all of us.

The security and **inviolibility** of our **freedom** & Democracy is at the fore front of our aspirations and concerns.

We should create a movement on the internet that can influence our elected policy makers to pay attention to our real & not imaginary fears at the threat of Muhammadan Islam from within & without.

This movement will also make it difficult for anyone on the internet to silence or prohibit us from expressing our freedom of expression.

As far as we are concerned, we shall continue our program of **educating, enlightening** and **exposing** the **facts & reality** of Muhammadan Islam to the whole world of so called Believers & Unbelievers, based entirely upon the very Arabic sources themselves and no other.

We shall once more upload all our previous chapters with new ones and hope you will once again spread the word about us and save our chapters in your blogs out of harm's way.

We would like to take this opportunity to thank ALL of you who have come to our defense in an outstanding and heartwarming show of wrath and disgust at our treatment and for the right of all of us to have a free and unfettered ability to express our opinions.

#97. Muhammad & Gabriel

Q: According to Muhammad, he received Allah's revelations not directly, unlike Moses, kalimu^allah, but indirectly through the agency of the angel Gabriel.

From my own research, I have no doubt that Muhammad did not know who Gabriel actually was, what his name meant and where & when he first appeared in the Bible.

What has your research determined?

A: I have to concur absolutely with **all** your conclusions.

To start with, neither Muhammad nor his Pagan Arabs had any knowledge of the Bible nor obviously of the characters that filled it, as **confirmed** by Muhammad himself in:

al-tirmidhi hadith 2215 narrated by ubayy ibn ka'b

Ubayy told of Allah's Messenger meeting Gabriel and saying, "I have been sent, Gabriel, **to a people who are unlettered**, among whom are old women and old men, boys and girls, and men who have never read a book." He replied, "The Qur'an, Muhammad, has been sent down in seven modes."

From our extensive research, we have shown and will continue to prove that this was the case, and that Muhammad's alleged revelations were based **entirely** upon stories that he had heard recited by Rabbis, Priests or story tellers especially during the **Ukaz** fairs as well as from his wife Khadijah and her Christian uncle Waraqa bin Nawfal.

None the less, Muhammad got most of them jumbled up in Time & Space as we have been proving.

In the Quran Gabriel is called Jibril - which is a Syriac and not an Arabic word - derived from the Hebrew (Gibbor-El), meaning 'God is Mighty'.

His name first appeared in the Bible in:

daniel 8 "15: *When I, Daniel, saw the vision I sought understanding, then, behold! There stood before me the likeness of a man. 16: I heard a human voice in the middle of the Ulai; he called out and said ' Gabriel, explain the vision to that (man). 17: So he came to where I was standing.* **When he came I was terrified, and I fell face down.** *He said to me ' Understand, Son of Man, that the vision concerns the time of the End"*

Luke1:18 *"And Zacharias said unto the angel, Whereby shall I know this? ...*

19 *And the angel answering said unto him,* **I am Gabriel, that stand in the presence of God...**

Mathew 1: 20 *" But while he thought on these things, behold, the angel of the Lord appeared unto him in a dream, saying, Joseph, thou son of David, fear not to take unto thee Mary thy wife: for that which is conceived in her is of the Holy Ghost.*

Gabriel is the same named angel who gave the 'good tidings' to Mary in **(Luke 1:19; & 26)** and who is now allegedly bringing a new 'good but **BLOODY** tidings' to Muhammad.

The following are Surahs that name or allude to Gabriel as being the messenger of Revelations:

Al Baqara 2: 97 *Say: Whoever is an enemy to Gabriel for he brings down the (revelation) to thy heart by Allah's will a confirmation of what went before and guidance and glad tidings for those who believe.*

98 *Whoever is an enemy to Allah and His angels and apostles to Gabriel and Michael ...*

Al Takwir 81:19 *Verily this is the word of a most honorable Messenger (Gabriel)*

20 *Endued with Power with rank before the Lord of the Throne*

<u>One should ask the following relevant but simple question:</u>

Why would Gabriel, who allegedly foretold the coming of Jesus, as the Messiah & the **redeemer** of all mankind, now announces the arrival of another different *'redeemer'*?

I repeat again to our readers/listeners, Believers & Unbelievers, that they should be aware that neither Muhammad nor the pagan Arabs had any idea who Gabriel was, where his name first appeared, whom he had met, whom he had inspired and what the meaning of his name is.

The followers of Muhammad of today, even after the lapse of almost 1400 years, are as ignorant of **previous revelations (ummiyoon)** as their forefathers were in the days of the **jahiliah paganism.**

Sahih Al-Bukhari Hadith 1.3 Narrated by Aisha

(the mother of the faithful believers) said: The commencement of the Divine Inspiration to Allah's Apostle was in the form of dreams... the Truth descended upon him while he was in the cave of Hira. The angel Gabriel came to him and asked him to read. The Prophet replied, "I do not know how to read."

The Prophet added, "The angel caught me (forcefully) and pressed me so hard that I could not bear it any more. He then released me and again asked me to read .... Thereupon he caught me for the third time and pressed me, and then released me and said,

"Iqraa bismi rabbika^allaththee khalqa

khalqa^l Insana min alaq

Iqraa wa rabbuka^l akramoo "

Al Alaq 96:1

'Read in the name of thy Lord, who has created

has created man from a clot.

Read! And your Lord is the Most Generous."

Then Allah's Apostle returned with the Inspiration and with his heart beating severely.... to his wife Khadija... who accompanied him to her cousin Waraqa bin Naufal who, during the **Pre-Islamic Period** became a **Christian** and used to write the writing with Hebrew letters.

He would write from the **Gospel in Hebrew** as much as Allah wished him to write. He was an old man and had lost his eyesight.

Khadija said to Waraqa, "Listen to the story of your nephew, O my cousin!" Waraqa asked, "O my nephew! What have you seen?"

Allah's Apostle described whatever he had seen.

Waraqa said, "This is the same one who keeps the secrets (angel Gabriel) whom Allah had sent to Moses.......

The most glaring difference between Gabriel's appearances to Zakhariah and Mary as compared to that with Muhammad is the violence and intimidation in the latter vis a vis the peaceful and gentle ones with the former.

With Zakharia and Mary, Gabriel introduced himself with assurances to both that they had nothing to fear and then explained to them the purpose of his intercession.

Not so in the story of his alleged encounter with Muhammad.

In the case of Muhammad, Gabriel, without any introduction whatsoever, merely ordered Muhammad to 'read' something that he, Gabriel, should have definitely known

- being the angel of Allah, the all knowing- that the allegedly illiterate Muhammad could not read.

Besides being an ignorant angel, he, contrary to his previous modus operandi, used physical violence against Muhammad to press his point.

More over, if Waraqa were truly a Christian and well read in the Bible, he could not have ever said the stupid and untrue statements put in his mouth by the Hadith writers, that Gabriel also appeared to Moses when in reality God spoke **directly** to Moses without the need of any intermediaries.

Waraqa would have known that **no angel** ever came to Moses and definitely not Gabriel.

Like so many errors, falsehoods, misrepresentations and downright lies in the Quran, the Ahadith have no choice but to follow suite ***

According to the Ahadith reports, Gabriel was in constant and repeated touch with Muhammad justifying every action and utterance through an Aya/Verse that invariably 'descended' very conveniently **AFTER** each event and not **BEFORE**.

There is no doubt that the manner with which these stories are recited shows that Muhammad actually believed that the Gabriel that he himself created in his own mind - split personality syndrome - was real and was giving him his instructions from Allah; he was thus justifying all his actions of broken treaties, murder, hatemongering, warmongering, destruction, enslavement and plunder besides the enormous amounts of plagiarized theology pirated from the Christians, Jews, pagan Arabs and others.

Sahih Al-Bukhari Hadith 4.431 Narrated by Abu Huraira

The Prophet said, "If Allah loves a person, He calls Gabriel saying, 'Allah loves so and-so; O Gabriel! Love him.' Gabriel would love him and make an announcement amongst the inhabitants of the Heaven."

*** How could Muhammad have known what Allah does and does not do without having communicated directly with him especially since Gabriel - according to all the records that we have - did not inform him of Allah's private affairs ? ***

Sahih Al-Bukhari Hadith 5.112 Narrated by Abu Salama

'Aisha said, "Once Allah's Apostle said (to me), 'O Aish ('Aisha)! This is Gabriel greeting you.' I said, 'Peace and Allah's Mercy and Blessings be on him, you see what I don't see.'

Sahih Al-Bukhari Hadith 5.373 Narrated by Ibn Abbas

On the day of Uhud. the Prophet said, "This is Gabriel holding the head of his horse and equipped with war material.'

*** Throughout the Quran and Ahadith, Muhammad and his followers **only** won battles because of the **support** they received from **thousands** of angels against the vastly **outnumbered** victims of Muhammad.

All these battles were **unfair** and **one-sided** since Allah's hordes were supporting Muhammad and his followers ***

Sahih Al-Bukhari Hadith 6.513 Narrated by Abdullah bin Abbas

Allah's Apostle said, "Gabriel recited the Qur'an to me in one way. Then I requested him (to read it in another way), and continued asking him to recite it in other ways, and he recited it in several ways till he ultimately recited it in seven different ways."

Sahih Al-Bukhari Hadith 7.843 Narrated by Salims father

Once Gabriel promised to visit the Prophet but he delayed and the Prophet got worried about that. At last he came out and found Gabriel and complained to him of his grief (for his delay). Gabriel said to him, "We do not enter a place in which there is a picture or a dog."

*** Ladies & Gentlemen, **contrary** to what the Quran and Ahadith **falsely** assert, the angel Gabriel **never** appeared to any of the characters in the Torah nor to anyone else in the Hebrew Bible except Daniel, and to Zakharia & Mary in the Gospels ***

#98. Paradise is Under the Shades of Swords

Q: I truly find the level of Hypocrisy practiced by the so called scholars of Muhammadan Islam not only abysmal but also disturbing since these scholars are supposed to be the harbingers of truths and historical facts.

What is your opinion?

A: What you have just said is not only disturbing but also frightening since they are doing so in spite of the incredible ease with which people are able to investigate on the Internet any and all subjects known to mankind at the click of a mouse.

It is frightening because they are deceiving new generations of the followers of Muhammad into believing their Falsehood & Mendacities while forbidding them from studying any other Scriptures beyond the Quran.

They are forbidden from reading these other scriptures lest they are then able to Compare & Contrast them with the utterly **false** Quranic versions, thus inducing in their minds the beginnings of **doubt**.

Doubt would make people think, investigate and question even more. These intellectual exercises are expressly forbidden in Muhammad's Quran for the very exact reason that Muhammad did not want anyone to ask him questions that he could not possibly have logical answers for.

Muhammad had a huge problem regarding veracity. Neither the pagan Quraysh nor the Jews accepted his version of Islam, and when they questioned him about the differences between the Biblical versions of events and his, he became upset, angry and full of ignorant replies. His anger manifested itself because he could not answer the questions truthfully since his versions of events were entirely invented by him as he went along.

All those who deceive & lie exhibit the same symptoms of agitation and upset whenever they are found out.

Lifting the Veil

Muhammad did not want his followers – or any one else for that matter - to ask questions that he could not answer satisfactorily. To eliminate such an event from ever happening he created the following verse/Aya and as usual ascribed it to the unsuspecting Allah hence making it a divine and inviolate ordinance.

Al Ma^ida 5:101 O ye who believe! **ask not questions about things which if made plain to you may cause you trouble.** But if ye ask about things when the Qur'an is being revealed they will be made plain to you

102 Some people before you did ask such questions and on that account lost their faith.

*** Ladies & Gentlemen, can any Believer listening to this chapter explain why if a question is answered clearly would cause the questioner trouble?

If so, why would the next verse assert, that the Quran would make it clear?

It is **obvious** that one is asking a question precisely **because** the Quran has **not** made it clear in the first place and hence requires a proper answer ***

Sahih Al-Bukhari Hadith 2.555 Narrated by Ash shabi

"Muawiya wrote to Al-Mughira bin Shu'ba:

Write to me something which you have heard from the Prophet

" So Al-Mughira wrote: I heard the Prophet saying, "Allah has hated for you three things:

1. Vain talks, (useless talk)
2. Wasting of wealth (by extravagance).
3. And askingtoo many questions (in disputed religious matters).

Sahih Al-Bukhari Hadith9.394 Narrated by Abu Musa Al Ashari

Allah's Apostle was asked about things which he disliked, and when the people asked too many questions, he became angry

Sahih Al-Bukhari Hadith 4.73 Narrated by Abdullah bin Abi Aufa

Allah's Apostle said, "Know that Paradise is under the shades of swords."

He then said, "O Allah! The Revealer of the (Holy) Book, the Mover of the clouds, and Defeater of Al-Ahzab (i.e. the clans of infidels), defeat them infidels and bestow victory upon us."

Muhammad and his Quran never miss an opportunity to show their warmongering, hate filled and abominable natures in hundreds of verses wishing death, destruction, plundering or subjugation on most of humanity unless and until they believe in Allah **and** in Muhammad as the messenger of Allah.

There is absolutely nothing in the Quran which shows a path to true salvation or redemption especially since all of Allah's creation is predestined and has no free will or choice.

Sahih Al-Bukhari Hadith 4.210 Narrated by Salim Abu An Nadr

"Once Allah's Apostle (during a holy battle), waited till the sun had declined and then he got up among the people and said, "O people! Do not wish to face the enemy (in a battle) and ask Allah to save you (from calamities) but if you should face the enemy, then be patient and let it be known to you that Paradise is under the shades of swords."

*** According to the Muhammadan Muslim traditions, **all** of Muhammad's so called battles, actually piratical raids for plunder, were holy.

Even Muhammad's paradise is subject to the tyranny and terror of swords; the symbols of death and destruction.

There is not an iota of spirituality, of mercy or compassion in the whole of Muhammad's Quran or the Ahadith ***

#99. Safa & Marwa

Q: The followers of Muhammad tell the world that Muhammad destroyed all the Pagan Arabian beliefs & traditions and brought them the new religion of Islam.

How accurate and true are these claims?

A: It is incumbent upon us to repeat as many times as necessary, that almost **all** their claims are **untrue, unsubstantiated, false & deceptive** because the moment they are put under scrutiny, based **entirely** upon the **Muhammadan** records themselves, all these **mendacities** can be and are **uncovered**.

Let us start with the **fact** that all **Muhammadan scholars** agree, that the practice of pilgrimage existed centuries before the rise of **Muhammadan Islam**. **Muhammad** & his pagan tribe of **Quraysh** (as well as other **pagan Arabs**) were accustomed to celebrating this pilgrimage.

Even after **Muhammad** declared himself the apostle of **Allah**, he and his followers continued to perform the pilgrimage's rites with the pagans at the **Ka'ba which was still a house of idolatry since it still contained all 360 idols of stones.**

In the final analysis, **Muhammad** only changed a few items from the pagan traditions & fetishes **BUT** successfully wrapped each one of them with his version of **Islam**.

Almost every major **'Islamic'** history book documents these facts. After the conquest of **Mecca,** the pilgrimage was turned by **Muhammad** into one of the **FIVE pillars** of **Muhammadan Islam.**

Muhammad banned the Arab polytheists from the Hajj after the year of the conquest. They were given four months either to embrace his Cult of Islam or be slaughtered. Thus will always be with Peaceful Muhammadan Islam.

After that, Muhammad made very slight changes in the ceremonial rituals of the pilgrimage although he destroyed all the idols of the Ka'ba. **Yet Muhammad himself continued to practice many pagan rituals.** He did not abolish them nor reject them. This created some consternation among some of his followers who expected him to completely uproot these idolatrous rudiments.

Muhammadan Muslims continued - and continue to date - to practice many of the pre-Islamic, pagan rituals such as running between the two hills of Safa and Marwa or kissing the Black Stone.

In the first case, **Arab polytheists** were accustomed to running between the two hills to glorify the idols that they erected whom they called **Isaf and Na'ila.** When Muhammad destroyed the idols, his followers were ashamed to continue this practice, and asked Muhammad about it. Soon, he claimed that a Quranic verse was **'revealed'** to him in which this **practice was re-ordained.**

Hadith Bukhari 2. 195 for instance, remarks:

"One of the companions said to Anas ibn Malik, 'Did you use to hate running between the **Safa and Marwa**?' He said, 'Yes, because it was part of the **pre-Islamic** rituals until Allah gave Muhammad this verse and proclaimed that it was also one of **Allah's ceremonial rites'**"

We also read in the **Sahih Muslim 3. 411**

"Adherents of the prophet, (when) they were still in the **pre-Islamic** period, used to come up to visit two idols, **Isaf** and **Na'ila**, then they would go and run between **Safa** and **Marwa**, then they would have their hair cut. When Islam was established, they hated to run between them, but Allah sent down this verse

Al Baqra 2:158 Behold! Safa and Marwa are among the Symbols of Allah. So if those who visit the house in the season or at other times should compass them round it, there is no sin in them...

In *Asbab al-Nuzul* by Imam al Suyuti, page 27

Ibn 'Abbas himself said "The demons in the **Jahiliyya** used to circumnavigate all night around these two mountains. The idols (were erected) between them. When **Islam** came, they (Muslims) said, 'O, apostle of Allah, we would never run between the **Safa and Marwa** because this is an **unfavorable matter** which we were accustomed to do in the **Jahiliyya.**' Thus, **Allah** gave the verse above"

So, this **"unfavorable matter"** was strongly related to idolatry, but even so, Muhammad refused to abolish it and several Quranic verses were given to confirm it. Muhammad himself performed it and Muhammadan Muslims are still practicing it today.

Fiqh-us-Sunnah **5.85** attempts to explain the historical background for the **Sa'i/Running** between **Safa And Marwah**

Ibn 'Abbas said: 'Prophet Ibrahim brought Hajar, his wife, and her son Isma'il whom she was still nursing, and left them at (the site of) the **House of Allah** under a tree above the **Zamzam. Makkah** at that time was a place where **there was neither water nor any dweller.** He left a bag of dates and a container of water for them.

Hajar sat under the tree with her baby next to her. She drank from her water container hanging nearby, and nursed her baby, until all the water she had was gone, her milk dried out. Her son grew hungrier and hungrier. She could hardly bear to look at him. She went and stood at Safa - the hill nearest to her. She looked down the valley to see if there was someone around to help. She could see no one. So, she climbed down **Safa** and reached the valley. She struggled hard, crossed the valley and reached **Marwa**. She stood on Marwah, and looked around. Still she could see no one around. She repeated this seven times. Ibn 'Abbas added, "The Prophet said: 'It is (to commemorate this walk) that pilgrims walk between *Safa and Marwa*.'"

*** Our readers/ steners should be made aware that the above story was **concocted** by Muhammad and his followers since the Bible has no knowledge of Abraham, Ishmael & Hagar of ever having visited Arabia or Mecca.

In fact, the names Allah, Mecca, Ka'ba, Zamzam etc do not **exist** anywhere in the Bible.

Moreover, why would Allah have a **house** in Mecca where there wan no water and no people?

Why does the Quran assert that it was Abraham & Ishmael who actually put up the foundations of the House, if there already was a House in situ?

Can any one among the **believers** dispute what we are saying? ***

Sunan of Abu-Dawood Hadith 1867 Narrated by Abu Hurayrah

The Apostle of Allah entered **Mecca,** and after the Apostle of Allah had gone forward to the **Stone,** and touched it, he went round the **House (the Ka'bah).** He then went to **as-Safa** and mounted it so that he could look at the **House.** Then he raised his hands began to make mention of **Allah** as much as he wished and make supplication.

Al-Tirmidhi Hadith 2624 Narrated by Aisha

The Prophet said, "Throwing pebbles at the **jamrahs** and running between **as-Safa** and **al-Marwah** were appointed only for the remembrance of Allah."

*** Ladies & Gentlemen, not a single word in the above hadiths represents any theological truth or fact based on any documentary evidence or even upon any Oral pagan Arabian tradition.

The agenda of the Muhammadan scholars had been and continues to be, the creation for the Arabs and Muhammad a worthy genealogy, an ancestry and a history connecting the Hebrews, Abraham & Ishmael to themselves.

They were and are still willing to go to any length of perversity, mendacity, deception and any depth of stupidity and illogic to achieve this goal.

Every alleged *'tradition'* of theirs is mere chimera and mirage of their fertile imagination as far away from any truth as the furthest galaxy is from the Earth.

It is a pitiful and a pitiable sight when so called *'learned'* Muhammadan scholars stoop to such levels of intellectual and theological depravity against all facts and all of documented history.

To prove my point, let us decipher the above stories, item by item:

1 Abraham, Hagar and Ishmael, according to the original story in the Bible, never went to Mecca or Arabia. Ishmael resided in the land of Paran.

2 The well that was revealed to Hagar was in Beersheba in the land of Canaan and not in Mecca in Arabia and was not called Zamzam.

3 Abraham, Hagar and Ishmael, had no knowledge of any god called Allah.

4 When Hagar and Ishmael were dismissed from Abraham's household, Ishmael was a teenager of at least 14 years of age and was definitely **NOT** a suckling baby.

(Genesis 21: 12-21)-

***Genesis 21:12** And God said unto Abraham, Let it not be grievous in thy sight because of the lad, and because of thy bondwoman; in all that Sarah hath said unto thee, hearken unto her voice; for in Isaac shall thy seed be called.*

*14 And Abraham rose up early in the morning, and took bread, and a bottle of water, and gave it unto Hagar, putting it on her shoulder, and the child and sent her away: and she departed, and **wandered in the wilderness of Beersheba**.*

15 And the water was spent in the bottle, and she cast the child under one of the shrubs.

17 And God heard the voice of the lad; and the angel of God called to Hagar out of heaven, and said unto her

18 Arise, lift up the lad, and hold him in thine hand; for I will make him a great nation.

*19 And God opened her eyes, **and she saw a well of water;** and she went, and filled the bottle with water, and gave the lad drink.*

*21 And he dwelt in the **wilderness of Paran:** and his mother took him a **wife** out of the **land of Egypt**.*

5 By what standard of logic should one believe that a holy place existed (House of Allah), in a place called Mecca where no one lived since there was no water to sustain life?

6 According to other traditions, Zamzam was a well in the valley where Mecca was, and **not** above the town; hence what is the Zamzam referred to here if it is not a well?

7 All that Muhammad and his followers perform during the Hajj, up to the present time, such as the running between Safa & Marwa, the kissing or touching of the Black Stone, the Ihram, the Umrah, etc, etc., were **Pagan Arabian** traditions and fetishes long before Muhammad and his Quran.

8 Since, according to the Quran, the Bible is Allah's revelations to the People of Israel, then how is it possible that the stories as depicted in the Quran contradict every one of these divine revelations?

Muhammad had no choice but to incorporate all the pagan Arabian traditions & fetishes into his new **Cult Beliefs**, otherwise, his Quraysh tribe and the other pagan Arabs would not have followed him. That is, he very conveniently **'Islamized'** them and gave them a Biblical background to make them sanctified and holy.

I leave any further comments and conclusions to the intelligent and inquisitive mind of the listeners to come to ***

#100. Muhammad's Megalomania

Q: Based upon my research of both the Quran and Hadiths, I have come to the conclusion that Muhammad was a delusional megalomaniac. Everything that is allegedly revealed to him in his Quran centered entirely upon himself, his own selfish persona.

Will you verify this based upon the Muhammadan records?

A: In fact, it is almost impossible for any thinking human being to come to any other conclusion based entirely on a small sample of the following verses from the Quran & Hadiths that are self evident in their meaning:

Al Baqara 2:104 *"You of Faith, say not (to the Prophet) words of ambiguous import like 'Listen to us,' but words of respect;* **and obey (him)***: To those who don't submit there is a grievous punishment."*

Al Nisa 4:12 *"Those who* **obey Allah and His Messenger** *will be admitted to Gardens to abide therein and that will be the supreme achievement. But those who* **disobey Allah and His Messenger** *and transgress...will be admitted to a Fire, to abide therein...*

65 *"They can have no Faith, until they make you* **(Muhammad) judge in all disputes***, and find in their souls no resistance against Your decisions, accepting them with complete submission."*

80 *"He who* **obeys the Messenger obeys Allah***."*

114 *"He who* **disobeys the Apostle** *after guidance has been revealed will burn in Hell."*

Al Ahhzab 33:36 *"No Muslim has any choice after* **Allah and His Apostle** *have decided a matter."*

51 *"***You [Muhammad] may have whomever you desire***; there is no blame."*

53 "O ye who believe! **Enter not the Prophet's apartments** until leave is given you for a meal. ... Linger not for conversation. Lo! that would cause annoyance to the Prophet. Such (behavior) bothers him. He is ashamed to dismiss you, but **Allah is not ashamed (to tell you) the truth.**

56 "**Allah and His angels shower blessings on the Prophet.** So believers, send your blessings on him, and salute him with all respect...

57 "Those who speak negatively of **Allah and His Apostle shall be cursed.**"

Al Fathh 48:10 "Verily those who **swear allegiance to you (Muhammad)**, indeed swear their allegiance to Allah."

*** It is evident from the verses above, that Muhammad and Allah are on the same level of importance and reverence. Whatever does not please Muhammad, the same with Allah***

Qaf 49:1 "Believers, be not forward in the presence of **Allah and His Messenger**...Raise not your voices **above the voice of the Prophet**, nor speak loudly around him...

Al Hhashr 59:6 "**Allah gives his Messenger Lordship and Power over whomever He wills.**"

Al Tahhreem 66:1 "O Prophet! **Why forbid yourself that which Allah has made lawful to you**? You seek to please your consorts... Allah has already sanctioned for you the dissolution of your vows."

This verse, very conveniently, justifies Muhammad to have sex with as many and any women that his heart desires

Al Qalam 68:4 "You [Muhammad] are an **exalted character of tremendous morality**

Al Kawthar 108:3 "For he who insults you (Muhammad) **will be cut off.**"

Bukhari 1.14 "The Prophet said, 'None of you will have faith till he loves me more than **his father, his children and all mankind.**'"

Bukhari 1.331 "The Prophet said, '**I have been given five things which were not given to any one else before me**.

1. Allah made me victorious by **terror**
2. The earth has been made for me.
3. **Booty** has been made lawful for me yet it was not lawful for anyone else before me.
4. I have been given the right of intercession.
5. Every Prophet used to be sent to his nation only but I have been sent to all mankind.'"

*** I refrain from making any comment on this and would very much like to read what our listeners think ***

Bukhari 4.203 "I heard Allah's Apostle saying, '**He who obeys me, obeys *Allah*, and he who disobeys me, disobeys Allah...**

*** **Muhammad and Allah are One & the same*****

Bukhari 4.732 "Allah's Apostle said, 'I have five names:

I am Muhammad and Ahmad, the praised one;

I am **al-Mahi** through whom Allah will eliminate infidelity [by killing every infidel];

I am **al-Hashir** who will be the first to be resurrected **[beating Jesus]**;

and I am also **al-Aqib,** because there will be no prophet after me.'"

Al-Tirmidhi Hadith 5761 Narrated by Abu Sa'id

Allah's Messenger said, "I shall be pre-eminent among the descendants of **Adam** on the **Day of Resurrection,** and **this is no boast;**

and in my hand will be the banner of praise, and **this is no boast;**.

There will be no prophet, Adam or any other, who will not be under my banner.

I shall be the first from whom the **Earth** will be cleft open, and **this is no boast**"

*** **This is after all, Muhammad at his most HUMBLE** ***

Bukhari 6.504 "Allah's Apostle said, 'Every Prophet was given miracles because of which people believed, but what I have been given is Divine Inspiration which Allah has revealed to me. **So I hope that my followers will outnumber the followers of the other Prophets.'"**

*** Muhammad was correct:

his followers became numerous through **terror** and **conquests** but as we all know, **quantity** does not represent **quality** ***

Bukhari 8.610 ... Allah's Apostle actually saw with his own eyes the vision of all the things which were shown to him on the **Night Journey to (the Temple of Solomon) in Jerusalem.** It was not a dream."

*** Muhammmad, the **humble, the sincere,** the **noble,** the **praised** & the **truthful,** declared **publicly** to his followers - with commendable **veracity** - that he had just recently visited the Temple of Solomon at Jerusalem, when in reality, such a temple had ceased to exist 550 years earlier ***

Bukhari 9.384 "Allah's Apostle said, '**Whoever obeys me will enter Paradise....**'"

Ishaq:53 "(Muhammads's) authority among the **Quraysh** was **like a religion** which the people followed and which could not be infringed; **they always acted in accordance with its laws**

Ishaq:205 "'If you are loyal to this undertaking it will profit you in this world and the next.'

They said, 'We will accept you as a **Prophet** under these conditions, but we want to know specifically what we will get in return for our loyalty.'

Muhammad said, '**I promise you Paradise.'"**

*** Muhammad usurped the power of Allah – if Allah were God - by promising those gullible, unlearned, illiterate and superstitious pagans Arabs who would believe in him as the messenger of Allah, that they would end up in Paradise ***

Lifting the Veil

Ishaq:231 "Whenever you differ about a matter it must be referred to **Allah and Muhammad**."

Ishaq:391 "O people, this is **Allah's Apostle** among you. **Allah has honored and exalted you by him.** So help him and strengthen him. Listen to his commands and obey them."

Tabari VI:134 "'Men of the **Khazraj,** do you know what you are pledging yourselves to in swearing allegiance to this man **(Muhammad)?**' 'Yes,' they answered.

'In swearing allegiance to him we are pledging ourselves to wage war against all mankind.'"

*** Even **1400 years ago,** some of the most unlearned, illiterate and simple people among the pagan Arabs **concluded** that they were **declaring total war** against all human beings who do not believe as they do.

They were more realistic and intelligent than most of our political & theological leaders of **today** ***

Ishaq:471 "We were steadfast trusting in Him. **We have a Prophet by whom we will conquer all men.**"

Ishaq:580 "Allah's religion is the religion of Muhammad.

*** Ladies & gentlemen, Believers & Unbelievers, the above sample verses reflect the state of mind of one who is a

Pathological Narcissist

especially as we have shown, that every letter, verse & chapter of the Quran are the product of Muhammad's own imagination, his

Alter Ego

projected into the unsuspecting mouth of Allah to give them **sanctity** ***

REFERENCES

Abu Muhammad 'Abd al-Malik bin Hisham, or Ibn Hisham: *Sirat al Nabi*; Translated by A. Guillaume "Life of Muhammad" from Ibn Ishaq; Oxford University Press, 1955.

Al Rasafi, Ma'roof: *Kitab al Shakhs'iya al Muhammadiya*; Al Jamal Publications, Koln 2002, Germany.

Ali, Abdullah Yusuf: *The Meaning of the Holy Quran*; 6th edition; Amana Corporation,1989; USA.

Asad, Muhammad: *The Message of the Quran*; 5th Edition; Oriental Press; Dubai, 2003.

Azumah, John Alembillah: *The Legacy of Arab-Islam in Africa*; Oneworld, Oxford,2001

Bukhari, Muhammad ibn Ismail al: The English Translation of **Sahih Al Bukhari** With the Arabic Text; Translators Muhammad Ibn Ismail Bukhari and Muhammad Muhsin Khan; Apex Books Concern, December 1980.

Bukhari, Muhammad ibn Ismail al: Sahih al Bukhari; Mahmood Muhammad Mahmood Hussain Nassar; Dat al Kotob Al-ilmiyah, 4th Edition, 2004; Beirut, Lebanon.

Gilchrist, John*: Jam' Al-Qur'an - The Codification of the Qur'an Text*; T.M.F.M.T. ; Warley; UK

Ginzberg, Louis: The Legends of the Jews; The Jewish Publications Society of America, 1968; Philadelphia

Hitler, Adolf: *Mein Kampf;* Translated by Ralph Manheim; Pimlico Publication, 2006; London.

Hitti, Philip K: *History of the Arabs;* 7th Edition; Macmillan & Co, 1960; London.

Jeffrey, Arthur: *The Foreign Vocabulary of the Quran;* Baroda, 1938.

Lane, Andrew J: *A Traditional Mu'tazilite Qur'an Commentary:* The Kashshaf of Jar Allah Al-Zamakhshari (Texts & Studies on the Qur'an) ; Brill 2005.

Lings, Martin: *Muhammad;* George Allen & Unwin, 1983.

New King James Version: *Holy Bible;* Thomas Nelson Publishers; Nashville, 1991, USA.

Muslim, Abul Husain: *al-Jami' al-] Sahih,* ed. by M.F. 'Abdul Baqi, Cairo, 1374.

Nicholson, Reynold A: *Literary History of the Arabs;* Curzon Press Ltd., 1993; Richmond, Surrey, UK.

Rasafi, Ma'roof Al: *Kitab al Shakhssiyah al Muhammadiyah;* Al Jamal Publications,2002; Al-Kamel Verlag, Koln, Germany.

Scherman, Rabbi Nosson: *Stone Edition Tanach;* 1st Edition, 1996; Mesorah Publications Ltd.. USA.

Segal, Ronald: *Islam's Black Slaves;* Atlantic Books, London 2002.

Suyuti, Abu al-Fadl 'Abd al-Rahman ibn Abi Bakr Jalal al-Din: Edited by Abu al-Fadhl Ibrahim; al-Maktabah al-Asreyah, Lebanon.

Suyuti, Abu al-Fadl 'Abd al-Rahman ibn Abi Bakr Jalal al-Din:Muhammad Salim Hasim; Dar Al Kotob Al-ilmiyah; 2nd Edition, 2007; Lebanon.

Tabari, Abu Ja'far Muhammad Ibn Jarir: *History;* Et All; State University of New York Press, 1986/90.

Waqidi , Abu `Abdullah Muhammad al: *Kitab al Maghazi;* Editior: Marsden Jones; Oxford University Press, 1967.

Waqidi : Et All; Ta Ha Publishers, 2000.

Zamakhshari, Abu al-Qasim Mahmud ibn 'Umar al:

Persian-born Arabic scholar whose chief work is Al-Kashshaf ("The Discoverer of Revealed Truths"), his exhaustive linguistic commentary on the Qur'an.

LINKS

www.YouTube.com/ahmadsquran3

We welcome any comments and recommendations you may make.

We also have put up our own **BLOG** containing every chapter of U-Tube for safety, just in case they terminate our site again:

www.the-koran.blogspot.com

Investigate Islam is kind enough to put our chapters on his:

www.muhammadtube.com

Made in the USA
Middletown, DE
14 April 2017